EXAM

CompTIA®

Practice Questions

Essentials, Exams 220-602, 220-603, 220-604

Second Edition

Charles J. Brooks

CompTIA® A+ Practice Questions Exam Cram
(Essentials, Exams 220-602, 220-603, 220-604), Second Edition

Copyright © 2008 by Pearson Education, Inc.

ISBN-13: 978-0-7897-3566-9

ISBN-10: 0-7897-3566-0

Library of Congress Cataloging-in-Publication Data

Brooks, Charles J.
  CompTIA A+ practice questions exam cram (exams 220-602, 220-603, 220-604, essentials) / Charles J. Brooks.
    p. cm.
  ISBN-13: 978-0-7897-3566-9 (pbk. w/cd)
  ISBN-10: 0-7897-3566-0 (pbk. w/cd)
  1. Electronic data processing personnel--Certification. 2. Computer technicians--Certification--Study guides. 3. Microcomputers--Maintenance and repair--Examinations--Study guides. I. Title.
  QA76.3.B7765 2008
  004.165--dc22
                    2007045222

Printed in the United States of America

Third Printing, April 2009

Trademarks

Warning and Disclaimer

Bulk Sales

Que Publishing offers excellent discounts on this book when ordered in quantity for bulk purchases or special sales. For more information, please contact:

U.S. Corporate and Government Sales
1-800-382-3419
corpsales@pearsontechgroup.com

For sales outside of the U.S., please contact:

International Sales
+1-317-581-3793
international@pearsontechgroup.com

Publisher
Paul Boger

Associate Publisher
David Dusthimer

Senior Development Editor
Christopher Cleveland

Managing Editor
Patrick Kanouse

Technical Editor
Toby Skandier

Project Editor
Mandie Frank

Copy Editor
Chuck Hutchinson

Proofreader
Mike Henry

Publishing Coordinator
Vanessa Evans

Multimedia Developer
Dan Scherf

Designer
Gary Adair

Page Layout
Trudy Coler

Safari BOOKS ONLINE ENABLED · **This Book Is Safari Enabled**

The Safari® Enabled icon on the cover of your favorite technology book means the book is available through Safari Bookshelf. When you buy this book, you get free access to the online edition for 45 days.

Safari Bookshelf is an electronic reference library that lets you easily search thousands of technical books, find code samples, download chapters, and access technical information whenever and wherever you need it.

To gain 45-day Safari Enabled access to this book

- Go to http://www.quepublishing.com/safarienabled.
- Complete the brief registration form.
- Enter the coupon code 3WH6-G6XH-2TQC-KGHG-2Y6M.

If you have difficulty registering on Safari Bookshelf or accessing the online edition, please email customer-service@safaribooksonline.com.

Contents at a Glance

Table of Contents

About the Author

Charles J. Brooks (A+, Network+, I-Net+, Server+, HTI+, MCP) is currently co-owner and vice president of Educational Technologies Group Inc., as well as co-owner of eITPrep, LLP, an online training company. He is in charge of research and product development at both organizations. A former electronics instructor and technical writer with the National Education Corporation, Charles taught and wrote on post-secondary EET curriculum, including introductory electronics, transistor theory, linear integrated circuits, basic digital theory, industrial electronics, microprocessors, and computer peripherals. Charles has authored several books, including the first five editions of *A+ Certification Training Guide*, *The Complete Introductory Computer Course*, and *IBM PC Peripheral Troubleshooting & Repair*. He currently also writes about networking, residential technology integration, and convergence.

About the Reviewer

Toby Skandier is a self-employed consultant with Talskan Technologies, LLC. Formerly, he worked for 12 years as a technical-training developer and instructor for Embarq and Sprint. Toby has authored and performed technical editing on several books by Pearson and other publishers. He holds CCSI, CCNP, CCDP, MCSE, MCP+I, Network+, i-Net+, Server+, CTT+, and all three A+ certifications.

Dedication

Thanks to my wife, Robbie—as always, you're the best. I couldn't do this without you. I thank my dad, Ralph, who has taken up personal computing a little later in life than some and knows exactly what he wants out of it. Finally, Robert, Jamaica, Michael, and Joshua—you guys light up my life.

Acknowledgments

I want to thank Dave Dusthimer, Jeff Riley, Chris Cleveland, and all the folks at Que Publishing for its excellent support on this and our other Que publication efforts. Also thanks to Toby for really wringing out the best technical information for this book. It's a real privilege to work with high-quality people and a high-quality organization.

I also want to thank all the people who have purchased our products in the past and were willing to give us feedback to make them better. As always, good luck with your certification efforts—although I hope you don't need any luck after using our materials to prepare.

We Want to Hear from You!

As the reader of this book, *you* are our most important critic and commentator. We value your opinion and want to know what we're doing right, what we could do better, what areas you'd like to see us publish in, and any other words of wisdom you're willing to pass our way.

As an associate publisher for Que Publishing, I welcome your comments. You can email or write me directly to let me know what you did or didn't like about this book—as well as what we can do to make our books better.

Please note that I cannot help you with technical problems related to the topic of this book. We do have a User Services group, however, where I will forward specific technical questions related to the book.

When you write, please be sure to include this book's title and author as well as your name, email address, and phone number. I will carefully review your comments and share them with the author and editors who worked on the book.

Fax: 317-581-4770

Email: feedback@quepublishing.com

Mail: David Dusthimer
         Que Publishing
         800 East 96th Street
         Indianapolis, IN 46240 USA

Reader Services

Visit our website and register this book at www.quepublishing.com/register for convenient access to any updates, downloads, or errata that might be available for this book.

Introduction

What Is This Book About?

Welcome to *A+ Practice Questions Exam Cram*! The sole purpose of this book is to provide you with practice questions complete with answers and explanations that will help you learn, drill, and review for the 220-601 Essentials, 220-602 IT Technician, 220-603 Remote Support Technician, and 220-604 Depot Technician certification exams. The book offers a large number of questions to practice each exam objective and will help you assess your knowledge before you write the real exam. The detailed answers to every question will help you reinforce your knowledge about different issues involving installing, configuring, and troubleshooting personal computer systems.

Who Is This Book For?

If you have studied the content material for one of the A+ exams and feel you are ready to put your knowledge to the test, but you're not sure that you want to take the real exam yet, this book is for you! Maybe you have answered other practice questions or unsuccessfully taken the real exam, reviewed, and want to take more practice questions before going to take the real exam. In that case, this book is for you, too! Even when the exam is done and you have passed with flying colors and have the A+ certificate in your pocket, keep this book handy on your desktop to provide answers to your everyday PC installation, configuration, and troubleshooting issues.

What Will You Find in This Book?

As we mentioned earlier, this book is all about practice questions! The practice questions in the book, some very easy and others with a little complicated problem scenario, all are aimed at raising your confidence level before writing the real exam. You will find questions that, in fact, you will face in real life.

This book is organized according to the four exams presented by the Computer Technology Information Association (CompTIA) for A+ certification. Each chapter corresponds to one of these exams, beginning with the prerequisite Essentials exam, followed by the IT Technician exam, the Remote Support Technician exam, and concluding with the Depot Technician exam. The content of each chapter is organized to follow the order of the exam's objectives, and in every chapter you will find the following three elements:

- ▶ *Practice Questions*—These are the numerous questions that will help you learn, drill, and review exam objectives. All the questions in this section are multiple-choice type. Choose the correct answer based on your knowledge of PC servicing.

- ▶ *Quick-Check Answer Key*—After you have finished answering the questions, you can quickly grade your exam from this section. Only correct answers are given in this section. No explanations are offered yet! Even if you have answered a question incorrectly, do not be discouraged. Just move on! Keep in mind that this is not the real exam. You can always review the topic and do the questions again.

- ▶ *Answers and Explanations*—This section provides you with correct answers as well as further explanations about the content posed in that question. Use this information to learn why an answer is correct and reinforce the content in your mind for the exam day.

NOTE

It is not possible to reflect a real exam on a paper product. As mentioned earlier, the purpose of this book is to help you prepare for the exam and not provide you with real exam questions. Neither the author nor Que Publishing can guarantee that you will pass the exam only by memorizing the practice questions given in this book.

Hints for Using This Book

Because this book is a paper practice product, you might want to complete your exams on a separate piece of paper so that you can reuse the exams over and over without having previous answers in your way. Also, a general rule of thumb across all practice question products is to make sure that you are scoring well into the high 80% to 90% range in all topics before attempting the real exam. The higher percentages you score on practice question products, the better your chances for passing the real exam. Of course, we cannot guarantee a passing score on the real exam, but we can offer you plenty of opportunities to practice and assess your knowledge levels before you enter the real exam.

When you have completed the exam on paper, use the companion MeasureUp CD to take a timed exam. This will further help you gain confidence and make a self-assessment in case you need more study. Your results will indicate the exam objectives in which you need further study or hands-on practice.

Need Further Study?

Are you having a hard time correctly answering these questions? If so, you probably need further review of all exam objectives. Be sure to see the following products related to this book from Que Publishing:

- *CompTIA A+ Exam Cram* by Charles J. Brooks (ISBN 0-7897-3564-4).

- *A+ Exam Prep (Exams 220-401, 220-402)* by Charles J. Brooks (ISBN 0-7897-3565-2).

CHAPTER ONE

Essentials Exam

Practice Questions

Domain 1.0: Personal Computer Components

Objective 1.1: Identify the fundamental principles of using personal computers

1. During the startup of the system, the PnP process collects information about all the intelligent devices in the system. Where is this information stored?

    ⊘ **A.** In the Extended System Configuration Data (ESCD) area of the CMOS RAM

    ○ **B.** In the Flash portion of the system BIOS

    ○ **C.** In the Flash portion of the BIOS extension (BIOSE)

    ○ **D.** In the Registry of the operating system

Quick Answer: **76**
Detailed Answer: **82**

2. What factors must be taken into account when ordering a new power supply for a desktop PC?

    ⊘ **A.** Form factor and wattage

    ○ **B.** Total BTUs and amperage

    ○ **C.** Voltage and form factor

    ○ **D.** Noise and total BTUs

Quick Answer: **76**
Detailed Answer: **82**

3. What is the purpose of parity?

Quick Answer: **76**
Detailed Answer: **82**

   ○ **A.** To detect operating system problems

   ○ **B.** To remove bad sectors

   ○ **C.** To delete corrupt files

   ⊘ **D.** To detect memory errors

4. What does ECC RAM do that other RAM types do not?

Quick Answer: **76**
Detailed Answer: **82**

   ○ **A.** ECC RAM stores system configuration settings.

   ⊘ **B.** ECC RAM detects memory errors and corrects them.

   ○ **C.** ECC RAM stores cached data on the module.

   ○ **D.** ECC RAM runs at twice the bus speed of other RAM types.

5. When you are discussing the memory capacity of a memory module, the capacity is specified in

Quick Answer: **76**
Detailed Answer: **82**

   ○ **A.** Qwords

   ○ **B.** Megabits

   ⊘ **C.** Bytes

   ○ **D.** Dibits

6. How many devices can a single USB hub support?

Quick Answer: **76**
Detailed Answer: **82**

   ○ **A.** 7

   ○ **B.** 15

   ⊘ **C.** 127

   ○ **D.** 128

7. You are helping a nontechnical user over the telephone, and you need to have the user plug in his SVGA monitor. How would you describe the connector and number of pins in the SVGA connector?

Quick Answer: **76**
Detailed Answer: **82**

   ⊘ **A.** 15-pin, 3-row D-shell

   ○ **B.** 9-pin, 3-row D-shell

   ○ **C.** 50-pin 2-row D-shell

   ○ **D.** 6-pin, round mini-DIN

8. How is information stored in the system's BIOS updated? (Select all that apply.)

   ○ **A.** By physically removing and replacing the BIOS device on the system board.

   ○ **B.** By replacing the RTC module so that the variable information stored in CMOS will update the BIOS on startup.

   ⊘ **C.** By electronically flashing the BIOS with new information.

   ○ **D.** By electronically removing the information from the BIOS, using new downloaded BIOS software to rewrite the BIOS, and then restoring it to the BIOS chip.

9. Which one of the following types of memory can be used to permanently store data and instructions that do not change?

   ○ **A.** SRAM devices

   ○ **B.** ROM devices

   ○ **C.** Magnetic memory

   ○ **D.** SDRAM devices

10. What is the stated clock speed for a DDR 3200 double-pumped DIMM?

   ○ **A.** 133MHz

   ○ **B.** 200MHz

   ○ **C.** 233MHz

   ○ **D.** 400MHz

11. You have upgraded a user's PC significantly and need to install an upgrade power supply to handle all the new equipment you've installed. You use the Internet to check pricing and features and find thousands of power supply listings. What specification is key in choosing a new power supply for the system?

   ○ **A.** Amperage

   ○ **B.** Amp hours

   ○ **C.** Voltage

   ○ **D.** Wattage

12. What system board structure makes it easy to install upgrade processors in a system?

Quick Answer: **76**
Detailed Answer: **82**

- ○ **A.** A removable ROM BIOS
- ○ **B.** A ZIF socket
- ○ **C.** A PGA socket
- ○ **D.** A PnP BIOS

13. How many wires are there in a standard IDE signal cable?

Quick Answer: **76**
Detailed Answer: **82**

- ○ **A.** 50
- ○ **B.** 40
- ○ **C.** 25
- ○ **D.** 8

14. The mechanism in a CD-ROM/DVD drive responsible for positioning the drive's Read mechanism in the correct position is the _____.

Quick Answer: **76**
Detailed Answer: **82**

- ○ **A.** collimator
- ○ **B.** spindle
- ○ **C.** stepper motor
- ○ **D.** head actuator

15. Which of the following devices is based on Flash memory technology?

Quick Answer: **76**
Detailed Answer: **82**

- ○ **A.** SD cards
- ○ **B.** Floppy disks
- ○ **C.** CD-ROMs
- ○ **D.** DVDs

16. Which of the following would a high-level game player most likely choose for a video card?

Quick Answer: **76**
Detailed Answer: **82**

- ○ **A.** A 16MB PCI-X card
- ○ **B.** A 256MB PCIe card
- ○ **C.** A 256MB AGP card
- ○ **D.** A 128MB AGP card

17. You have been called to upgrade a PC at a customer's business, and no one can remember the Supervisor password to get into the machine. How can you reset this password so that you can access the system and perform the upgrade?

Quick Answer: **76**
Detailed Answer: **84**

- ○ **A.** Remove the BIOS chip from the system.
- ○ **B.** Remove the CMOS chip from the system.
- ○ **C.** Remove the CMOS backup battery and unplug the system from the power source for several minutes.
- ○ **D.** Remove the processor from the system for several minutes.

18. What part of a hard disk drive (HDD) reads the information stored on a disk?

Quick Answer: **76**
Detailed Answer: **84**

- ○ **A.** The spindle
- ○ **B.** The R/W head mechanism
- ○ **C.** The platter
- ○ **D.** The drive controller

19. A computer system with a 1GHz CPU installed is operating at only 700MHz. What is most likely the problem?

Quick Answer: **76**
Detailed Answer: **84**

- ○ **A.** The processor is employing CPU throttling to operate more efficiently.
- ○ **B.** The wrong speed processor is installed on the mother board.
- ○ **C.** Operation of 1GHz can be obtained only if the processor is overclocked.
- ○ **D.** The CPU's core speed multiplier has not been configured correctly.

20. What is a 3-1/2″ floppy disk best used for?

Quick Answer: **76**
Detailed Answer: **84**

- ○ **A.** Installing OEM printer drivers
- ○ **B.** Booting a failing system into Safe Mode
- ○ **C.** Loading third-party device drivers into a Windows system
- ○ **D.** Booting a failing system to a command prompt environment

21. How many pins are in a USB connector?

Quick Answer: **76**
Detailed Answer: **84**

- ○ **A.** 2
- ○ **B.** 4
- ○ **C.** 8
- ○ **D.** 15

22. How many pins are in an SVGA connector?

Quick Answer: **76**
Detailed Answer: **84**

- ○ **A.** 9
- ○ **B.** 15
- ○ **C.** 25
- ○ **D.** 50

23. Which portion of the PC system is responsible for controlling the operating temperature of the microprocessor?

Quick Answer: **76**
Detailed Answer: **84**

- ○ **A.** The Processor Management portion of the PCI chipset
- ○ **B.** The Temp Management portion of the microprocessor
- ○ **C.** The Processor Management portion of the operating system
- ○ **D.** The Health Management portion of the BIOS

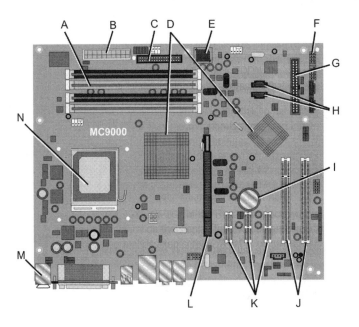

24. From the figure depicting an ATX motherboard, identify the PCIe X1 expansion slots.

Quick Answer: **76**
Detailed Answer: **84**

- ○ **A.** A
- ○ **B.** J
- ○ **C.** K
- ○ **D.** L

25. From the figure depicting an ATX motherboard, identify the DIMM slots.

○　**A.** A

○　**B.** J

○　**C.** K

○　**D.** L

Quick Answer: **76**
Detailed Answer: **84**

26. From the figure depicting an ATX motherboard, identify the PATA connectors.

○　**A.** B

○　**B.** C

○　**C.** G

○　**D.** H

Quick Answer: **76**
Detailed Answer: **84**

27. Cache memory is used to _____.

○　**A.** increase the speed of memory access

○　**B.** increase the size of memory available to programs

○　**C.** store data in nonvolatile memory

○　**D.** augment the memory used for the operating system kernel

Quick Answer: **76**
Detailed Answer: **84**

28. What type of device would you expect to find in an AGP slot?

○　**A.** A sound card

○　**B.** An internal modem card

○　**C.** A network interface card

○　**D.** A video adapter card

Quick Answer: **76**
Detailed Answer: **84**

Objective 1.2: Install, configure, optimize, and upgrade personal computer components

1. One of your customers is having problems with a new CD-RW drive he has installed on his system. The system originally contained a single PATA HDD and a 52x CD-R drive. When your customer attempts to make copies of a disc using the CD-RW drive, he receives buffer underrun errors. What suggestions can you give him to improve his copy operations? (Select all that apply.)

   ○ **A.** Place the CD-ROM or DVD writer on an IDE channel of its own. This keeps the drive from competing with other drives for the channel's available bandwidth.

   ○ **B.** Conduct the write operation on the same drive as the read operation and use reduced write speed options.

   ○ **C.** Locate a Flash program for the drive's BIOS to upgrade it so that it provides better support for the write function.

   ○ **D.** Switch the master/slave settings on the HDD and CD-RW drive so that the CD-RW drive has first position for the primary controller.

Quick Answer: **76**
Detailed Answer: **85**

2. When you are installing a ribbon cable for a disk drive, the color stripe should point to _____.

   ○ **A.** the red dot on the board

   ○ **B.** pin 34

   ○ **C.** the white dot on the connector

   ○ **D.** pin 1

Quick Answer: **76**
Detailed Answer: **85**

3. You have just installed a 500GB HDD in a Windows XP Professional machine. When you start up the system, it recognizes only 137GB of drive space. What are the most likely causes of this problem? (Select all that apply.)

   ○ **A.** The system needs a new HDD driver for Windows XP to handle this size drive.

   ○ **B.** The firmware on the HDD needs to be updated to work with Windows XP Pro.

   ○ **C.** The system needs to have Service Pack 1 (SP1) or higher installed to handle this size drive.

   ○ **D.** The system needs to have the BIOS flashed with a version that can accommodate the new drive.

Quick Answer: **76**
Detailed Answer: **85**

4. You are installing a printer for a customer at her office. The printer is new and features USB connectivity. The host system is an old Pentium II system with two USB ports on the back panel. After you connect the printer and turn it on, the system recognizes it, but the printer doesn't work. What is the most likely cause for this situation?

- ○ **A.** The USB cable is a USB 2.0 version that is not compatible with the computer port.

- ○ **B.** The USB cable is a USB 1.1 version that is not compatible with the new printer port.

- ○ **C.** The new printer is a USB 2.0 device, but the host computer has a USB 1.1 port.

- ○ **D.** The USB drivers need to be updated to USB 2.0 drivers.

5. Which of the following types of cable specifications can be used to connect hard drives to a typical BTX system board? (Select all that apply.)

- ○ **A.** EIDE (PATA) cables

- ○ **B.** SATA cables

- ○ **C.** SCSI cables

- ○ **D.** IEEE-1284 cables

6. You've installed one PATA hard drive, and it is working fine. You install a second PATA drive, and neither drive works when you start the system. What is the most likely cause for this problem?

- ○ **A.** The drives are connected in the wrong order on the PATA signal cable.

- ○ **B.** The second drive is on the secondary IDE channel with its jumper set in the slave position.

- ○ **C.** Both drives are connected to the primary IDE channel, and the jumpers on both drives are set as masters.

- ○ **D.** One drive is connected as primary master and the other as secondary master, but the power connector isn't connected to the secondary master.

7. What part does the hard disk drive play in Windows memory management?

Quick Answer: 76
Detailed Answer: 85

   ○ **A.** The operating system's extended memory management (EMM) file is located on the hard disk drive.

   ○ **B.** Extended memory storage is located on the hard disk drive.

   ○ **C.** The operating system's memory registers are located on the hard disk drive.

   ○ **D.** The operating system's swap file is located on the hard disk drive.

8. After the USB function has been enabled and the device has been plugged into the system, what action must be performed to fully install the device?

Quick Answer: 76
Detailed Answer: 85

   ○ **A.** Run the Add New Hardware Wizard from the Control Panel.

   ○ **B.** Run the Add/Remove Programs Wizard to install the drivers for the new device.

   ○ **C.** Use the Have Disk option to install proprietary USB drivers from the device manufacturer's disk.

   ○ **D.** Start the system and let the operating system detect it through the PnP process.

9. A user needs to connect a FireWire-compatible video camera with his workstation. However, before he requests a purchase for all required devices, he wants to make sure that the cable segment is long enough so that he can place the video camera on a tripod in a specific place in his office and still be connected to the workstation. Which of the following is the maximum segment length for an IEEE-1394 connection?

Quick Answer: 76
Detailed Answer: 85

   ○ **A.** 14 feet
   ○ **B.** 20 feet
   ○ **C.** 30 feet
   ○ **D.** 63 feet

10. What action should be taken when upgrading an AGP card or system board containing an AGP slot?

- ○ **A.** Set the CMOS setting for the AGP function to Autodetect so that the system automatically establishes compatibility between the slot and the card.
- ○ **B.** Always install Universal AGP cards so that you can always be sure the slot and card are compatible.
- ○ **C.** Consult the system board and AGP adapter card's documentation to verify their compatibility with the other component.
- ○ **D.** Obtain the correct BIOS Flash routine for the new AGP device so that you can upgrade the BIOS to work with the adapter.

Objective 1.3: Identify tools, diagnostic procedures, and troubleshooting techniques for personal computer components

1. You have been called in to troubleshoot a new Windows XP Media Center Edition installation that is not supporting USB devices from any of its USB ports. What should you do first to correct this problem?

- ○ **A.** Enable USB support in the CMOS Setup utility.
- ○ **B.** Get new USB 2.1 devices so that they are compatible with the MCE system.
- ○ **C.** Test the USB devices in other machines.
- ○ **D.** Check the Windows XP MCE HCL to determine whether the components are compatible with the new operating system.

2. A user tells you that her laptop's cooling fan is making an unusual amount of noise. Later, she reports the noise has completely stopped. What has most likely happened?

- ○ **A.** The BIOS's Health monitor has corrected the fan's speed.
- ○ **B.** The dust buildup blocking the fan's operation has cleared itself.
- ○ **C.** The system has reached proper operating temperature, and the fan has settled into proper operation.
- ○ **D.** The fan has completely stopped working, and the unit should be shut down and checked for heat damage.

3. At bootup, one of your computer systems makes a loud noise and begins to produce smoke through its vent openings. What is the first thing you should do?

- ◯ **A.** Call the manufacturer and check warranty status.
- ◯ **B.** Shut down the system and vent the room.
- ◯ **C.** Try to boot the system in Safe Mode.
- ◯ **D.** Remove power from the computer.

4. Your coworker has installed a floppy disk drive (FDD) unit in a machine so that he can upload some old company data that has been stored on floppies. When he turns on the machine, it does not work, and the FDD activity light stays on all the time. What is the most likely problem given this information?

- ◯ **A.** The FDD signal cable is installed incorrectly.
- ◯ **B.** The system needs drivers for the floppy drive.
- ◯ **C.** The FDD is the wrong size. He needs to flash the BIOS to accommodate the floppy drive.
- ◯ **D.** The floppy drive needs to be configured using the jumpers on the back of the drive.

5. You are trying to implement procedures to increase the productivity of your repair and maintenance staff. What activity can you have each member perform to prevent redundant steps and efforts in troubleshooting a problem?

- ◯ **A.** Document each troubleshooting step and its outcome.
- ◯ **B.** Identify the source of the problem before beginning the troubleshooting process.
- ◯ **C.** Start at the beginning of the troubleshooting process and do not skip troubleshooting steps.
- ◯ **D.** Interrogate the user to determine how to conduct your troubleshooting process efficiently.

6. A customer wants you to install an additional PATA drive in her system so that she can move her growing collection of digital pictures off her main drive. After you install the second drive and start the system, it refuses to recognize the second drive. What is the most likely problem?

- ○ **A.** The new drive's jumpers have not been configured properly for its position in the system.
- ○ **B.** The new drive has not been low-level formatted.
- ○ **C.** The new drive has not been configured in the CMOS Setup utility.
- ○ **D.** The new drive has not been partitioned.

7. You have been asked to troubleshoot a PC that does not start up and does not show any signs of life. You decide to install a new power supply, and it still does not operate. Which of the following should you do first?

- ○ **A.** Check the power supply's system board connection.
- ○ **B.** Check the power supply's On/Off switch connection.
- ○ **C.** Check the voltage setting on the back of the unit.
- ○ **D.** Use a multimeter to check for AC voltage.

8. Which of the following must you do first when troubleshooting a customer's equipment?

- ○ **A.** Gather information from the user and assess the problem systemically.
- ○ **B.** Inspect each component related to the possible cause.
- ○ **C.** Test each component involved and evaluate the results of each test.
- ○ **D.** Document the possible causes of the problem the system is displaying.

9. While typing on your notebook computer, numbers and strange characters show up on the screen instead of the letters you type. What is the most likely cause of this problem?

- ○ **A.** The Fn key is stuck.
- ○ **B.** The Shift key is stuck.
- ○ **C.** The Windows Character Map is configured incorrectly.
- ○ **D.** The NumLk key has been depressed.

10. After you finish building a new computer, you notice that none of the USB devices functions at startup. What is the first thing you should do to troubleshoot this problem?

Quick Answer: **76**
Detailed Answer: **87**

- ○ **A.** Remove the USB devices and install them one at a time while the system is running so that the hot swap function can detect them and install the proper drivers.
- ○ **B.** Disconnect all the USB devices, reconnect them, and let the system detect them through the PnP process.
- ○ **C.** Start the system in Safe Mode and use the Device Manager to troubleshoot each device's driver configuration.
- ○ **D.** Check the CMOS Setup utility and enable the USB ports in the Integrated Peripherals page.

11. What questions should you ask the user when you are first examining a defective unit? (Select all that apply.)

Quick Answer: **76**
Detailed Answer: **87**

- ○ **A.** What were you doing when the problem occurred?
- ○ **B.** Is the unit new? Did it ever work?
- ○ **C.** Was there an error message? What did it say?
- ○ **D.** How much experience do you have with this type of computer?

12. Which symptom would the POST not identify?

Quick Answer: **76**
Detailed Answer: **87**

- ○ **A.** A CMOS RAM error
- ○ **B.** A stuck keyboard key
- ○ **C.** A hard drive failure
- ○ **D.** A RAM chip that fails at high temperature

Objective 1.4: Perform preventative maintenance on personal computer components

1. While servicing a PC, you open a system unit case and discover that a lot of dust has accumulated inside. Which of the following are the best ways for safely removing it? (Select all that apply.)

   ○ **A.** Vacuum it out with a static-free vacuum.

   ○ **B.** Gently wash it out with a damp soft cloth.

   ○ **C.** Use compressed air to remove the dust.

   ○ **D.** Shake it out of the system.

Quick Answer: **76**
Detailed Answer: **88**

2. What is the best type of cleaning tool for use on the exterior of computers and peripheral components?

   ○ **A.** A vacuum cleaner

   ○ **B.** A damp cloth

   ○ **C.** A soft brush

   ○ **D.** A can of antistatic spray

Quick Answer: **76**
Detailed Answer: **88**

3. What type of cleaning solution should be used on the exterior of computer components?

   ○ **A.** Bleach and water

   ○ **B.** Window cleaner

   ○ **C.** Soap and water

   ○ **D.** Citrus-based cleaners

Quick Answer: **76**
Detailed Answer: **88**

4. At what point does heat buildup become a problem for most PCs?

   ○ **A.** Room temperatures above 85° F

   ○ **B.** Room temperatures above 90° F

   ○ **C.** Room temperatures above 95° F

   ○ **D.** Room temperatures above 100° F

Quick Answer: **76**
Detailed Answer: **88**

Objective 2.0: Laptops and Portable Devices

Objective 2.1: Identify the fundamental principles of using laptops and portable devices

1. What type of RAM do you typically find in a notebook PC?

   O **A.** RIMM

   O **B.** SODIMM

   O **C.** PCMCIA

   O **D.** SD memory

Quick Answer: **77**
Detailed Answer: **89**

2. Which PCMCIA slot type can handle all the different PC Card device formats?

   O **A.** Type I

   O **B.** Type II

   O **C.** Type III

   O **D.** Mini PCI

Quick Answer: **77**
Detailed Answer: **89**

3. What happens when you press the Windows Logo key along with the L key?

   O **A.** It bypasses the Windows logo when the system starts up.

   O **B.** It brings the Windows Logon dialog box to the display.

   O **C.** It brings the network Logon dialog box to the screen.

   O **D.** It locks the system until the logged-in user unlocks it.

Quick Answer: **77**
Detailed Answer: **89**

4. What are the main differences between desktop and notebook PC designs? (Select all that apply.)

   O **A.** Thermal handling

   O **B.** Power consumption

   O **C.** Processor speeds

   O **D.** Memory size

Quick Answer: **77**
Detailed Answer: **89**

5. The LCD display on a portable computer is powered by _____.

- ◯ **A.** low-voltage AC
- ◯ **B.** high-voltage AC
- ◯ **C.** low-voltage DC
- ◯ **D.** high-voltage DC

Objective 2.2: Install, configure, optimize, and upgrade laptops and portable devices

1. Which Windows tool is used to safely remove hot-swappable devices in Windows XP?

- ◯ **A.** The Safely Remove Hardware utility
- ◯ **B.** The MSCONFIG utility
- ◯ **C.** The Add New Hardware Wizard
- ◯ **D.** The Device Manager

2. A salesperson from your company has contacted you asking how she can configure her new notebook PC to go into Hibernate mode to conserve her battery life on long trips. How can she get to the Hibernate configuration page from the Windows XP desktop?

- ◯ **A.** Start/All Programs/System Tools/Power Options/Hibernate
- ◯ **B.** Start/Control Panel/Power Options/Hibernate Tab/Enable Hibernation
- ◯ **C.** Start/Control Panel/Power Options/Advanced Tab/Enable Hibernate Support
- ◯ **D.** Start/Settings/Power Options/Hibernate/Enable

3. Which power-saving mode provides the best power savings and still permits the computing session to be activated later?

- ◯ **A.** Hibernate mode
- ◯ **B.** Suspend mode
- ◯ **C.** Standby mode
- ◯ **D.** Shutdown mode

4. Which type of interface would you normally expect to encounter when installing an external CD-ROM/DVD drive? (Select all that apply.)

Quick Answer: **77**
Detailed Answer: **89**

- ○ **A.** USB
- ○ **B.** IDE
- ○ **C.** Bluetooth
- ○ **D.** SCSI

5. Before you remove a PC Card device from a PCMCIA slot in a working computer, you should _____.

Quick Answer: **77**
Detailed Answer: **90**

- ○ **A.** Do nothing. PCMCIA devices are hot swappable and can be removed from the system at any time.
- ○ **B.** Open the Device Manager and click the PC Card node. Then select the option to disable the PC Card you want to remove.
- ○ **C.** Access the Add New Hardware applet in the Control Panel and start the Add New Hardware Wizard. When the wizard starts, select the option to disable the PC Card device. Then remove the card from the system.
- ○ **D.** Click the PC Card status indicator on the taskbar and then select the option to stop the operation of the PC Card you want to remove.

6. Which BIOS-based power conservation mode can be enabled in portable PCs to turn off selected components, such as the hard drive and display, until a system event such as a keyboard entry or a mouse movement occurs?

Quick Answer: **77**
Detailed Answer: **90**

- ○ **A.** Hibernate mode
- ○ **B.** Suspend mode
- ○ **C.** Standby mode
- ○ **D.** Shutdown mode

Objective 2.3: Identify tools, basic diagnostic procedures, and troubleshooting techniques for laptops and portable devices

1. You have just installed a new processor in a laptop PC. When you restart the system, you discover that the keyboard works properly but the touchpad does not. What should you do to overcome this problem?

Quick Answer: **77**
Detailed Answer: **90**

- ○ **A.** Use the keyboard to start the operating system installation. When the process moves into the GUI phase, the touchpad becomes active.

- ○ **B.** You have installed an incompatible processor type that must be replaced.

- ○ **C.** The touchpad connector may have been loosened during the installation. Reconnect it.

- ○ **D.** The portion of the system board responsible for the touchpad has shorted out. You need to install a USB touchpad or mouse.

2. You have installed 1GB of RAM in a notebook used by the sales staff. After some time, one of the sales people tells you that the notebook is only showing 700MB available. What should you tell the salesperson?

Quick Answer: **77**
Detailed Answer: **90**

- ○ **A.** Someone must have removed a memory module, so you need to check the machine before it goes back into the field.

- ○ **B.** One of the machine's modules must have gone bad, so it needs to be replaced before it goes back into the field.

- ○ **C.** The machine has BIOS shadowing configured in the CMOS, so the missing RAM capacity is being used to hold a copy of the BIOS so that the system can access it faster.

- ○ **D.** Notebooks often use shared video memory, which uses a portion of the system's installed memory capacity for video display support.

3. Which of the following is the best way to detect a bad battery in a Windows XP–based laptop PC?

Quick Answer: **77**
Detailed Answer: **90**

- ○ **A.** Check the voltage with a multimeter.

- ○ **B.** Check the battery indicator in the systray portion of the taskbar.

- ○ **C.** Disconnect the AC adapter and measure the time it takes for the system to fail.

- ○ **D.** Check the battery level in the Control Panel's ACPI applet.

4. A customer can't configure the correct resolution for his notebook's LCD display and cannot make out any images on the display. What can you do to fix his problem?

Quick Answer: **77**
Detailed Answer: **90**

- ○ **A.** Use the Device Manager to verify that the installed video driver is correct for the installed video adapter.

- ○ **B.** Connect a video projector to the external VGA connector.

- ○ **C.** Install a PC Card-based video adapter card.

- ○ **D.** Connect an external monitor to the external VGA connector.

5. What item needs to be checked on an external CD-R/DVD drive that is not normally checked on an internal drive when installing the drive on a notebook PC?

Quick Answer: **77**
Detailed Answer: **90**

- ○ **A.** Its signal cable
- ○ **B.** Its power supply
- ○ **C.** Its disk drive controller
- ○ **D.** Its hard drive

Objective 2.4: Perform preventative maintenance on laptops and portable devices

1. Which of the following offers the best thermal protection solution for using a notebook PC?

   ○ **A.** It should be configured to go into Hibernate mode if it doesn't detect input activity for more than a minute.

   ○ **B.** It should be placed on a hard, flat surface when it is in operation.

   ○ **C.** It should have at least its front vent openings clear while it is turned on to allow the fan to pull cool air into the case.

   ○ **D.** It should be used in an air-conditioned environment as much as possible.

Quick Answer: **77**
Detailed Answer: **90**

2. What is the best preventative maintenance that can be given a notebook PC?

   ○ **A.** Cleaning the LCD display panel regularly

   ○ **B.** Having a spare battery on hand

   ○ **C.** Protecting it from being dropped

   ○ **D.** Regularly blowing the dust and debris out of it

Quick Answer: **77**
Detailed Answer: **90**

3. After completing the delivery and setup of new notebook PCs to a client's sales department, you must give the client's staff a presentation for how to care for their new PCs. When you get to the cleaning and routine PM portion of the discussion, what should you tell them about applying cleaning agents to the LCD displays on their notebook PCs?

   ○ **A.** Household cleaning agents can be applied directly to display's the plastic screen guard.

   ○ **B.** Commercial cleaning agents should be applied to a cloth or cleaning rag that will be used to clean the LCD panel.

   ○ **C.** Household cleaning agents should be applied to a sponge that will be used to clean the LCD panel.

   ○ **D.** Commercial cleaning agents should not be used on an LCD display.

Quick Answer: **77**
Detailed Answer: **91**

Quick Check

Quick Answer: **77**
Detailed Answer: **91**

4. What is the suggested cleaning solution for portable displays?

    ◯ **A.** Water and mild soap

    ◯ **B.** Water and citrus-based cleaning solutions

    ◯ **C.** Water and ammonia

    ◯ **D.** Water and antistatic spray

Objective 3.0: Operating Systems

Objective 3.1: Identify the fundamentals of using operating systems

1. The file that guides the Windows 2000/XP boot process is
_____.

   - ○ **A.** NTIO.SYS
   - ○ **B.** NTLDR.EXE
   - ○ **C.** NTBOOT.SYS
   - ○ **D.** BOOTSECT.DOS

Quick Answer: **77**
Detailed Answer: **92**

2. What is the purpose of the NTBOOTDD.SYS file in the Windows 2000 operating system?

   - ○ **A.** It enables SCSI hardware during the Windows 2000 boot process.
   - ○ **B.** It detects hardware during the Windows 2000 boot process.
   - ○ **C.** It configures PATA hard drives during the Windows 2000 boot process.
   - ○ **D.** It creates the Emergency Repair Disk (ERD) during the installation process.

Quick Answer: **77**
Detailed Answer: **92**

3. Under which of the following conditions would you select FAT32 as the file system to be used in a Windows XP installation?

   - ○ **A.** To maintain compatibility with older systems
   - ○ **B.** To save the expense and lost productivity involved in training the users in NTFS functions
   - ○ **C.** With systems that have relatively small hard drives
   - ○ **D.** With systems that routinely handle large files

Quick Answer: **77**
Detailed Answer: **92**

4. Which command prompt operation can be used to compare the contents of two disks?

   - ○ **A.** DISKCOPY
   - ○ **B.** DISKCOMP
   - ○ **C.** DISKCMD
   - ○ **D.** DISKCMF

Quick Answer: **xxx**
Detailed Answer: **xxx**

5. What key combination opens the Start menu in Windows XP?

Quick Answer: **77**
Detailed Answer: **92**

- ○ **A.** Ctrl+Esc
- ○ **B.** Alt+Esc
- ○ **C.** Ctrl+Alt+Esc
- ○ **D.** Shift+Esc

6. Which Windows utility can be used to automate many routine or periodic functions?

Quick Answer: **77**
Detailed Answer: **92**

- ○ **A.** The Scheduled Tasks tool
- ○ **B.** The Task Manager utility
- ○ **C.** The Device Manager
- ○ **D.** The MSCONFIG utility

7. What type of kernel structure does the Mac OS X operating system employ?

Quick Answer: **77**
Detailed Answer: **92**

- ○ **A.** Linux
- ○ **B.** UNIX
- ○ **C.** New Technology
- ○ **D.** Longhorn

8. To view the status of a local area network (LAN) connection in a Windows XP Professional system, you should check under _____.

Quick Answer: **77**
Detailed Answer: **92**

- ○ **A.** My Network Places/Network Monitor
- ○ **B.** Network Neighborhood/Network Monitor
- ○ **C.** My Computer/Network Connections
- ○ **D.** Control Panel/Network Connections

9. What action occurs if you type **Del *.*** at the Windows command prompt?

Quick Answer: **77**
Detailed Answer: **92**

- ○ **A.** The entire contents of the current directory are deleted from the drive.
- ○ **B.** The entire contents of the drive are deleted.
- ○ **C.** The current directory and all its subdirectories are deleted.
- ○ **D.** The current file is deleted from the folder.

10. What is the proper way to remove a USB mass storage device?

Quick Answer: **77**
Detailed Answer: **93**

  - ○ **A.** Click the Safely Remove Hardware icon in the systray.

  - ○ **B.** USB devices are hot-swappable and can be installed or removed at any time.

  - ○ **C.** Use the New Hardware Wizard to remove the device from the system and then disconnect it.

  - ○ **D.** Disable the device in the Device Manager and then physically remove it from the system.

11. What is the native file system for Windows 2000 and Windows XP Professional?

Quick Answer: **77**
Detailed Answer: **93**

  - ○ **A.** NTFS4

  - ○ **B.** FAT32

  - ○ **C.** FAT16

  - ○ **D.** NTFS5

12. What Windows XP command-line utility can be used to create and manage disk partitions?

Quick Answer: **77**
Detailed Answer: **93**

  - ○ **A.** FDISK

  - ○ **B.** FORMAT

  - ○ **C.** DISKPART

  - ○ **D.** DISKPERF

13. How many logical drives can be created on a FAT drive?

Quick Answer: **77**
Detailed Answer: **93**

  - ○ **A.** 8

  - ○ **B.** 23

  - ○ **C.** 38

  - ○ **D.** 44

14. Where does the bootstrap loader look for the operating system boot files?

Quick Answer: **77**
Detailed Answer: **93**

  - ○ **A.** The dynamic partition

  - ○ **B.** The active partition

  - ○ **C.** The extended partition

  - ○ **D.** The primary partition

15. How do you create a new folder using Windows Explorer?

- ○ **A.** Select a parent directory, click the Edit menu, select New, and then select Folder.
- ○ **B.** Select a parent directory, click the Edit menu, and then select New Folder.
- ○ **C.** Select a parent directory, click the File menu, select New, and then click Folder.
- ○ **D.** Select a parent directory, click the File menu, and then select New Folder.

Quick Answer: **77**
Detailed Answer: **93**

16. Which method is used to change file attributes from the Windows Explorer?

- ○ **A.** Edit the appropriate Registry entry with RegEdt32.
- ○ **B.** Right-click the file and select Properties.
- ○ **C.** Highlight the file and choose the Select Options entry from the System Tools menu.
- ○ **D.** Highlight the file and choose the Select Options entry from the View menu.

Quick Answer: **77**
Detailed Answer: **93**

17. The command used to set the attributes of a file is _____.

- ○ **A.** APPEND
- ○ **B.** ASSIGN
- ○ **C.** ATTRIB
- ○ **D.** AUTOEXEC

Quick Answer: **77**
Detailed Answer: **93**

Objective 3.2: Install, configure, optimize, and upgrade operating systems

(References to upgrading from Windows 95 and NT may be made.)

1. What is the default setting for Driver Signing in Windows XP?

- ○ **A.** Warn
- ○ **B.** Block
- ○ **C.** Ignore
- ○ **D.** None

Quick Answer: **78**
Detailed Answer: **93**

2. Select two ways to improve the performance of a system that has never been connected to the Internet or a local area network.

- ○ **A.** Run the Defrag utility to optimize the read and write operations of the system's drives.
- ○ **B.** Delete the Recycle Bin.
- ○ **C.** Use the Windows Cleanup utility to delete files from the Windows\Temporary folder.
- ○ **D.** Delete cookies from the system to free up additional disk space.

3. You are planning to perform a fresh install of Windows XP Professional on an existing PC. Before you remove the old operating system from the PC, which tools can you use to make sure that Windows XP can be used on the computer you intend to upgrade? (Select all that apply.)

- ○ **A.** The Microsoft Hardware Compatibility List (HCL) web page
- ○ **B.** The computer's Installation and User's Manual documentation
- ○ **C.** The Checkupgradeonly utility on the Windows XP distribution CD
- ○ **D.** The Windows XP Help and Support page

4. You have been sent to a residential customer for whom you are supposed to upgrade his operating system to Windows XP Home. When you arrive and inspect the PC, you find that it is running Windows 95a. What must you do to upgrade the system to Windows XP Home?

- ○ **A.** You simply need to install Windows XP Home directly over the existing Windows 95 operating system.
- ○ **B.** You must remove Windows 95 from the system first.
- ○ **C.** The system is too old to upgrade to Windows XP. The customer must purchase a newer system to run XP.
- ○ **D.** You must upgrade the system to Windows 98 or Windows Me before you can upgrade to Windows XP Home.

5. How do you install dual monitors on a Windows XP laptop?

Quick Answer: **78**
Detailed Answer: **94**

- ○ **A.** Right-click the desktop display, select the Dual monitors option from the menu, and extend the desktop.

- ○ **B.** Click the Display icon in the Control Panel and configure the settings for multiple monitors.

- ○ **C.** Click the Add Hardware icon in the Control Panel, select the Dual Monitor option, and configure the dual monitor settings.

- ○ **D.** Navigate to the Device Manager, expand the Display node, and configure the options under the Dual Monitor tab.

6. If TCP/IP is missing from a Windows 2000 Professional installation, how can it be restored?

Quick Answer: **78**
Detailed Answer: **94**

- ○ **A.** Use the Network and Dial-up Connections page to add and configure the protocol.

- ○ **B.** Use the Add/Remove Programs Wizard to reinstall the TCP/IP suite.

- ○ **C.** Use the Add New Hardware Wizard to install the TCP/IP port settings.

- ○ **D.** Use the Add/Remove Windows components utility to reinstall the protocol suite.

7. Which of the following media are typically used to perform local, attended Windows XP installs? (Select all that apply.)

Quick Answer: **78**
Detailed Answer: **94**

- ○ **A.** CD-ROMs
- ○ **B.** IrDA connections
- ○ **C.** LAN connections
- ○ **D.** USB drives

8. Patch management is defined as _____.

Quick Answer: **78**
Detailed Answer: **94**

- ○ **A.** installing new operating system releases to keep systems up-to-date

- ○ **B.** downloading antivirus definition updates to keep systems safe from virus attacks

- ○ **C.** removing software patches that are installed automatically when new applications are downloaded and installed on the system to recover wasted drive and memory capacity

- ○ **D.** keeping the operating system up-to-date and secure

9. You have been asked to hook up an old dot-matrix printer to a new Windows XP system. What is the best place to check to determine whether the printer will work with the new system?

- ○ **A.** Check the Microsoft HCL on the Microsoft website.
- ○ **B.** Check the printer manufacturer's documentation.
- ○ **C.** Check the Microsoft HCL on the Windows XP distribution disc.
- ○ **D.** Check the computer manufacturer's documentation.

Quick Answer: **78**
Detailed Answer: **94**

10. Windows XP Professional can support up to _____ RAM.

- ○ **A.** 4GB
- ○ **B.** 16GB
- ○ **C.** 32GB
- ○ **D.** 64GB

Quick Answer: **78**
Detailed Answer: **94**

11. Which of the following utilities lets you directly edit Registry entries in Windows XP Professional?

- ○ **A.** RegEdit
- ○ **B.** Device Manager
- ○ **C.** Add New Hardware Wizard
- ○ **D.** MSCONFIG

Quick Answer: **78**
Detailed Answer: **94**

12. A computer system installed several months ago is showing signs of increasingly slow operation. What steps can be performed to improve system performance? (Select all that apply.)

- ○ **A.** Delete temporary files from the hard drive.
- ○ **B.** Defrag the primary hard disk drive.
- ○ **C.** Run the FDISK utility to revitalize the operating system.
- ○ **D.** Run the CHKDSK utility to clear unused files from the system.

Quick Answer: **78**
Detailed Answer: **94**

13. What is the minimum amount of memory required to install Windows 2000 Professional?

- ○ **A.** 8MB
- ○ **B.** 16MB
- ○ **C.** 32MB
- ○ **D.** 64MB

Quick Answer: **78**
Detailed Answer: **94**

14. What is the minimum amount of RAM that needs to be installed in the system to install Windows XP Professional?

   Quick Answer: **78**
   Detailed Answer: **94**

   ○ **A.** 128MB

   ○ **B.** 32MB

   ○ **C.** 64MB

   ○ **D.** 256MB

15. You are preparing to conduct a departmentwide disk-cloning operation to install Windows XP. Which Windows tool is used to prepare the reference computer for cloning?

   Quick Answer: **78**
   Detailed Answer: **94**

   ○ **A.** RIPrep

   ○ **B.** Unattend.exe

   ○ **C.** Sysprep

   ○ **D.** Ghost

16. What is the proper order of operations for preparing a disk drive for use?

   Quick Answer: **78**
   Detailed Answer: **94**

   ○ **A.** Format, partition, run Setup, reboot, load drivers

   ○ **B.** Partition, format, run Setup, load drivers, reboot

   ○ **C.** Format, partition, run Setup, load drivers, reboot

   ○ **D.** Partition, format, run Setup, reboot, load drivers

17. Which Windows operating system versions can be upgraded directly to Windows XP? (Select all that apply.)

   Quick Answer: **78**
   Detailed Answer: **94**

   ○ **A.** Windows 2000 Professional

   ○ **B.** Windows NT 4.0 Workstation

   ○ **C.** Windows 98SE

   ○ **D.** Windows NT 3.51

Objective 3.3: Identify tools, diagnostic procedures, and troubleshooting techniques for operating systems

1. If a computer running Windows XP Professional generates a disk error during the system startup operation, which Event Viewer log file should be checked for the error?

   ○ **A.** Application

   ○ **B.** Security

   ○ **C.** System

   ○ **D.** Hardware

Quick Answer: **78**
Detailed Answer: **94**

2. In Windows 2000 and XP, which utility can be used to access hard drives and command-line utilities when the system does not boot?

   ○ **A.** Recovery Console

   ○ **B.** Computer Management console

   ○ **C.** Device Manager

   ○ **D.** REGEDT32.EXE

Quick Answer: **78**
Detailed Answer: **96**

3. Which Windows XP utility enables support personnel to take control of a remote computer and perform troubleshooting steps without involving the user in the actual troubleshooting process?

   ○ **A.** Internet Help

   ○ **B.** Remote Desktop

   ○ **C.** Telnet services

   ○ **D.** Remote Assistance

Quick Answer: **78**
Detailed Answer: **96**

4. Which function key can be used to access the Advanced Startup Options menu in Windows 2000 or XP systems?

   ○ **A.** F1

   ○ **B.** F4

   ○ **C.** F6

   ○ **D.** F8

Quick Answer: **78**
Detailed Answer: **96**

5. If the PC system briefly shows a blue screen and continuously reboots, which of the following is likely causing this condition?

Quick Answer: **78**
Detailed Answer: **96**

- ○ **A.** The hard drive is full.
- ○ **B.** The system has a defective RAM module.
- ○ **C.** The operating system has not been activated.
- ○ **D.** The system is low on both RAM capacity and HDD space.

6. You are upgrading a user in the production department to a new Windows XP system. The user wants you to move all her documents and picture files from her old Windows 2000 Professional environment to the new installation of Windows XP. What Windows XP tool should be used to do this?

Quick Answer: **78**
Detailed Answer: **96**

- ○ **A.** The Windows XP Fast User Transport utility
- ○ **B.** The Windows XP User State Migration tool
- ○ **C.** The System State Backup option
- ○ **D.** The ASR Restore option

7. When you started your desktop PC this morning, it rebooted itself during the POST process. You tried to start the system again, but it continued to automatically reboot before it could load the Windows splash screen. Where should you begin checking the system for the source of this problem?

Quick Answer: **78**
Detailed Answer: **96**

- ○ **A.** Check the microprocessor's fan and heat sink assembly; the microprocessor is overheating.
- ○ **B.** Boot the system to the ERD and check for the presence of the `pagefile.sys` file. Windows cannot
  create a swap file on the primary disk drive.
- ○ **C.** Check the system's installed RAM; one of the modules is failing and causing the system to lock up and reboot.
- ○ **D.** Boot the system to the Recovery Console on the Windows distribution CD and check the operating system's boot files; they may have been corrupted.

Quick Answer: **78**
Detailed Answer: **96**

8. Which Windows command-line utility is used to move files from `driver.cab` on a Windows distribution CD or recovery disk to repair a corrupted disk drive?

- ○ **A.** Expand
- ○ **B.** Extract
- ○ **C.** Move
- ○ **D.** Extend

9. Which Windows utility can be used to selectively turn off items during the startup process for diagnostic purposes?

    ○ **A.** Safe Mode

    ○ **B.** MSCONFIG

    ○ **C.** SFC

    ○ **D.** Dr. Watson

Quick Answer: **78**
Detailed Answer: **96**

10. Which of the following actions writes a new boot sector into the system volume?

    ○ **A.** Running the ASR Restore operation

    ○ **B.** Running the Diagnostic Startup option from the Startup tab of the MSCONFIG utility

    ○ **C.** Running the FIXBOOT command from the Recovery Console's command line

    ○ **D.** Running the SYS C: command from the Windows command interpreter

Quick Answer: **78**
Detailed Answer: **97**

11. After you upgrade a video adapter card's driver in Windows XP, the video display is scrambled. What action should you take to revert to the old driver version?

    ○ **A.** Boot into Safe Mode with command prompt only and remove the driver.

    ○ **B.** Boot into Safe Mode and run the Driver Rollback feature from the Device Manager.

    ○ **C.** Use the SFC utility to start up the system and roll back the driver.

    ○ **D.** Use the Recovery Console to reboot the system and then roll back the driver.

Quick Answer: **78**
Detailed Answer: **97**

12. During the boot process, your computer stalls and produces a blue screen displaying the words NTLDR missing. Which of the following best fixes this problem?

    ○ **A.** Boot to the Advanced Options menu and start the system in Last Known Good Configuration.

    ○ **B.** Boot to Safe Mode and run the Roll Back feature from the Device Manager.

    ○ **C.** Boot to the Windows distribution CD and use the Recovery Console's FIXMBR command to replace the master boot record (MBR).

    ○ **D.** Boot to Safe Mode and run the MSCONFIG utility.

Quick Answer: **78**
Detailed Answer: **97**

13. You need to reinstall Windows 2000 Professional in an existing system that has failed. The system has a set of four Setup disks and an Emergency Repair Disk. Which of the following must occur so that the disks can be used to start the system, enabling you to carry out the repair function?

   ○ **A.** Change the HDD driver settings to the default value.

   ○ **B.** Change the boot sequence in the CMOS to include the FDD in the startup process.

   ○ **C.** Change the boot order in the BOOT.INI file.

   ○ **D.** The device driver for the FDD must be enabled.

14. A user boots into Windows 2000 and receives an error message stating that one or more services did not start. Where can she go to examine which services did not start?

   ○ **A.** Device Manager

   ○ **B.** Task Manager

   ○ **C.** Dr. Watson

   ○ **D.** Event Viewer

15. What utility can be used to restore the Windows XP Registry from a backup if you cannot boot to a GUI?

   ○ **A.** Backup

   ○ **B.** Regrestore

   ○ **C.** Recovery Console

   ○ **D.** ScanReg

16. Your Windows XP system refuses to start up. You have been unable to recover the system using other methods, including Safe Mode, Last Known Good Configuration mode, and the Recovery Console. What else can be done in a Windows XP system to recover the system?

   ○ **A.** Run the Automated System Recovery (ASR) backup operation.

   ○ **B.** Run the Automated System Recovery (ASR) restore operation.

   ○ **C.** Run the Windows XP Repair Disk program (RDISK.EXE) from the command line of the ASR disk.

   ○ **D.** Run the Windows XP recovery program WINNT /ox at the command prompt.

17. Under what conditions should you consider manually establishing a Restore Point? (Select all that apply.)

   ○   **A.** Whenever you can't get into Safe Mode to reconfigure the driver loading process

   ○   **B.** Before you install a new application program and it creates problems with the system that uninstalling it does not resolve

   ○   **C.** Anytime you need to get back to a point where you know the system was functioning correctly

   ○   **D.** Before you update a driver and it appears to cause problems with the system that rolling back the driver does not resolve

18. In Windows, how do you test the print spooler if the printer won't print?

   ○   **A.** Use BOOTCFG to check the disk integrity.

   ○   **B.** Print directly to the printer port.

   ○   **C.** Change the printer cable.

   ○   **D.** Print from the command line.

19. Under what conditions should the standard Safe Mode startup option be used?

   ○   **A.** When an application does not start from the desktop or the command line

   ○   **B.** When Windows displays a `Registry Failure` error message

   ○   **C.** When Windows does not start after the `Starting Windows...` message appears

   ○   **D.** When Windows needs to load Real Mode drivers for a device instead of its embedded virtual drivers

20. Which of the following items are loaded in a standard Safe Mode startup?

   ○   **A.** `BOOT.INI`, `CONFIG.SYS`, `NTLDR`

   ○   **B.** Basic processor, DRAM, and HDD drivers

   ○   **C.** Basic mouse, keyboard, and standard VGA drivers

   ○   **D.** Standard network adapter, mouse, and keyboard drivers

21. In Windows, which utility can you use to control programs that run at startup?

    ○ **A.** STARTREG.EXE

    ○ **B.** MSCONFIG.EXE

    ○ **C.** REGEDIT.EXE

    ○ **D.** REGEDT32.EXE

22. What condition is indicated by the Missing Operating System error messages?

    ○ **A.** The drive is not formatted.

    ○ **B.** The MBR is missing or corrupt.

    ○ **C.** Operating system files are missing or corrupt.

    ○ **D.** The HDD cable is not attached.

23. What action can be taken when you encounter an Invalid Drive or Drive Specification error message? (Select the best answer.)

    ○ **A.** Replace the drive.

    ○ **B.** Reset the drive configuration in the CMOS Setup.

    ○ **C.** Repartition and reformat the drive.

    ○ **D.** Reinstall the operating system.

24. One of your applications fails to start when you click its icon on the desktop. What action should you take to correct this problem?

    ○ **A.** Right-click the icon and open the application's Properties to check its executable filename and path information.

    ○ **B.** Right-click the desktop and select the Properties option from the pop-up menu to check for proper command syntax and path information.

    ○ **C.** Move into the Control Panel and open the Add/Remove Software applet so that you can use the Add/Remove Software Wizard to repair the icon link to the application.

    ○ **D.** Try to execute the application's Install file from Windows Explorer.

25. After you install a device driver, the system becomes unstable. You try to reboot the system, but nothing happens. Then you perform a second reboot and select the Last Known Good Configuration option from the Advanced Options menu. However, the system does not reset to the old configuration. What is the problem?

  ○ **A.** The Last Known Good Configuration file is overwritten after each successful login, so there is no Good Configuration to revert to after the second reboot.

  ○ **B.** The driver has been corrupt for some time and cannot be rolled back.

  ○ **C.** The Last Known Good Configuration is rewritten at each logout or shutdown, so the old configuration no longer exists.

  ○ **D.** You should use the Recovery Console's Rollback feature before selecting the Last Known Good Configuration option.

Objective 3.4: Perform preventative maintenance on operating systems

1. Your Windows 2000 system is working with SP2 and you want to upgrade to SP4. What do you need to know about this operation?

  ○ **A.** You must remove SP2 and then install SP4.

  ○ **B.** You must install SP3 before going to SP4.

  ○ **C.** SP4 includes SP3, so you can simply install it.

  ○ **D.** You should install SP4 only if the system is having problems using just SP2.

2. You are responsible for 75 Windows XP Professional–based PCs in your organization. To minimize the amount of time you need to use keeping these systems updated, you decide to configure all the systems to receive automatic updates from Microsoft. How can you configure the Automatic Updates feature for Windows XP? (Select all that apply.)

  ○ **A.** Use the Add Components utility to add the Automatic Updates feature to the system.

  ○ **B.** Double-click Automatic Updates in the Control Panel and then click Automatic.

  ○ **C.** Use the Add/Remove Programs utility to install the Windows Automatic Updates utility.

  ○ **D.** Select the Automatic Updates tab under the Control Panel's System icon and configure the Automatic Updates options.

3. You are preparing to install a new scanner on one of your Windows XP Professional production computers. In case there is a problem with installing the new device, you decide to establish a Restore Point that you can return to. Where can you establish a Restore Point in Windows XP Professional?

Quick Answer: **78**
Detailed Answer: **99**

- ○ **A.** Control Panel/Administrative Tools/System Restore
- ○ **B.** Control Panel/System/System Restore
- ○ **C.** Start/All Programs/Accessories/System Tools/System Restore
- ○ **D.** Control Panel/System/Hardware/Device Manager/System Restore

4. Microsoft typically releases patches in the form of updates, or in collections that include additional functionality or new device drivers, that it refers to as _____.

Quick Answer: **78**
Detailed Answer: **99**

- ○ **A.** Service packs
- ○ **B.** OEM patches
- ○ **C.** Releases
- ○ **D.** Updates

Objective 4.0: Printers and Scanners

Objective 4.1: Identify the fundamental principles of using printers and scanners

1. What type of printer is used to print continuous-feed, multipart forms?

   ○ **A.** Dot-matrix printers

   ○ **B.** Inkjet printers

   ○ **C.** Laser printers

   ○ **D.** Dye-sublimation printers

Quick Answer: **78**
Detailed Answer: **100**

2. You have been asked to install a printer in a customer's office. When you arrive, you find that a number of connectivity options are available with the printer, including wireless RF, infrared, parallel SCSI, and USB connections. Which printer interface is fastest for a local printer?

   ○ **A.** SCSI

   ○ **B.** 802.11g

   ○ **C.** USB

   ○ **D.** IrDA

Quick Answer: **78**
Detailed Answer: **100**

3. Which of the following printers can produce photographic-quality, continuous-tone images?

   ○ **A.** Dot-matrix printer

   ○ **B.** Dye-sublimation printer

   ○ **C.** Direct thermal printer

   ○ **D.** Thermal wax transfer printer

Quick Answer: **78**
Detailed Answer: **100**

4. What printer type produces print by squirting ink at the page?

   ○ **A.** Laser

   ○ **B.** Thermal

   ○ **C.** Inkjet

   ○ **D.** Dot-matrix

Quick Answer: **78**
Detailed Answer: **100**

5. Which of the following statements is correct regarding direct thermal printers and thermal wax transfer printers?

Quick Answer: **78**
Detailed Answer: **100**

- ○ **A.** Thermal wax transfer printers require special thermal paper on which to print.
- ○ **B.** In the thermal printer, the print head moves across the page.
- ○ **C.** The early fax machine technology was based on direct thermal printing.
- ○ **D.** Both direct thermal printers and thermal wax transfer printers are available in monochrome version only.

6. What type of printer delivers ink to the page by applying power to an electromagnet, which in turn forces a wire to strike an inked ribbon?

Quick Answer: **78**
Detailed Answer: **100**

- ○ **A.** A laser printer
- ○ **B.** A drum printer
- ○ **C.** An inkjet printer
- ○ **D.** A dot-matrix printer

7. In a laser printer, a positive charge on the transfer corona wire causes _____.

Quick Answer: **78**
Detailed Answer: **100**

- ○ **A.** the positive image to appear on the print drum
- ○ **B.** the toner to be transferred from the drum to the paper
- ○ **C.** the excess toner to be dislodged from the drum after printing
- ○ **D.** the negative image to appear on the print drum

8. What are the two functions of the two corona wires in a laser printer?

Quick Answer: **78**
Detailed Answer: **100**

- ○ **A.** They transfer toner from the drum to the paper.
- ○ **B.** They fuse the toner to the paper.
- ○ **C.** They condition the drum to be written on.
- ○ **D.** They clean the drum.

9. What is the function of the fuser unit in a laser printer?

Quick Answer: **78**
Detailed Answer: **100**

- ○ **A.** It transfers the image from the drum to the paper.
- ○ **B.** It melts toner to the paper.
- ○ **C.** It transfers image to the drum.
- ○ **D.** It cleans the drum.

10. What is the order of operations of a laser printer?

Quick Answer: **78**
Detailed Answer: **101**

- ○ **A.** Conditioning, cleaning, writing, developing, fusing, transferring
- ○ **B.** Cleaning, conditioning , writing, developing, transferring, fusing
- ○ **C.** Writing, conditioning, cleaning, developing, fusing, transferring
- ○ **D.** Conditioning, cleaning, writing, developing, transferring, fusing

11. Which component of a laser printer transfers toner to the paper?

Quick Answer: **78**
Detailed Answer: **101**

- ○ **A.** The drum
- ○ **B.** The transfer corona wire
- ○ **C.** The fuser assembly
- ○ **D.** The platen

12. What is the main circuit board in a dot-matrix printer called?

Quick Answer: **78**
Detailed Answer: **101**

- ○ **A.** Main control board
- ○ **B.** Printhead board
- ○ **C.** Control panel
- ○ **D.** Sensor board

Objective 4.2: Identify basic concepts of installing, configuring, optimizing, and upgrading printers and scanners

1. After printing out a picture you have downloaded from your digital camera, you notice that the color on the printed version is very different from that of the picture displayed on the camera and the PC's monitor. What action can you take to make the printed copy more closely resemble the copy in the camera?

Quick Answer: **79**
Detailed Answer: **101**

- ○ **A.** Install new ink cartridges.
- ○ **B.** Register the printer colors with the monitor.
- ○ **C.** Calibrate the printer to match the monitor.
- ○ **D.** Clean the printer's print head mechanism.

2. You are asked to install a parallel printer on a standalone Windows XP desktop system that supports this standard through a 25-pin D-shell connector. Which of the following is the best installation method for this printer?

Quick Answer: **79**
Detailed Answer: **101**

- ○ **A.** Connect the printer to the LPT1 interface, turn on the printer, turn on the PC, and then let its PnP process detect the attached printer.

- ○ **B.** Connect the printer to the COM1 interface, turn it on, turn on the PC, open the Add New Hardware applet, and then install the correct printer driver from the Windows list.

- ○ **C.** Connect the printer, turn it on, turn on the PC, insert the printer's OEM disk or CD in the appropriate drive, and then install the correct printer driver using the Windows Have Disk function.

- ○ **D.** Connect the printer to the PC's parallel port interface, turn it on, turn on the PC, access Windows, click on the Add Printer option, and then use the Add Printer Wizard to install the correct printer drivers.

3. You are tasked with the install of a new USB printer in a Windows XP Home system. Which of the following methods are commonly used for installing this type of printer? (Select all that apply.)

Quick Answer: **79**
Detailed Answer: **101**

- ○ **A.** Enable USB printers in the CMOS Setup and let the system autodetect the printer.

- ○ **B.** Connect the printer to the host PC, boot the computer system, and allow the Windows PnP process to discover and install the proper driver.

- ○ **C.** Turn on the PC, use the Add Printer Wizard, and select a generic printer driver. Then turn on the printer.

- ○ **D.** Insert the manufacturer's driver disc in the CD drive and allow the system to configure the printer when Windows starts up.

4. Which of the following is not a type of interface connection commonly used with printers?

Quick Answer: **79**
Detailed Answer: **102**

- ○ **A.** USB
- ○ **B.** SCSI
- ○ **C.** SATA
- ○ **D.** IrDA

5. Which two of the following indicate the presence of a network-ready printer?

- ○ **A.** A UTP network cable connected to the printer
- ○ **B.** An RJ-45 jack on the back of the printer
- ○ **C.** An RS-232 port on the back of the printer
- ○ **D.** An RJ-11 jack on the back of the printer

Objective 4.3: Identify tools, basic diagnostic procedures, and troubleshooting techniques for printers and scanners

1. Typically, the first test to perform when a printer won't print is the _____.

- ○ **A.** signal cable-check
- ○ **B.** printer self-test
- ○ **C.** port loopback test
- ○ **D.** configuration check

2. A customer has brought his laser printer into your repair area because it produces a paper feed error when he tries to print a document. Where is the first place to check given this symptom?

- ○ **A.** The pickup rollers
- ○ **B.** The compression rollers
- ○ **C.** The developing rollers
- ○ **D.** The registration mechanism

3. One of your customers reports that she is getting poor quality output from her color printer. She indicates that the inkjet printer is producing disfigured graphics. What actions should you take to identify the source of this problem? (Select all that apply.)

- ○ **A.** Calibrate the printer.
- ○ **B.** Install a new print head and ink cartridges.
- ○ **C.** Check the printer's paper thickness settings.
- ○ **D.** Check the wear on the printer's paper-handling mechanisms.

4. If an inkjet printer is printing text correctly but leaves a line through each character, what is the most likely cause of this problem?

Quick Answer: **79**
Detailed Answer: **102**

- ○ **A.** One of the printhead nozzles is partially clogged and needs to be cleaned out.
- ○ **B.** One of the ink cartridges needs to be refilled.
- ○ **C.** The printer driver software has been corrupted and must be replaced.
- ○ **D.** The paper-handling mechanism is malfunctioning.

5. Your first activity of the morning is to print out a report that gets compiled each night and downloaded to your computer. The printer was working properly when you left the office last night, but now it does not print. What should you check first in this situation?

Quick Answer: **79**
Detailed Answer: **102**

- ○ **A.** Determine whether there is paper in the printer.
- ○ **B.** Check the printer driver to see if it has become corrupt.
- ○ **C.** Determine whether the printer driver is missing from the system due to a virus.
- ○ **D.** Check to see if the building maintenance crew may have disconnected the power cord from your printer during the evening.

6. You have been called to a new advertising firm that has just set up shop. The firm has a new flatbed scanner that does not scan. When you test it, the scanning light is on, but it does not move across the page. Which of the following is the most likely cause of the problem?

Quick Answer: **79**
Detailed Answer: **102**

- ○ **A.** The resolution setting of the scanning software is not compatible with the size of the picture being scanned.
- ○ **B.** The picture being scanned is too big for the resolution setting and memory available in the host system.
- ○ **C.** The scanner's light positioning mechanism is locked.
- ○ **D.** The scanner's signal cable is faulty.

Quick Check

7. A user is having problems printing to his local printer. It was working fine until he sent several documents to the printer one after the other. The printer turned out a few pages but then stopped printing. The user can no longer print to that printer from his computer. When you attempt to print a test page from the printer, it prints successfully. What item should you check next?

Quick Answer: **79**
Detailed Answer: **103**

   ○ **A.** The printer signal cable

   ○ **B.** The Windows Print spooler

   ○ **C.** The printer driver

   ○ **D.** The printer port enabling in the CMOS Setup

8. You have been called to a print shop to troubleshoot its new flatbed scanner. After you unlock the light bar mechanism, you discover that the light comes on and runs during its self-test. However, it does not move when the software application initiates an actual scan operation. What is the most likely reason for this?

Quick Answer: **79**
Detailed Answer: **103**

   ○ **A.** The scanner's application software is configured incorrectly.

   ○ **B.** The scanner's signal cable is disconnected.

   ○ **C.** The scanner's TWAIN driver is corrupted.

   ○ **D.** The I/O port the scanner is connected to has been configured incorrectly in the PC's CMOS Setup.

9. After handling a printed document from a laser printer, you notice the letters smudge and the toner rubs off. What is most likely the problem?

Quick Answer: **79**
Detailed Answer: **103**

   ○ **A.** The primary corona wire is bad.

   ○ **B.** The fuser is bad.

   ○ **C.** The developing roller is bad.

   ○ **D.** The transfer corona is bad.

Objective 5.0: Networks

Objective 5.1: Identify the fundamental principles of networks

1. A CAT5 UTP cable consists of _____.

   ○ **A.** Four twisted wires inside

   ○ **B.** Four pairs of twisted wires inside

   ○ **C.** Two pairs of twisted wires inside

   ○ **D.** Four sets of four twisted wires inside

Quick Answer: **79**
Detailed Answer: **104**

2. What is the maximum range for low-power Bluetooth devices?

   ○ **A.** 1 meter

   ○ **B.** 3 meters

   ○ **C.** 10 meters

   ○ **D.** 100 meters

Quick Answer: **79**
Detailed Answer: **104**

3. What frequency does the 802.11a standard uses to conduct wireless network connectivity?

   ○ **A.** 2.4MHz

   ○ **B.** 900MHz

   ○ **C.** 5.2GHz

   ○ **D.** 54MHz

Quick Answer: **79**
Detailed Answer: **104**

4. You are setting up a home office network for your family business, but you have no router or server to automatically supply network addresses for your three computers and a laser printer. You know you need to manually set the IP address and subnet mask information for all the systems, so you are looking for documentation about how to accomplish this. What is the term you should be looking for to find information about manually configuring an IP address?

   ○ **A.** Static IP addresses

   ○ **B.** APIPA

   ○ **C.** Classful IP addressing

   ○ **D.** Dynamic IP addresses

Quick Answer: **79**
Detailed Answer: **104**

5. Which of the following connectivity methods are used with 802.11g?

Quick Answer: **79**
Detailed Answer: **104**

- ○ **A.** CAT5 cabling with RJ-45 connectors
- ○ **B.** Fiber-optic cables and SC connectors
- ○ **C.** RF signals and antennas
- ○ **D.** Coaxial cables and BNC connectors

6. Which of the following network types is best for a small business?

Quick Answer: **79**
Detailed Answer: **104**

- ○ **A.** LAN
- ○ **B.** WAN
- ○ **C.** MAN
- ○ **D.** CAN

7. Which network component types are compatible with 802.11g systems?

Quick Answer: **79**
Detailed Answer: **104**

- ○ **A.** 802.11a
- ○ **B.** 802.11b
- ○ **C.** Bluetooth
- ○ **D.** 802.3

8. A residential customer who has just switched Internet access over to a satellite system has called to find out why she sometimes experiences delays in the satellite system delivering Internet connectivity. How do you explain this delay to the customer?

Quick Answer: **79**
Detailed Answer: **104**

- ○ **A.** Modern satellite systems should not have a delay period.
- ○ **B.** There is a downlink delay time associated with connecting to the satellite source.
- ○ **C.** The dish requires an azimuth correction period to switch to a different satellite.
- ○ **D.** This is due to connection latency caused by additional parties in the communications link.

9. What networking technology supports several peripherals communicating with a PC simultaneously?

Quick Answer: **79**
Detailed Answer: **105**

- ○ **A.** Bluetooth
- ○ **B.** Ethernet
- ○ **C.** IrDA
- ○ **D.** Wi-Fi

10. Which of the following network types does not have to interact with a dedicated server?

   ○ **A.** A domain-based LAN

   ○ **B.** A peer-to-peer LAN

   ○ **C.** An intranet

   ○ **D.** An Internet

11. You are setting up a small peer-to-peer network in your home office and have decided to use simple private IP addressing with static addresses. Which of the following IP addresses is reserved specifically for use as a private address?

   ○ **A.** 192.168.0.1

   ○ **B.** 170.124.0.1

   ○ **C.** 169.254.0.1

   ○ **D.** 135.254.0.1

12. What general advantage does an 802.11g network have over an 802.11b network?

   ○ **A.** Better data transfer rate

   ○ **B.** Greater useful transmission distance

   ○ **C.** Better frequency range

   ○ **D.** More simultaneous users

13. What is the maximum communicating speed of an 802.11g-rated wireless access point?

   ○ **A.** 2Mbps

   ○ **B.** 54Mbps

   ○ **C.** 5.5Mbps

   ○ **D.** 11Mbps

14. A customer wants to install a 1Gbps local area network in his facility. Which of the following cabling types will meet the user's expectations?

   ○ **A.** CAT3 cabling

   ○ **B.** CAT5 Cabling

   ○ **C.** CAT6 cabling

   ○ **D.** Coaxial cabling

15. The 802.11x standard is used to identify which type of network?

- ○ **A.** Ethernet
- ○ **B.** Wi-Fi wireless
- ○ **C.** Fiber-optic
- ○ **D.** Bluetooth wireless

16. Which wireless networking option offers the fastest communications? (Select all that apply.)

- ○ **A.** 802.11a
- ○ **B.** 802.11b
- ○ **C.** 802.11g
- ○ **D.** 802.15.1

17. Which of the following is an advantage of peer-to-peer networks?

- ○ **A.** It's easy to share information.
- ○ **B.** It's easy to implement security.
- ○ **C.** They centralize user accounts.
- ○ **D.** It's easy to implement standards across the system.

18. What type of network typically employs SC connectors?

- ○ **A.** Client/server STP-based networks
- ○ **B.** Peer-to-peer UTP-based networks
- ○ **C.** Ethernet fiber-optic-based networks
- ○ **D.** CAT7 UTP-based networks

19. An RJ-45 connector is most commonly used with _____.

- ○ **A.** disk drive units
- ○ **B.** fiber-optic cabling
- ○ **C.** coaxial cabling
- ○ **D.** unshielded twisted-pair cabling

20. Where is single mode fiber cable most likely to be employed?

- ○ **A.** In fiber-optic-based local area networks
- ○ **B.** In networks with connections ranging up to 20 kilometers
- ○ **C.** In VOIP connections
- ○ **D.** In fiber cabling drops from the street to residential customers

21. You join a new division as part of the technical staff of a large company. This new division integrates Windows XP workstations with an older network that uses NetWare 4.0 and older software. Due to software incompatibility, TCP/IP is not a viable option. Which of the following networking protocols should the Windows XP workstation be using in this network?

  ○ **A.** NetBEUI

  ○ **B.** IPX/SPX

  ○ **C.** NWLink

  ○ **D.** AppleTalk

22. Which of the following is not an advantage associated with using TCP/IP as the network protocol?

  ○ **A.** It enables messages to be fragmented and reassembled.

  ○ **B.** It enables messages to be routed to a specific computer.

  ○ **C.** It can service networks that include a wide variety of computer types.

  ○ **D.** It provides a high level of encryption to data packets.

23. Why are you required to use plenum-rated cable in air returns?

  ○ **A.** To minimize the spread of toxic gases throughout the facility

  ○ **B.** To avoid additional heat buildup in the air space

  ○ **C.** To reduce EMI caused by air-handling equipment

  ○ **D.** To protect the cabling from oxidation

24. Which of the following modem types is not considered a high-speed broadband communications device?

  ○ **A.** A DSL modem

  ○ **B.** An ISDN modem

  ○ **C.** An analog modem

  ○ **D.** A cable modem

Objective 5.2: Install, configure, optimize, and upgrade networks

1. A traveling user needs to access the company's network through a wireless access point when he is in the office. What type of hardware do you recommend?

Quick Answer: **79**
Detailed Answer: **106**

- ○ **A.** An IrDA card

- ○ **B.** An IEEE-1394 adapter

- ○ **C.** An 802.3 adapter

- ○ **D.** An 802.11 adapter

2. You have been asked to make a recommendation to improve the performance of a client's network. When you examine the network architecture, you find that it is based on low-speed hubs. What should you suggest to improve the LAN's performance?

Quick Answer: **79**
Detailed Answer: **106**

- ○ **A.** Install higher speed hubs to minimize system upgrade costs and maintain compatibility with the existing network structure.

- ○ **B.** Install high-speed switches to replace the old hubs. This provides more intelligent transmission of the information around the network.

- ○ **C.** Install routers to replace the hubs. Router performance is so much better than hubs that the network performance increase is very noticeable.

- ○ **D.** Install a router to better control information movement in the network and replace the hubs with switches to improve network traffic.

3. What Windows tool can be used to configure most modern routers?

Quick Answer: **79**
Detailed Answer: **107**

- ○ **A.** The Windows Explorer interface

- ○ **B.** The Device Manager utility

- ○ **C.** The MSCONFIG utility

- ○ **D.** The Internet Explorer web browser

4. You are trying to determine the best place to locate your desk in a large open office area. You communicate with the office network through a wireless 802.11b PC Card adapter in your notebook computer. There are three different access points (APs) positioned more or less equally around the periphery of the office. What is the easiest way to determine where to put your desk?

Quick Answer: **79**
Detailed Answer: **107**

○ **A.** Use the power meter in the wireless device's configuration program to view the relative signal strength as you move your portable around the office. Put the desk in the area of the room where the meter shows the highest signal strength.

○ **B.** Use the power meter in the wireless device's configuration program to view the relative signal strengths of the different APs and then place your desk near the strongest one.

○ **C.** Use the power meter in the wireless device's configuration program to view the relative signal strengths of the different APs and then configure your notebook card to communicate with the strongest one. You can put the desk anywhere in the office you like.

○ **D.** Obtain a handheld power meter to take high-quality samples of the signal strengths produced by the different APs and then configure your wireless card to communicate with the AP that has the highest signal strength. Then place the desk in the area where that AP is strongest.

5. Your boss has called you into his office to look at his Internet Explorer. He is having trouble getting a current copy of his favorite online news website since another technician upgraded his system to IE7 yesterday. Under the new Internet Explorer version, he can view only yesterday's page and cannot access more current information for that web page. What do you need to do to get him today's version of the news site?

Quick Answer: **79**
Detailed Answer: **107**

○ **A.** Reset his Windows Date and Time Properties to display today's time and date information.

○ **B.** Access the Services console in the Microsoft Management Console and restart the IE History cache.

○ **C.** Access Internet Options in the IE Tools menu and then click the Settings button. In the Browser history area, set the Check for Newer Version of Stored Pages to Every Time I Visit the Web page.

○ **D.** Access Internet Options in the IE Tools menu and then click the Settings button. In the History area, reduce the Days to Keep Pages in History Setting to 0 to force the system to display only today's web history.

6. You are traveling and you want to add yourself to the wireless network in your hotel. What do you need to do to join yourself to the hotel's hot spot using your laptop with built-in Wi-Fi? (Select all that apply.)

   ○ **A.** Configure the SSID on your laptop to match the local access point.

   ○ **B.** Confiure WEP on your laptop to match the local AP.

   ○ **C.** Configure the Proxy Server settings in Internet Explorer.

   ○ **D.** Configure your Wi-Fi channel setting to match the local AP.

7. A cable modem is attached to a router using _____ connector.

   ○ **A.** a Type-F

   ○ **B.** an RJ-11

   ○ **C.** an RJ-45

   ○ **D.** a BNC

8. Which of the following network types would not employ a dedicated DHCP server for automatic addressing functions?

   ○ **A.** Peer-to-peer

   ○ **B.** Intranet

   ○ **C.** Internet

   ○ **D.** Extranet

Objective 5.3: Identify tools, diagnostic procedures, and troubleshooting techniques for networks

1. Which of the following indicates that an operating "physical" connection is in place to a local area network?

   ○ **A.** Link lights are present and operating on the back of the network adapter card.

   ○ **B.** You can ping the local host.

   ○ **C.** You can view the network adapter's connection status in the Device Manager of the local machine.

   ○ **D.** You can ping IP address 127.0.0.1.

2. You are working on a client computer that cannot see any other computers on the network. You check the TCP/IP configuration for the computer and find that it is set for 169.254.0.2. What is the most likely cause of the computer's network problem?

Quick Answer: **79**
Detailed Answer: **107**

   ○ **A.** You have an unplugged network cable.

   ○ **B.** You have a missing DHCP server or bad router configuration.

   ○ **C.** The DNS function is not configured correctly on this client.

   ○ **D.** TCP/IP is not configured properly.

3. Which of the following can be used to check the operation of a network adapter card?

Quick Answer: **79**
Detailed Answer: **107**

   ○ **A.** A cable tester

   ○ **B.** An Ethernet loopback cable

   ○ **C.** A digital mulitmeter

   ○ **D.** A time domain reflectometer

4. You have been sent to troubleshoot an Internet connectivity problem. When you try to ping the site's FQDN, the site cannot be located; however, you can ping its IP address. What network function should be checked?

Quick Answer: **79**
Detailed Answer: **108**

   ○ **A.** DNS

   ○ **B.** DHCP

   ○ **C.** WINS

   ○ **D.** FTP

5. When you enter IPCONFIG in the Run dialog box, you momentarily see a black box on the display followed by an immediate return to the normal desktop screen. What is occurring with this command?

Quick Answer: **79**
Detailed Answer: **108**

   ○ **A.** This is a normal response for running a TCP/IP utility from the Run dialog box.

   ○ **B.** The network adapter is bad. Therefore, there is no information for the IPCONFIG utility to return.

   ○ **C.** The local host is not communicating with the client computer. Therefore, there is no information for the IPCONFIG utility to report.

   ○ **D.** The TCP/IP utility has not been configured on the local machine.

6. After statically assigning an IP address and subnet mask to a Windows XP machine, you try to ping the local adapter's IP address, but you receive a `Destination host unreachable` message. What does this indicate?

   ○ **A.** TCP/IP has not been loaded into the system.

   ○ **B.** The local adapter's IP address has not been initialized.

   ○ **C.** TCP/IP is not working on the gateway device.

   ○ **D.** The default gateway is not functional.

Quick Answer: **79**
Detailed Answer: **108**

7. A flashing indicator light on the back of a network adapter card indicates which of the following?

   ○ **A.** Network activity is occurring.

   ○ **B.** Data is being transferred from the NIC to the network media.

   ○ **C.** A connection exists to an active network.

   ○ **D.** The NIC has been configured properly for TCP/IP operations.

Quick Answer: **79**
Detailed Answer: **108**

Objective 6.0: Security

Objective 6.1: Identify the fundamental principles of security

1. You install a new wireless network for a client. However, your client has been reading about network security and asks you to increase the security of the network while maintaining the wireless nature of the network. What do you suggest to accomplish this?

   ○ **A.** Connect all the wireless clients to the wireless access point using CAT5.

   ○ **B.** Enable Wired Equivalent Privacy.

   ○ **C.** Install more wireless access points throughout the network.

   ○ **D.** Change encryption from 40-bit keys to 16-bit keys.

Quick Answer: **80**
Detailed Answer: **109**

2. A _____ is used to block unauthorized outside users from accessing an intranet site.

   ○ **A.** hub

   ○ **B.** router

   ○ **C.** gateway

   ○ **D.** firewall

Quick Answer: **80**
Detailed Answer: **109**

3. Performing a System State Backup backs up _____.

   ○ **A.** the entire operating system along with user configuration settings

   ○ **B.** key operating system configuration settings and data so that the system can be rebuilt quickly in the event of a failure

   ○ **C.** data that has changed since the last major backup

   ○ **D.** tagged files and folders

Quick Answer: **80**
Detailed Answer: **109**

4. You are setting up a SOHO network by connecting several Windows XP computers to a router, which in turn provides access to a broadband Internet connection. What steps should be taken to protect the network from attack?

   ○ **A.** Enable the Windows Firewall feature on each machine.

   ○ **B.** Establish a unique SSID on each machine.

   ○ **C.** Enable a unique WEP key for each machine.

   ○ **D.** Configure MS-CHAP authentication on each machine.

Quick Answer: **80**
Detailed Answer: **109**

5. Which of the following are wireless encryption protocols? (Select all that apply.)

- ○ **A.** WPA
- ○ **B.** WEP
- ○ **C.** SSID
- ○ **D.** CHAPS

6. A member of the Power Users group has been trying to access the files of a user who has left the company. However, she can't get into them. Why is this?

- ○ **A.** Power Users don't have access rights to user's files and folders unless they created the user or they have been granted permissions through some other source.
- ○ **B.** Only a file's owner or an administrator can access secured files.
- ○ **C.** Power User members have access only to their own files and system hardware configuration functions.
- ○ **D.** Power Users have access only to files allowed by an administrator.

7. You have been asked to connect a single Windows XP system to a broadband modem for Internet access. Which of the following actions should you take to protect the PC from the Internet?

- ○ **A.** Turn on Windows Firewall and enable the file sharing option.
- ○ **B.** Turn on ICS and enable file and printer sharing.
- ○ **C.** Configure the firewall function in the modem.
- ○ **D.** Install spam blocker, adware, and antivirus protection software.

8. A technician is in the server room when you enter, and you notice that the door has been braced open. What should you do?

- ○ **A.** Tell the technician to close the door when he leaves.
- ○ **B.** Report the security breach to the network supervisor.
- ○ **C.** Close the door and note the security breach in the server room log book.
- ○ **D.** Tell the technician he is creating a security breach and close the door yourself.

9. Which of the following is considered malicious software?

- ○ **A.** Adware
- ○ **B.** Pop-ups
- ○ **C.** Spam
- ○ **D.** Worms

Quick Answer: **80**
Detailed Answer: **110**

10. Which of the following is considered a virus?

- ○ **A.** Trojan
- ○ **B.** Spam
- ○ **C.** Worm
- ○ **D.** Spyware

Quick Answer: **80**
Detailed Answer: **110**

11. Where would you establish a Supervisory password on a computer that will be installed in an Internet kiosk so that users can access the system but not modify its configuration?

- ○ **A.** In CMOS.
- ○ **B.** In the BIOS.
- ○ **C.** In Windows.
- ○ **D.** If you set a password in this environment, users will not be able to access the system.

Quick Answer: **80**
Detailed Answer: **110**

12. What is one way to completely remove data from a hard disk drive?

- ○ **A.** Partition and completely reformat the drive.
- ○ **B.** Reinstall the operating system over the existing OS structure.
- ○ **C.** Delete all the files on the drive and perform a disk defrag operation.
- ○ **D.** Physically destroy the drive's platters with a hammer or acid.

Quick Answer: **80**
Detailed Answer: **110**

13. Which of the following steps can be taken to protect a wireless network from unauthorized user access? (Select all that apply.)

- ○ **A.** Set up MAC address filtering on each card.
- ○ **B.** Configure the AP so that it doesn't broadcast the SSID.
- ○ **C.** Set up WEP on all network nodes.
- ○ **D.** Minimize the distance between network connections.

Quick Answer: **80**
Detailed Answer: **110**

14. Which of the following are advantages associated with using NTFS? (Select all that apply.)

- ○ **A.** Data security
- ○ **B.** Support for larger drives
- ○ **C.** 64-bit entries to keep track of items
- ○ **D.** Handling small drives efficiently

Objective 6.2: Install, configure, upgrade, and optimize security

1. A user wants to back up his system information to a CD, but he doesn't have any CD burner software to work with. How does he do this in Windows XP Home Edition?

- ○ **A.** Use the Windows Backup utility to save to a CD.
- ○ **B.** Windows XP Home does not back up to a recordable CD.
- ○ **C.** Use the System State Backup utility.
- ○ **D.** Use the grandfather/father/son technique to back up the data.

2. You have just installed a new high-speed tape drive in a customer's server and backed up her entire system. How can you be sure that the new drive has done this successfully?

- ○ **A.** Check the size of the backup file to make sure that it is large enough to represent the stored data.
- ○ **B.** Check the backup log to make sure that everything indicated was backed up to the tape.
- ○ **C.** Place the backup tape in another drive and see if it can be read from a secondary storage device in case the first drive fails.
- ○ **D.** Verify the backup by performing a restore operation from the tape.

3. You are searching online for a new high-end video card that you want to purchase for your game machine. When you go to one of the sites that have listed this product in your favorite search engine, you receive a message warning you that the site's SSL certificate has expired. Which of the following actions should you take first?

Quick Answer: **80**
Detailed Answer: **111**

- ○ **A.** Leave the site immediately because there is no security connection present at this time.

- ○ **B.** In Internet Explorer, access the Internet Options page, select the Contents tab, and access Certificates. Click the Clear the SSL State option.

- ○ **C.** Examine the certificate to determine whether it comes from a trustworthy authority and determine whether you trust it before doing business on this site.

- ○ **D.** Reconfigure the Windows Date and Time Properties to show the correct date and time.

4. What backup method requires the most time to perform?

Quick Answer: **80**
Detailed Answer: **111**

- ○ **A.** Incremental
- ○ **B.** Full
- ○ **C.** Differential
- ○ **D.** Selective

5. After a system becomes infected with a virus, what actions can be taken to remove viruses from an infected system? (Select all that apply.)

Quick Answer: **80**
Detailed Answer: **111**

- ○ **A.** Run an antivirus program to detect and remove the virus.

- ○ **B.** Reinstall the operating system over the current OS structure to replace the infected file.

- ○ **C.** Partition the drive and reinstall the operating system.

- ○ **D.** Install the antivirus software CD and run it.

Objective 6.3: Identify tool, diagnostic procedures, and troubleshooting techniques for security

1. Your company is sponsoring an Internet café at a local trade show, and you are responsible for setting up six PCs that trade show attendees can walk up to and use to browse the Web or check their email. Because these machines are open to public use, what type of BIOS password should be established on them?

   Quick Answer: **80**
   Detailed Answer: **111**

   ○ **A.** User access

   ○ **B.** Remote access

   ○ **C.** Admin access

   ○ **D.** Supervisory access

2. You are responsible for maintaining and administering 35 PCs in your area of the building. You need to secure them so that employees cannot change CMOS settings. What types of passwords should be set to provide secured logons for users in the CMOS while still protecting the system configuration? (Select all that apply.)

   Quick Answer: **80**
   Detailed Answer: **111**

   ○ **A.** User access

   ○ **B.** Remote access

   ○ **C.** Admin access

   ○ **D.** Supervisory access

Objective 6.4: Perform preventative maintenance for computer security

1. A friend has contacted you with questions about his Windows XP Professional PC. He uses it to perform Internet research for his home business, in addition to preparing reports, creating documents, and managing finances. Other than the applications he is familiar with, your friend is basically PC illiterate. However, he is worried that his system is not up-to-date because he has heard about updates to Windows XP, but the has no idea of how to acquire or install them. What can you tell your friend about acquiring and installing updates and patches for his computer system?

Quick Answer: **80**
Detailed Answer: **112**

- ○ **A.** Your friend should use the Internet to access the Microsoft Windows Update page where he can obtain and install the latest updates and service packs for his operating system through the Windows Update service.

- ○ **B.** Offer to prepare your friend an update disc created using a Windows XP PC that is completely updated with the latest patches and service pack.

- ○ **C.** Tell your friend to download SP2 for Windows XP Professional from the Microsoft website because all other Windows XP patches are unnecessary.

- ○ **D.** Tell your friend not to worry because Windows XP Professional comes with the Automatic Updates feature enabled by default. Therefore, he has been receiving Windows Updates in the background as he has been browsing the Internet.

Quick Check

Quick Answer: **80**
Detailed Answer: **112**

2. You run your own computer management company and would like to expand your business. However, it seems that you are constantly handling emergency calls from your established customers and can't find the time to investigate better business activities for your company. After reviewing your call log for the past year, you conclude that a large portion of your time has been spent removing viruses, spyware, and adware from customers' systems, which is included in their annual service fee. If you could reduce the number of calls you must handle performing these types of services, you could investigate more profitable business activities. What can you do to protect PC systems against malware like your customers have been encountering so that you can pursue these other activities?

   ○ **A.** Configure their firewalls to block the user access to the Internet.

   ○ **B.** Educate users about how these types of programs are encountered and how they can be avoided.

   ○ **C.** Use file and folder permission settings to limit user interactions with their PCs.

   ○ **D.** Use the Sharing feature to limit access to the operating system kernel files.

Objective 7.0: Safety and Environmental Issues

Objective 7.1: Describe the aspects and importance of safety and environmental issues

1. You have just installed a replacement system board in a customer's PC, and you drop the last screw into the system unit. Which is the best way to retrieve the screw from the system unit?

   ○ **A.** Use plastic tweezers.

   ○ **B.** Use long needle-nose pliers.

   ○ **C.** Use an extension magnet.

   ○ **D.** Use a magnetic screwdriver.

Quick Answer: **80**
Detailed Answer: **113**

2. You are preparing to install new adapter cards in a desktop PC. Which of the following actions should you take first?

   ○ **A.** Put on an antistatic wrist strap and connect it to the chassis of the system unit.

   ○ **B.** Unplug the computer from the AC power source.

   ○ **C.** Unplug the power supply from the system board's power connector.

   ○ **D.** Roll back any existing drivers for the cards that you will be installing.

Quick Answer: **80**
Detailed Answer: **113**

3. What are all hazardous materials required to have that accompany them when they change hands?

   ○ **A.** Disposal bags

   ○ **B.** Material Safety Data Sheets (MSDS)

   ○ **C.** Red flags

   ○ **D.** Mr. Yuk stickers

Quick Answer: **80**
Detailed Answer: **113**

Objective 7.2: Identify potential hazards and implement proper safety procedures including ESD precautions and procedures, safe work environment, and equipment handling

1. You are preparing to travel to a job to upgrade the RAM in a customer's PC. Which of the following statements is correct concerning the handling of the RAM modules?

Quick Answer: **80**
Detailed Answer: **113**

- ○ **A.** Lay the RAM devices on a sheet of foil while they are waiting to be installed.
- ○ **B.** Store the RAM devices in antistatic bags to transport them.
- ○ **C.** Unplug the power supply from the system board while installing the RAM modules.
- ○ **D.** Use compressed air to blow any dust accumulation off the modules before installing them.

2. You enter a customer's server room and see water on the floor and stained ceiling tiles. What should you do first?

Quick Answer: **80**
Detailed Answer: **113**

- ○ **A.** Shut down the servers and notify the network administrator immediately.
- ○ **B.** Notify the building maintenance supervisor.
- ○ **C.** Notify the security supervisor.
- ○ **D.** Clean up the water immediately and look for the source of the leak.

3. What is the purpose of the antistatic wrist strap?

Quick Answer: **80**
Detailed Answer: **113**

- ○ **A.** To protect the equipment from electrostatic discharge
- ○ **B.** To protect the technician from injury
- ○ **C.** To place the technician's body at the same electrical potential as the system board
- ○ **D.** To protect technicians working on high-voltage equipment such as power supplies and CRT monitors

Objective 7.3: Identify proper disposal procedures for batteries, display devices, and chemical solvents and cans

1. What is the recommended method for handling an empty toner cartridge?

   Quick Answer: **81**
   Detailed Answer: **113**

   ○ **A.** Recycle it through the original manufacturer.

   ○ **B.** Throw it in the trash.

   ○ **C.** Burn it in a certified incinerator.

   ○ **D.** Turn it in to a licensed computer retailer.

2. What is the recommended method for handling a dead battery?

   Quick Answer: **81**
   Detailed Answer: **114**

   ○ **A.** Recycle it.

   ○ **B.** Throw it in the trash.

   ○ **C.** Burn it in a certified incinerator.

   ○ **D.** Recharge it.

3. Which of the following are legitimate ways of disposing of chemical solvents and cans?

   Quick Answer: **81**
   Detailed Answer: **114**

   ○ **A.** If they are not listed on the MSDS, dispose of them in your normal trash-disposal system.

   ○ **B.** Open the containers and allow the liquids to evaporate so that they can be buried.

   ○ **C.** If your local code calls for it, dispose of the items in a Subtitle-D dumpsite.

   ○ **D.** Burn them in an acceptable disposal oven.

4. _____ are those substances that can pass through a standard paint filter.

   Quick Answer: **81**
   Detailed Answer: **114**

   ○ **A.** Color liquids

   ○ **B.** Acoustic liquids

   ○ **C.** Free liquids

   ○ **D.** Geomantic liquids

5. CRT monitors contain which of the following elements that cause their disposal to be considered hazardous?

   Quick Answer: **81**
   Detailed Answer: **114**

   ○ **A.** Copper

   ○ **B.** Lead

   ○ **C.** Tin

   ○ **D.** Aluminum

Quick Check

Quick Answer: **81**

Detailed Answer: **114**

6. When disposing of a CRT, you should first _____.

- ○ **A.** pack it in its original container and dispose of it in the normal garbage

- ○ **B.** discharge the HV anode and dispose of it in the normal garbage pickup

- ○ **C.** check applicable local ordinances and dispose of it in accordance with local regulations

- ○ **D.** smash the CRT's glass envelope with a hammer and dispose of it in a Subtitle-D dumpsite

Objective 8.0: Professionalism and Communication

Objective 8.1: Use good communication skills including listening and tact/ discretion, when communicating with customers and colleagues

1. You have just been moved into the customer service area of your company and will be the first contact for many customers with service issues. Your new manager has told you the most important thing you can do is practice active listening. Which of the following describes active listening?

   ○ **A.** Participating in discussions with customers and letting them know they are being heard

   ○ **B.** Listening until customers completely finish their explanation and then recapping their conversation to make sure you got it all

   ○ **C.** Guiding the customers' conversation so that it ends where you need it to

   ○ **D.** Interjecting your feedback into the discussion as soon as you have a good idea as to the cause of the problem

Quick Answer: **81**
Detailed Answer: **115**

2. After troubleshooting a customer's PC, you determine it has a bad RAM module that needs to be replaced. After you explain your findings to the customer several times, she still disagrees with your findings and doesn't understand why the module needs to be replaced. Which of the following should you do?

   ○ **A.** Prepare the customer a step-by-step description of your troubleshooting process.

   ○ **B.** Offer to let the customer speak to your immediate supervisor.

   ○ **C.** Install the RAM and then show the customer the difference in the system's operation.

   ○ **D.** Go online with the customer or use a troubleshooting reference to back up your diagnosis of the problem.

Quick Answer: **81**
Detailed Answer: **115**

3. You have been called into your service manager's office and told that your communications with your subordinates tend to be overly assertive at times. The manager explains that some of your assertiveness is good and some is counterproductive. Which of the following is an example of good assertive communication?

Quick Answer: **81**
Detailed Answer: **115**

- ○ **A.** Telling a coworker "I don't think you know what you're doing"

- ○ **B.** Telling an employee "If you don't get this job finished today, I will fire you"

- ○ **C.** Saying "Your work makes you look incompetent" to a coworker

- ○ **D.** Saying "You will have to stay on task to get this project done on schedule" to an employee

4. A customer spends several minutes telling you the problems he is having with his PC. You are reasonably sure that you comprehend the problem, so how should you handle the customer at this point?

Quick Answer: **81**
Detailed Answer: **115**

- ○ **A.** Repeat each portion of the problem back to the customer for verification.

- ○ **B.** Report the problem to your supervisor to let her know why your call is taking so long to complete.

- ○ **C.** Tell the customer the service is no longer available.

- ○ **D.** Tell the customer you understand and fix the problem without any further delay.

Objective 8.2: Use job-related professional behavior including notation of privacy, confidentiality, and respect for the customer and customers' property

1. When you arrive at a remote service call, you find that the business manager is very upset about the situation. What key thing do you need to remember to successfully deliver service to this customer?

Quick Answer: **81**
Detailed Answer: **115**

- ○ **A.** Stay calm and refer the customer to your supervisor.

- ○ **B.** Stay calm and do the job as efficiently as possible.

- ○ **C.** Think of something nice to block out the tension created by the angry customer.

- ○ **D.** Avoid dealing with the customer directly and do the job as efficiently as possible.

2. You are working remotely at a customer's office when you receive a call on your cell phone. The phone display indicates that the call is coming from a friend. How should you handle this situation?

- ○ **A.** Ignore the call and let it go to voicemail for later.

- ○ **B.** Tell the customer you have to take the call, step away from the work space, and handle it as quickly as possible.

- ○ **C.** Answer the call, tell the friend you will have to speak later, and end the call.

- ○ **D.** Leave the customer's office and return the call.

3. When dealing with customers over the telephone, you should _____.

- ○ **A.** control the call and gather important information about the problem

- ○ **B.** allow the customers to guide the call because they saw the problem

- ○ **C.** let the customers explain everything and write it down

- ○ **D.** take control of the conversation as soon as you have a good idea of what the problem is

4. An angry customer returns a computer that she brought in several times for the same problem, but it still does not work. What is the best way to handle this situation?

- ○ **A.** Tell the customer that you have not worked on this computer before but you're the best and you are sure you will get it fixed.

- ○ **B.** Tell the customer that the machine qualifies as a lemon under the "lemon law" and replace it with a new unit.

- ○ **C.** Offer to send off the machine to a depot facility for a detailed troubleshooting process.

- ○ **D.** Try to calm the customer, review all the problems with her, perform a standard troubleshooting process based on the information and symptoms you receive and correct the problem.

Quick Check

Quick Answer: **81**
Detailed Answer: **116**

5. While working on a user's computer, his phone rings. Which of the following should you do?

- ○ **A.** Answer the phone and take a message for the person.
- ○ **B.** Don't touch the phone; let the message system get the call.
- ○ **C.** Answer the call and ask the caller to wait so that you can find the user.
- ○ **D.** Answer the call and tell the caller to call back later.

Quick Check Answer Key

Objective 1.1

1. A	11. D	21. B
2. A	12. B	22. B
3. D	13. B	23. D
4. B	14. D	24. C
5. C	15. A	25. A
6. C	16. B	26. C
7. A	17. C	27. A
8. A, C	18. B	28. D
9. B	19. A	
10. B	20. D	

Objective 1.2

1. A, B, C	5. A, B	9. A
2. D	6. C	10. C
3. C, D	7. D	
4. C	8. D	

Objective 1.3

1. A	5. A	9. D
2. D	6. A	10. D
3. D	7. D	11. A, B, C
4. A	8. A	12. D

Objective 1.4

1. A, C	3. C
2. B	4. A

Quick Check Answer Key

Objective 2.1

1. B	3. D	5. C
2. C	4. A, B	

Objective 2.2

1. A	3. A	5. D
2. B	4. A, D	6. C

Objective 2.3

1. C	3. C	5. B
2. D	4. D	

Objective 2.4

1. B	3. D
2. C	4. A

Objective 3.1

1. B	7. A	13. B
2. A	8. D	14. B
3. C	9. A	15. C
4. B	10. A	16. B
5. A	11. D	16. C
6. A	12. C	

Quick Check Answer Key

Objective 3.2

1. A	7. A, D	13. D
2. A, C	8. D	14. C
3. A, C	9. A	15. C
4. D	10. A	16. B
5. B	11. A	17. A, B, C
6. A	12. A, B	

Objective 3.3

1. C	10. C	19. C
2. A	11. B	20. C
3. D	12. C	21. B
4. D	13. B	22. B
5. A	14. D	23. C
6. B	15. C	24. A
7. C	16. B	25. A
8. B	17. B, C, D	
9. B	18. B	

Objective 3.4

1. C	3. C
2. B, D	4. A

Objective 4.1

1. A	5. C	9. B
2. A	6. D	10. B
3. B	7. B	11. B
4. C	8. A, C	12. A

Quick Check Answer Key

Objective 4.2

1. C
2. D

3. B, D
4. C

5. A, B

Objective 4.3

1. B
2. A
3. C, D

4. A
5. D
6. C

7. B
8. C
9. B

Objective 5.1

1. B
2. A
3. C
4. A
5. C
6. A
7. B
8. D

9. A
10. B
11. A
12. A
13. B
14. C
15. B
16. A, C

17. A
18. C
19. D
20. B
21. C
22. D
23. A
24. C

Objective 5.2

1. D
2. B
3. D

4. A
5. C
6. A, B

7. C
8. A

Objective 5.3

1. A
2. B
3. B

4. A
5. A
6. B

7. A

Quick Check Answer Key

Objective 6.1

1. B	6. A	11. A
2. D	7. D	12. D
3. B	8. B	13. B, C
4. A	9. D	14. A, B, C
5. A, B	10. A	

Objective 6.2

1. B	3. B	5. A, C, D
2. D	4. B	

Objective 6.3

1. D
2. A, D

Objective 6.4

1. A
2. B

Objective 7.1

1. A
2. B
3. B

Objective 7.2

1. B
2. B
3. A

Quick Check Answer Key

Objective 7.3

1. A
2. A

3. C
4. C

5. B
6. C

Objective 8.1

1. A
2. C

3. D
4. A

Objective 8.2

1. B
2. A

3. A
4. D

5. B

Answers and Explanations

Objective 1.0

Objective 1.1

1. **Answer: A.** The BIOS stores the PnP information it collects from the devices in a special section of the CMOS RAM known as the *ESCD area*.

2. **Answer: A.** The major difference between power supply types is in their form factors. Different power supply form factors produce power supplies that are smaller in size than other power supply form factors, and their hole patterns are different. Another point that differentiates power supplies is their power (or wattage) rating. Typical power ratings include 450 watt, 500 watt, and greater versions. Voltage is generally not a decision point. When you buy a power supply for a PC you generally do not have the option to buy a 110 Vac versus a 220 Vac supply. Typically, PC power supplies offer a voltage selector switch and exchangeable power cable connection to handle this function.

3. **Answer: D.** Parity checking is a simple self-test used to detect RAM read-back errors.

4. **Answer: B.** The ECC RAM detects and corrects errors in the information it processes.

5. **Answer: C.** The capacity of memory modules is specified in bytes. However, the geometry of the device involves an x-by-y format that corresponds to word size. A 512MB memory module designed to work directly with a 64-bit microprocessor would be designed to deliver data in 8-byte words (64 bits × 8 million words). Under this format, the capacity of the device (in bytes) is derived by multiplying the two numbers and then dividing by eight (or nine for parity chips).

6. **Answer: C.** The universal serial bus (USB) is a high-speed serial interface that has been developed to provide a fast, flexible method of attaching up to 127 peripheral devices to the computer. USB peripherals can be daisy-chained or networked together using connection hubs that enable the bus to branch out through additional port connections.

7. **Answer: A.** The monitor is attached to the video adapter card in the system unit via a signal cable or cables. The signal cable permits the monitor to be positioned away from the system unit if desired. With most CRT monitors, the signal cable is permanently attached to the monitor and plugs into the video adapter card using a 3-row, 15-pin D-shell connector. (In some cases, the monitor may use a signal cable that can be disconnected at both ends.)

8. **Answers: A, C.** When the microprocessor is upgraded, the BIOS should be flashed with the latest compatibility firmware. If the BIOS does not possess the flash option and does not support the new microprocessor, a new BIOS chip that does support it must be obtained and installed. If not, the entire system board needs to be replaced.

9. Answer: B. ROM devices store information permanently and are used to hold programs and data that do not change. RAM devices retain the information stored in them only as long as electrical power is applied to the IC. This is referred to as *volatile memory*. ROM, on the other hand, is nonvolatile. It retains the information even if power is removed from the device. Although hard disk drives are capable of storing data on a long-term basis, they are not considered to be permanent storage devices; they are designed to be read from and written to. In addition, the magnetic charges that are used to store the information on the disk will dissipate over time, and eventually (about 10 years) the data may become unreadable.

10. Answer: B. The PC3200 (3.2GBps/400MHz) Double Data Rate (DDR) module is designed for use with a double-pumped front-side bus that runs on a 400MHz effective FSB. To understand this relationship, consider that DDR memory chips used to make DDR modules are designed to transfer data on both the rising and falling edges of the memory bus's squarewave clock signal. This means that these devices transfer data at a rate of twice the actual bus speed frequency. The DDR 400 devices that make up the PC3200 memory modules work on a memory bus speed of 200MHz, so its effective and nominal rate is 400MHz. Then you must multiply the effective clock rate and the bus size (8 bytes—or 64 bits) together to produce an effective data transfer rate of 3200MBps (3.2GBps).

11. Answer: D. When you are upgrading power supplies, power consumption (expressed as wattage rating) is important so that enough power is delivered to drive all components installed.

12. Answer: B. Special Zero Insertion Force (ZIF) sockets are designed to allow the microprocessor to be set in the socket without force and then be clamped in place. An arm-activated clamping mechanism in the socket shifts to the side, locking the pins in place.

13. Answer: B. The original IDE interface used a single 40-pin ribbon cable to connect the hard drive to the host adapter card or system board and supported a maximum throughput of 8.3MBps.

14. Answer: D. CD-ROM/DVD drives have an actuator motor that moves the laser/detector module in and out under the disc.

15. Answer: A. Secure Digital (SD) is a Flash memory card format used in a variety of different portable devices, including digital cameras, notebook computers and PDAs. SD cards generally measure 1.26″ × 0.94″ × 0.08″ (32mm × 24mm × 2.1mm), but can be as thin as 0.055″ (1.4mm).

16. Answer: B. PCI Express (PCIe) slots are a collection of high-speed serial versions of the PCI bus standard. These PCI versions employ new slot specifications that are not compatible with older PCI devices. PCIe pushes performance levels to 2.5GHz and data transfer rates to between 250MBps and 32GBps. High-end video adapter cards such as those used by artists and serious game players are designed to plug into more advanced PCI-X or PCIe slots (although PCIe has largely eclipsed the PCI-X standard).

17. **Answer: C.** You must remove the backup battery (or short across its reset jumper) to reset the CMOS information. It is also necessary to unplug the power from the commercial outlet to reduce the voltage to the CMOS registers. When the content of the CMOS is reset, you must manually restore any nondefault CMOS settings being used by the system.

18. **Answer: B.** To perform a read or write operation, the address of the particular track and sector to be accessed is applied to a stepper motor, which moves a Read/Write (R/W) head over the desired track. As the desired sector passes beneath the R/W head, the data transfer occurs.

19. **Answer: A.** Enhanced Intel SpeedStep Technology (EIST) enables the operating system software to dynamically control the clock speed of a processor. This feature allows the system to speed up the processor when higher performance is required and then slow it down to a lower power consumption speed when the demands on the processor are lower. This throttling technique is used to conserve battery power in notebooks, extend processor life, and reduce noise from cooling devices. Like the dual-core Intel processors, the Athlon 64 X2 supports a 64-bit extension to the x86 Instruction set, enhanced virus protection with supported operating systems, and speed throttling features.

20. **Answer: D.** Few new desktop and tower PCs include a floppy disk drive as a standard component. Rewritable CDs and Flash drives have replaced the floppy disk in many cases. However, floppies are still widely used to boot older failing PC systems to a command prompt for troubleshooting purposes.

21. **Answer: B.** USB transfers are conducted over a four-wire cable. The signal travels over a pair of twisted wires (D+ and D−) in a 90-ohm cable. The four wires are connected to four pins within the connector end.

22. **Answer: B.** The most widely used display device for current PCs is the color VGA/SVGA display. The display monitor's signal cable normally connects to a 15-pin, 3-row female D-shell (DE-15F) connector at the back of the system unit.

23. **Answer: D.** The BIOS controls the cooling system through its Health Management system. This includes monitoring the actual temperature of the microprocessor and manipulating the cooling system to maintain a designated temperature level.

24. **Answer: C.** K points to the PCIe X1 expansion slots; J identifies the conventional PCI expansion slots; L is the PCIe x16 expansion slot; A is the DIMM slots.

25. **Answer: A.** A identifies DIMM slots; K points to the PCIe X1 expansion slots; J identifies the conventional PCI expansion slots; L is the PCIe x16 expansion slot.

26. **Answer: C.** G points to this board's single PATA connector, which controls hard drives and CD/DVD drives. G points at two of the board's SATA interface connectors, B is the system board power connector, and C is the FDD connector.

27. **Answer: A.** Cache memory is a fast RAM system used to hold information that the microprocessor is likely to use.

28. **Answer: D.** Many Pentium system boards include an Accelerated Graphics Port (AGP) interface connector for video adapter cards.

Objective 1.2

1. **Answers: A, B, C.** (A) To minimize buffer underruns, place the CD-ROM or DVD writer on an IDE channel of its own. This keeps the drive from competing with other drives for the channel's available bandwidth. (B) Conducting the write operation on the same drive as the read operation and using reduced write speed options in the R/W application software can minimize data flow problems. (C) Because the drive has already been purchased and installed, check its documentation for suggestions and check the drive manufacturer's website for newer R/W applications and driver versions. You might also be able to locate a Flash program for the drive's BIOS to upgrade it so that it provides better support for the write function.

2. **Answer: D.** When you are connecting a ribbon cable to the system board, pin 1 of the connector must line up with the signal cable's indicator stripe.

3. **Answers: C, D.** With the rapid increase that occurs in hard disk drive capacities, it is not uncommon for a new drive to show up as something less when the system is started. The most common reason for this is that the system's BIOS version does not support the size of the new drive and reverts to its maximum support capabilities. You may need to flash the BIOS with the latest upgrade version to support the new drive. You may also gain additional support by updating the operating system with the latest patches and service packs. In the case of Windows XP Professional, the move to Service Pack 1 (SP1) increased the capability of Windows to handle larger drives beyond 137GB.

4. **Answer: C.** You may encounter situations in which incompatible USB ports and devices refuse to work together. Some older PCs that have USB 1.1 ports may not be able to work with some newer USB 2.0 devices. In these cases, the system may recognize the device but do not work with it.

5. **Answers: A, B.** Most internal hard drives and CD-ROM/DVD drives typically connect to one of the system board's parallel IDE/EIDE-ATA (PATA) interface connections, or one of its Serial ATA (SATA) interface connections. On some system boards you find only PATA connectors, on others you find only SATA connectors, and on some you find a mixture of both.

6. **Answer: C.** If a working PATA hard drive fails because a second PATA drive has been installed, they probably are connected to the same IDE channel, and both drives are set as master. With the IDE interface, there can only be one master drive selection on each IDE channel.

7. **Answer: D.** A heavily used, heavily fragmented hard drive can affect the system's virtual memory (in particular, the swap file) and produce memory shortages as well.

8. **Answer: D.** Wait for the operating system to recognize the device and configure it through the PnP process. Microsoft's Windows 2000 and Windows XP operating systems detect the presence of the USB or FireWire device and start their Found New Hardware Wizard program to guide you through the installation process.

9. **Answer: A.** A single IEEE-1394 connection can be used to connect up to 63 devices to a single port with the maximum segment length of 4.5 meters (15 feet).

10. **Answer: C.** When upgrading an AGP card or system board containing an AGP slot, you should always consult the system board and AGP adapter card's documentation to verify their compatibility with each other.

Objective 1.3

1. **Answer: A.** The first step in troubleshooting USB problems is to check the CMOS Setup screens to make sure that the USB function is enabled there. If the USB function is enabled in BIOS, check in the Windows Control Panel/System/ Device Manager to make certain that the USB controller appears there.

2. **Answer: D.** Listen to the system. Listen for the sounds of the power supply and processor fans, the hard drive spindle motor turning, and the sounds coming from the system speaker. If the fan has completely stopped working, you should shut down the unit down and check for heat damage.

3. **Answer: D.** Anytime you see smoke coming from a PC or one of its peripherals, you should remove power from it as quickly as possible. This should be done first to avoid additional damage to the unit or to yourself. Having smoking components is one of those obvious (and dangerous) conditions that requires immediate attention and does not fall into a troubleshooting sequence.

4. **Answer: A.** If the FDD activity light stays on constantly, this indicates that the FDD signal cable is reversed or not installed properly.

5. **Answer: A.** Take the time to document the problem, including all the tests you perform and their outcomes. This recorded information can prevent you from making repetitive steps that waste time and may cause confusion. This information is also very helpful when you move on to more detailed tests or measurements.

6. **Answer: A.** The most likely reason the system does not recognize the second drive is that both drives are connected to the same IDE channel and are configured as master. With PATA drives, there can be only one master drive selection on each IDE channel. You should never need to perform a low-level format on any modern disk drive. Even if the drive were not partitioned, the system's PnP function should recognize the presence of the drive, show it in the CMOS configuration, and create a drive letter for it. That's how you set up brand new PCs and install operating systems on them.

7. **Answer: D.** When the system exhibits no signs of life, including the absence of lights, the best place to start looking for the problem is at the power supply. Having replaced the power supply (with a known good unit), you should have covered the supply's system board connector and the 110/220 voltage setting on the back of the power supply unit (if it has one). Unless someone was working inside the unit, the original power supply problem should not have been caused by a missing or loose on/off switch connection to the system board. Therefore, the *first* thing you should do is check the power being supplied to the unit from the power outlet; you can do this using a working lamp or a multimeter.

8. **Answer: A.** First, you must gather information to identify the nature of the problem. This can involve questioning the user and identifying any changes that have been made to the system. After the problem has been identified, you should assess the problem systematically and divide complex problems into smaller components to be analyzed individually.

9. **Answer: D.** The condition of the NumLk (NumLock on desktop keyboards) key can cause portable PCs to produce incorrect characters. Notebook PCs do not have separate 10-key numeric keypads. If the NumLk key function is engaged, the system remaps different keys to the locked numbers. In some cases, the only indicator that the NumLk key function is engaged is a small light near a small icon representing a numeric keypad. With some notebook models, if you don't look closely, you probably won't realize that there is a numeric keypad associated with the keyboard (small numbers are embossed on the alpha keys). Some notebook models call out the NumLk feature on a specific key, whereas others only include an icon on one of the function keys. With the latter arrangement, you can disable the NumLk-On setting using the Fn key along with a designated function key (also denoted by a small numeric keypad icon).

10. **Answer: D.** The first step in troubleshooting USB problems is to check in the CMOS Setup utility to make sure that the USB function is enabled there. If the USB function is enabled in BIOS, check in the Windows Control Panel/System/Device Manager to make certain that the USB controller appears there.

11. **Answers: A, B, C.** (A) Ask the user to demonstrate the procedures that led to the malfunction in a step-by-step manner. This communication can help you narrow down a problem to a particular section of the computer. (B) Determine if the unit ever works. If the unit has been working, take note of the environment in which the equipment is being used and how heavy its usage is. If the unit has never been used, the problem might occur during the installation and configuration. (C) Most PCs have reasonably good built-in self-tests that run each time the computer is powered up. These tests can prove beneficial in detecting hardware-oriented problems within the system. A numerically coded error message or written description of the error is issued for a self-test failure or configuration mismatch.

12. **Answer: D.** During the POST, the operation of the keyboard, hard disk drive, and CMOS is tested. Therefore, most problems with these hardware devices should show up during the POST. However, a RAM chip that fails at high temperature could not be detected at this stage; the symptom will not appear until the system has had an opportunity to heat up.

Objective 1.4

1. **Answers: A, C.** Dust buildup inside the system can be taken care of with a soft brush. A static-free vacuum or compressed air can also be used to remove dust from inside cases and keyboards. Be sure to use a static-free vacuum because normal vacuums are, by their nature, static generators. The static-free vacuum has special grounding to remove the static buildup it generates. Dust covers are also helpful in holding down dust problems. These covers are placed over the equipment when the equipment is not in use and are removed when the device is needed. Dust is statically attracted to electronic components. Therefore, it would be very difficult to shake the system vigorously enough to remove dust from it. In addition, the forces exerted on the system unit's components during vigorous shaking could be great enough to damage some parts or loosen some connections.

2. **Answer: B.** A damp cloth is easily the best general-purpose cleaning tool for use with computer equipment.

3. **Answer: C.** Outer-surface cleaning can be accomplished with a simple soap-and-water solution, followed by a clear water rinse. Care should be taken to make sure that none of the liquid splashes or drips into the inner parts of the system.

4. **Answer: A.** PCs are designed to run at normal room temperatures. If the ambient temperature rises above 85° F, heat buildup can become a problem. High humidity can also lead to heat-related problems.

Objective 2.0

Objective 2.1

1. **Answer: B.** Notebook and other portable computer manufacturers do not use traditional DIMM modules in their designs. Special form factor DIMMs, called *small outline DIMMs (SODIMMs)*, were developed specifically for use in notebook computers.

2. **Answer: C.** PCMCIA Type III cards are being produced. These cards are 10.5mm thick and are intended primarily for use with removable hard drives. Both Type I and Type II cards can be used in a Type III slot.

3. **Answer: D.** The Windows logo key provides specialized Windows functions such as locking the system when pressed in combination with the L key. The locked condition requires the user who locked the computer to enter his password to unlock it (administrators can also unlock the computer). When unlocked, the system returns to the state it was in when the user locked it (the programs that were in use are still open).

4. **Answers: A, B.** Because of the difference in free air space, desktop power supplies and their fans are not included in notebook PC designs; separate fans and power supplies are designed to decrease power consumption and thermal heat buildup.

5. **Answer: C.** The power consumption of LCD displays is very low. The screen is scanned by sequentially activating the panel's row and column electrodes. The pixels appear to be continuously lit because the scanning rate is very high. The electrodes can be controlled using very low DC voltage levels.

Objective 2.2

1. **Answer: A.** The Safely Remove Hardware utility is used to notify the operating system in advance of the removal. Because some devices have write caching enabled, corruption or data loss may occur.

2. **Answer: B.** In Windows 2000 and XP, the power management functions are located in the Control Panel under the Power Options icon. These functions include options for configuring hard drive and display shutdown times, standby mode timing, and the hibernate functions. Standby settings are confgured under the Power Schemes tab, and the hibernation function is enabled under the Hibernate tab (Enable Hibernate Support in Windows 2000 and Enable Hibernation in Windows XP).

3. **Answer: A.** Hibernate mode saves the computing session that is stored in RAM to the hard disk and then shuts down the system. When the system is reactivated, the computing session is fully restored back into memory and restarted at the place it left off.

4. **Answers: A, D.** Historically, most external CD-ROM/DVD drives have employed SCSI interface connectors. However, newer external CD-ROM/DVD drives tend to employ USB connections.

5. **Answer: D.** The proper procedure for removing a PC Card from the computer begins with clicking on the Remove Hardware Safely icon on the taskbar. Then select the command to stop the operation of the PC Card you want to remove. When the operating system prompts you, physically remove the PC Card from the system.

6. **Answer: C.** Many BIOS versions provide a Standby power saving mode that turns off selected components, such as the hard drive and display, until a system event, such as a keyboard entry or a mouse movement, occurs.

Objective 2.3

1. **Answer: C.** Examine the I/O port connection (or internal connector) and configuration to make sure that it is properly set up to support the pad. As with other internal portable connections, internal touch pad connections may be loosened whenever the system is taken apart for repair purposes.

2. **Answer: D.** Under shared memory, the system uses a portion of its main memory to hold screen information for the display. In desktop PCs, this memory is distributed to the video adapter card. The disadvantage of shared memory is that it takes up RAM that applications would normally use. If you are upgrading memory in the portable system, you must take into account that the amount of RAM available for use by the system will not be the same as the installed RAM.

3. **Answer: C.** The system shutting down earlier than normal indicates that either the battery is bad or that it is having a battery memory problem in which it becomes internally conditioned to run for less time than the designed capacity.

4. **Answer: D.** If you cannot find a working resolution, you should plug an external display into the notebook's external VGA port to determine whether the problem is with the display or the display adapter. If the problem does not appear on the external display, there is some problem either with the LCD panel or the video signal ribbon cable that connects the LCD panel to the adapter.

5. **Answer: B.** Internal CD/DVD drives attach to the system with a signal cable and obtain their power from one of the system's options power connectors. However, external CD/DVD drives employ a separate power adapter of their own. You must check this item to make sure it is functional when troubleshooting an external drive problem.

Objective 2.4

1. **Answer: B.** With notebooks and other portable PCs, make sure that they are sitting on a hard, flat surface. Placing portables on soft or uneven surfaces can block airflow that is designed to exit underneath the unit.

2. **Answer: C.** Portable computers are designed to endure the minor jolts and jars associated with travel and mobility. However, this doesn't include being dropped on the floor, or even a short drop onto a tabletop. Such occurrences typically damage portable PCs and can often totally disable them. Therefore, one of the best preventative activities you can engage in is to take steps to reduce the likelihood of dropping the portable PC.

3. **Answer: D.** Typically, you should avoid aerosol sprays, solvents, and commercial cleaners when cleaning LCD displays because they can damage the screen and cabinet.

4. **Answer: A.** The screen should be cleaned periodically with a glass cleaner and a soft, lint-free cloth. You can also use clean water and a mild soap to clean the display. Take care that you do not oversaturate the cloth with water and allow it to drip down into the frame of the display. Stronger cleaning agents such as citrus-based and ammonia-based cleansers can damage the viewing screen and should not be used. Never spray the cleaner directly on the screen.

Objective 3.0

Objective 3.1

1. **Answer: B.** The NT Loader program named NTLDR guides the Windows 2000/XP boot process before the Windows operating system takes control.

2. **Answer: A.** If the Windows system employs a SCSI disk drive, a driver file named NTBOOTDD.SYS must be present in the root directory of the system partition. This condition must also be noted in the BOOT.INI file by placing a numerical ID in its SCSI(x) or MULTI(x) locations. When the operating system encounters the MULTI() designator during the boot process, it relies on the PC's BIOS to support the drive, whereas it refers to the NTBOOTDD.SYS driver file to access the boot partition on the SCSI device when a SCSI() designator is encountered.

3. **Answer: C.** In most situations, the NTFS system offers better performance and features than a FAT16 or FAT32 system. The exceptions to this occur when smaller drives are being used. (The NTFS system is more complex than the FAT systems and, therefore, is not as efficient for smaller drives.)

4. **Answer: B.** The DISKCOMP command is used to compare the contents of two disks. It compares the data on the disks not only to see that they are alike, but also to verify that the data is in the same place on both disks. This command is normally used to verify the contents of backup disks and is typically performed after a DISKCOPY operation has been performed.

5. **Answer: A.** Pressing the Ctrl+Esc key combination pops up the Start menu along with the taskbar in Windows 2000/XP.

6. **Answer: A.** The Windows utility for scheduling tasks is located under the Control Panel's Scheduled Tasks icon. This utility is used to schedule operating system and application operations so that they start and run automatically. This enables users and technicians to schedule routine tasks such as backups and defragmentation operations to occur without a user or technician being involved. Also, these tasks can be scheduled to run at the most convenient times, such as the middle of the night when no one is using the machine. Tasks can be scheduled to run daily, weekly, monthly, or at prescribed times and dates.

7. **Answer: A.** All Apple computers originally ran proprietary versions of the Apple operating system. However, newer Apple Macintosh computers run on a proprietary version of UNIX named Mac OS X. Although the structure of OS X is UNIX based, the user interaction portions of the system employ Apple's trademark GUI-based desktop.

8. **Answer: D.** In Windows 2000, the Control Panel's Network and Dial-up Connections icon is used. In Windows XP, the Networking icon has been changed to the Network Connections icon.

9. **Answer: A.** The DEL command allows the user to remove unwanted files from the disk when typed in at the command prompt. When used with the wildcard *.*, this command tells the system to perform the command on any file found in the current or specified directory.

10. **Answer: A.** The Safely Remove Hardware utility is used to notify the operating system in advance of the removal of USB devices. This is necessary because some devices use write caching techniques, and corruption or data loss may occur if this cache is not stored before removing the device from the system.

11. **Answer: D.** The Windows 2000 and XP operating systems support several file management system formats, including FAT, FAT16, FAT32, CDFS (the compact disk file system is used on CD-ROMs), and NTFS4, along with its own native NTFS5 format.

12. **Answer: C.** In Windows XP, the DISKPART command is used to execute disk management tasks from a command line. This includes creating and managing disk partitions.

13. **Answer: B.** Under the FAT file system, there is room for one primary partition and the extended partition on a hard disk drive. The extended partition can be created on any unused disk space after the primary partition has been established and properly configured. The extended partition can be subdivided into 23 logical drives (the letters of the alphabet minus a, b, and c).

14. **Answer: B.** When the system checks the MBR of the physical disk during the boot process, it also checks to see which partition on the disk has been marked as active. It then jumps to that location, reads the information in that partition boot record, and boots to the operating system in that logical drive.

15. **Answer: C.** To create a new folder in Explorer, select a parent directory by highlighting it in the left window. Then click the File menu button, move the cursor to the New entry, slide across to the Folder option, and click on it. A new unnamed folder icon appears in the right Explorer window.

16. **Answer: B.** To change file attributes from the Explorer, right-click the desired file, select the Properties option from the pop-up list, move to the General page, and click the desired attribute boxes.

17. **Answer: C.** To change the file's attribute, use the ATTRIB command along with the proper switch to add or remove the desired attribute from the designated file.

Objective 3.2

1. **Answer: A.** The Warn setting causes Windows to notify the user when an unsigned driver has been detected. It also produces an option to load or not load the driver. This is the default setting for driver signing.

2. **Answers: A, C.** The Windows Cleanup utility can be used to identify optional applications and certain types of temporary files that are not required for operation of the system. The DEFRAG utility realigns files on the drive that may have become fragmented by erase and write/rewrite operations. The defrag operation moves fragmented files into the pattern that provides the most efficient reading operation (the drive requires time to process the sector of information it just read from the disk—during this period, sectors are passing under the R/W heads—therefore, placing the next section of the file in the sector that passes under the R/W heads when it is ready again provides the best performance). The Recycle Bin cannot be removed in any modern versions of Windows.

3. **Answers: A, C.** Before you install or upgrade hardware devices included in a Windows XP Professional system, they must be listed on the Microsoft Windows XP Hardware Compatibility List (HCL) page. You can find comprehensive listings of Windows 2000– and Windows XP-compatible products on the Microsoft website under the Windows Quality Online Services page at http://winqual.microsoft.com/hcl. This collection is a complete reference for products that have been tested for Windows compatibility. You should also run the Windows XP version of the Checkupgradeonly utility for possible hardware/software compatibility conflicts.

4. **Answer: D.** Systems running Windows 95a or Windows NT Workstation 3.51 operating systems cannot upgrade directly to Windows XP. Instead, they must have intermediate upgrades to bring them up to a Windows version that does support direct upgrading to Windows XP.

5. **Answer: B.** Most notebook PCs provide a VGA port connector that permits a CRT, a better LCD display, or a video projector to be used instead of the built-in display unit. Windows XP provides built-in support for dual displays. To add a CRT VGA display to a system, simply open the Display icon on the Control Panel and configure the system for dual display operation.

6. **Answer: A.** In Windows 2000, the TCP/IP protocol can be uninstalled and installed. If the TCP/IP protocol is missing, someone either removed it, or the system did not detect a network adapter during the setup process. To install TCP/IP, you must access the Properties of the network connection that should be using the protocol. On the General tab, verify that TCP/IP is not present. Then click Install/Protocol/Add and the Internet Protocol (TCP/IP) option in the Select Network Protocol dialog box. Under Windows XP, it is not possible to remove the TCP/IP protocol from the system (it can be disabled but not removed).

7. **Answers: A, D.** Local, attended installations can be conducted from a Windows distribution CD or from a USB Flash drive.

8. **Answer: D.** Rather than provide customers with a new version of the operating system when new features are added or major problems are corrected, software manufacturers provide updates and patches for their products. Microsoft typically releases patches in the form of updates, or in collections that include additional functionality or new device drivers that referred to as *service packs*. Patch management refers to evaluating and deploying these updates and patches to keep the system current and protected. For the most part, patch management has become a formal security-based process to protect the operating system (and the rest of the computer's software) from attack.

9. **Answer: A.** The Microsoft Hardware Compatibility List (HCL) found on the operating system's distribution CD and the Microsoft website (http://winqual.microsoft.com/hcl) were the definitive list of Windows-compatible hardware products. For a short time, Microsoft moved away from the HCLs as the definitive list of compatible products; however, it has once again turned to HCLs for compatibility. All hardware devices included in a Windows XP Professional system must be listed on Microsoft's Windows XP HCL. These devices have been tested and are supported by Microsoft. Windows XP makes no claim to maintaining compatibility with a variety of hardware devices. The HCL on the website is likely to contain a more current list of compatible devices than the version on the distribution CD.

10. **Answer: A.** In Windows XP, the maximum supported RAM is 4GB. The required RAM is 64MB, and 128MB is recommended. Generally, the more memory installed, the better. However, there does come a point when more RAM fails to add better performance.

11. **Answer: A.** Windows 2000 includes two Registry editors: RegEdit and Regedt32. RegEdit is an older Registry editor that was used with previous Windows versions but retains some features not available in the newer RegEdit version. Both utilities enable you to add, edit, and remove Registry entries and to perform other basic functions. Under Windows XP, the Regedt32 option has been reduced simply to a small program that launches `Regedit.exe`.

12. **Answers: A, B.** If the operation of the system begins to show signs of slowing down over time, you should consider removing unnecessary files from the disk to free up space and then defrag the drive to realign the contents of the disk in an optimal pattern for accessing the drive. If these actions do not provide an increase in performance, you should consider checking the system for viruses and other malware products that may be slowing the system.

13. **Answer: D.** The minimum hardware requirements for installing Windows 2000 Professional on a PC-compatible system are a Pentium (P5 equivalent or better) microprocessor running at 133MHz, recommended RAM is minimum 64MB (4GB maximum), and HDD space is 650MB or more free on a 2GB drive.

14. **Answer: C.** The minimum requirement of RAM for installing Windows XP Professional on a PC-compatible is 64MB required/128MB recommended. Generally, the more memory installed, the better. Maximum supported RAM is 4GB.

15. **Answer: C.** The SYSPREP tool is used to prepare the reference computer for cloning.

16. **Answer: B.** Installing a new operating system on a hard drive has evolved into the five basic steps that follow: Partition the drive for use with the operating system. Format the drive with the basic operating system files. Run the appropriate Setup utility to install the complete operating system. Load all the drivers necessary for the operating system to function with the system's installed hardware devices. Reboot the system to activate all the system components.

17. **Answers: A, B, C.** Computers running Windows 98, Windows Me, Windows NT Workstation 4.0 (with Service Pack 5 installed), or Windows 2000 Professional can be upgraded directly to Windows XP. However, systems running Windows 95 or Windows NT Workstation 3.51 operating systems cannot upgrade directly to XP. Instead, they must have intermediate upgrades to bring them up to a Windows version that does support direct upgrading to Windows XP.

Objective 3.3

1. **Answer: C.** In Windows XP systems, access the Event Viewer utility and expand the System node to view the event log of system events, such as loading the networking services. Even if no desktop is available, you can restart the system in Safe Mode and access the Event Viewer to use this log to isolate the cause of the error.

2. **Answer: A.** The Recovery Console is a command-line interface that provides you with access to the hard disks and many command-line utilities when the operating system does not boot. The Recovery Console can access all volumes on the drive, regardless of the file system type. However, if you have not added the Recovery Console option prior to a failure, you cannot employ it and need to use the Windows Setup disks instead.

3. **Answer: D.** Remote Assistance enables you to get online with the user and share his desktop. While connected, you can chat with him, send and receive files, and manipulate the remote system as if you were physically sitting at it. This includes manipulating drivers, launching applications, and viewing event logs. Although the user is not involved in the troubleshooting process, he is often required to participate initially to grant access.

4. **Answer: D.** Prior to the `Starting Windows 2000/XP` message, the user has the option to access the Advanced Boot Menu by pressing the F8 function key. This action is
normally taken to enter a diagnostic startup mode.

5. **Answer: A.** In Windows XP, stop errors may produce a condition where the system reboots seemingly for no reason. This is caused by a combination of a blue screen error and an Auto Restart setting in Windows XP. The setting is designed to automatically reboot Windows when it detects a critical error in the system such as a hard drive being full.

6. **Answer: B.** Windows 2000 and XP both have special tools called the *user state migration tools (USMTs)* that administrators can use to transfer user configuration settings and files from systems running Windows 9x/Me and NT/2000 systems to a clean Windows 2000 or Windows XP installation. This enables user information to be preserved without going through the upgrade process.

7. **Answer: C.** When a parity error occurs, the system generates a Non-Maskable Interrupt (NMI) signal, causing the BIOS to execute its NMI handler routine. This routine normally places a parity error message onscreen, along with an option to shut down the system or to continue. In other cases, the system shows a short memory count during the POST and locks up without an error message. Another possible outcome when a parity error occurs is that the system counts the memory, locks up, and reboot itself.

8. **Answer: B.** In addition to the necessary system files required to start the system in a minimal, real-mode condition, the Windows distribution disc provides a number of driver files and diagnostic programs that are stored in the `.CAB` file format. The CAB files can be pulled out of the cabinets using the `EXTRACT.EXE` program.

9. **Answer: B.** The Selective Startup option located on the General tab of the System Configuration Utility dialog page interactively loads device drivers and software options according to the check boxes enabled on the General tab. Start the troubleshooting process with only one box checked. If the system starts up with that box checked, add another box to the list and restart. When the system fails to start, move into the tab that corresponds to the last option you enabled and step through the check boxes for that file one at a time until the system fails again.

10. **Answer: C.** The Recovery Console's FIXBOOT command writes a new boot sector to the system volume. You can run the Recovery Console from the Windows distribution CD.

11. **Answer: B.** Windows XP includes an option that can be used to revert to an older device driver when a driver upgrade causes problems with a device. This feature is called *Device Driver Rollback* and can be implemented through the Windows XP Device Manager.

12. **Answer: C.** A Missing Operating System error, such as the Missing NTLDR error message, indicates a problem with the master boot record. In Windows 2000 and XP, you can use the Recovery Console's FIXMBR command to replace the master boot record.

13. **Answer: B.** Make sure that the system is configured in the CMOS Setup utility to check the floppy disk drive as part of the boot sequence. You must enable this setting before you can boot the system from the setup floppy so that you can use the Emergency Repair Disk to fix the problem.

14. **Answer: D.** In Windows 2000 systems, access the Event Viewer utility and expand the System node to view the event log of system events, such as loading the networking services. Even if no desktop is available, you can restart the system in Safe Mode and access the Event Viewer to use this log to isolate the cause of the error.

15. **Answer: C.** The Recovery Console available in Windows 2000 and Windows XP is a command-line interface that provides you with access to the hard disks and many command-line utilities when the operating system does not boot. After the Last Known Good Configuration and Safe Mode options have been tried, you can use the Recovery Console to copy files from a floppy disk, CD, or another hard disk to restore the Registry.

16. **Answer: B.** In Windows XP, the ASR tool is used to back up and restore the System State information, along with all the files stored on the system volume. The ASR feature is considered to be the last resort that is used when you have been unable to recover the system using other methods, including Safe Mode, Last Known Good Configuration Mode, and the Recovery Console.

17. **Answers: B, C, D.** You should actually create a Restore Point any time that you are making changes to the system that might make it unstable or that might disable it. Restore Points can be created manually as a method of preserving the current state of the operating system prior to performing management activities including when (B) you have installed a new software application and it appears to cause problems with the system that removing it does not resolve, (C) anytime you need to get back to a point where you know the system was functioning correctly, and (D) when you update a driver and it appears to cause problems with the system that rolling back the driver does not resolve.

18. **Answer: B.** If a printer is not printing in Windows, check the print spooler to see whether it causes the problem. Select the Print Directly to the Printer option on the Advanced tab of the printer's properties page. If the print job goes through, there is a spooler problem. If not, the hardware and printer driver are suspect.

19. **Answer: C.** Safe Mode should be used when the system does not start after the `Starting Windows` message is displayed, when the system stalls repeatedly or for long periods of time, when the system cannot print to a local printer after a complete troubleshooting sequence, when the system has a video display problem, and whenever the system slows down noticeably or does not work correctly.

20. **Answer: C.** In Safe Mode, only the essential device drivers and system services are loaded. In Safe Mode, Windows 2000 and Windows XP load the following: Drivers for serial or PS/2 mouse devices, standard keyboards, hard disks, CD-ROM drives, and standard VGA devices. Your system firmware must support universal serial bus (USB) mouse and USB keyboard devices in order for you to use these input devices in safe mode. System services for the Event Log, Plug and Play, remote procedure calls (RPCs), and Logical Disk Manager.

21. **Answer: B.** The system configuration utility (`MSCONFIG.EXE`) is useful for controlling which programs are automatically loaded at startup.

22. **Answer: B.** A `Missing Operating System` message typically indicates that the disk's master boot record is missing or has become corrupt. Other possible causes for this message include an incorrect CMOS setting that prevents the system from recognizing the drive with the system partition, the system partition not being marked as Active, or a misconfigured `BOOT.INI` file.

23. **Answer: C.** If the system cannot see a hard drive after booting from an alternative source, an `Invalid Drive...` or `Invalid Drive Specification` error message is returned in response to any attempt to access the drive. This message indicates that the hard drive controller cannot find a recognizable track/sector pattern on the drive. Therefore, you might need to repartition the drive and then reformat it with an operating system. However, you should be aware that there are some products, such as Partition Commander, that can hide a partition until you unhide it. This leads to the same result.

24. **Answer: A.** As with other GUI-based environments, Windows applications hide behind icons. The properties of each icon must correctly identify the filename and path of the application's executable file; otherwise, Windows is not able to start it. Likewise, when a folder or file accessed by the icon or by the shortcut from the Windows Start menu is moved, renamed, or removed, Windows is not able to find it when asked to start the application. If an application does not start in Windows, you have several possibilities to consider: The application is missing or its path is incorrect; part or all of the application is corrupted; the application's executable file is incorrectly identified; the application's attributes are locked; incorrect application properties (filename, path, and syntax); missing or corrupt Registry entries; or conflicting DLL files. When an application does not start after you click its desktop icon, the first action you should take is to check its properties. You can access these properties by right-clicking on the icon and selecting the Properties option from the pop-up menu that appears.

25. **Answer: A.** The Last Known Good Configuration option starts Windows XP using the settings that existed the last time a successful user logon occurred. All system setting changes made since the last successful startup are lost. This is a useful option if you have added or reconfigured a device driver that is causing the system to fail.

Objective 3.4

1. **Answer: C.** Windows 2000 eventually generated a list of four service packs before Microsoft stopped mainstream support for this operating system. Windows 2000 SP4 contained all the updates delivered in the previous service packs. In addition to security fixes and application compatibility improvements, Windows 2000 SP4 delivered USB 2.0 and 802.1x wireless networking support to the Windows 2000 platform. The Windows Automatic Updates service was delivered in SP3, and 128-bit encryption was delivered in SP2.

2. **Answers: B, D.** (B) To turn on Automatic Updates in Windows XP, simply access the Automatic Updates icon in the Control Panel. (D) You can also turn on Automatic Updates by accessing the System icon in the Control Panel and clicking the Automatic Updates tab. Using either method, you can configure Automatic Updates to download and install updates on a specified schedule or to notify the user when high-priority updates become available. You can click the Automatic (Recommended) option button and then enter day and time settings for Windows to install the updates under the Automatically Download Recommended Updates for My Computer and Install Them option.

3. **Answer: C.** To activate the Windows XP System Restore utility, navigate the Start/All Programs/Accessories/System Tools path and then select the System Restore option from the menu.

4. **Answer: A.** Microsoft typically releases patches in the form of updates, or in collections that include additional functionality or new device drivers, that it refers to as *service packs*.

Objective 4.0

Objective 4.1

1. **Answer: A.** Tractor feeds are used with very heavy forms, such as multiple-part continuous forms, and are most commonly found on dot-matrix printers.

2. **Answer: A.** Full-speed USB devices operate under the USB 2.0 specification (also referred to as *high-speed USB*) and support data rates up to 480Mbps. The IrDA-SIR standard infrared protocol is used to provide a standard serial port interface with transfer rates ranging up to 115kbps. The IrDA-FIR fast infrared protocol is used to provide a high-speed serial port interface with transfer rates ranging up to 4Mbps. The parallel ULTRA160/320/640 SCSI specifications provide data throughputs up to 160, 320, and 640MBps (or 1280, 2560, and 5120Mbps), respectively. The 802.11g wireless specification delivers data transfer rates in excess of up to 54Mbps.

3. **Answer: B.** In the dye-sublimation printer, a heating element strip is used to transfer the color substance on a plastic film to the paper. The heating element contains thousands of small heat points, which creates fine patterns of color dots. Different temperatures can be applied to the element to produce different shades.

4. **Answer: C.** Inkjet printers produce characters by squirting a precisely controlled stream of ink drops onto the paper. The drops must be controlled very precisely in terms of their aerodynamics, size, and shape; otherwise, the drop placement on the page becomes inexact, and the print quality falters.

5. **Answer: C.** The print wires are heated in the direct thermal printer so that they can burn dot patterns into special thermal paper. Thermal printers are widely used for barcode printing, battery-powered handheld printing devices, and credit card receipt printers.

6. **Answer: D.** The printhead in a dot-matrix printer is a vertical column of print wires that are controlled by electromagnets. Dots are created on the paper by energizing selected electromagnets, which extend the desired print wires from the printhead. The print wires impact an ink ribbon, which impacts the paper.

7. **Answer: B.** The toner is transferred to the paper from the drum because of the highly positive charge the transfer corona wire applies to the paper. The positive charge attracts the negatively charged toner particles away from the drum and onto the page.

8. **Answers: A, C.** (A) The transfer corona wire (transfer roller) is responsible for transferring the toner from the drum to the paper. The toner is transferred to the paper because of the highly positive charge the transfer corona wire applies to the paper. (C) A high voltage, applied to the primary corona wire, creates a highly charged negative field that conditions the drum to be written on by applying a uniform negative charge (<600V) to it.

9. **Answer: B.** After the image has been transferred to the paper, a pair of compression rollers in the fusing unit melts and presses the toner particles into the paper.

10. **Answer: B.** Before the laser writes on the drum, it is cleaned and conditioned. The laser is used to create a charged image on the drum, which attracts toner expelled by the developer roller. The toner attracted to the drum is then transferred to paper that has been given a different charge. After being transferred from the drum to the paper, the toner is then pressed and fused into the paper.

11. **Answer: B.** The transfer corona wire (transfer roller) is responsible for transferring the toner from the drum to the paper. The toner is transferred to the paper because of the highly positive charge the transfer corona wire applies to the paper.

12. **Answer: A.** The primary component of a dot-matrix printer is a main control board. It contains the logic circuitry required to convert the signals, received from the computer's adapter card, into character patterns, as well as to generate the control signals to position the printhead properly on the page.

Objective 4.2

1. **Answer: C.** You must calibrate the printer's colors to match those of the monitor and camera. First, check to make sure that you are using the correct device driver for the printer. The printer driver provides color adjustments for that printer through its properties. You must select a Custom Mode option and click the Advanced button to access the color management functions. This page enables you to adjust brightness, contrast, saturation, and CMYK color settings. You must adjust these settings and print test pages until you achieve the print output you want. Most often, you do this by matching the output of the monitor/printer and digital camera to special test images that can be obtained from the Web or hardware/software manufacturers.

2. **Answer: D.** Because this printer is being connected to the PC through a legacy parallel printer port, you should connect the printer to the parallel port and turn it on before trying to configure it through Windows. To install local printers in Windows XP, access the Printers and Faxes option from the Start menu. Next, click the Add a Printer option to access the Add Printer Wizard. Then choose the Local Printer (Local Printer Attached to This Computer in XP) option and click on the Next button. In the Windows XP dialog window, you should also select the Automatically Detect and Install My Plug and Play Printer option. Normally, the LPT1 options should be selected from the list of Printer Port options. Next, the Add Printer Wizard produces a list of manufacturers and models to choose from.

3. **Answers: B, D.** (B) To install a USB printer, connect the USB signal cable to the computer and to the printer, plug in the printer's power cord, and then allow the system to detect the printer through the PnP process when it is started up. When the operating system detects the new printer, it may automatically install the printer's drivers without any additional efforts. If the operating system does not recognize the printer, a Found New Hardware Wizard appears, and you need to select the proper driver from a Windows list or supply an OEM driver from a disc. If the operating system does not detect the printer, you must install it using the Add Hardware Wizard. (D) Increasingly, manufacturers of USB printers instruct you to run their installation software that comes with the device before connecting it to the computer and turning on the printer.

4. **Answer: C.** Printers can be installed using USB buses, SCSI buses, or infrared ports, but not the SATA bus. The SATA interface is a systems-level interface that is a standard disk drive interface. However, this interface has not been adapted as an external interface for printers.

5. **Answers: A, B.** (A) It is relatively easy to determine whether a printer is networked by the presence of a coaxial or a twisted-pair network signal cable connected directly to the printer. (B) The presence of the RJ-45 jacks on the back of the printer also indicates that the printer is network capable, even if it is not being used in that manner.

Objective 4.3

1. **Answer: B.** Nearly every printer is equipped with a built-in self-test. The easiest way to determine whether a printer is at fault is to run its self-test. If the self-test runs and prints clean pages, most of the printer has been eliminated as a possible source of problems.

2. **Answer: A.** Most paper feed errors are related to the paper feed rollers (pickup rollers). Given the symptoms, you first should check the rollers for proper alignment and wear.

3. **Answers: C, D.** If the printer's paper thickness selector is set improperly, or the rollers in its paper feed system become worn, the paper can slip as it moves through the printer and cause disfigured graphics to be produced. Check the printer's paper thickness settings. If they are correct and the print output is disfigured, you need to replace the paper feed rollers.

4. **Answer: A.** If a single inkjet is not firing, the output appears as white lines on the page. To correct this problem, replace the cartridge that is not working. If one of the jets is activated all the time, black or colored lines are produced on the page. To correct this problem, either clean the printhead or replace it. Apply alcohol to the inkjet nozzle using a fiber-free swab to manually clean the printhead. Afterward, use the printer's built-in cleaning process to remove any additional ink buildup from the nozzles. In some printer models, the printhead is built into the ink cartridges. This provides the printer with a fresh printhead each time the ink cartridge is replaced.

5. **Answer: D.** This question indicates that the printer was working when you left the office the previous day. Therefore, you should first check for things that may have changed since then. The preliminary steps for troubleshooting printer problems includes checking for simple causes, such as the printer not being plugged in to the power source, or not being connected to the host computer. In this case, the nighttime cleaning crew may have disconnected the printer to clean and then simply forgotten to plug it back in.

6. **Answer: C.** Some scanners have locking mechanisms that prevent the light source from moving inside the housing during transportation. If the light source is on but does not move when the system applies a scan request, refer to the scanner's documentation to determine whether your scanner has a locking mechanism. If so, check to make sure that the scanner is unlocked.

7. **Answer: B.** From the printer's properties window, select Spool Settings and select the Print Directly to the Printer option. If the print job goes through, there is a spooler problem. If not, the hardware and printer driver are suspect. To check spooler problems, examine the system for adequate hard disk space and memory. Also try canceling the top print job in the spooler and then try to print again. If an Enhanced Metafile (EMF) Spooling option is selected in the Print Processor page, change it to a RAW format option and try printing again.

8. **Answer: C.** One of the most common types of drivers associated with scanners is the TWAIN driver. The TWAIN interface specification was designed to enable different types of image acquisition devices to communicate with TWAIN-compatible applications. If a TWAIN file is missing or damaged, the TWAIN application generates an error message when you try to perform a scan operation. The scanner application software installs the TWAIN drivers when it is installed. You should uninstall and reinstall the scanner's TWAIN software.

9. **Answer: B.** Smudged print is usually a sign of failure in the fusing section. If the fusing roller's temperature is not sufficient to bond the toner to the page, the print smudges when touched.

Objective 5.0

Objective 5.1

1. **Answer: B.** Unshielded twisted-pair (UTP) networking cable contains four pairs of color-coded, individually insulated wires.

2. **Answer: A.** Bluetooth devices use low-power consumption, short-range radio frequency signals to provide a low-cost, secure communication link. The specification provides three power level/range options that include 100 mW/100 meters, 2.5 mW/10 meters, and 1 mW/1 meter.

3. **Answer: C.** The 802.1a specification provides up to 54Mbps data rates. It operates in the 5GHz frequency range.

4. **Answer: A.** If you are setting up a relatively small network, such as a residential or small office network, consider using static IP addressing and assigning each computer a unique address. In this case, there is no router or DHCP server to perform the dynamic host configuration process to provide automatic IP addressing. So, static IP addressing is the best option available.

5. **Answer: C.** A typical wireless LAN, 802.11g/b consists of a device known as an *access point* and any number of wireless network-capable devices. The wireless access point acts as a bridging device that connects the wireless network computers with the wired network. The access point uses antennas and a radio receiver/transmitter to communicate with the other devices through radio frequency signals.

6. **Answer: A.** Local area networks (LANs) have become the backbone of small- and medium-size businesses because they enable people to share and control business resources and information in a highly efficient manner. LANs also play a major role in large businesses, tying users together with each other and with other networks within the organization.

7. **Answer: B.** The 802.11g devices are fully compatible with 802.11b devices. The 802.11g specification delivers data transfer rates up to 54Mbps in the 2.4GHz band while the 802.11b uses the same 2.4GHz band to provide data transfer rates between 4.3 and 11Mbps. The presence of an 802.11b device in an 802.11g network causes the entire network to slow down considerably. The practical distance for 802.11g signals is the same as that of the 802.11b specification.

8. **Answer: D.** Instead of sending web page requests to a web server on the Internet, the uplink service routes the request to the satellite system's network operation center. The network operation center then requests the desired page from the real web server and returns it to the user through the satellite's downlink. The page request operation can occur only at the speed of the uplink connection, and the additional steps to get the page to the user may result in a noticeable delay known as *latency*.

9. **Answer: A.** Bluetooth can use up to eight devices, which can be grouped together to form a piconet. Any device can become the master device and assume control of the network by issuing a request broadcast. The other seven devices become slave devices until the master device releases its position. The master device uses time division multiplexing to rapidly switch from one slave device to another around the network.

10. **Answer: B.** Although peer-to-peer networks enable users to share resources and have a limited amount of local control over resources, they do not typically provide networking services for the different computers and devices attached to the network. In a client/server-based network, special dedicated computers running server operating systems can be tasked with automatically providing these services to the network's clients.

11. **Answer: A.** The following IP address ranges are available for private IP addressing: Class A addresses between 10.0.0.0 and 10.255.255.255, Class B addresses 172.16.0.0 through 172.31.255.255, and Class C addresses 192.168.0.0 through 192.168.255.255. However, the APIPA default range of 169.254.0.0 through 169.254.255.255 should not be used for private static addressing. Microsoft uses this range for dynamic auto-configuration in the absence of a DHCP server.

12. **Answer: A.** The 802.11b specification provides data transfer rates only up to 11Mbps, with fallback operations at 5.5Mbps, 2Mbps, and 1Mbps. Typically, the effective range of the 802.11b signal is from 100 to 300 feet (30 to 90 meters), assuming a direct line of sight (the practical indoor range is about 150 feet or 35 meters). The 802.11g specification delivers data transfer rates up to 54Mbps in the 2.4GHz band. The practical distance for 802.11g signals is the same as the 802.11b specification.

13. **Answer: B.** The 802.11g wireless networking specification delivers data transfer rates of up to 54Mbps in the 2.4-GHz band.

14. **Answer: C.** CAT6 cabling is a 250MHz, 100-ohm UTP specification that is capable of data transfers up to 1.2Gbps over 1000BASE-T wiring.

15. **Answer: B.** Wi-Fi wireless networking standards fall under the designation of 802.11x. Current standard versions include 802.11a, b, and g. These are sometimes referred to as *wireless ethernet* standards; however, true ethernet protocols are classified under IEEE 802.3 specifications.

16. **Answers: A, C.** The 802.11a specification provides up to 54Mbps data rates in the 5GHz frequency range. The 802.11g wireless networking specification delivers data transfer rates of up to 54Mbps in the 2.4GHz band.

17. **Answer: A.** In a typical peer-to-peer network arrangement, the users connected to the network can easily share access to different network resources, such as hard drives and printers. These resources can be shared at the discretion of the individual user.

18. **Answer: C.** The SC connector is the dominant connector for fiber-optic ethernet networks. The connector is designed so that it correctly aligns the end of the fiber cable with the receiver.

19. **Answer: D.** UTP LAN cable connects a computer and a switch using RJ-45 connectors.

20. **Answer: B.** A multimode fiber cable transmits light over sufficient distances for use in local area networks (less than 3000 feet). A single-mode fiber cable is normally reserved for use in high-speed, long-distance cable runs (up to 24 miles/40km in point-to-point configurations, 5km in an ethernet installation).

21. **Answer: C.** NWLink is Microsoft's version of the Internetwork Packet Exchange/Sequenced Packet Exchange (IPX/SPX) network protocol used in older Novell NetWare environments. Although NetWare has used IPX/SPX for the majority of its networking functions, with the release of NetWare 5.0, Novell changed NetWare's primary protocol from IPX/SPX to TCP/IP. Even so, the majority of the installed NetWare networks continue to run IPX/SPX for at least some networking functions. NWLink is relatively easy to install and manage and is also a routable protocol.

22. **Answer: D.** The TCP/IP packet is designed primarily to allow for message fragmentation and reassembly. TCP/IP calls for data to be grouped together in bundles called *network packets*. Because of its capability to connect to many types of computers and servers, TCP/IP is used in the majority of all computer networks and is the preferred network protocol for all current Windows operating system versions. However, the basic TCP/IP protocol does not offer a high level of encryption for the IP packet, although additional protocols from the TCP/IP suite of protocols, such as IPSec, can be added to perform this function.

23. **Answer: A.** Plenum-rated cables are suitable for use in plenum and other spaces used for environmental air because of their fire-resistant and low-smoke-producing characteristics. If catching fire, the cables located in a plenum area give off toxic gases, which spread throughout the facility via the air circulation system.

24. **Answer: C.** Analog modems are used for dial-up networking through the traditional telephone lines. Their maximum transmission speed tops out at 56kbps. Also, they do not use broadband transmission techniques. The other technologies employ digital modems and are all considered high-speed broadband devices (with the exception of an ISDN BRI connection that operates at sub-T1 speeds, which sets the limit for broadband badging, making BRI a narrowband technology).

Objective 5.2

1. **Answer: D.** Wireless network computers use a network interface card (802.11a, b, or g adapter card) that has a radio transmitter, receiver, and antenna integrated into the card. Each computer that has a wireless card installed can communicate with other wireless-equipped computers or with the access point.

2. **Answer: B.** Instead of repeating received messages to all its other ports, the switch can direct the information to its intended receiver if the address of the receiver is known. Because the information is sent only to the port where it is intended, the performance of the entire network is improved greatly. For this reason, switches have largely replaced hubs as the most basic connectivity device in local area networks. If the address is not known, the switch broadcasts the information to all its ports in the same manner as a hub does.

3. **Answer: D.** After the router has been connected, you must configure it for operation. Routers typically employ a browser-based wizard for this purpose. To begin the configuration process, start one of the computers in the network and open its browser. Next, enter the router's IP address in the browser's navigation window. The normal default value for most routers is the private network address 192.168.0.1.

4. **Answer: A.** Many wireless configuration applications include a built-in power meter program that shows the relative signal strength being received from the access point. When you're positioning a computer that has a wireless network card, you should use this tool to maximize the location of the computer. Likewise, if you are operating in a multiple access point environment, you can use this tool to identify the best access point to use in a given location.

5. **Answer: C.** This problem occurs because the Check for Newer Versions of Stored Pages setting in IE has been set to Never. Using this setting, Internet Explorer does not check for a newer version of a page; it simply pulls it from the history cache until the page has been removed from the history.

6. **Answers: A, B.** Information you need to configure your system with includes a service set identifier (SSID) name and possibly encryption information (none, WEP, WPA, or WPA2). This information must match that of the host AP you are connecting to.

7. **Answer: C.** The cable modem typically features two main connections: one to the host computer's USB port or an ethernet network adapter and the other to the CATV coaxial cable outlet on the wall. A CAT5 UTP cable/RJ-45 connector normally provides the communication path between the cable modem and the router, as well as between the router and the PC's network adapter. The cable modem has an F-Type connector that is used to attach the coaxial cable from the cable system to the cable modem.

8. **Answer: A.** Although peer-to-peer networks enable users to share resources and have a limited amount of local control over resources, they do not use dedicated server computers to provide services for the different computers and devices attached to the network. Internets, extranets, and intranets are all domain-based, client/server network configurations that employ dedicated computers running server versions of operating systems to provide network services to the network members such as automatically assigning TCP/IP settings (DHCP) and domain name services (DNS).

Objective 5.3

1. **Answer: A.** Check the activity light on the back plate of the LAN card (if available) to see whether the network recognizes the adapter. If the light is active, the connection is alive.

2. **Answer: B.** If the clients have an IP address of 169.254.xxx.xxx, it is because they cannot communicate with the DHCP server. Windows 2000 automatically assigns the computer an IP address in the 169.254 range if it cannot be assigned one from a DHCP server.

3. **Answer: B.** You can use an ethernet loopback cable to make the network adapter think it is attached to a network connection. This cable is made by looping wires from pin 1 to pin 3 and pin 2 to pin 6 of the RJ-45 plug. When the loopback cable is inserted into the NIC's RJ-45 jack, the link light should appear in a few seconds.

4. **Answer: A.** To ping the site's FQDN, your DNS must submit a name resolution request to a DNS server. The server searches through its DNS database and, if necessary, through the hierarchical DNS system until it locates the hostname or FQDN that was submitted to it. At this point, it resolves the IP address of the requested hostname and returns it back to the client.

5. **Answer: A.** This is a normal response for running a TCP/IP utility from the Run dialog box. Because these utilities are troubleshooting tools that return information to the screen, they cannot simply be initiated from the Start/Run dialog box; they must be run from the command prompt.

6. **Answer: B.** The PING utility can be used for testing TCP/IP functions. Pinging the local adapter's IP address in a Windows XP machine and receiving a Destination host unreachable message indicates that the adapter's IP address has not been initialized. This is typically due to a bad or disconnected network cable. However, the system will also fail to initialize the adapter's IP address if a duplicate address is assigned. In this case you should receive a notice that a duplicate address exists, and the IPCONFIG utility will return an address of 0.0.0.0 for the adapter.

7. **Answer: A.** The activity light blinks when the NIC is transmitting or receiving data to/from the LAN, indicating that there is network activity present. A solid light indicates no activity is present.

Objective 6.0

Objective 6.1

1. **Answer: B.** To minimize the risk of security compromise on a wireless LAN, the IEEE802.11 standard provides a security feature called Wired Equivalent Privacy (WEP). WEP provides a method for encrypting data transmissions and authenticating each computer on the network.

2. **Answer: D.** A hardware or software firewall is typically employed to block unauthorized, outside users from accessing the intranet site.

3. **Answer: B.** In addition to backing up data files and applications, it is often convenient to back up the key system configuration settings and data information as well. This type of data is called *system state data* and is stored so that the system can be rebuilt quickly in case of a failure.

4. **Answer: A.** The Windows Firewall feature is designed to provide protection from outside attacks by preventing unwanted connections from Internet devices. Computers connected directly to the Internet are always vulnerable to attacks from the outside.

5. **Answer: A, B.** The IEEE-802.11 standard provides a security feature called Wired Equivalent Privacy (WEP). WEP provides a 128-bit mathematical key encryption scheme for encrypting data transmissions and authenticating each computer on the network. Enabling the WEP function adds security for data being transmitted by the workstations. Although WEP is a strong encryption method, serious hackers can crack it. This has led the wireless industry to create a stronger Wi-Fi Protected Access (WPA) standard. WPA adds improved data encryption using Temporary Key Integrity Protocol (TKIP) and IEEE 802.1X Extensible Authentication Protocol (EAP) user authentication protocol to provide increased security. A newer version of WPA, called *WPA2*, is supported in Windows XP. This WPA version fully implements the security mechanisms for wireless networks called for in the IEEE-802.11i standard. WPA2 mandates both TKIP and AES encryption capabilities for secure data transmissions. WPA2 provides excellent wireless LAN security using a high level of encryption along with choice of strong and stronger authentication protocols.

6. **Answer: A.** Power Users is a special group that has permissions to perform many management tasks on the system but does not have the full administrative privileges of the Administrator account. Power Users can create and manage users and groups they create.

7. **Answer: D.** A networked or online computer has more opportunity to contract a virus or encounter grayware (including spyware and adware) than a standalone PC because these programs can enter the unit over the network or through the network connection. In particular, all computers with connections to the Internet should be protected by at least an antivirus solution, as well as spyware and adware blockers, before they are ever attached to the Internet. Conducting regular virus scans of the system's memory and HDD is critical when using the Internet.

8. **Answer: B.** The network administrator is generally responsible for determining which personnel can have access to the server room and may require a logbook entry for anyone working inside the server room. The presence of unauthorized individuals in the server room should be reported to the network administrator. Violations of any server room security measures should be reported to the network administrator for corrective action.

9. **Answer: D.** *Malware* is the term used to describe programs designed to be malicious in nature. The common malware programs are viruses, Trojan horses, and worms.

10. **Answer: A.** Computer viruses such as a Trojan horse virus are destructive programs designed to replicate and spread on their own. After they infiltrate one machine, they can spread into other computers through infected disks that friends and coworkers pass around or through local and wide area network connections.

11. **Answer: A.** Most BIOSes offer a variety of security options that can be set through the CMOS Setup utility. The Supervisory password option establishes a password that must be used to access the CMOS Setup utility (where the User and Supervisory password options are configured).

12. **Answer: D.** If a hard disk drive is not going to be reused, it should be damaged to the point where it is physically unusable—not just logically unusable. This can involve opening the outer cover of the drive and physically scarring its disk surfaces: scratching the surface with a sharp implement, hammering the disks, or pouring acid on the disk surfaces.

13. **Answers: B, C.** All the computers in the network must be configured to use the same key to communicate. Therefore, if you enable WEP on the AP, you need to enable the same WEP key on each computer in the network. In addition, you should disable the SSID Broadcast option so that outsiders do not use SSID to acquire your address and data.

14. **Answers: A, B, C.** The NTFS system offers more efficient drive management, support for very large drives made possible by its 64-bit clustering arrangement, increased folder and file-security capabilities, disk quotas, disk compression, file encryption, recoverable file system capabilities, and built-in RAID support.

Objective 6.2

1. **Answer: B.** The Windows XP Removable Storage Management system does not recognize CD-R, CD-RW, or DVD-R devices as backup media, even though there are options to add these devices through the utility.

2. **Answer: D.** You should periodically perform Restore operations from backups to diverse locations. This enables you to validate the backups. You do not want to wait until the system fails to find out that the backups you've been making on a regular basis don't work. Also, the worst time to learn how to restore data is when you are in the middle of a crisis.

3. **Answer: B.** The first step to take after receiving this notice is to clear the SSL history (cache) on your local machine. This forces your browser to request a new certificate from the SSL server. If the new certificate is still expired, the SSL encryption is still active, provided the site is a legitimate site. Therefore, any information passed between the browser and the site's web server is secure. If you select the option to continue, an authenticated and encrypted SSL session is established. However, in some cases, sites with expired certificates can be exploitation or redirected malicious sites. Check the certificate to see if you can determine whether the certifying body is a trusted company. Anyone can generate a certificate; the value in certificates for SSL is that trustworthy authorities issue them. You should also check the date setting on your local machine to make sure that it is correct. An incorrect date could fall outside the certificate's assigned life cycle and cause this message to appear.

4. **Answer: B.** The full backup process backs up the entire contents of the disk. This includes directory and subdirectory listings and their contents. This backup method requires the most time each day to back up but requires the least time to restore the system after a failure.

5. **Answers: A, C, D.** If you can access your antivirus program, immediately run a scan on your PC using the current virus definitions. If this does not identify the virus and stop its operation, download the latest virus signatures from the manufacturer and rescan your system. If you can reach the Internet from the infected machine, you can download any of several free removal tools and scanning utilities and run them to identify and possibly remove viruses from your infected machine. If the virus has made it impossible for you to access updated virus signatures and utilities, you may need to obtain an antivirus tool on a CD. You can use this CD to boot the system and then run a virus scan from it. This will probably require that you create the CD from an uninfected PC and download the newest security patches and definitions. In cases of severe infections, your only option may be to repartition your drive and reinstall the operating system and applications. Hopefully, you have a recent backup copy of your important files.

Objective 6.3

1. **Answer: D.** These computers are intended for use by the general public so it is not reasonable to configure a User password for the system. The Supervisory password option establishes a password that must be used to access the CMOS Setup utility (where the User and Supervisory password options are configured). This will prevent the users from changing the configuration of the system.

2. **Answers: A, D.** Most BIOSes offer a variety of security options that can be set through the CMOS Setup utility. The User password option enables administrators to establish passwords that users must enter during the startup process to complete the boot process and gain access to the operating system. This provides a secure logon environment for the users. On the other hand, the Supervisory password option establishes a password that must be used to access the CMOS Setup utility (where the User and Supervisory password options are configured).

Objective 6.4

1. **Answer: A.** The Windows Update service is offered through the Internet and enables the system to periodically check the Microsoft Updates site for enhancements. When the system connects with the site, the service compares the current status of the local Windows installation to the latest information on the site. It then provides a list of available updates for the computer. Users can select which updates are applicable to their use. Users can also access the Windows Update service at any time through the Start menu or through the Internet Explorer Tools menu. The Windows Update service is also used to obtain service packs. These additions are important because they address major issues that have been detected in the operating system version since it was launched (or since the last service pack was issued). An even better friend would make sure that he was set up with automatic updates so that he did not need to remember how to access the updates site and make choices beyond his abilities.

2. **Answer: B.** There are some malicious computer activities for which the only prevention method is to educate customers about them. They must be educated about the fact that these attacks occur and given examples of strategies that can be used to prevent them from working.

Objective 7.0

Objective 7.1

1. **Answer: A.** The plastic tweezers are the best tool for retrieving screws and other objects that fall into the system. This tool can save a lot of disassembly/reassembly time when metal objects get loose in the system. Although many computer technicians carry a telescopic magnet in their tool kits for retrieving screws and nuts that get dropped into the system unit or printer, this tool can adversely affect the operation of disk drives and CRT-based monitors.

2. **Answer: B.** Most adapter card manufacturers' installation guides will advise you to unplug the power to the unit before installing any adapter card. However, for an antistatic strap to work correctly, you need to connect the strap to the chassis of the case before the grounded, three-pronged power cable is removed from the wall outlet. Without this connection, the built-up static on your body has nowhere to go. As soon as your body is at the same electrical potential as the chassis, you can unplug the power cable from the outlet.

3. **Answer: B.** All hazardous materials are required to have Material Safety Data Sheets (MSDS) that accompany them when they change hands. They are also required to be on-hand in areas where hazardous materials are stored and commonly used.

Objective 7.2

1. **Answer: B.** PC boards containing static-sensitive devices are normally shipped in special antistatic bags. These bags are good for storing ICs and other computer components that may be damaged by ESD. They are also the best method of transporting PC boards with static-sensitive components.

2. **Answer: B.** The presence of water in the work area from other sources, such as leaking pipes or ceilings, should always be a cause for alarm and correction. Water leaks in the work area are generally the responsibility of the building maintenance supervisor. If the business does not have someone on staff who is responsible for building infrastructure, you should report the situation to whoever is responsible for the PCs and/or network so that person can properly shut down the systems.

3. **Answer: A.** Technicians protect the equipment from electrostatic discharge by using grounding strap devices that are placed around the wrists or ankles to ground the technicians to the system being worked on. These straps release any static present on a technician's body and pass it harmlessly to ground potential.

Objective 7.3

1. **Answer: A.** Laser printer toner cartridges should be refilled and recycled. The preferable method is to return the cartridge to the original manufacturer. However, many third-party refill organizations refill toner cartridges as part of their business.

2. **Answer: A.** As with toner cartridges, the desired method of disposal for batteries is recycling.

3. **Answer: C.** Check with your local waste management agency before disposing of them. Some landfills do not accept chemical solvents and cans. In this case, these items must be disposed of in a Subtitle-D dumpsite.

4. **Answer: C.** Free liquids are those substances that can pass through a standard paint filter. If the liquid passes through the filter, it is free liquid and cannot be disposed of in the landfill.

5. **Answer: B.** Most computer components contain some level of hazardous substances. CRTs contain glass, metal, plastics, lead, barium, and rare earth metals.

6. **Answer: C.** Local regulations concerning acceptable disposal methods for computer-related components should always be checked before disposing of any electronic equipment, such as a CRT display.

Objective 8.0

Objective 8.1

1. **Answer: A.** Active listening involves participation in the discussion customers are communicating to you so that you can pinpoint what they mean.

2. **Answer: C.** Sometimes explaining the problem to the customer is not enough. In this case, showing the customer the actual problem by replacing the bad RAM with the good RAM helps her to understand your findings by seeing the difference that it makes in the system's operation.

3. **Answer: D.** Recognize that there is a professional way to communicate with customers. There is a difference between saying "You broke this PC" and "Help me understand how the computer got to this point." The first statement is overly assertive and judgmental, whereas the second is inquiring and nonjudgmental. The assertive statement sets up a level of separation between the technician and the user, whereas the inquisitive statement brings the two together to investigate the problem. Overly assertive conversations with coworkers can create adversarial conditions. If you have a personality that tends to use this approach with people, work on controlling and minimizing this trait.

4. **Answer: A.** Mentally (and maybe physically) identify key points as the customer describes the nature of the problem. Don't interrupt customer descriptions before you have all the details, but do verify your understanding of what the customer is telling you by repeating his main points as he is describing them to you. Even if you are sure that you know what is going on after the first sentence, have patience to listen to the complete description. Then fix the problem.

Objective 8.2

1. **Answer: B.** Avoid arguing with the customer. When you do reply, remain calm, talk in a steady voice, and avoid making inflammatory comments. Also, try to avoid taking a defensive stance, as this signals a conflict point.

2. **Answer: A.** When using a cell phone, you should set it to silent or vibrate mode before entering a customer's site. Unless an emergency or your supervisor is trying to reach you about the current job, you should let your messaging service answer the call. All personal calls should be made or received while offsite.

3. **Answer: A.** The ability to communicate clearly is the other trait most looked for in service people. Allow customers to talk through their problems, but try to guide and control the discussion to make certain that it stays focused. If you simply let the conversation go in any direction, you may waste a significant amount of the customers' and your time. Also, you're the one with the knowledge of what might cause problems. The customers may not have good diagnostic skills or system knowledge, so they will not know how to optimize the conversation.

4. **Answer: D.** Avoid arguing with the customer. When you do reply, remain calm, talk in a steady voice, and avoid making inflammatory comments. After the customer has poured out the full story, try to redirect the conversation to creating solutions to the problems. Go over the important details one at a time and explain how you will handle each concern or whom you must turn to for a final answer.

5. **Answer: B.** Avoid distracting employees while you are working at a customer's site. Ask permission to use the customer's facilities, such as the telephone, copier, or other equipment. In this case there is no reason for you to answer someone else's telephone unless he has specifically asked you to.

CHAPTER TWO

IT Technician Exam

Practice Questions

Domain 1.0: Personal Computer Components

Objective 1.1: Install, configure, optimize, and upgrade personal computer components

1. After you upgrade your system board processor from a 2.8GHz Pentium D 820 to a 3.6GHz Pentium D 960, the system tries to start up but shuts down in the middle of the POST. Which of the following causes the system to automatically shut down after installing a new processor?

   ○ **A.** The processor overheats because the fan unit is not connected properly.

   ○ **B.** The processor has been installed incorrectly, so a wrong voltage is being applied to the wrong pins.

   ○ **C.** The wrong microprocessor driver has been installed.

   ○ **D.** The BIOS does not recognize the new processor type.

Quick Answer: **179**
Detailed Answer: **184**

2. While observing a PC's screen during the boot process, you believe that the system has insufficient memory installed to handle the applications typically being run on the machine. You decide to upgrade the memory. How do you determine the correct type of memory to use in this computer? (Select all that apply.)

Quick Answer: **179**
Detailed Answer: **184**

- ○ **A.** Consult the PC manufacture's website for proper memory types and configuration information.

- ○ **B.** Open the computer and check the type of physical memory currently installed.

- ○ **C.** Check the Internet for information about the types of RAM available for the system.

- ○ **D.** Consult the system board's Installation and Users documentation for proper memory types and configuration.

3. You have been tasked with refurbishing old computers your company is donating to a technical school. You must install new hard drives in the systems so that there is no chance that important data could be recovered from the original drives. The systems all have EIDE/PATA drive support built in, but none offers SATA support. You must search through a pile of signal cables to connect the new PATA drives to the system boards. Also, you know that there are two types of IDE signal cables and that you need the ones for newer UltraDMA drives. How many pins does a PATA hard drive connection have?

Quick Answer: **179**
Detailed Answer: **184**

- ○ **A.** 80
- ○ **B.** 40
- ○ **C.** 20
- ○ **D.** 10

4. One of your service technicians has called you from a customer's office to request that you ship a new power supply to him so that he can replace a dead unit in one of the customer's PCs. Which of the following is important information to gather about the power supply unit?

Quick Answer: **179**
Detailed Answer: **184**

- ○ **A.** Wattage rating
- ○ **B.** Output voltages
- ○ **C.** Current capacity
- ○ **D.** Country selectable switch information

5. Your company is sending you to Europe to work for an extended period of time. Your desktop PC is being shipped to your new location. What step should you take to prepare your PC for operation in your new location?

Quick Answer: **179**
Detailed Answer: **184**

   ○ **A.** Obtain the correct DC power adapter for the country you are going to visit.

   ○ **B.** Download language support and character codes for the country you are going to.

   ○ **C.** Change the voltage selector switch position on the power supply.

   ○ **D.** Install a native language version of your operating system for the location where you will be working.

6. You are installing a PATA CD-ROM drive into a PC system that already has a single PATA HDD installed. How should the new drive be configured?

Quick Answer: **179**
Detailed Answer: **184**

   ○ **A.** Primary master

   ○ **B.** Primary slave

   ○ **C.** Secondary master

   ○ **D.** Secondary slave

7. Your manager has asked you to research RAID technology to recommend a solution for providing data security through redundancy. Which RAID types provide fault tolerance through redundant drives that allow the array to continue operating if one drive fails?

Quick Answer: **179**
Detailed Answer: **184**

   ○ **A.** RAID0

   ○ **B.** RAID1

   ○ **C.** RAID3

   ○ **D.** RAID5

8. Which of the following PC components offer the fastest data access?

Quick Answer: **179**
Detailed Answer: **184**

   ○ **A.** DRAM devices

   ○ **B.** SATA hard disk drives

   ○ **C.** USB flash drives

   ○ **D.** Floppy disk drives

9. How many PATA devices can be installed in a typical ATX or BTX system?

- ○ **A.** 1
- ○ **B.** 2
- ○ **C.** 4
- ○ **D.** 8

Quick Answer: **179**
Detailed Answer: **185**

10. What is the data transfer speed of a USB 2.0 interface?

- ○ **A.** 100Mbps
- ○ **B.** 480Mbps
- ○ **C.** 1Gbps
- ○ **D.** 12Mbps

Quick Answer: **179**
Detailed Answer: **185**

11. What is the minimum number of disks required for a RAID5 system?

- ○ **A.** 2
- ○ **B.** 3
- ○ **C.** 5
- ○ **D.** 32

Quick Answer: **179**
Detailed Answer: **185**

12. You have been asked to install a SATA hard drive in a computer that already has a PATA HDD and CD-ROM drive installed. Which cable should you connect the new drive to?

- ○ **A.** The secondary signal cable ′
- ○ **B.** The primary signal cable
- ○ **C.** The 15-pin SATA signal cable
- ○ **D.** The 7-pin SATA signal cable

Quick Answer: **179**
Detailed Answer: **185**

13. What is the maximum capacity of a single-sided, dual-layer DVD-R disc?

- ○ **A.** 4.7GB
- ○ **B.** 9.4GB
- ○ **C.** 2.1GB
- ○ **D.** 8.5GB

Quick Answer: **179**
Detailed Answer: **185**

14. You are using a Windows 2000 Emergency Start Disk with no USB support to boot a failing computer. Where must you go to enable USB support in a PC?

- ○ **A.** In the startup program on the Windows ESD disk
- ○ **B.** In the CMOS Setup utility
- ○ **C.** Windows Control Panel/Ports
- ○ **D.** Windows Device Manager

15. What type of standard I/O device uses a 3-row, 15-pin female connector?

- ○ **A.** Monitor
- ○ **B.** Joystick
- ○ **C.** Printer
- ○ **D.** Modem

16. You want to upgrade your existing computer to play exotic games. In particular, you want to install a dual processor system board, additional high-speed DDR2-RAM, a high-end video display card, and a Windows XP Professional operating system. Your current system uses a 350W power supply, a Pentium II microprocessor, 512MB of SDRAM-RAM, a 30GB EIDE drive, and a 52X CD-RW drive. What other equipment do you need to upgrade to reach the desired function for this system?

- ○ **A.** A faster HDD unit is needed.
- ○ **B.** A larger power supply is needed.
- ○ **C.** A larger HDD unit is needed.
- ○ **D.** A DVD drive should be installed to replace the CD-ROM drive.

17. What type of equipment should be used to minimize the chances of ESD during normal computer maintenance work?

- ○ **A.** Surge protector
- ○ **B.** Terrycloth towel
- ○ **C.** Wrist strap
- ○ **D.** Screwdriver

18. The most effective tool for protecting the PC system from dangerous static buildup is _____.

Quick Answer: 179
Detailed Answer: 186

   ○ **A.** an ESD wrist or ankle strap

   ○ **B.** the safety ground plug at a commercial AC receptacle

   ○ **C.** the ground plane of the system board

   ○ **D.** the chassis ground provided by the brass standoff(s)

19. Which of the following is the best way to optimize the cooling system in a desktop PC?

Quick Answer: 179
Detailed Answer: 186

   ○ **A.** Use fewer devices.

   ○ **B.** Drill holes in the side panels.

   ○ **C.** Remove the side panels.

   ○ **D.** Add additional case fans to increase airflow through the computer.

20. What type of socket is used for an AMD Athlon XP microprocessor?

Quick Answer: 179
Detailed Answer: 186

   ○ **A.** Socket 462

   ○ **B.** Socket 423

   ○ **C.** Socket 370

   ○ **D.** Slot 1

Objective 1.2: Identify tools, diagnostic procedures, and troubleshooting techniques for personal computer components

1. After you install a new video driver on your notebook PC, the system does not display anything on the LCD screen. What action should you take?

Quick Answer: 179
Detailed Answer: 186

   ○ **A.** Connect a monitor to the external VGA connector and reboot the system. After gaining visual access to the system, open the Device Manager and use the Device Driver Rollback feature.

   ○ **B.** Use the ASR function to restore the system to its previous state.

   ○ **C.** Restart the system in Safe Mode, access the Device Manager, expand the Display Adapters node, and use the Driver Rollback feature.

   ○ **D.** Press the Fn and the Screen function keys several times until the LCD display comes on.

2. After you install two SCSI hard drives, a SCSI CD-ROM drive, and a SCSI CD-R/W drive in a system, none of them work when you start the system. What actions should you take to get the SCSI interface and devices working properly with the system?

Quick Answer: **179**
Detailed Answer: **186**

- ○ **A.** Make sure that consecutive addresses have been assigned to the drives.
- ○ **B.** Ensure that the SCSI host adapter is configured as ID-7 or ID-15.
- ○ **C.** Make sure that the boot drive is configured as ID=0.
- ○ **D.** Make sure that the termination is correct and that each device has a unique address.

3. What could cause a video system to be limited to a 16-color output?

Quick Answer: **179**
Detailed Answer: **186**

- ○ **A.** The wrong video driver has been installed.
- ○ **B.** The video adapter and the display are incompatible.
- ○ **C.** The Color Quality setting of the Display Properties is incorrect.
- ○ **D.** You have installed the wrong video cable.

4. One of your customer's PCs periodically shuts itself off and then comes back on. What is the most likely cause of this problem?

Quick Answer: **179**
Detailed Answer: **186**

- ○ **A.** The processor has a broken pin that makes intermittent contact with the socket.
- ○ **B.** The power supply needs to be upgraded to furnish enough power to keep the system running when the peripherals are active.
- ○ **C.** The processor's cooling fan is not working.
- ○ **D.** The ACPI timing function is set incorrectly.

5. A customer is complaining that her video display is dead and doesn't show anything. Which of the following should you do first when you arrive at her workstation?

Quick Answer: **179**
Detailed Answer: **187**

- ○ **A.** Determine whether it's plugged in to the power outlet.
- ○ **B.** Determine whether it's turned on and just in sleep mode.
- ○ **C.** Determine whether the display drivers are correct.
- ○ **D.** Replace the video adapter card with a known good unit.

6. What causes the system to perform a memory dump?

    ○ **A.** The system encounters a condition that it cannot recover from.

    ○ **B.** The system has been shut down incorrectly.

    ○ **C.** The DLL file of an unsigned driver conflicts with the DLL file of another driver in the system.

    ○ **D.** Dr. Watson detects a memory usage error and stops the system to prevent data contamination.

7. Which device produces several beeps and causes the system to fail during the POST?

    ○ **A.** Hard disk drive

    ○ **B.** Microprocessor

    ○ **C.** Power supply

    ○ **D.** Video display

8. Which components cause the system to not complete the POST if they are defective? (Select all that apply.)

    ○ **A.** RAM

    ○ **B.** Microprocessor

    ○ **C.** Power supply

    ○ **D.** Network adapter

9. A user in your area has a notebook PC whose keyboard intermittently produces incorrect characters on the screen. What's the most likely cause of this problem?

    ○ **A.** His Fn key has been depressed by mistake.

    ○ **B.** His keyboard driver is corrupt.

    ○ **C.** The numeric keypad feature is enabled.

    ○ **D.** The Windows Character Map is configured incorrectly.

10. You have been asked to install a printer in a customer's office. When you arrive, you find that there are a number of connectivity options available with the printer, including wireless RF, infrared, enhanced parallel, and USB connections. Which printer interface is fastest for a local printer?

    ○ **A.** USB 2.0

    ○ **B.** 802.11b

    ○ **C.** ECP

    ○ **D.** IrDA

11. Which of the following would cause a keyboard error at bootup? (Select two correct answers.)

Quick Answer: **179**
Detailed Answer: **188**

- ○ **A.** Keys are stuck.
- ○ **B.** The keyboard is unplugged.
- ○ **C.** The typematic rate is set too high in CMOS.
- ○ **D.** The keyboard has been disabled in CMOS.

12. What is the first thing you should check when a customer complains of a machine that was working yesterday and is completely dead today?

Quick Answer: **179**
Detailed Answer: **188**

- ○ **A.** AC outlet for power
- ○ **B.** Power supply
- ○ **C.** Motherboard
- ○ **D.** Power switch

13. Which of the following is the first step you would perform when checking out a video display that appears dead?

Quick Answer: **179**
Detailed Answer: **188**

- ○ **A.** Check to see that the power cord is plugged in.
- ○ **B.** Check the connection to the video adapter.
- ○ **C.** Check the power supply connection to the motherboard.
- ○ **D.** Check to see that the power light is on.

14. To measure voltage, a multimeter should be connected _____.

Quick Answer: **179**
Detailed Answer: **188**

- ○ **A.** in series with the item being checked
- ○ **B.** in line with the item being checked
- ○ **C.** in parallel with the item being checked
- ○ **D.** in place of the item being checked

15. A user complains that his monitor displays the wrong colors and that his screen is distorted. He has just installed a new video card and a new sound card and attached a set of speakers to the sides of his monitor. What is the most likely cause of this problem?

Quick Answer: **179**
Detailed Answer: **188**

- ○ **A.** The speakers are unshielded.
- ○ **B.** The video card is defective.
- ○ **C.** The refresh rate is set to low.
- ○ **D.** The monitor is defective.

Objective 1.3: Perform preventative maintenance of personal computer components

1. You are installing a new hard drive inside a mini-tower case. The space inside the system unit is limited. What action should you take during the installation to maximize the operational life of the new drive?

    ○ **A.** Ensure adequate airflow around the drive unit to prevent it from overheating.

    ○ **B.** Lubricate the spindle bearing on the bottom of the drive twice a year.

    ○ **C.** Reseat the drive's signal cable periodically to remove any corrosion that may build up during normal operation.

    ○ **D.** Run the CHKDSK and DEFRAG utilities on the drive each week.

Quick Answer: **179**
Detailed Answer: **188**

2. A couple of hours after you install a new processor upgrade in a desktop system, it is overheating. What is the most likely cause of this?

    ○ **A.** You forgot to apply thermal compound to the heat sink.

    ○ **B.** You installed an incompatible processor.

    ○ **C.** You installed the wrong driver for the new processor.

    ○ **D.** You forgot to attach the fan's power connector.

Quick Answer: **179**
Detailed Answer: **188**

3. You can use the _____ utility to free up hard drive space by removing temporary Internet files and removing installed components and unused programs.

    ○ **A.** MSCONFIG

    ○ **B.** Disk Manager

    ○ **C.** DEFRAG

    ○ **D.** Disk Cleanup

Quick Answer: **179**
Detailed Answer: **188**

4. What command-line utility can you use to rearrange the data on an HDD so that it is located in contiguous efficient links?

    ○ **A.** SFC.EXE

    ○ **B.** CHKDSK.EXE

    ○ **C.** MSCONFIG.EXE

    ○ **D.** DEFRAG.EXE

Quick Answer: **179**
Detailed Answer: **188**

5. Which of the following should be used to clean dust out of the interior of a desktop PC?

   ○ **A.** A special dust cleaning solution on a chamois cloth

   ○ **B.** A household vacuum cleaner

   ○ **C.** A can of compressed air

   ○ **D.** A nylon bristle paintbrush

Quick Answer: **179**
Detailed Answer: **189**

6. Which item is best suited for general cleaning of monitors?

   ○ **A.** An antistatic spray

   ○ **B.** A common flower mister

   ○ **C.** A glass cleaner

   ○ **D.** A damp cloth

Quick Answer: **179**
Detailed Answer: **189**

7. Which of the following are common sources of heat buildup that can be found around a PC installation? (Select all that apply.)

   ○ **A.** Direct sunlight

   ○ **B.** Location of heaters

   ○ **C.** Excess body heat

   ○ **D.** Papers piled on equipment

Quick Answer: **179**
Detailed Answer: **189**

8. What surge-suppressor rating describes how quickly its protective circuitry can react to changes in the incoming line and limit the amount of current that passes through?

   ○ **A.** Clamping voltage

   ○ **B.** Clamping speed

   ○ **C.** Filter value

   ○ **D.** Surge limiting

Quick Answer: **179**
Detailed Answer: **189**

9. What product is recommended for manual cleaning of tape drive R/W heads?

   ○ **A.** Soft cloths

   ○ **B.** Cotton swabs

   ○ **C.** A pencil eraser

   ○ **D.** Foam swabs

Quick Answer: **179**
Detailed Answer: **189**

Quick Check

Quick Answer: **179**
Detailed Answer: **189**

10. Which of the following can be done to reduce the risk of thermal failure caused by the accumulation of dust particles? (Select two correct answers.)

    ❍ **A.** Remove the side panels from the chassis.

    ❍ **B.** Optimize the speed of the fan.

    ❍ **C.** Replace the fans with foam filters.

    ❍ **D.** Install foam filters at chassis openings.

Objective 2.0: Laptops and Portable Devices

Objective 2.1: Identify fundamental principles of using laptops and portable devices

1. One of your technical representatives calls you because she left the AC power adapter for her notebook PC in her last hotel room in a different city. She has a presentation to give tomorrow, and there is no way to get the adapter from the old hotel. There is also no time to order an exact replacement from the manufacturer. You tell your rep that she needs to buy a generic replacement from a local retail store, and all she needs to do is get the correct voltage and current specifications. Where can she find information about her laptop's correct DC input voltage and current requirements? (Select all that apply.)

   Quick Answer: **179**
   Detailed Answer: **190**

   ○ **A.** On the power adapter manufacturer's website

   ○ **B.** On the body of the AC power adapter

   ○ **C.** On the bottom of the notebook PC

   ○ **D.** In the notebook's Installation and Users documentation

2. Your national sales director spends a considerable amount of time on airplanes each month. It is time to upgrade his notebook PC. You have settled on the fact that he needs one of the low-power consumption chipsets and processors, and now you are evaluating which battery types might be available to provide power over the duration of longer flights. Which battery type offers the longest battery life in a portable PC?

   Quick Answer: **179**
   Detailed Answer: **190**

   ○ **A.** NiCD

   ○ **B.** NiMH

   ○ **C.** Lead acid

   ○ **D.** Alkaline

3. You are working with a small advertising firm whose art development person will be traveling a lot over the next six months in conjunction with a big project she is working on. The art developer needs a notebook PC to travel with, but the display has to be very good for her to prepare the types of artwork required for the project. What should you recommend as the best display type for this notebook PC?

- ○ **A.** Dual-scan technology
- ○ **B.** Active-matrix TFT technology
- ○ **C.** Passive-matrix technology
- ○ **D.** CSTN/DSTN technology

4. What is the size of a Type II PC card?

- ○ **A.** 5mm
- ○ **B.** 7.5mm
- ○ **C.** 3.3mm
- ○ **D.** 10.5mm

5. What is another name for a PC Card device?

- ○ **A.** A PC Bus card
- ○ **B.** A smart card
- ○ **C.** A PCMCIA card
- ○ **D.** An I/O bus card

6. What type of power does a notebook PC receive from the wall outlet?

- ○ **A.** Low-voltage alternating current
- ○ **B.** Low-voltage direct current
- ○ **C.** High-voltage alternating current
- ○ **D.** High-voltage direct current

7. What functions are performed by the external power supply of a portable computer system?

- ○ **A.** Increase the voltage of commercial power for the computer.
- ○ **B.** Convert commercial DC voltage into AC voltage for system usage and battery charging.
- ○ **C.** Store commercial power to recharge the battery.
- ○ **D.** Convert commercial AC voltage into DC voltage for system usage and battery charging.

Objective 2.2: Install, configure, optimize, and upgrade laptops and portable devices

1. You have just completed a major upgrade of a notebook PC. You upgraded the notebook's processor to a faster version and doubled the RAM capacity by installing an additional 512MB of new DDR2 RAM. When you start up the system, it shows only 956MB of memory installed. What is the cause of this discrepancy?

   ○ **A.** One of the new memory modules is bad.

   ○ **B.** The new memory modules do not match the existing modules.

   ○ **C.** The system is set up to use split bank addressing.

   ○ **D.** The system is using shared video memory.

Quick Answer: **179**
Detailed Answer: **190**

2. Which of the following portable PC components is hot-swappable?

   ○ **A.** An external CD/DVD R/W drive

   ○ **B.** A PS/2 keyboard

   ○ **C.** A DDR2 module

   ○ **D.** An internal SATA drive

Quick Answer: **179**
Detailed Answer: **191**

3. Before you remove a USB device from a working PC, you should _____.

   ○ **A.** Do nothing. USB devices are hot-swappable and can be removed from the system at any time.

   ○ **B.** Open the Device Manager and click the USB node. Then select the option to disable the USB device you want to remove.

   ○ **C.** Access the Add New Hardware applet in the Control Panel and start the Add New Hardware Wizard. When the wizard starts, select the option to disable the USB device. Then remove the card from the system.

   ○ **D.** Click the Safely Remove Hardware status indicator on the taskbar and then select the option to stop the operation of the USB device you want to remove.

Quick Answer: **179**
Detailed Answer: **191**

Objective 2.3: Use tools, diagnostic procedures, and troubleshooting techniques for laptops and portable devices

1. Which of the following are functions normally associated with the Fn key on a notebook PC? (Select all that apply.)

   Quick Answer: **180**
   Detailed Answer: **191**

   ○ **A.** To access hidden functions on the hard drive

   ○ **B.** To access additional functions from the keyboard

   ○ **C.** To access additional display devices attached to the system

   ○ **D.** To access additional Windows features from the keyboard

2. Your customer complains of a dim LCD panel after plugging the unit into a receptacle and getting a spark. What is most likely the problem?

   Quick Answer: **180**
   Detailed Answer: **191**

   ○ **A.** The Inverter module is damaged.

   ○ **B.** The AC power converter has been damaged.

   ○ **C.** The battery has been weakened.

   ○ **D.** The LCD panel is beginning to wear out.

3. A coworker has asked you to upgrade the memory in his notebook computer. He has purchased appropriate SODIMM modules for the unit, which are stored in an antistatic bag. You first unplug the AC power adapter from the notebook. Which of the following should you do next?

   Quick Answer: **180**
   Detailed Answer: **191**

   ○ **A.** Put on an antistatic strap.

   ○ **B.** Remove the battery from the notebook.

   ○ **C.** Remove the installed memory modules from the notebook.

   ○ **D.** Remove the new memory modules from the storage bag.

4. After you return from presenting a technology briefing where you used an overhead projector with your notebook PC, you find the notebook goes through the boot process but produces no display on the LCD. How do you activate the display?

Quick Answer: **180**
Detailed Answer: **191**

- ○ **A.** Restart the system in Safe Mode, access the Device Manager, expand the Display Adapters node, and use the Driver Rollback feature.

- ○ **B.** Press the Fn and the Screen function keys several times until the LCD display appears.

- ○ **C.** Connect an external display to the system to regain visual access to the system. Then access the Display Control Panel and reset the output port for the video.

- ○ **D.** Connect an external display to the system to regain visual access to the system. Then open the Device Manager and use the Device Driver Rollback feature to return the display output to the LCD.

5. Which of the following may cause a permanently distorted image on an LCD screen? (Select all that apply.)

Quick Answer: **180**
Detailed Answer: **191**

- ○ **A.** Magnets
- ○ **B.** Pressure on the screen
- ○ **C.** Extreme cold
- ○ **D.** Extreme heat

6. What is the most common repair for a failed LCD monitor?

Quick Answer: **180**
Detailed Answer: **191**

- ○ **A.** Replace the signal cable.
- ○ **B.** Replace the LCD panel.
- ○ **C.** Demagnetize the LCD screen.
- ○ **D.** Replace the computer.

Objective 3.0: Operating Systems

Objective 3.1: Identify the fundamental principles of operating systems

1. What command-line statement is used to convert a FAT32 partition to an NTFS partition in a Windows XP system?

   Quick Answer: **180**
   Detailed Answer: **192**

   ○ **A.** `Change C:/FS:NTFS`

   ○ **B.** `Convert C:/FS:NTFS`

   ○ **C.** `Format C:/FS:NTFS`

   ○ **D.** `Connect C:/FS:NTFS`

2. How do you get a list of the options that can be used with the COPY command at the command prompt?

   Quick Answer: **180**
   Detailed Answer: **192**

   ○ **A.** `COPY ?`

   ○ **B.** `COPY /?`

   ○ **C.** `COPY *`

   ○ **D.** `COPY /Help`

3. Which of the following can you use to restart the print spooler from the command prompt?

   Quick Answer: **180**
   Detailed Answer: **192**

   ○ **A.** `Start /Spooler`

   ○ **B.** `Run /Spooler`

   ○ **C.** `Spoolsv.exe`

   ○ **D.** `Spooler.com`

4. The _____ is used to copy and paste special characters such as special mathematical characters and characters from other languages into Windows programs.

   Quick Answer: **180**
   Detailed Answer: **192**

   ○ **A.** Windows Font Manager

   ○ **B.** Control Panel's Fonts applet

   ○ **C.** Control Panel's Regional and Language Options applet

   ○ **D.** Start menu's Character Map

5. Under what condition is it better to create a FAT32 partition than an NTFS partition?

Quick Answer: **180**
Detailed Answer: **192**

❍ **A.** For systems that are using non-NTFS-aware operating systems that require access to the partition being established

❍ **B.** On systems that already have file systems that employ larger cluster sizes

❍ **C.** On systems where file security is a high priority for the disk drive file system

❍ **D.** Where the system is likely to be used only by a single user

6. Which of the following causes a mapped drive to disappear from a system when it is shut down and restarted?

Quick Answer: **180**
Detailed Answer: **192**

❍ **A.** The Reconnect at Startup option is not checked in the mapped drive's Properties.

❍ **B.** The name of the mapped drive has been changed.

❍ **C.** The path to the mapped drive has changed.

❍ **D.** No one is logged in to the host computer for the mapped drive.

7. Your company is gaining an international presence, and you are investigating the possibility of producing your product documentation in several languages. You understand that Windows is already capable of dealing with foreign language character sets. What character code does Windows use for this?

Quick Answer: **180**
Detailed Answer: **192**

❍ **A.** Unicode

❍ **B.** ASCII

❍ **C.** TRON

❍ **D.** HTML

8. One of your customers is expanding its staff and needs to establish network accounts for the new people. At this point the company feels financially strapped by the cost of adding the employees and wants to minimize any expenses related to new equipment. Because increasing the disk drive capacities of the server is not an option, you suggest limiting the amount of disk space each new employee can use. Which NTFS feature enables administrators to monitor and control disk usage for each user?

Quick Answer: **180**
Detailed Answer: **193**

❍ **A.** Disk Management

❍ **B.** EFS

❍ **C.** NTFS Permissions

❍ **D.** Disk Quotas

9. What Windows command is used to compare directories from two drives in the same machine?

Quick Answer: **180**
Detailed Answer: **193**

  ○ **A.** DISKCOMP

  ○ **B.** DISKCOPY

  ○ **C.** FORMAT

  ○ **D.** DC

10. In Windows XP, where can you find a standard set of tools for managing the system's disk drives?

Quick Answer: **180**
Detailed Answer: **193**

  ○ **A.** In the Disk Manager snap-in

  ○ **B.** In the Computer Management Console

  ○ **C.** In the Device Manager utility

  ○ **D.** In the Task Manager utility

11. Where would you locate information about conflicts found in the Device Manager?

Quick Answer: **180**
Detailed Answer: **193**

  ○ **A.** Open the Device Manager and then click the Resources tab.

  ○ **B.** Navigate Start/Programs/Accessories/System Tools, select System Information, and then click the Resources tab.

  ○ **C.** Navigate Start/Settings/Control Panel, double-click System, and select the Resources tab.

  ○ **D.** Open the Device Manager and double-click the device driver's name; then click the Resources tab.

12. What is the proper path to activate the Windows XP System Restore Wizard?

Quick Answer: **180**
Detailed Answer: **193**

  ○ **A.** Start/All Programs/Administrative Tools/Backup/System Restore

  ○ **B.** Start/All Programs/Administrative Tools/System Restore

  ○ **C.** Start/All Programs/Accessories/System Tools/System Restore

  ○ **D.** Start/All Programs/Backup/System Restore

13. What are the primary characteristics of an active partition?

Quick Answer: **180**
Detailed Answer: **193**

○ **A.** It is the logical drive that the system boots to.

○ **B.** It can be divided into 23 logical drives.

○ **C.** It cannot be deleted if logical drives have been defined within it.

○ **D.** It is the first partition on the drive.

14. What are the primary characteristics of an extended partition? (Select two correct answers.)

Quick Answer: **180**
Detailed Answer: **193**

○ **A.** It can be divided into 23 logical drives.

○ **B.** It is the first partition on the drive.

○ **C.** It cannot be deleted if logical drives have been defined within it.

○ **D.** It is the logical drive that the system boots to.

15. Which command-line function can be used to graphically display the directory structure of the disk?

Quick Answer: **180**
Detailed Answer: **193**

○ **A.** DIR

○ **B.** CHDIR

○ **C.** DIR/ALL

○ **D.** TREE

16. You want to copy a group of folders and subfolders—including empty folders—from one place to another in a PC you are working on. You are working from the command prompt, so you need to use the XCOPY command. Which XCOPY switch enables you to perform this operation?

Quick Answer: **180**
Detailed Answer: **193**

○ **A.** XCOPY /s

○ **B.** XCOPY /h

○ **C.** XCOPY /e

○ **D.** XCOPY /CMDLINE

17. Which of the following file systems is not supported under Windows XP Professional?

Quick Answer: **180**
Detailed Answer: **193**

○ **A.** HPFS

○ **B.** NTFS5

○ **C.** FAT

○ **D.** FAT32

Objective 3.2: Install, configure, optimize, and upgrade operating systems

1. You use your Windows XP notebook in the office and when you travel. To shorten the startup time and extend the useful battery time when you are flying, you want to stop certain Windows services from loading when you start up the system on the airplane. Which Windows tool would you use to accomplish this task?

   ○ **A.** The Services snap-in

   ○ **B.** The Startup snap-in

   ○ **C.** The Security snap-in

   ○ **D.** The Performance snap-in

Quick Answer: **180**
Detailed Answer: **194**

2. You are about to install Windows XP Professional on an older SCSI drive in one of your home office PCs. The SCSI drive is larger than any of your other drives, and you want to take advantage of its features. When you check the Windows XP Marketplace Tested Product page, you do not find the drive listed there. You know that the XP Setup procedure will ask you to enter OEM drivers for the drive at some point. Which function key is required in the Windows XP Setup to install the drivers for the SCSI boot drive?

   ○ **A.** F2

   ○ **B.** F4

   ○ **C.** F6

   ○ **D.** F9

Quick Answer: **180**
Detailed Answer: **194**

3. You have two PATA hard drives in a system that keeps getting slower. The system is used to create and manipulate large multimedia files. How can you improve the system's disk drive subsystem performance?

   ○ **A.** Set the virtual memory setting to maximum.

   ○ **B.** Move the system's swap file to the D: drive where there is less traffic and more room to expand.

   ○ **C.** Set the virtual memory setting to variable so that Windows can make the swap file as large as necessary.

   ○ **D.** Set the virtual memory setting to minimum so that the system has to directly interface with the application, eliminating an extra processing step.

Quick Answer: **180**
Detailed Answer: **194**

4. One of your coworkers is having an operation and will be out of the office for several weeks. The company has decided to upgrade her system with a new dual core processor system board and SATA hard drive with Windows XP Professional installed. The company has tasked you with installing the upgrade components and transferring the user's data to the new drive. When backing up a user's existing HDD before an upgrade, what types of files are irreplaceable for most users? (Select all that apply.)

- ○ **A.** Email
- ○ **B.** Pictures
- ○ **C.** System State files
- ○ **D.** Registry files

5. Your supervisor wants you to install an application that automatically starts for all users whenever they log on to a Windows computer in your facility. Where do you do this in Windows XP?

- ○ **A.** Documents & Settings/Administrator/Start Menu/Programs/Startup
- ○ **B.** Control Panel/Add or Remove New Programs/Set Program Access and Defaults
- ○ **C.** Start/Programs/Startup
- ○ **D.** Documents & Settings/All Users/Start Menu/Programs/Startup

6. Which Windows XP utilities work to keep the system's hard drive running at its optimum capabilities? (Select all that apply.)

- ○ **A.** The CHKDSK utility
- ○ **B.** The DEFRAG utility
- ○ **C.** The Disk Management utility
- ○ **D.** The Device Manager

7. Where in Windows 2000/XP can you optimize virtual-memory management?

- ○ **A.** Help and Support Center
- ○ **B.** Programs/Accessories/System Tools
- ○ **C.** System Tools/Control Panel/Advanced tab
- ○ **D.** Control Panel/System

8. What Windows 2000 tool can be used to prepare disk images?

Quick Answer: **180**
Detailed Answer: **195**

- ○ **A.** Disk Manager
- ○ **B.** DISKCOPY
- ○ **C.** SYSPREP
- ○ **D.** FDISK

9. What is the first portion of the Windows 2000 or Windows XP installation process called?

Quick Answer: **180**
Detailed Answer: **195**

- ○ **A.** Text mode
- ○ **B.** GUI mode
- ○ **C.** Visual mode
- ○ **D.** Interactive mode

10. Which of the following methods can be used to upgrade a Windows 95 computer to Windows 2000? (Select all that apply.)

Quick Answer: **180**
Detailed Answer: **195**

- ○ **A.** Open the command prompt, navigate to the CD-ROM drive, change to the I386 subdirectory, enter the command **SETUP,** and then click Install Windows 2000.
- ○ **B.** Boot to the desktop, insert the Windows 2000 CD, and then click Install Windows 2000.
- ○ **C.** Open the command prompt, navigate to the CD-ROM drive, change to the I386 subdirectory, and then enter the command **WINNT32.**
- ○ **D.** Open the command prompt, navigate to the CD-ROM drive, type **cd** at the prompt, enter the command **SETUP,** and then click Install Windows 2000.

11. You are preparing to install a new copy of Windows XP on a network computer in your company. However, the user wants to retain his My Documents, My Pictures, Desktop, and Favorites folders, along with his display properties, mapped network drives, network printers, browser settings, and folder options from his old Windows Me system. What can you do to achieve both goals?

- ○ **A.** Access the Windows XP user state migration tools (USMT) to transfer the user configuration settings and files to a clean Windows XP installation without going through the upgrade process.

- ○ **B.** Run the Windows XP Recovery Process utility to move the files to a server on the network and then reinstall them after the operating system installation has been completed.

- ○ **C.** Run the Windows XP Automated System Recovery (ASR) utility to move the files to a server on the network and then reinstall them after the operating system installation has been completed.

- ○ **D.** Run the Windows XP Backup/Restore utility from NTBACKUP to move the files to a server on the network and then reinstall them after the operating system installation has been completed.

12. When you are uninstalling an application in a Windows system, what is the best response to a message about the possibility of deleting shared files?

- ○ **A.** Remove all files.
- ○ **B.** Remove the file.
- ○ **C.** Keep all files.
- ○ **D.** Keep the file.

Objective 3.3: Identify tools, diagnostic procedures, and troubleshooting techniques for operating systems

1. Which of the following utilities can be used to control the boot process in a Windows XP system?

- ○ **A.** BOOTCFG.EXE
- ○ **B.** BOOT.INI
- ○ **C.** BOOTSECT.DOS
- ○ **D.** NTBOOTDD.SYS

2. Which Windows utility can be used to verify the integrity of the Windows XP operating system files?

- ○ **A.** SFC
- ○ **B.** CHKDSK
- ○ **C.** Dr. Watson
- ○ **D.** MSCONFIG

3. Which Windows utility is used to isolate conflicting items in the startup sequence?

- ○ **A.** Task Manager
- ○ **B.** MSCONFIG
- ○ **C.** SFC
- ○ **D.** Device Manager

4. Which of the following is a valid bootup option when using Windows 2000 and Windows XP Professional distribution CDs to start the system?

- ○ **A.** Last Known Good Configuration
- ○ **B.** Automatic System Recovery
- ○ **C.** Recovery Console
- ○ **D.** MSCONFIG

5. Using unsigned drivers in a Windows system can_____.

- ○ **A.** cause the system to become unstable and lock up
- ○ **B.** create cross-linked files in the system
- ○ **C.** allow viruses attached to the driver to attack your system
- ○ **D.** corrupt different operating system core files

6. If you received an `Event log full` message in Windows XP, where can you go to clear it?

- ○ **A.** In the System Monitor utility
- ○ **B.** In the Device Manager
- ○ **C.** In the Microsoft Management Console
- ○ **D.** In the Event Viewer

7. A customer's PC does not boot up to the Windows 2000 Professional desktop. When you try to start the system using the Windows 2000 ERD, the system does not recognize the disk. Which of the following actions should you take next?

- ○ **A.** Reset the system and hold down the F8 key when requested to boot the system into Safe Mode.
- ○ **B.** Insert the Windows 2000 distribution CD in the drive and reboot the system to the CD.
- ○ **C.** Reboot the system, enter the CMOS Setup utility, and change the Boot Seek Sequence to check the floppy disk drive.
- ○ **D.** Reboot the system and use the ASR utility to recover the system.

8. Where can you find the exact wording of error codes and messages created by the Windows system when significant occurrences in the system or its programs need to be reported to the user?

- ○ **A.** The manufacturer's website
- ○ **B.** In the System Information utility
- ○ **C.** In the Windows Event Viewer
- ○ **D.** In the Microsoft Management Console

9. What condition is indicated by the `Invalid Media Type` error messages?

- ○ **A.** The MBR is missing or corrupt.
- ○ **B.** The drive is not formatted.
- ○ **C.** Operating system files are missing or corrupt.
- ○ **D.** The HDD cable is not attached.

10. Booting to Windows results in a distorted image that prevents you from manipulating the operating system. What can you do to correct this problem?

- ○ **A.** Boot to Safe Mode and reinstall/configure the driver.
- ○ **B.** Reboot the system to the command line.
- ○ **C.** Replace the video card.
- ○ **D.** Replace the monitor.

11. A Windows XP Professional workstation has had problems during operation lately. Which of the following applications enables you to review conflicts and problems that have occurred over time?

- ○ **A.** Services and Applications
- ○ **B.** AUTOEXEC.BAT
- ○ **C.** CONFIG.SYS
- ○ **D.** Event Viewer

12. The Windows 2000 Emergency Repair process is designed to _____ and cannot be of assistance in repairing application or data problems.

- ○ **A.** repair the desktop configuration
- ○ **B.** repair the file system
- ○ **C.** repair the network configuration
- ○ **D.** repair the operating system

13. Windows 2000/XP Recovery Console does all the following except _____.

- ○ **A.** copy files
- ○ **B.** control startup of services
- ○ **C.** format volumes
- ○ **D.** uninstall programs

14. Under what conditions would you select a Safe Mode Command Prompt Only option for starting a computer?

- ○ **A.** When the system fails to start in standard Safe Mode
- ○ **B.** When the system fails to start in Step-by-Step Confirmation mode
- ○ **C.** When the System Recovery tool does not start Windows
- ○ **D.** When the Emergency Repair Disk does not start Windows

15. What types of problems is the MSCONFIG.EXE utility used for?

- ○ **A.** Hardware configuration
- ○ **B.** System configuration
- ○ **C.** Network configuration
- ○ **D.** Desktop configuration

Objective 3.4: Perform preventative maintenance for operating systems

1. How do you configure the Automatic Updates feature for Windows 2000?

   ○ **A.** Use the Add Components utility to add the Automatic Updates feature to the system.

   ○ **B.** Double-click Automatic Updates in the Control Panel and then click Automatic.

   ○ **C.** Use the Add/Remove Programs utility to install the Windows Automatic Updates utility.

   ○ **D.** Access the Microsoft Windows Update web page and click the Automatic Updates option.

2. Before installing a new software program on your supervisor's Windows XP Professional computer, you think it wise to establish a Restore Point that you can return to in case something goes wrong with the installation. Where do you set up a Restore Point in Windows XP Professional?

   ○ **A.** Control Panel/Administrative Tools/System Restore

   ○ **B.** Control Panel/System/System Restore

   ○ **C.** Start/All Programs/Accessories/System Tools/System Restore

   ○ **D.** Control Panel/System/Hardware/Device Manager/System Restore

3. You have just completed the physical installation of a PC in a retirement community. You intend to set up the system to automatically update itself so that the residents don't have to remember to do it. Which Windows 2000/XP service automatically delivers security updates, critical updates, and service packs to help protect computers against viruses and other security threats?

   ○ **A.** Windows WQHL

   ○ **B.** Automatic Updates

   ○ **C.** Add Windows Components/Updates

   ○ **D.** Windows Security Center

4. A new customer has called you to remove a virus that infected his machine. After successfully removing the virus, you notice that the system is still running an original version of Windows XP Professional without any updates or service packs. What is the best way to update/patch this Windows XP Professional computer system?

Quick Answer: **180**
Detailed Answer: **198**

○ **A.** Use the online Windows Update service to find all applicable service packs and patches for this machine.

○ **B.** Find a computer with the same operating system that is completely updated and burn all the patches onto an update CD that can be transferred onto the original PC.

○ **C.** Download SP2 from Microsoft's website because all other patches are unnecessary.

○ **D.** Use the Task Scheduler utility to look for patches and updates on a regular schedule.

5. After you download and install a new web browser in your Windows XP Professional system with Service Pack 2 installed, the system does not access any network resources. What should you do to correct this problem?

Quick Answer: **180**
Detailed Answer: **198**

○ **A.** Configure the Windows Firewall setting to permit the application to access the network.

○ **B.** Stop and restart the operating system's networking services one at a time.

○ **C.** Simply reinstall SP2.

○ **D.** Use the Add or Remove Programs utility to remove the new service pack.

6. One of your technicians has contacted you to get help deciding how to have his customer perform network backups from his server. The customer needs to back up more than 100 gigabytes every day. The server is unusual because it offers USB ports that can be used to attach an array of different external storage devices. Which of the following backup options should he recommend to his customer?

Quick Answer: **180**
Detailed Answer: **198**

○ **A.** A SCSI DLT tape drive

○ **B.** An external ZIP drive

○ **C.** A USB flash drive

○ **D.** An internal CD-RW drive

7. A customer has asked you to update her Windows XP
   Professional system. When you run the Windows update scan on
   the machine, you find that it is running only SP1 and the update
   service is recommending that you download and install SP2. What
   additional features will your customer receive by installing SP2?

   ○ **A.** The Windows Security Center

   ○ **B.** Windows antivirus software

   ○ **C.** Windows Internet Connection Firewall

   ○ **D.** Windows Automatic Updates

8. A customer's Windows XP computer is having intermittent printer
   delay problems. When you check the PC system, you find that it is
   also performing poorly. You also note that it does not have any
   security updates or patches installed. How can the intermittent
   printing delay problem be fixed?

   ○ **A.** By updating the printer's firmware

   ○ **B.** By replacing the processor

   ○ **C.** By installing additional memory modules in the printer

   ○ **D.** By checking for viruses and other forms of malware
             and then updating the operating system

Objective 4.0: Printers and Scanners

Objective 4.1: Identify the fundamental principles of using printers and scanners

1. Which of the following printer types requires special paper?

   ○ **A.** Laser

   ○ **B.** Thermal

   ○ **C.** Dot-matrix

   ○ **D.** Inkjet

   Quick Answer: **181**
   Detailed Answer: **199**

2. What Windows structure allows multiple files to be loaded onto a printer for printing?

   ○ **A.** The Print Manager

   ○ **B.** The Print Spooler

   ○ **C.** The Print Buffer

   ○ **D.** The Print Queue

   Quick Answer: **181**
   Detailed Answer: **199**

3. In a network printing environment, what Windows structure controls printing for everyone on the network?

   ○ **A.** The Print Spooler

   ○ **B.** The Print Manager

   ○ **C.** The Print Buffer

   ○ **D.** The Printer Queue

   Quick Answer: **181**
   Detailed Answer: **199**

4. Which of the following standards establishes high-speed, bidirectional capabilities for a parallel printer port?

   ○ **A.** IEEE-1284

   ○ **B.** IEEE-1394

   ○ **C.** 802.3

   ○ **D.** 802.11

   Quick Answer: **181**
   Detailed Answer: **199**

5. Which printer type uses a photosensitive drum?

   ○ **A.** Dot-matrix

   ○ **B.** Inkjet

   ○ **C.** Laser

   ○ **D.** Dye-sublimation

   Quick Answer: **181**
   Detailed Answer: **199**

6. Which of the following printers can produce photographic-quality, continuous-tone images?

- ❍ **A.** Dot-matrix printer
- ❍ **B.** Dye-sublimation printer
- ❍ **C.** Direct thermal printer
- ❍ **D.** Thermal wax transfer printer

7. What type of printer uses a multicolored waxed ribbon that small pins heat up to melt the wax onto the paper?

- ❍ **A.** Dye-sublimation
- ❍ **B.** Thermal wax
- ❍ **C.** Solid ink
- ❍ **D.** Thermal auto chrome

Objective 4.2: Install, configure, optimize, and upgrade printers and scanners

1. After you install a printer and print a test page from an application on the host computer, what should you do next?

- ❍ **A.** Educate the user about the operation of this printer model.
- ❍ **B.** Go over the user's manual with the customer and read the most important parts verbatim.
- ❍ **C.** Go over the user's manual with the customer and highlight the most important parts.
- ❍ **D.** Clean up any mess you've created and have the customer sign off on the work order.

2. You have just installed a new laser printer that is connected to the network in a small office environment. You are supposed to make this printer the default for the office users. How do you set up a printer to be the default printer in a network environment?

- ○ **A.** Access each user's Add Printer Wizard to locate and install the new printer. Then open the local printer queue on each machine and click the Set as Default Printer option in the Printer menu.

- ○ **B.** Establish this setting while configuring the new printer through the Add Printer Wizard on each machine.

- ○ **C.** Access the print spooler on the print server computer and click the Set as Default Printer option in the Printer menu.

- ○ **D.** Access each user's Add Printer Wizard to locate and install the new printer. Then right-click the new printer in the Printer and Faxes dialog box and select the Properties option from the menu. Click on the Set as Default Printer radio button.

3. Which of the following is not a proper method to use when explaining printer operations to a user?

- ○ **A.** Using the user's manual to highlight key information he will need when you're not there

- ○ **B.** Using pictures and illustrations to highlight your instructions as you go through the different processes with the user

- ○ **C.** Using the actual printer to demonstrate the operation of the system because you may invalidate the customer's warranty when you perform some steps

- ○ **D.** Using industry jargon and acronyms so that the user will become aware of these industry-accepted terms

4. Which of the following is a common scanner driver format?

- ○ **A.** TWAIN
- ○ **B.** PCL
- ○ **C.** PCX
- ○ **D.** JPG

5. How can you access the Add Printer Wizard in Windows 2000? (Select all that apply.)

- ○ **A.** Select Start/Settings/Printers and then click the Add Printer icon.

- ○ **B.** Select Start/Programs/Accessories/Windows Explorer/Printers and then click the Add Printer icon.

- ○ **C.** Double-click My Network Places on the desktop and then double-click Computers Near Me.

- ○ **D.** Select Control Panel/Printers and then click the Add Printer icon.

Objective 4.3: Identify tools and diagnostic procedures to troubleshoot printers and scanners

1. A laser printer is printing faded text in your documents. The toner cartridge has just been replaced and is not the problem. What is most likely the problem?

- ○ **A.** A bad primary corona wire.

- ○ **B.** A bad transfer corona wire.

- ○ **C.** A bad laser-scanning module.

- ○ **D.** The rotating drum is not getting completely discharged.

2. A user reports that she can't print to her local inkjet printer; no paper comes out and nothing is printed. When you examine the Printers and Faxes page of her Windows XP system, you see that only an HP Laser 1100 printer is showing on the page. What is the most likely cause of this problem?

- ○ **A.** The printer is not installed in the system.

- ○ **B.** The printer spooler has been disabled on the system.

- ○ **C.** The wrong printer driver has been installed in the system.

- ○ **D.** The default printer setting has been set incorrectly on the printer.

3. After installing a new USB scanner, you scan a sample color document. The output on the video display looks okay, but when you print it out, the image on the page looks odd because the four color dots (CMYK) do not line up correctly for each pixel. What can you do to correct this problem?

Quick Answer: **181**
Detailed Answer: **200**

- ○ **A.** Calibrate the scanner and monitor.
- ○ **B.** Reduce the resolution of the scanner and scan the sample again.
- ○ **C.** Scan a smaller graphic to test the scanner.
- ○ **D.** Install TWAIN drivers for the scanner.

4. You are troubleshooting a laser printer that is producing a `Fuser Error` message. Which of the following should you do first?

Quick Answer: **181**
Detailed Answer: **200**

- ○ **A.** Replace the fuser assembly.
- ○ **B.** Turn the printer off and on to see whether the error goes away.
- ○ **C.** Replace the paper in the printer.
- ○ **D.** Replace the transfer corona wire.

5. After installing a new printer, you discover that it prints odd characters in places. What should you do to correct this problem?

Quick Answer: **181**
Detailed Answer: **200**

- ○ **A.** Download the latest drivers for this printer from the manufacturer's website.
- ○ **B.** Patch the operating system from the Microsoft Windows Updates site.
- ○ **C.** Download and install updated third-party drivers for this printer.
- ○ **D.** Obtain new flash code from the printer manufacturer to update the printer's firmware.

6. What type of failure would cause your laser printer to start up in an offline condition?

Quick Answer: **181**
Detailed Answer: **200**

- ○ **A.** The offline button has been pressed.
- ○ **B.** The printer's interface cable might be defective.
- ○ **C.** The printer driver is incorrect.
- ○ **D.** The toner cartridge is empty.

7. Your laser printer has started to produce documents that have long white stripes down the length of the page. What type of problem is indicated by this symptom?

Quick Answer: **181**
Detailed Answer: **201**

  ○ **A.** The drum is failing.

  ○ **B.** The fuser is not heating evenly.

  ○ **C.** The conditioning roller has a spot on it.

  ○ **D.** The toner cartridge is not evenly distributing toner.

8. When you retrieve a copy of a document from the office laser printer, your touch smears the type on the page. What type of problem is indicated by this symptom?

Quick Answer: **181**
Detailed Answer: **201**

  ○ **A.** The drum is going bad.

  ○ **B.** An incorrect type of replacement toner has been used.

  ○ **C.** The transfer corona wire has failed.

  ○ **D.** The fusing roller has failed.

9. If a standalone printer passes the self-test and the user still cannot print, what else could be the cause of the problem?

Quick Answer: **181**
Detailed Answer: **201**

  ○ **A.** Fuse error

  ○ **B.** Laser error

  ○ **C.** Pickup roller

  ○ **D.** Printer interface

Objective 4.4: Perform preventative maintenance of printers and scanners

1. For the best quality output from a laser printer, what should you recommend to your customers?

Quick Answer: **181**
Detailed Answer: **201**

  ○ **A.** Use toner cartridges produced by the printer manufacturer.

  ○ **B.** Use high-quality toner in a refill cartridge to get good quality and low prices.

  ○ **C.** Use only the highest quality printer paper.

  ○ **D.** Tell customers to reload their own cartridges so they know that they have high-quality materials to work with.

2. A new laser printer in your Hawaiian warehouse is consistently picking up too many sheets of paper. The warehouse is open to the outside atmosphere when large trucks are backed up to its loading docks to load or unload products. What is the most likely cause of this problem?

   ○ **A.** Dust from the outside air is defeating the page thickness sensors so that the printer cannot determine the correct thickness of the paper being used.

   ○ **B.** Temperature changes caused by the large doors opening and closing are causing the printer's pickup sensors to incorrectly read the thickness of the paper.

   ○ **C.** Humidity caused by the open atmosphere of the warehouse is causing the pages to stick together so that they cannot be picked up properly by the printer's separation mechanism.

   ○ **D.** The wrong paper setting is being used in the warehouse printer, and a simple adjustment to the tray settings should correct the problem.

3. As part of your company's maintenance agreement with your customers, you have just serviced a customer's three-tray laser printer that has been having paper jam problems. You installed a standard service kit and loaded new paper into all the trays. What steps should you take to complete the job? (Select all that apply.)

   ○ **A.** Print test pages from all trays to determine whether the jam problem is still present.

   ○ **B.** Print a registration page to make sure that the print is correctly aligned on the page.

   ○ **C.** Cycle the printer on and off to see whether any errors appear.

   ○ **D.** Have the customer sign off on the job to verify your work.

4. After completing the installation of a new laser printer and walking the user through its operation, you want to establish a suggested maintenance schedule for the printer with the customer. Where are you most likely to find a maintenance schedule for a given laser printer?

   ○ **A.** Under the main access cover where it can be read each time the printer is open for preventative maintenance, upgrading, or repair.

   ○ **B.** The printer manufacturer's website

   ○ **C.** The printer's driver page in Windows Device Manager utility

   ○ **D.** The printer's Installation and Service Guide

Objective 5.0: Networks

Objective 5.1: Identify the fundamental principles of networks

1. One of your coworkers is trying to solve an Internet connection problem for a customer. When he tries to access a website using its name, the system cannot find the page. However, when he tries to connect to the numeric IP address he has on the customer's work order, it connects. He doesn't know where to look for the problem. What can you tell him about which TCP/IP service resolves IP addresses to domain names?

Quick Answer: **181**
Detailed Answer: **202**

- ○ **A.** DNS
- ○ **B.** DHCP
- ○ **C.** FTP
- ○ **D.** TCP

2. Which of the following IP address examples can actually be used on the Internet?

Quick Answer: **181**
Detailed Answer: **202**

- ○ **A.** 192.168.0.101
- ○ **B.** 127.0.0.1
- ○ **C.** 147.0.1.20
- ○ **D.** 10.0.0.1

3. What is the purpose of the NAT service? (Select all that apply.)

Quick Answer: **181**
Detailed Answer: **202**

- ○ **A.** To represent the network as a single entity to the Internet environment
- ○ **B.** To prevent internal users from accessing outside Internet locations
- ○ **C.** To configure safe communications between two remote systems without using encryption services.
- ○ **D.** To prevent outsiders on the Internet from making direct contact with internal network users

4. You are setting up a small office network for a business client and using private IP addressing in the range of 192.168.X.X. When you begin to configure the first PC, you enter **192.168.0.1**. What is the standard subnet mask you would use for this IP address?

   ○ **A.** 255.0.0.0

   ○ **B.** 255.255.0.0

   ○ **C.** 255.255.255.0

   ○ **D.** 255.255.255.254

Quick Answer: **181**
Detailed Answer: **202**

5. Which of the following protocols work at the network and transport levels of the OSI model? (Select all that apply.)

   ○ **A.** Ethernet

   ○ **B.** IPX/SPX

   ○ **C.** TCP/IP

   ○ **D.** 802.11x

Quick Answer: **181**
Detailed Answer: **202**

6. At what OSI level do MAC addresses work?

   ○ **A.** Physical layer

   ○ **B.** Data Link layer

   ○ **C.** Network level

   ○ **D.** Transport level

Quick Answer: **181**
Detailed Answer: **202**

7. What networking protocol should you use to set up direct connections between a Tablet PC and a properly equipped printer?

   ○ **A.** Bluetooth

   ○ **B.** 802.3

   ○ **C.** 802.11b

   ○ **D.** IrDA

Quick Answer: **181**
Detailed Answer: **202**

8. What OSI layer does a lack of link lights signal as a problem?

   ○ **A.** Network

   ○ **B.** Session

   ○ **C.** Physical

   ○ **D.** Presentation

Quick Answer: **181**
Detailed Answer: **203**

9. How many bits make up an IPv4 address?

- ○ **A.** 32
- ○ **B.** 64
- ○ **C.** 128
- ○ **D.** 256

10. Which TCP/IP utility can be used to control a remote Linux PC from a local Windows 2000 Professional PC?

- ○ **A.** FTP
- ○ **B.** Telnet
- ○ **C.** SNMP
- ○ **D.** Remote Access

11. One of your customers has installed a Windows XP MCE machine in his family room and connected it to use his large-screen LCD television as the video output. He has no problem viewing the screen from across the room, but his hardwired keyboard and mouse do not have long enough signal cables to get him far enough away from the display. He has asked you for a recommendation for wireless keyboards and mouse devices that will enable him to use the TV display from his sofa. Which wireless technology is best suited for using wireless keyboards and mouse devices over a short distance like this?

- ○ **A.** Bluetooth
- ○ **B.** IrDA
- ○ **C.** 802.11a
- ○ **D.** 802.11g

12. A technician notices that a user has a different IP address each week when he performs routine preventative maintenance for the customer. Why is this?

- ○ **A.** The user's network is set up to use APIPA.
- ○ **B.** The user has contracted a virus that manipulates his IP address to avoid getting caught.
- ○ **C.** The user's network is set up to use DHCP.
- ○ **D.** The user's network is set up to use DNS.

13. Your company moves to a new location. Because your company is very small, you use a DSL connection to connect all users to the Internet. When setting up the network, you connect the DSL modem using an RJ-11 connector to the phone outlet, connect the DSL modem to a router using a CAT5 cable, and plug the DSL modem into a power source. You connect all the workstations to the router using CAT5 cable and put line filters on all phone lines and the phone line used for the DSL modem. When you test the system, no users can connect to the Internet. However, after you unplug the DSL modem and remove all the line filters, the phone line is still operational. What is the most likely solution to this situation?

Quick Answer: **181**
Detailed Answer: **203**

- ○ **A.** Replace the DSL modem.
- ○ **B.** Remove the line filter for the phone line for the DSL modem.
- ○ **C.** Connect the DSL modem using an RJ-45 connector to the phone outlet instead.
- ○ **D.** Replace the CAT5 cable with coaxial cable.

14. A client complains that, after replacing his DSL modem, his home DSL connection isn't working. When you inspect his computer, you notice that none of the lights on the DSL modem are on, and the only two cables that plug into the DSL modem connect via the RJ-11 and RJ-45 connectors. You are able to ping port 127.0.0.1. What is the most likely problem with the DSL?

Quick Answer: **181**
Detailed Answer: **203**

- ○ **A.** The network interface card (NIC) is improperly set up.
- ○ **B.** The phone line is not plugged into the DSL modem.
- ○ **C.** The ethernet cable is not plugged into the DSL modem.
- ○ **D.** The power cord is not plugged into the DSL modem.

15. Which of the following services is responsible for performing dynamic IP addressing?

Quick Answer: **181**
Detailed Answer: **203**

- ○ **A.** LMHOST
- ○ **B.** IMAP
- ○ **C.** DHCP
- ○ **D.** DNS

16. What type of device is commonly used to make checks on a LAN cable?

   ○ **A.** OTDR

   ○ **B.** Multimeter

   ○ **C.** Voltmeter

   ○ **D.** Cable tester

17. What protocol is required for Internet access?

   ○ **A.** NetBEUI

   ○ **B.** FTP

   ○ **C.** TCP/IP

   ○ **D.** HTTP

18. What protocol is typically used to transfer large files over a remote network connection?

   ○ **A.** NNTP

   ○ **B.** DTP

   ○ **C.** HTTP

   ○ **D.** FTP

19. Which protocol type is used specifically for authenticating users in a credit-card-based e-commerce setting?

   ○ **A.** HTTP

   ○ **B.** SSSP

   ○ **C.** SSL

   ○ **D.** SMTP

Objective 5.2: Install, configure, optimize, and upgrade networks

1. A traveling user who works for a customer that employs static IP addresses at the office has called to complain that she cannot connect to the Internet while on the road. She typically stays in motels that offer free Internet connections in the room, but she cannot take advantage of the service. What should you tell her to do?

   ○ **A.** Tell her that she must configure her network connection to automatically obtain an IP address when traveling and then change it back to the static address in her office.

   ○ **B.** Tell her to get a wireless network card.

   ○ **C.** Tell her to wait until her company switches to DHCP.

   ○ **D.** Tell her to set up Automatic Private IP Addressing in the TCP/IP Properties page.

Quick Answer: **182**
Detailed Answer: **204**

2. What is the typical speed of data transfers for hardwired, network printers?

   ○ **A.** 54Mbps

   ○ **B.** 10/100/1000Mbps

   ○ **C.** 24Mbps

   ○ **D.** 480Mbps

Quick Answer: **182**
Detailed Answer: **204**

3. What pieces of information are required to establish a static IP address? (Select all that apply.)

   ○ **A.** Gateway address

   ○ **B.** DNS server address

   ○ **C.** DHCP address

   ○ **D.** IP address

Quick Answer: **182**
Detailed Answer: **204**

4. What does the presence of an active activity light on a network adapter card indicate?

   ○ **A.** The NIC sees network traffic.

   ○ **B.** It is downloading data.

   ○ **C.** It is uploading data.

   ○ **D.** The NIC driver is functioning.

Quick Answer: **182**
Detailed Answer: **204**

5. A workstation can share its printer with other nodes on the network. What type of networking is this?

- ○ **A.** Client/server network
- ○ **B.** Peer-to-peer network
- ○ **C.** Star network
- ○ **D.** Ring network

6. In a client/server network, _____.

- ○ **A.** At least one unit depends on the other units for its information
- ○ **B.** At least one unit is reserved just to serve the other units
- ○ **C.** Each unit has its own information and can serve as either client or server
- ○ **D.** Each unit handles some information for the network

Objective 5.3: Use tools and diagnostic procedures to troubleshoot network problems

1. After setting up a new segment on the corporate network, one of the users complains that he can access resources on other network PCs but can't access the Internet. What is the most likely cause of this problem?

- ○ **A.** the subnet mask configuration is incorrect.
- ○ **B.** the TCP/IP protocol is not enabled on this machine.
- ○ **C.** the DHCP service is not working.
- ○ **D.** the gateway address is configured incorrectly.

2. If you know the hostname of a PC on a network, how can you find its IP address?

- ○ **A.** Ping / *hostname*
- ○ **B.** IPCONFIG / *hostname*
- ○ **C.** FIND / *hostname*
- ○ **D.** TRACERT / *hostname*

3. If you try to ping the loopback address and nothing happens, what is most likely the problem?

Quick Answer: **182**
Detailed Answer: **205**

○ **A.** TCP/IP is not working on the local machine.

○ **B.** The network cable is bad.

○ **C.** The local connectivity device is turned off.

○ **D.** The NIC in the local machine is defective.

4. Generally, whenever a user tells you that her LAN connection is not working, what is the first thing to check?

Quick Answer: **182**
Detailed Answer: **205**

○ **A.** Check the network adapter drivers to see that they are configured properly.

○ **B.** Ping a known IP address to see whether the network cable and connectivity are good.

○ **C.** Check for the presence of link lights on the back of the NIC.

○ **D.** Run `IPCONFIG` to see whether the local network hardware is functioning.

5. Which IP address invokes the TCP/IP loopback test function?

Quick Answer: **182**
Detailed Answer: **205**

○ **A.** 127.0.0.1

○ **B.** 10.0.0.1

○ **C.** 169.192.0.1

○ **D.** 172.254.0.1

6. A user has called to report that one of the network's printers previously worked, but now it doesn't. When you inspect the printer, you find that its signal and power cables are all connected properly. You can ping the printer's gateway from the user's computer but cannot ping the printer's IP address. What is the most likely cause of this problem?

Quick Answer: **182**
Detailed Answer: **205**

○ **A.** The user has a bad network adapter card.

○ **B.** The user has a corrupt NIC driver.

○ **C.** The local network cable is bad.

○ **D.** The TCP/IP protocol has been disabled on the printer.

7. You have just finished configuring a notebook PC that has a built-in wireless NIC. However, when you start the system, you find that you can't connect to any wireless network. What should you check first?

○ **A.** Run IPCONFIG /ALL to check the local network configuration settings.

○ **B.** Check the notebook for an external button to enable its internal radio module and antenna.

○ **C.** Check the notebook's TCP/IP configuration.

○ **D.** Run PING 127.0.0.1 to ensure that the local network adapter's IP address has been initialized.

8. Link lights on a network switch are blinking rapidly even with all the other switch ports disconnected. What two items could be causing this condition?

○ **A.** There is a bad network card in the computer attached to the switch port.

○ **B.** TCP/IP is not configured properly in the computer.

○ **C.** The network cable between the NIC and the switch is cross-wired.

○ **D.** There is a bad port in the switch.

9. What TCP/IP command would be used to reestablish network connectivity?

○ **A.** IPCONFIG /all

○ **B.** IPCONFIG /release

○ **C.** IPCONFIG /renew

○ **D.** IPCONFIG /registerdns

10. In general, what is the first TCP/IP tool used to begin troubleshooting network connectivity problems?

○ **A.** IPCONFIG

○ **B.** ARP

○ **C.** NET VIEW

○ **D.** PING

11. Which TCP/IP utility can be used to locate a slow router on a wide area network, such as the Internet?

Quick Answer: **182**
Detailed Answer: **205**

- ○ **A.** ARP
- ○ **B.** TRACERT
- ○ **C.** NETSTAT
- ○ **D.** IPCONFIG

Objective 5.4: Perform preventative maintenance of networks including securing and protecting network cabling

1. What preventative activity should be performed on any computer that has access to the Internet?

Quick Answer: **182**
Detailed Answer: **206**

- ○ **A.** Disable all port settings on the router's firewall.
- ○ **B.** Disable all port settings in the Windows Firewall.
- ○ **C.** Disable cookies in the web browser.
- ○ **D.** Conduct regular virus scans of the system's memory and HDD.

2. Which of the following is the best way to improve privacy on an 802.11 wireless network?

Quick Answer: **182**
Detailed Answer: **206**

- ○ **A.** Configure WEP to encrypt network transfers.
- ○ **B.** Remove all 2.4GHz cordless phones from the area.
- ○ **C.** Locate the network computers as close as possible to the AP.
- ○ **D.** Install a unidirectional antenna on the AP and each wireless adapter card.

3. One of your customers has had to set up a temporary office due to a fire in the company's normal office building. You have been called in to get replacement computers configured with the software and backup data required to get the staff back in business. When you get to the customer's office, you observe that network cables have been strung on the floor in different areas of the workplace. Some are run behind tables and chairs, and others cross over walkways. What should you do about this situation?

- ○ **A.** Tape down the cables so that they are not a trip or catch hazard.

- ○ **B.** Remove the cables from the walkways.

- ○ **C.** Recommend that the customer replace these cables with cables that can be routed out of the way.

- ○ **D.** Disconnect the cables and run new cables that can be run out of the walkway.

Objective 6.0: Security

Objective 6.1: Identify the fundamentals and principles of security

1. Which type of computer activity involves another person taking control of a legitimate user's web application session while it's in progress?

Quick Answer: **182**
Detailed Answer: **207**

   - ○ **A.** Social engineering
   - ○ **B.** Denial of Service attack
   - ○ **C.** Session hijacking
   - ○ **D.** Phishing

2. You are performing an upgrade on a desktop PC at a customer's site. Upgrades often require several reboots, and each time you will need to enter the user's ID and password. How can you address this issue?

Quick Answer: **182**
Detailed Answer: **207**

   - ○ **A.** Ask permission to use the customer's ID and password.
   - ○ **B.** Use your admin capabilities and change the user's password.
   - ○ **C.** Have the customer stand by and enter the password each time you need it.
   - ○ **D.** Ask the customer to write down the ID and password information for you.

3. Your employer wants a listing of when anyone logs in to the company network. Where can you find this information?

Quick Answer: **182**
Detailed Answer: **207**

   - ○ **A.** In System Information
   - ○ **B.** In the Event Viewer
   - ○ **C.** In the System Monitor
   - ○ **D.** In Dr. Watson

4. You have configured your children's account on your Windows XP Home computer as a limited account so that they cannot access your financial and personal data. What else will the children not be able to do as members of this group? (Select all that apply.)

Quick Answer: **182**
Detailed Answer: **207**

   - ○ **A.** Create additional users
   - ○ **B.** Create new folders
   - ○ **C.** Delete folders and files
   - ○ **D.** Install applications

5. Which of the following is required to access a network share in an NTFS system?

Quick Answer: **182**
Detailed Answer: **207**

- ○ **A.** Share permissions
- ○ **B.** A password
- ○ **C.** Access rights
- ○ **D.** User permissions

6. What is the default lockout value of Windows XP Professional for bad login attempts?

Quick Answer: **182**
Detailed Answer: **208**

- ○ **A.** 0
- ○ **B.** 3
- ○ **C.** 6
- ○ **D.** 9

7. Your company is expanding and has hired 15 new employees to provide telephone support for your technical service staff. They will all be using a new database application that tracks call information for the entire group. What is the most efficient way to install this application and provide access to it for the entire group of new employees, as well as the existing technical support personnel?

Quick Answer: **182**
Detailed Answer: **208**

- ○ **A.** Install the application and provide Full Control permissions to the program through the Everyone group.
- ○ **B.** Install the application on each user's machine so that access to the data can be controlled through the normal Windows logon process.
- ○ **C.** Install the application and create a Group Policy Object that will install the application on the desired users' machines when they log in and provide them with access to the designated program and its data.
- ○ **D.** Install the application, create a group account for the new employees, and give all the appropriate network users membership in the group.

Objective 6.2: Install, configure, upgrade, and optimize security

1. A Windows XP Professional customer asks you to show him how to set up file and folder encryption to protect his private information on his disk drive. How do you do this?

Quick Answer: 182
Detailed Answer: 208

- ○ **A.** Click on the Encrypt option of the drive's Properties menu and choose Encrypt Files on This Drive.

- ○ **B.** Tell the user that file and folder encryption is performed automatically on NTFS5 disks.

- ○ **C.** Click the Encrypt Contents to Secure Data check box in the folder's Advanced Attributes windows.

- ○ **D.** Click on the Encrypt option of the drive's Properties menu and choose Encrypt Folders on This Drive.

2. What is it called when people make emails appear to come from somewhere other than their real address?

Quick Answer: 182
Detailed Answer: 208

- ○ **A.** Spoofing
- ○ **B.** Hacking
- ○ **C.** Social engineering
- ○ **D.** Spamming

3. A customer is using an unencrypted wireless network in his condominium. What can you do to protect this user's data? (Select all that apply.)

Quick Answer: 182
Detailed Answer: 208

- ○ **A.** Set up WEP encryption.
- ○ **B.** Select one of the nondefault channels on the access point.
- ○ **C.** Don't broadcast the SSID.
- ○ **D.** Set up a firewall on the access point.

4. Your friend is setting up the Windows Firewall utility in his new Windows XP Professional machine, and he wants to make sure that his email can be sent and received. What does he need to know to make sure that these services can pass through the firewall?

Quick Answer: 182
Detailed Answer: 208

- ○ **A.** Open TCP/UDP port 144.
- ○ **B.** Open TCP/UDP ports 20 and 21.
- ○ **C.** Open TCP/UDP ports 25 and 110.
- ○ **D.** Open TCP/UDP port 80.

Objective 6.3: Identify tool, diagnostic procedures, and troubleshooting techniques for security

1. What user group must you be a member of to install a non-hot-swappable device in a Windows XP system?

   ○ **A.** Administrators

   ○ **B.** Guest

   ○ **C.** Users

   ○ **D.** Power Users

2. One of your customers has bought a new wireless access point. Which of the following options should you configure to make her network most secure?

   ○ **A.** WEP

   ○ **B.** WPA2

   ○ **C.** SSID

   ○ **D.** MS-CHAP

Objective 6.4: Perform preventative maintenance for security

1. Which type of computer activity exploits people's human nature to fool them into providing information about themselves, their business, or their computer/network?

   ○ **A.** Session highjacking

   ○ **B.** Social engineering

   ○ **C.** Spoofing

   ○ **D.** Spamming

2. While checking your company email, you receive an email saying that the company is trying to confirm all its email accounts and its needs you to email your account information. What should you do?

   ○ **A.** Ignore the request by deleting the email.

   ○ **B.** Encrypt your information and return it.

   ○ **C.** Send the reply as an email attachment.

   ○ **D.** Forward the email to your supervisor for follow-up.

Objective 7.0: Safety and Environmental Issues

Objective 7.1: Identify potential hazards and proper safety procedures including power supply, display devices, and environment

1. What is the best way to protect PC equipment from destructive ESD? (Select all that apply.)

   Quick Answer: **183**
   Detailed Answer: **210**

   ○ **A.** Wear an antistatic wrist strap.

   ○ **B.** Place the PC on an antistatic mat.

   ○ **C.** Wash your hands to remove ESD.

   ○ **D.** Unplug the PC from the power outlet.

2. What action should be taken prior to cleaning the exterior of a CRT monitor?

   Quick Answer: **183**
   Detailed Answer: **210**

   ○ **A.** Unplug the monitor from the system unit.

   ○ **B.** Turn off the monitor.

   ○ **C.** Wipe the display with an antistatic cloth.

   ○ **D.** Unplug the monitor from the power source.

3. You are setting up computers in a 911-response center in a community near a power-generating station. The incoming power is known to frequently have significant surges and sags in the line voltage. What device should you install to protect the office computers from damage, keep them online during emergencies, and prevent loss of data from the power line surges and sags?

   Quick Answer: **183**
   Detailed Answer: **210**

   ○ **A.** A power line filter

   ○ **B.** A power strip

   ○ **C.** A surge suppressor

   ○ **D.** A UPS system

4. You find water dripping from the ceiling in the server room, which of the following should you do first?

- O **A.** Notify building maintenance.
- O **B.** Notify the network administrator.
- O **C.** Place a note in the server room logbook.
- O **D.** Immediately turn off the servers.

5. You live in a brownout-prone area. What precaution should you take to protect your Windows XP Home system and data?

- O **A.** Install a UPS.
- O **B.** Install a power strip.
- O **C.** Install a surge suppressor.
- O **D.** Install a power filter.

Objective 8.0: Professionalism and Communication

Objective 8.1: Use good communication skills including listening and tact/ discretion when communicating with customers and colleagues

1. You have been called to work on a PC in the back office of a small retail store. When you arrive, you find that you are unable to speak the same language as the proprietor. What can you do considering the language barrier that exists? (Select all that apply.)

   ○ **A.** Use illustrations and graphics to communicate with the customer (after you notify the supervisor).

   ○ **B.** Get an appropriate translation dictionary so that you can conduct basic conversations with the proprietor.

   ○ **C.** Contact your management to see if there is someone in the organization that has the ability to interact with this customer.

   ○ **D.** Ask if the customer knows anyone who can speak your language so that she can interpret.

Quick Answer: **183**
Detailed Answer: **211**

2. A customer asks you to install an application on his machine from a CD that has no label on it and no licensing or other documentation. How should you handle this request?

   ○ **A.** Tell the customer it is illegal to use unlicensed software and refuse to install the material on his machine.

   ○ **B.** Confiscate the disc and report the user to his supervisor.

   ○ **C.** Refuse to install the software but let the user know that it is okay if he does so himself.

   ○ **D.** Report the user to the software manufacturer to make sure that you have no legal liability in this matter.

Quick Answer: **183**
Detailed Answer: **211**

3. A customer asks you to perform work outside the scope of the contract the organization has with your company. What should you do?

Quick Answer: **183**
Detailed Answer: **211**

   ○ **A.** Call your supervisor, describe the requested additional work, and proceed as directed.

   ○ **B.** Offer to do the work after hours because this is such an important customer.

   ○ **C.** Refuse the work because it is not part of the scope of work you have been given.

   ○ **D.** Inform the customer that the additional work will cost extra and perform the requested work.

4. While troubleshooting a customer's computer, you discover that it is infected with a virus, and after several unsuccessful attempts to remove the virus, you decide that you need to reformat the drive and start over. What is the best way to tell the customer that you must reinstall the operating system?

Quick Answer: **183**
Detailed Answer: **211**

   ○ **A.** Tell the customer you must kill and then reinstall the system.

   ○ **B.** Tell the customer that you cannot remove the viruses and must reinstall the operating system and that some data might be lost.

   ○ **C.** Tell the customer that you must reinstall the operating system and this would be a good time to upgrade the system.

   ○ **D.** Tell the customer that she needs to take better precautions with the systems because this problem requires that the operating system be replaced and data may be lost.

5. Which of the following is the proper method of coaching a customer on the operation and care of the new peripheral device you've installed?

Quick Answer: **183**
Detailed Answer: **211**

- ○ **A.** Sit down beside the customer and address him at his level as you explain the operation of the device.
- ○ **B.** Make sure to include appropriate industry slang and acronyms in your coaching so that the customer will become familiar with these terms.
- ○ **C.** Go over the user's manual with the customer and carefully read the most important parts.
- ○ **D.** Always remain standing while you are explaining the operation of the device so that you have a psychologically authoritative position with reference to the customer.

6. When you go to a customer's location to work on equipment, which of the following should you do first?

Quick Answer: **183**
Detailed Answer: **211**

- ○ **A.** Ask the user if she is ready to have you work on the equipment.
- ○ **B.** Ask to see the manager so that someone knows you are working in the facilities.
- ○ **C.** Go directly to equipment specified in your work order and get straight to work so that the customer does not think you are running up the bill.
- ○ **D.** Turn on the equipment to see how it is working. This is the beginning of the Inspection portion of the troubleshooting or upgrading processes.

7. A user in your organization asks you to install a program on her machine after you've installed a new antivirus product. What should you do with the user's request?

Quick Answer: **183**
Detailed Answer: **212**

- ○ **A.** Refuse to install the software.
- ○ **B.** Check company policy about the software and proceed accordingly.
- ○ **C.** Tell the user that you do not have authority to install the requested program, so she will have to install it herself.
- ○ **D.** Install the software as requested.

8. You must reconfigure the user accounts on a computer that was set up by another technician who has limited user account setup experience. What should you do after fixing the problem?

  O **A.** Report the technician to your supervisor and explain that you had to fix his problem.

  O **B.** Tell the technician he needs user account setup lessons.

  O **C.** Prepare written instructions for setting up user accounts and give them to the technician.

  O **D.** Demonstrate the proper process for setting up user accounts for the other technician.

Objective 8.2: Use job-related professional behavior including notation of privacy, confidentiality, and respect for the customer and customer's property

1. You receive an urgent page while working at a customer's facility. How should you handle this situation?

  O **A.** Tell the customer you must respond to the page and excuse yourself from the customer's presence to respond to the page.

  O **B.** Answer the page and find out whether the call is urgent or not before you leave the work area.

  O **C.** Ignore the page, return to work, and finish the job as quickly as possible. Then you can respond to the page afterward.

  O **D.** Answer the page, take care of the call, and then return to work.

2. While recovering the HDD on a customer's computer, you discover illegal software on the drive. What action should you take?

  O **A.** Tell the customer that it is illegal to pirate software.

  O **B.** Delete the illegal software from the drive.

  O **C.** Report the copyright violation to your supervisor.

  O **D.** Report the copyright violation to the company that manufactures the software.

3. While repairing a customer's computer, you break a pin on the CD-ROM drive, which is eight years old. Which of the following should you do?

Quick Answer: **183**
Detailed Answer: **212**

○ **A.** Reinstall the broken CD-ROM drive in the computer and tell the customer the unit is fixed. Don't disclose the broken device.

○ **B.** Report the broken device to your supervisor and replace it at your company's expense.

○ **C.** Tell the customer that due to the age of the device it no longer works and needs to be replaced.

○ **D.** Tell the customer that the pin broke while you were working on the system, but that it is not covered under your service agreement.

4. A customer tells you she must leave the residence where you will be working, but her 12-year-old will be there to give you access to the place. What should you do?

Quick Answer: **183**
Detailed Answer: **212**

○ **A.** Reschedule the appointment for a time when the customer will be available.

○ **B.** Inform the customer that you cannot be responsible for anything in the house if she isn't going to be present.

○ **C.** Ask the customer to be present when you arrive to start work.

○ **D.** Tell the customer that she must be in the house or you are not coming.

5. While working at a customer's residence, his misbehaving children are preventing you from getting the job completed. What do you do to handle this?

Quick Answer: **183**
Detailed Answer: **212**

○ **A.** Ask the parent or guardian to remove the children from the work area.

○ **B.** Pack up and come back later when the children are asleep.

○ **C.** Ask the children to leave the immediate work area.

○ **D.** Ask your supervisor to assign an additional person to the job.

6. A coworker calls you on your cell phone with a complicated question while you are working in the customer's home. How do you handle it?

Quick Answer: **183**
Detailed Answer: **213**

- ○ **A.** Tell your coworker to call later and keep working on the problem.
- ○ **B.** Leave the residence and take the call.
- ○ **C.** Ask the customer's permission to take the call.
- ○ **D.** Determine the urgency of the call and decide whether it is important enough to require immediate response.

7. While repairing a customer's computer, you discover that it is infected with a virus and several types of malware. The customer has no virus protection, so what should you do to get the customer back in operation?

Quick Answer: **183**
Detailed Answer: **213**

- ○ **A.** Download freeware versions of an antivirus program and install it. Run the program and then remove the malware.
- ○ **B.** Install your antivirus software and clean the machine. Then remove the malware items from the computer.
- ○ **C.** Tell the customer to purchase virus software from a vendor so that you can install it and remove their viruses.
- ○ **D.** Reformat the disk drive and reinstall the customer's applications.

8. A customer is irate about a problem with his PC and tells you this is not the first time this problem has occurred. How do you handle this customer?

Quick Answer: **183**
Detailed Answer: **213**

- ○ **A.** Tell the customer to leave until he can speak rationally to you.
- ○ **B.** Ask the customer to explain the problem in more detail and assure him you'll get to the bottom of it. Then fix his computer and return it in proper working order.
- ○ **C.** Work with the customer to reassure him that you are capable, fix the computer, and return it in working order.
- ○ **D.** Find out from the customer who worked on the PC before and make notes about the continuation of the problem.

9. When you arrive at a customer's site to troubleshoot equipment, you find that the owner is already irate and is threatening to pull his business from your company and use a competitor's service. What should you do in this situation?

Quick Answer: **183**
Detailed Answer: **213**

- ○ **A.** Tell the customer good luck and leave the offices.
- ○ **B.** Do nothing because the customer has already decided to use another service.
- ○ **C.** Try to calm down the customer and fix the computer problem because this would be much faster than bringing in a new service.
- ○ **D.** Speak to the customer in a calm, reassuring manner and get him to start defining the problem for you.

10. A customer asks you to fix a network problem that is outside your area of expertise. How should you handle this request?

Quick Answer: **183**
Detailed Answer: **213**

- ○ **A.** Volunteer to fix the problem.
- ○ **B.** Assist the user in finding the proper channel to get the problem resolved.
- ○ **C.** Tell the user the problem is not within your area of expertise and that you can't help with this work.
- ○ **D.** Call your supervisor to get permission to work on the problem.

Quick Check Answer Key

Objective 1.1

1. D	8. A	15. A
2. B, D	9. C	16. B
3. B	10. B	17. C
4. A	11. B	18. B
5. C	12. D	19. D
6. C	13. D	20. A
7. B	14. B	

Objective 1.2

1. C	6. A	11. A, B
2. D	7. D	12. A
3. A	8. A, B	13. A
4. C	9. C	14. C
5. B	10. C	15. A

Objective 1.3

1. A	5. C	9. D
2. A	6. D	10. B, D
3. D	7. A, B, D	
4. D	8. B	

Objective 2.1

1. C, D	4. A	7. D
2. B	5. C	
3. B	6. C	

Objective 2.2

1. D	3. D
2. A	

Quick Check Answer Key

Objective 2.3

1. B, C	**3.** B	**5.** C, D
2. A	**4.** B	**6.** B

Objective 3.1

1. B	**7.** A	**13.** A
2. B	**8.** D	**14.** A, C
3. C	**9.** A	**15.** D
4. D	**10.** B	**16.** C
5. A	**11.** D	**17.** A
6. A	**12.** C	

Objective 3.2

1. A	**5.** D	**9.** A
2. C	**6.** A, B	**10.** B, C, D
3. B	**7.** D	**11.** A
4. A,B	**8.** C	**12.** C

Objective 3.3

1. A	**6.** D	**11.** D
2. A	**7.** C	**12.** D
3. B	**8.** C	**13.** D
4. C	**9.** B	**14.** A
5. A	**10.** A	**15.** B

Objective 3.4

1. B	**4.** A	**7.** A
2. C	**5.** A	**8.** D
3. B	**6.** A	

Quick Check Answer Key

Objective 4.1

1. B	4. A	7. B
2. D	5. C	
3. A	6. B	

Objective 4.2

1. A	3. D	5. A, D
2. A	4. A	

Objective 4.3

1. B	4. B	7. D
2. A	5. A	8. D
3. B	6. B	9. D

Objective 4.4

1. A	3. A, D
2. C	4. D

Objective 5.1

1. A	8. C	15. C
2. A	9. A	16. D
3. A, D	10. B	17. C
4. C	11. A	18. D
5. B, C	12. C	19. C
6. B	13. B	
7. A	14. D	

Quick Check Answer Key

Objective 5.2

1. A
2. B

3. A, B, D
4. A

5. B
6. B

Objective 5.3

1. D
2. A
3. A
4. C

5. A
6. D
7. B
8. A, D

9. C
10. A
11. B

Objective 5.4

1. D
2. A

3. A

Objective 6.1

1. C
2. C
3. B

4. A, D
5. A
6. A

7. C

Objective 6.2

1. C
2. A

3. A, C
4. C

Objective 6.3

1. A
2. B

Quick Check Answer Key

Objective 6.4

1. B
2. A

Objective 7.1

1. A, B
2. D
3. D
4. A
5. A

Objective 8.1

1. A, C
2. A
3. A
4. B
5. A
6. A
7. B
8. D

Objective 8.2

1. A
2. C
3. B
4. A
5. A
6. A
7. A
8. C
9. D
10. B

Answers and Explanations

Domain 1.0

Objective 1.1

1. **Answer: D**. Although both processors employ the LGA 775 socket, they are not identical. The physical microprocessor upgrade you've made should be accompanied by a logical upgrade to the system's BIOS. Later BIOS versions are developed to permit installation of faster processors and functions as they come on the market. If the new processor is not recognized by the system, check the system board manufacturer websites to obtain a compatible BIOS upgrade and support information.

2. **Answers: B, D**. You must ensure that the memory type and size you want to install is supported by the system board and that it does not already have the maximum amount of memory installed. The system board's documentation includes information on the type, configuration, and size of memory it can accept. In addition, verify that the memory you want to install is compatible with the memory currently installed on the board.

3. **Answer: B**. IDE enhancements called ATA-4/Ultra ATA 66 and Ultra ATA 100 provide high data throughput by doubling the number of conductors in the PATA signal cable. The PATA connector has remained compatible with the 40-pin IDE connection, but each pin has been provided with its own ground conductor in the cable.

4. **Answer: A**. When ordering a replacement power supply, you must remember to take into account its form factor and its wattage rating requirements. The wattage rating is a measurement of the total power the supply can deliver to the system. More heavily equipped systems (that is, more disk drives and peripherals) require power supplies with higher wattage ratings.

5. **Answer: C**. Change the setting of the 110/220 switch setting on the outside of the power supply. The normal setting for equipment used in the United States is 110 VAC. In many countries outside the United States, the voltage level is 220VAC 50Hz.

6. **Answer: C**. Because the hard drive is a single-drive system, its configuration jumpers are most likely set to primary master. The most efficient jumper setting for the CD-ROM drive is the secondary master setting. This places the CD-ROM drive on its own IDE channel and avoids potential bus contention issues between the drives.

7. **Answer: B**. RAID1 provides redundancy through a mirrored drive arrangement. The second drive has an exact copy of the first drive. If either drive fails, the system continues to operate, and the information can be copied back over to a replacement for the failed drive without interrupting the system's operation.

8. **Answer: A**. DRAM devices are the fastest accessed devices in the list. They must be quick enough to operate directly with the microprocessor and can be read from and written to as needed. Most secondary memory systems for computers have involved storing binary information in the form of magnetic charges on moving magnetic surfaces; however, optical storage methods such as CD-ROM and DVD have moved to rival magnetic storage for popularity. Magnetic storage has remained popular because of three factors: low cost-per-bit storage, intrinsically nonvolatile nature, and progressive evolution in capacity. However, secondary memory systems are not nearly as fast as lower capacity volatile memory devices used for primary memory systems.

9. **Answer: C**. Typical Pentium-based system boards include two independent, enhanced IDE controllers to handle the hard disk drive/CD/DVD hosting function. Each controller can handle up to two PATA drives. This provides the PC with the capability to control up to four PATA devices.

10. **Answer: B**. Full-speed USB devices operate under the USB 2.0 specification (also referred to as *high-speed USB*) and support data rates up to 480Mbps.

11. **Answer: B**. RAID5 is an array of independent data disks with distributed parity blocks (or striped array with parity disks). This requires a minimum of three disks to implement.

12. **Answer: D**. Newer system boards provide two or more 7-pin connectors to accommodate Serial ATA (SATA) drives. The flat 7-pin SATA signal cable has four wires used to form two differential signal pairs (A+/A– and B+/B–). The other three wires are used for shielded grounds. The cable is only 0.5 inch wide, which makes cable routing inside the system unit simpler and provides less resistance to airflow through the case. The maximum length for an internal SATA cable is specified as 39.37 inches (1 meter).

13. **Answer: D**. Recordable DVDs are available in DVD-R (write-once) and DVD-R/DVD+R/DVD+R DL (rewritable) formats. These discs have capacities that range between 4.7GB and 17GB of data. A single-sided, single-layer 120mm DVD can hold up to 4.7GB of data, whereas a single-sided, dual-layer DVD is boosted to a capacity of 8.5GB. Double-sided, single-layer DVDs hold up to 9.4GB, whereas double-sided, double-layer discs can hold 17.1GB.

14. **Answer: B**. All newer PCs rely on high-speed USB and/or IEEE-1394 ports as their major I/O connections. The controller functions for these ports are typically integrated into the system board's chipset circuitry and are enabled/disabled through its CMOS Setup utility.

15. **Answer: A**. The monitor's signal cable connects to a 3-row, 15-pin female D-shell connector at the back of the system unit.

16. **Answer: B**. Each time a new device is added to the system, more electrical power is required. For example, upgrading the processor can easily increase the power consumption by more than 20W. Replacing RAM with faster RAM devices increases power consumption as well. Simply increasing the installed memory from 128MB to 1GB more than doubles the power consumption of the system's memory (that is, from 6W to over 12W). Adding high-end video adapters used for games may consume up to 100W. A typical hard disk drive can require up to 20 or 30W each.

17. **Answer: C**. Professional service technicians use grounding straps to minimize the chances of electrostatic discharge (ESD) during normal computer maintenance work involving MOS devices. These antistatic devices can be placed around the wrists or ankle to ground the technician to the system being worked on. These straps release any static present on the technician's body and pass it harmlessly to ground potential.

18. **Answer: B**. The ground plug on a standard power cable is the best tool for overcoming ESD problems. The ground lead prevents hazardous charge buildups in the circuitry that protects property and life. To avoid damaging static-sensitive computer devices, ground yourself by touching the power supply housing with your finger before touching any components inside the system. This technique works safely only if the power cord is attached to a grounded power outlet.

19. **Answer: D**. Additional case fans can be installed to increase or redirect the airflow through the chassis.

20. **Answer: A**. The AMD Socket 462/Socket A specification has been used with Athlon, Duron, Athlon XP, Athlon XP-M, Athlon MP, and Sempron processors.

Objective 1.2

1. **Answer: C**. If the Windows video problem prevents you from being able to use the display, restart the system, press the F8 function key when the `Starting Windows` message appears, and select the Safe Mode option. After you have gained access to a usable display, you can move into the Device Manager, expand the Display Adapters node, select the Driver tab, and click the Roll Back Driver button to return to the driver that was in use before the update occurred.

2. **Answer: D**. Because the drive is a SCSI drive, check to see that its ID is set correctly and that the SCSI chain has been terminated correctly. Make sure that every SCSI device has a unique ID address. Any of these errors result in the system not being able to see the drive. Also, check the CMOS Setup utility to make sure that SCSI support has been enabled, along with large SCSI drive support. SCSI ID settings are suggestions and not requirements. ID 7 is the preferable ID for SCSI host adapters on all chains, and ID 15 is a middle-priority ID on chains with 16 IDs.

3. **Answer: A**. Having the wrong driver installed for a given video adapter card can cause limited color symptoms. If you cannot adjust the Color Quality setting through the Settings tab of the Control Panel's Display icon, use the Advanced button to continue to the adapter's properties. You can access this page by clicking the Properties button on the Adapter tab. Select the Driver tab to uninstall, roll back, or update the display adapter's driver. If you uninstall the current driver, you can simply restart Windows and allow it to detect the display adapter and attempt to install the correct driver. The Windows XP Roll Back Driver feature returns the system to the driver that was being used before the current video display driver. The Update Driver option asks you to select a driver to use from several options.

4. **Answer: C**. If the system consistently locks up after being on for a few minutes, this is a good indication that the microprocessor's fan is not running or that some other heat buildup problem is occurring. The key indicator here is that the failure is linked to time required to heat up and cool down.

5. **Answer: B**. If you suspect a video display hardware problem, the first task is to check the display's On/Off switch to see that it is in the on position. Also check the monitor's power cord to see that it is plugged either into the power supply's monitor outlet or into an active 120 VAC commercial outlet. Check the monitor's intensity and contrast controls to make certain that they are not turned down.

6. **Answer: A**. Under Windows, you can configure the system to write events to the System log when the system stops unexpectedly, such as when it encounters a condition it cannot recover from. These logs hold memory dump files that contain the contents of specified amounts of memory when the system failed (referred to as a *memory dump*). Administrators can configure this feature under the Advanced tab of the Control Panel's System icon. From the Startup and Recovery area of this tab, you can click the Settings button and configure the options available for System Failure, along with how much debugging information to store and where. The memory dump file can be examined with the DUMPCHK.EXE utility located on the Windows distribution CD. DUMPCHK displays basic information about the memory dump and verifies all the virtual and physical addresses in the file. If it detects any errors in the memory dump file, it displays them in the report. Programmers typically use this feature to debug their applications.

7. **Answer: D**. When a self-test failure or setup mismatch is encountered, the BIOS may indicate the error through a blank screen, a visual error message on the video display, or an audio response (*beep codes*) produced by the system's speaker. For example, the beep code message produced by one BIOS manufacturer's devices is "eight beeps indicate a video adapter memory error." Replace the video card.

8. **Answer: A, B**. The POST is actually a series of tests that are performed each time the system is turned on. The different tests check the operation of the microprocessor, keyboard, video display, floppy and hard disk drive units, as well as both RAM and ROM memory units.

9. **Answer: C**. The condition of the NumLk (NumLock on desktop and wide notebook keyboards) key can cause portable PCs to produce incorrect characters. Notebook PCs do not have separate 10-key numeric keypads. If the NumLk key function is engaged, the system remaps different keys to the locked numbers. In some cases, the only indicator that the NumLk key function is engaged is a small light near a small icon representing a numeric keypad. With some notebook models, if you don't look closely, you probably won't realize that there is a numeric keypad associated with the keyboard (small numbers are embossed on the alpha keys). Some notebook models call out the NumLk feature on a specific key, whereas others only include an icon on one of the function keys. With the latter arrangement, you can disable the NumLk-On setting using the Fn key along with a designated function key (also denoted by a small numeric keypad icon).

10. **Answer: C**. The enhanced ECP parallel ports employ DMA transfer techniques to conduct data transfers at rates up to 1.5MBps over an IEEE-1284 bidirectional parallel cable. Full-speed USB 2.0 devices operate under the USB 2.0 specification (also referred to as *high-speed USB*) and support data rates up to 480Mbps. The IrDA-SIR standard infrared protocol is used to provide a standard serial port interface with transfer rates ranging up to 115kbps. The IrDA-FIR fast infrared protocol is used to provide a high-speed serial port interface with transfer rates ranging up to 4Mbps. The 802.11g wireless specification delivers data transfer rates in excess of up to 54Mbps.

11. **Answers: A, B**. (A) The keys of the keyboard can wear out over time. This might result in keys maintaining electrical contact (sticking) even when pressure is removed. The stuck key produces an error message when the system detects it during bootup. (B) An unplugged keyboard, or one with a bad signal cable, produces a keyboard error message during startup.

12. **Answer: A**. When the system exhibits no signs of life, the first thing to do is confirm that the power supply cord is plugged into a functioning outlet.

13. **Answer: A**. If you suspect a video display hardware problem, first examine the power cord to see that it is plugged in and check to see that the monitor's power switch is in the on position.

14. **Answer: C**. The DC voltage function is used to take measurements in live DC circuits. It should be connected in parallel with the device being checked.

15. **Answer: A**. The speakers are unshielded. The magnetic waves generated by the operation of the speakers are interfering with the focusing of the electron beams the CRT uses to paint the display.

Objective 1.3

1. **Answer: A**. The primary preventative maintenance tasks associated with modern hard disk drives revolve around protecting them from shock hazards and overheating. Rough handling is responsible for more physical hard drive problems than anything else. Although hard drives are not any more susceptible to heat than other PC components, it is a good practice to ensure that there is ample room for airflow around the drive to cool it.

2. **Answer: A**. When you are installing a new processor, be aware that small air gaps exist between the heat sink and processor's surface. Because air conducts heat poorly, special heat-conducting grease (Thermal Compound) is typically used with snap-on heat sinks to provide good thermal transfer between the microprocessor and the heat sink. The fact that this system takes several hours to fail suggests that the overheating problem is due to a slow heating process such as the heat sink not being able to dissipate enough heat. A failed fan unit would take some time for the processor to overheat, but this should be a few minutes, not hours.

3. **Answer: D**. The Windows 2000/XP Windows Cleanup utility can be used to identify certain types of temporary files that are not required for operation of the system. The temporary files that you can normally afford to remove from the system to gain needed disk space include Windows, Internet, and multimedia temp files.

4. **Answer: D**. The DEFRAG utility realigns files on the drive that may have become fragmented by erase and write/rewrite operations. The defrag operation moves fragmented files into the pattern that provides the most efficient reading operation (the drive requires time to process the sector of information it just read from the disk—during this period, sectors are passing under the R/W heads—therefore, placing the next section of the file in the sector that passes under the R/W heads when it is ready again provides the best performance). The Recycle Bin cannot be removed in any modern versions of Windows.

5. **Answer: C**. You can take care of dust buildup inside the system with a soft brush. You also can use a static-free vacuum or compressed air to remove dust from inside cases and keyboards. Be sure to use a static-free vacuum because normal vacuums are, by their nature, static generators. The static-free vacuum has special grounding to remove the static buildup it generates.

6. **Answer: D**. A damp cloth is the best general-purpose cleaning tool for use with computer equipment, such as a monitor.

7. **Answers: A, B, D**. Sources of heat buildup around the computer and its peripherals include direct sunlight from an outside window, locations of portable heaters in the winter, and papers and books piled up around the equipment.

8. **Answer: B**. The surge suppressor's clamping speed rating describes how quickly it can react to changes in the incoming power level and act to minimize it.

9. **Answer: D**. To manually clean read/write heads, use isopropyl alcohol on a foam swab. Cotton swabs can shed fibers that can contaminate the drive and damage portions of its R/W head.

10. **Answers: B, D**. (B) Optimizing the speed of the fan lowers the relative dust accumulation that can lead to thermal failure. (D) The risk of thermal failure can also be reduced by installing foam filters at the chassis openings to filter the incoming air.

Domain 2.0

Objective 2.1

1. **Answers: C, D.** The specifications for the portable PC's DC power requirements should be located on the bottom of the PC. Another source of information related to obtaining a replacement AC adapter includes the portable PC's user's guide documentation. (This information is also typically located on the AC power adapter, but it is not present in this example.)

2. **Answer: B.** Most portable PC designs have switched to nickel metal-hydride (NiMH), lithium-ion (Li-ion), or lithium-ion polymer batteries. These batteries typically provide in excess of two or three hours of operation. The actual life of a laptop computer battery may vary from just under one hour to over six hours in each sitting, depending on the particular notebook PC type and configuration, the way it is being used (lots of disk/disc accesses), and the battery type and its age.

3. **Answer: B.** An improved type of LCD places a transistor at each of the matrix row-column junctions to improve switching times. This technology produces an active-matrix display that employs thin-film transistor (TFT) arrays to create displays that tend to be brighter and sharper than dual-scan displays. However, TFT-based LCD panels also tend to require more power to operate and are more expensive to produce than panels using other LCD technologies.

4. **Answer: A.** The PC Card Type II cards are 5mm thick and support virtually any traditional expansion function, except removable hard drive units.

5. **Answer: C.** The PCMCIA bus standard was introduced primarily to accommodate the notebook and subnotebook computer markets. Later, a small form-factor expansion-card format, referred to as the *PC Card standard*, was also adopted for use. Today, the terms *PC Card* and *PCMCIA* are used interchangeably when describing any portion of the PCMCIA standard, although the *PCMCIA* term has largely been abandoned in favor of the *PC Card* terminology.

6. **Answer: C.** Portable power supplies, also referred to as *AC adapters*, convert commercial 120VAC voltage into a single, low DC voltage that the portable computer can use to power its components and recharge its batteries.

7. **Answer: D.** The external power supply used with portable systems basically converts AC voltage into a DC voltage that the system can use to power its internal components and recharge its batteries.

Objective 2.2

1. **Answer: D.** Portable PCs typically use a technique called *shared video memory*. Under shared memory, the system uses a portion of its main memory to hold screen information for the display. One of the disadvantages of shared memory is that it takes up memory space that applications would normally use. It also causes the system to show less memory capacity than is installed because a portion has been reserved for use with the video display.

2. **Answer: A**. External read/write CD-ROM and DVD drives typically connect to the system through a USB port, a FireWire port, an external SCSI connector, or though a CardBus adapter. With the exception of the SCSI-based version, all these interfaces are hot swappable.

3. **Answer: D**. The proper procedure for removing a USB device from the computer begins with clicking the Safely Remove Hardware icon in the systray. Then select the command to stop the operation of the USB device you want to remove. When the operating system prompts you, physically remove the USB device from the system. The Safely Remove Hardware utility is used to notify the operating system in advance of the device removal. Because some devices have write caching enabled, corruption or data loss may occur.

Objective 2.3

1. **Answers: B, C**. The portable keyboard normally contains an Fn function key. This key activates special functions in the portable, such as display brightness and contrast. Other common Fn functions include Suspend mode activation and LCD/external-CRT device selection.

2. **Answer: A**. If you have a dim screen on a portable system, there are two likely candidates: the LCD panel and the inverter card. The inverter provides power for the LCD panel's backlight. In most cases of a dim screen, the inverter is the source of the problem. This unit is normally separate and is much less expensive to replace than an LCD panel. You can install a generic inverter to start the display running, but you must install the correct inverter for the display to receive optimal brightness and uniformity from the display. If replacing the inverter does not restore the brightness to the display, you are looking at replacing the LCD panel.

3. **Answer: B**. After turning off the notebook and unplugging it from the power source, you should remove the battery from the notebook to ensure that power has been completely removed form the system board and its memory slots.

4. **Answer: B**. The portable keyboard normally contains an Fn function key. This key activates special functions in the portable, such as display brightness and contrast. The Fn key of portable computers can be used to redirect the video output to the external VGA port. If you suspect this to be the case, you need to check the user's guide for directions in redirecting the video back to the main display.

5. **Answers: C, D**. The LCD screen should be shielded from bright sunlight and heat sources. Moving the computer from a cooler location to a hot location can cause damaging moisture to condense inside the housing (including the display). It should also be kept away from ultraviolet light sources and extremely cold temperatures. The liquid crystals can freeze in extremely cold weather. A freeze/thaw cycle may damage the display and cause it to be unusable.

6. **Answer: B**. When an LCD panel fails, the most common repair is to replace the entire display panel/housing assembly.

Domain 3.0

Objective 3.1

1. **Answer: B.** The CONVERT command is used in Windows 2000 and Windows XP to convert disks (volumes) from FAT-based disks into NTFS disks that typically provide more efficient disk management. The format for using this command is C:\> CONVERT C: /FS:NTFS. This converts a FAT-based drive C: into an NTFS-based disk drive C: by installing the NTFS file system on the disk.

2. **Answer: B.** You can modify the performance of various commands by placing one or more software switches at the end of the basic command. You add a switch to the command by adding a forward slash (/) and one or more letters that define how the command is to be implemented. Placing a question mark after the slash produces a list of switch options that can be used with the command.

3. **Answer: C.** You can restart any stopped application or file with an .EXE extension by entering its filename at the command prompt. For example, you can attempt to restart a stalled print spooler by entering **spoolsv.exe** at the command prompt and pressing Enter.

4. **Answer: D.** The Character Map utility enables you to move and insert special characters, such as symbols and mathematical characters into documents, as well as use, display, or print foreign characters from another language.

5. **Answer: A.** In most situations, the NTFS system offers better performance and features than a FAT16 or FAT32 system. The exceptions to this occur when smaller drives are being used (the NTFS system is more complex than the FAT systems and, therefore, is not as efficient for smaller drives) and when other non-NTFS-aware file systems are being used on the same system and require access to the partition being established.

6. **Answer: A.** The Reconnect at Logon option must be selected in the Map Network Drive page for the drive mapping to become a permanent part of the system. If the option is not selected when the user logs off, the mapped drive information disappears and needs to be remapped for any further use. If a red X appears on the icon of a properly mapped drive, this indicates that the drive is no longer available. Its host computer may be turned off, the drive may have been removed, or it may no longer be on the same path. If the drive was mapped to a particular folder, and the folder name has been changed, the red X also appears.

7. **Answer: A.** Windows supports the Unicode character set. Unicode is a character set standard established to represent nearly all the written languages of the world. This character set enables Windows to be a global tool that can be used around the world. *Unicode* is a 16-bit character code standard, similar to 8-bit ASCII, used to represent characters as integer numbers. The 16-bit format allows it to represent more than 65,000 different characters. This is particularly useful for languages that have very large character sets.

8. **Answer: D**. The NTFS5 structure includes a Quota Table for tracking allowable storage space on individual volumes for each user. This table enables administrators to establish disk quotas that limit the amount of hard drive space users can have access to.

9. **Answer: A**. The `DISKCOMP` command allows you to compare the contents of two disks. It compares the data on the disks not only to see that they are alike, but also to verify that the data is in the same place on both disks. This command is normally used to verify the contents of backup disks and is typically performed after a `DISKCOPY` operation has been performed.

10. **Answer: B**. The Computer Management/Storage Console provides a standard set of tools for managing the system's disk drives in Windows XP. This includes the Disk Management, Removable Storage, and Disk Defragmenter snap-ins. Disk Manager was the disk management utility provided in Windows NT versions prior to Windows 2000.

11. **Answer: D**. When a device conflict is suspected, simply access the Device Manager utility, double-click the offending device in the device listing, and then click the Resources tab in the selected device's properties page to examine the conflicting device's status.

12. **Answer: C**. To activate the Windows XP System Restore Wizard, navigate the Start/All Programs/Accessories/System Tools/System Restore path and then select the System Restore option from the menu. The Welcome screen is displayed. After you confirm the Restore Point, the system conducts the rollback and the system automatically restarts.

13. **Answer: A**. The active partition is the logical drive to which the system will boot. The system files must be located in this partition, and the partition must be set to Active for the system to boot up from the drive.

14. **Answer: A, C**. After the primary partition has been established, an additional partition, referred to as an *extended partition*, is also permitted. However, the extended partition may be subdivided into 23 logical drives. If logical drives have been defined within it, the extended partition cannot be deleted. FAT installations allow for a single primary partition and an extended partition, which can be subdivided into 23 logical drives. NTFS allows for up to three primary partitions to be created.

15. **Answer: D**. The TREE command lists all the directory and subdirectory names on a specified disk.

16. **Answer: C**. The XCOPY command copies all the files and directories (except hidden and system files) from the source drive (or location) to the destination drive (or location). The / s switch instructs the XCOPY command to copy directories and subdirectories. Similarly, the XCOPY / e command copies files, directories, and subdirectories, including the empty ones.

17. **Answer: A**. Windows 2000 and Windows XP support NTFS (NTFS5 is native to both OS versions). They also support the FAT, FAT16, and FAT32 file systems (along with the CDFS CD file system used with CD-ROMs).

Objective 3.2

1. **Answer: A**. Unused system services should be stopped or disabled to optimize system responsiveness and performance. In Windows XP, you can launch the Services control applet either through the Control Panel/Administrative Tools/Services path or by running the SERVICES.MSC command-line utility. This utility produces a listing of all the user-controllable services running in the system. From this list, you can stop or switch services to manual startup configuration; you should not disable any service unless you are absolutely sure that you will not need it and that no other vital service needs it.

2. **Answer: C**. When you are installing a SCSI drive in a Windows system, you should verify that the drive is on the Windows XP Marketplace Tested Product page. If the drive is not acceptable to the system, it is difficult to conduct the installation, and you receive errors during the text-based portion of the Windows XP setup routine. If the drive is not listed on the page, you can attempt to load OEM drivers for the devices from an OEM CD-ROM or floppy by pressing the F6 key when prompted and accessing the drivers on the disk.

3. **Answer: B**. It is possible to optimize the system's performance by distributing its swap file (PAGEFILE.SYS) space among multiple drives. It can also be helpful to relocate the swap file away from slower or heavily used drives. You should not place the swap file on mirrored or striped volumes. Also, don't create multiple swap files in logical disks that exist on the same physical drive.

4. **Answers: A, B**. Before you perform an OS upgrade, you should always back up the contents of the existing drive. Although you may not need to back up the current operating system files, you should always make sure to back up the users' personal files and settings. The new operating system, or a restored OS after a failure, starts the system running; however, files such as personal documents, pictures, illustrations, and user-specific settings and preferences cannot be recovered unless they have been backed up in some manner.

5. **Answer: D**. Applications placed in the Startup folder under the All Users path are executed when the system starts up, regardless of which user logs on to the system.

6. **Answers: A, B**. CHKDSK and DEFRAG utilities are designed primarily to optimize the performance of the system's disk drives. The CHKDSK command is a command-line utility that has remained in use with Windows 2000 and XP and is used to recover (and remove, if necessary) lost allocation units from the hard drive. The DEFRAG utility realigns files on the drive that may have become fragmented by erase and write/rewrite operations. The defrag operation moves fragmented files into the pattern that provides the most efficient reading operation (the drive requires time to process the sector of information it just read from the disk—during this period, sectors pass under the R/W heads—therefore, placing the next section of the file in the sector that passes under the R/W heads when it is ready again provides the best performance).

7. **Answer: D**. You can increase the performance of Windows 2000/XP by manipulating the size and placement of their virtual memory swap file. Page file manipulation in Windows 2000/XP can be handled in the Control Panel's System applet.

8. **Answer: C**. You use the Windows SYSPREP tool to prepare the disk image of a reference computer for cloning.

9. **Answer: A**. The Windows 2000 installation process, also called *Setup*, occurs in two distinct phases: a text-only phase and a graphical wizard-driven phase. The installation process begins with a text-based sequence of screens known as the Text Mode portion of Setup. This mode of operation continues until enough of the operating system structure is in place to switch to the GUI-based conclusion of the Setup process. After the basic Windows files have been copied into the system, the Setup process switches into GUI format and presents the Windows Setup Wizard to guide the completion of the Setup process.

10. **Answers: B, C, D**. (B) You can upgrade a Windows 95 computer to Windows 2000 by selecting the Install Windows 2000 option if the system detects the Windows 2000 Professional distribution CD in the drive. (C) When upgrading a Windows 95 computer to Windows 2000 at the command prompt, navigate to the location of the Winnt32.exe (d:\i386\) and then execute the file. (D) To upgrade a Windows 95 computer to Windows 2000, insert the Windows 2000 Professional distribution CD in the CD-ROM drive first. If the system doesn't detect the CD in the drive, start Setup through the Run command.

11. **Answer: A**. Windows XP has special tools, *called the user state migration tools (USMT)*, that administrators can use to transfer user configuration settings and files from
systems running Windows 9x/Me and Windows NT systems to a clean Windows XP installation. This enables user information to be preserved without going through the upgrade process.

12. **Answer: C**. The best response is to keep all these files to avoid disabling another application. If the files are to be deleted, you should make a backup before running the Uninstall utility so that the files can be replaced, if needed.

Objective 3.3

1. **Answer: A**. One of the major Windows 2000/XP Recovery Console commands is the BOOTCFG command. This command can be used to change the configuration of the BOOT.INI file or to recover from boot problems. The BOOTCFG file is available for use from the Recovery Console or directly from the command prompt.

2. **Answer: A**. The System File Checker utility (SFC.EXE) is a Windows 2000/XP command-line utility that checks the system's protected files for changed, deleted, or possibly corrupted files. If it finds such files, it attempts to extract the original correct versions of the files from Windows files in the \system32\dllcache folder. You can use SFC to verify that the protected system files are the appropriate versions and to verify and replace files in the dllcache folder. The latter ensures that files used to replace invalid operating system files are actually valid.

3. **Answer: B**. The Selective Startup option located on the General tab of the System Configuration Utility dialog box interactively loads device drivers and software options according to the check boxes enabled. Start the troubleshooting process with only one box checked. If the system starts up with that box checked, add another box to the list and restart. When the system fails to start, move into the tab that corresponds to the last option you enabled and step through the check boxes for that file one at a time until the system fails again.

4. **Answer: C**. You can run the Recovery Console from the distribution CD for both Windows 2000 and Windows XP. To do so, start the system with the distribution CD in the drive and choose the option to repair (press the R key) the installation. Enter the administrator's password to access the Recovery Console. Note: The ASR utility is valid only for Windows XP.

5. **Answer: A**. Prior to the Windows Driver Signing system, manufacturers often provided poorly written drivers with their equipment that would crash systems or cause conflicts with other peripheral devices. Some manufacturers continue to provide unsigned drivers to reduce the cost of their product. The results of using unsigned drivers ranges from no effect to system lockups and crashes.

6. **Answer: D**. If events are occurring so quickly that the logs fill up before the default time, this indicates that an excessive number of system errors (events) is occurring. The Event Viewer stops logging events until the predetermined amount of time has passed. You should examine the full event log to determine what activity is accounting for so many loggable events. To clear the event logs so that the system will continue logging, access the Event Viewer and select the Clear All Events option from the Action menu list.

7. **Answer: C**. To use the Windows 2000 Setup disks to boot the system so that the ERD disks can be used, you must make sure the system is configured to read the floppy disk drive through the CMOS Setup utility.

8. **Answer: C**. In the case of failure events, the system usually generates a user alert through a pop-up dialog box on the screen. The information in the box indicates the nature of the problem and refers you to the Event Viewer for details. The Event Viewer is available through the Start/Programs(All Programs in XP)/Administrative Tools/Event Viewer path. This tool can also be accessed through the Control Panel/Administrative Tools/Computer Management path.

9. **Answer: B**. An `Invalid Media Type` message appears when the controller cannot find a recognizable track/sector pattern on the drive. It indicates that the drive is not properly formatted. Therefore, you might need to repartition the drive and then reformat it with an operating system. However, you should be aware that some products, such as Partition Commander, can hide a partition until you unhide it. This leads to the same result.

10. **Answer: A**. If the Windows video problem prevents you from being able to work with the display, restart the system, press the F8 function key when the `Starting Windows` message appears, and select the Safe Mode option. This should load Windows with the standard VGA driver and should furnish a starting point for installing the correct driver for the monitor being used.

11. Answer: D. In Windows 2000 and Windows XP, significant events (such as system events, application events, and security events) are routinely monitored and stored. You can view these events through the Event Viewer utility, enabling you to review conflicts and problems that have occurred over time. This tool is located under the Control Panel/Administrative Tools/Computer Management path. The Event Viewer is also available through the Start/Programs(All Programs in XP)/Administrative Tools/Event Viewer path.

12. Answer: D. The Windows 2000 Emergency Repair process is designed to repair the operating system in which you can repair the boot sector, replace the system files, and repair the startup files.

13. Answer: D. You can use the Recovery Console to perform tasks such as copying files to the hard disk used for booting; controlling the startup state of services; adding, removing, and formatting volumes on the hard disk; repairing the MBR or boot sector of a hard disk or volume; and restoring the Registry. You cannot use it to uninstall programs.

14. Answer: A. You normally resort to using the Command Prompt Only mode when the system fails to start in standard Safe Mode.

15. Answer: B. If a startup problem disappears when the system is started using any of the Safe Modes, use the System Configuration utility (MSCONFIG.EXE) to isolate the conflicting items. Of course, you might need to enter this command from the command line.

Objective 3.4

1. Answer: B. In Windows 2000 you can double-click the Automatic Updates icon in the Control Panel. Automatic Updates can be configured to download and install updates on a specified schedule or to notify the user when high-priority updates become available. You can click the Automatic (Recommended) option button and then enter day and time settings for Windows to install the updates under the Automatically Download Recommended Updates for My Computer and Install Them option.

2. Answer: C. To activate the Windows XP System Restore utility, navigate the Start/All Programs/Accessories/System Tools path and then select the System Restore option from the menu.

3. Answer: B. You can configure Windows to automatically check the Windows Update Service. Enabling the Automatic Updates feature causes Windows to routinely check for updates. These updates include security updates, critical updates, and service packs.

4. **Answer: A.** The Windows Update service is offered through the Internet and enables the system to periodically check the Microsoft Updates web page (www. windowsupdate.microsoft.com) for enhancements. When the system connects with the site, the service compares the current status of the local Windows installation to the latest information on the site. It then provides a list of available updates for the computer. Users can select which updates are applicable to their use. The Windows Update service is also used to obtain service packs. These additions are important because they address major issues that have been detected in the operating system version since it was launched (or since the last service pack was issued).

5. **Answer: A.** Windows XP Service Pack 2 (SP2) introduced several security features to the Windows operating system such as the Windows Firewall, the Windows Security Center, and Pop-up Blocker for Internet Explorer. These enhancements were included to provide better protection from viruses, worms, and hackers. By default, the Windows Firewall service blocks all connection requests initiating from outside its network. It permits to come through only incoming traffic that it recognizes as a response to a request from inside the network. The firewall knows which responses are acceptable because it maintains a table of outgoing connection information for itself and any computers on the local network that are sharing the Windows Firewall connection.

6. **Answer: A.** All the other options lack enough capacity to hold the required volume of data to be backed up. Also, the Windows Removable Storage Management system does not recognize removable media such as ZIP drives, CD-R, CD-RW, or DVD-R discs as backup media, even though there are options to add these devices through the utility.

7. **Answer: A.** With the addition of Windows XP SP2, the Windows operating system implemented the Windows Security Center. Under this update, the Internet Connection Firewall (ICF) became known simply as the Windows Firewall and was moved under the Security Center icon in the Control Panel.

8. **Answer: D.** One of the symptoms associated with virus infections is slow or erratic printing. In this question, no operating system patches or service packs have been applied. This makes Windows less secure from attacks by viruses and other malware. Attempt to use antivirus and other malware detection and removal tools to clear any of these items from the machine. Then update the operating system with the latest service pack. Windows XP Service Pack 2 introduced several security features such as the Windows Firewall, the Windows Security Center, and Pop-up Blocker for Internet Explorer. These enhancements were included to provide better protection from viruses, worms, and hackers.

Domain 4.0

Objective 4.1

1. **Answer: B**. Nonimpact printers relied on special heat-sensitive or chemically reactive paper to form characters on the page. Thermal printing techniques were at one time widely used with PC printing. These printers use heated elements to burn or melt dot pattern characters on special paper. There are two types of thermal printers: direct thermal printers and thermal wax transfer printers.

2. **Answer: D**. The print queue structure allows multiple files to be loaded onto a print server for printing (which may or may not be located with the physical print device). Closing the print window does not interrupt the print queue in Windows 2000 or Windows XP. The print jobs in the queue are completed unless they are deleted from the list.

3. **Answer: A**. Windows 2000 and Windows XP employ a print spooler processing architecture that controls the flow of information between the host computer and the printer (*print device* under Microsoft's definition). In a local printing operation, the spooler consists of the logical blocks between the client computer and the print device. These blocks process threads in the background and pass them to the printer when it is ready to receive data. In essence, the application prints to the Windows printer driver, the driver controls the operation of the spooler, and the driver prints to the printer from the spooler. In a network printing operation, the print spooler must run on both the local server and remote client systems. The information passes from the remote client spooler to the print server's spooler, which manages the local printing for everyone sending print jobs to that printer.

4. **Answer: A**. The IEEE has established specifications for bidirectional parallel printer cables (IEEE-1284). These cables affect the operation of EPP and ECP parallel devices.

5. **Answer: C**. The laser printer modulates a highly focused laser beam to produce CRT-like raster-scan images on a rotating drum that is coated with a photosensitive plastic. This process is referred to as *electrophotographic reproduction*.

6. **Answer: B**. A variation of the thermal wax printer type, called *dye-sublimation printers*, has been produced to provide photographic quality, continuous tone images. These printers tend to be very slow and expensive. However, because of their capability to produce continuous-tone images, they are widely used by professional graphics businesses to produce posters and large-scale reproductions.

7. **Answer: B**. In a thermal wax transfer printer, a thermal printhead melts dots of wax-based ink from the transfer ribbon onto the paper. When the wax cools, it is permanently attached to the page.

Objective 4.2

1. **Answer: A**. After you have finished installing and configuring a printer, the final step is to educate the user about its operation. As with other training efforts, avoid using slang and jargon to instruct the user about the operation of the printer.

2. **Answer: A**. First, you must locate and configure the local machine to connect to and use the remote printer. The local Add Printer Wizard allows you to perform this task. Then the print queue window's Printer/Set as Default option permits you to designate the printer as the default printer to be used for print jobs. This action must be performed on each local machine and requires proper permission levels to configure the remote printer.

3. **Answer: D**. After you have finished installing and configuring a printer, the final step is to educate the user about its operation. As with other training efforts, avoid using slang and jargon to instruct the user about the operation of the printer.

4. **Answer: A**. Most scanners use drivers written to the TWAIN specification. This specification provides drivers specifically designed for use in digital imaging equipment. These drivers make diverse pieces of imaging equipment compatible with TWAIN support software applications.

5. **Answers: A, D**. (A) To access the Add Printer Wizard using the Start menu in Windows 2000, move to the Settings entry, click on Printers, and then double-click the Add Printer icon. (D) In Windows 2000, you can access the Add Printer Wizard through the Control Panel/Printers path.

Objective 4.3

1. **Answer: B**. Faint print in a laser printer can be caused by a number of things. If the contrast control is set too low, or the toner level in the cartridge is low, empty, or poorly distributed, the print quality can appear washed out. Other causes of faint print include a weakened corona wire or a weakened high-voltage power supply that drives it. Replace the unit that contains the corona wire. Also replace the high-voltage power supply.

2. **Answer: A**. Normally, if a printer is not producing anything in a Windows environment even though print jobs have been sent to it, you should check the print spooler to see whether any particular type of error has occurred. To view documents waiting to be printed, you double-click the desired printer's icon. While viewing the print spooler queue, you should check to make certain that the printer has not been set to the Pause Printing setting. However, in this scenario, the customer is trying to print to an inkjet printer, but only a laser printer has been defined for use. The local inkjet printer must be added and defined in the local computer's Printers and Faxes list using the Add Printer Wizard. Despite having the wrong printer driver installed in the system, the printer would still allow the printer to print something. It just wouldn't be correct.

3. **Answer: B**. If you receive printed images that appear to have speckled areas, you may have the scanner resolution set too high. Images scanned with the resolution set too high may appear fuzzy, blurry, or out of focus. Decrease the resolution setting and rescan the image.

4. **Answer: B**. In some cases, turning off the printer, waiting 10 minutes or so, and then turning it back on can clear fuser error messages. If the message continues, remove and reseat the fuser assembly. If this does not correct the error message, troubleshoot or replace the fuser assembly according to the manufacturer's guidelines.

5. **Answer: A**. Drivers delivered with Windows XP may not be the latest version for a given peripheral device (these drivers were added to XP when it was created), and they may not support the new printer's current firmware version. Therefore, for a new printer installation, you should always check for driver updates when you have problems. Check the manufacturer's website for newer versions.

6. **Answer: B**. When the printer starts up in an offline condition, there is probably some type of problem with the printer/computer interface that does not allow them to communicate. Disconnect the interface cable to see if the printer will start up in a Ready state.

7. **Answer: D**. White lines that run along the length of the page from a laser printer are normally a sign of poorly distributed toner. Remove the toner cartridge and shake it to distribute the toner more evenly. If this does not work, replace the toner cartridge with a new one.

8. **Answer: D**. If the output of the printer smudges when you touch it, the fuser has failed to bond the toner to the paper. The heating lamp in the fuser is broken or not receiving sufficient power to melt the toner.

9. **Answer: D**. If the printer runs the self-test and prints clean pages, most of the printer has been eliminated as a possible cause of problems. The problem could be in the computer, cabling, or interface portion of the printer.

Objective 4.4

1. **Answer: A**. Under most circumstances, it is best to recommend products specified by the manufacturer of the product. This typically involves using toner cartridges produced by the printer manufacturer or ones that have been approved by the manufacturer. You should never have a problem using manufacturer-recommended kits and supplies. Toner/cartridge information is usually found in the printer's documentation.

2. **Answer: C**. Using paper that is too heavy or too thick can result in jams, as can overloading paper trays. Similarly, using the wrong type of paper can defeat the separation pad and allow multiple pages to be drawn into the printer at one time. Multiple sheets can move through the printer together, or they may result in a jam somewhere in the printer. In high-humidity environments, paper can absorb moisture from the air and swell up. Also, the moist pages can stick together causing paper jams.

3. **Answers: A, D**. When you finish any type of printer maintenance, you should always verify the printer's functionality and have the customer sign off on the repair. In this example, you should verify that the printer works correctly from all the trays.

4. **Answer: D**. Most PC components have recommended maintenance programs and schedules designed by their manufacturers. These schedules are typically available in a device's documentation. You may also be able to obtain the manufacturer's maintenance schedule from its website.

Domain 5.0

Objective 5.1

1. **Answer: A**. To communicate with another computer in a TCP/IP network, a computer must have the IP address of the destination host. Users generally specify the name of a computer when establishing connections, not the IP address. These names must be converted into the IP address of the destination computer. The process of matching a computer name to an IP address is called *name resolution*. The domain name service (DNS) can be used to perform name resolution for any TCP/IP client provided the DNS database has the association registered.

2. **Answer: A**. Private network IP addresses include Class A addresses between 10.0.0.0 and 10.255.255.255, Class B addresses 172.16.0.0 through 172.31.255.255, and Class C addresses 192.168.0.0 through 192.168.255.255. However, the Automatic Private IP Address (APIPA) default range of 169.254.0.0 through 169.254.255.255 should not be used for private static addressing. Microsoft uses this range for dynamic autoconfiguration in the absence of a Dynamic Host Configuration Protocol (DHCP) server. Addresses in the 127.X.X.X range are reserved for testing network systems. The U.S. government owns some of these addresses for testing the Internet backbone. The 127.0.0.1 address is reserved for testing the bus on the local system.

3. **Answers: A, D**. The network address translation (NAT) service is a protocol that enables private IP addresses to be converted to a public IP address. One purpose for doing this is that it effectively hides the internal structure of the network from the Internet, making it harder for outsiders to gain access to a specific PC or network device. Outsiders see the network as a single entity represented by one public IP address. However, NAT can be configured to provide different public IP addresses for each outbound device in the network. These addresses can be manually or dynamically configured (static or dynamic NAT).

4. **Answer: C**. For a Class C address such as 192.168.0.1, which is typically used in a residential network, a subnet mask of 255.255.255.0 is employed. This can also be expressed as 192.168.0.1/24, indicating that the 24 most significant bits (three octets) are being used for the network portion of the address. This reserves the first three octets and leaves the addresses from the lower octet (254 of them) open for use in assigning IP addresses to hosts in the network.

5. **Answers: B, C**. Portions of the TCP/IP protocol suite operate at the Network and Transport layers of the OSI model, as does the IPX/SPX protocol associated with older Novell operating systems. Ethernet operates at the Data Link layer, as do the 802.11x wireless protocol versions.

6. **Answer: B**. MAC addresses are processed at the Data Link layer of the OSI model.

7. **Answer: A**. In the PC networking environment, the Bluetooth specification allows several Bluetooth peripheral devices to communicate with a PC simultaneously. In particular, Bluetooth is used with desktop PCs, notebooks, Tablet PCs, and PDAs to communicate with wireless input and output devices such as mouse devices, keyboards, and printers.

8. **Answer: C**. Link light operations are defined at the Physical layer of the OSI model.

9. **Answer: A**. IPv4 addresses exist in the numeric format XXX.YYY.ZZZ.AAA. Each address consists of four 8-bit (32 bits total) fields separated by dots (.). This format of specifying addresses is referred to as *dotted decimal notation*. The decimal numbers are derived from the binary address that the network devices and software understand.

10. **Answer: B**. Telnet is a client/server service that enables you to "telephone-net" into another computer so that you can utilize its resources in a command-line interface environment. Although most web browsers do not include a client for telnet access, most operating systems include a utility that enables you to launch telnet. Telnet enables users at remote computers to connect to a server. The client computer doesn't have to be running the same operating system as the remote server. This is a good solution for situations in which the PC environment is radically different from that of the other computer (such as a Linux or Novell system, or a mainframe computer).

11. **Answer: A**. Bluetooth is used with disktop PCs, notebooks, Tablet PCs, and PDAs to communicate with wireless input and output devices such as mouse devices, keyboards, and printers. IrDA keyboards and mouse devices have been developed for PDA and other handheld devices but have not gained widespread popularity for use with full-size PCs, especially those designed for use as media centers.

12. **Answer: C**. Many ISPs use the dynamic IP addressing function of DHCP to provide access to their dial-up users. The protocol automatically delivers IP addresses, subnet mask and default router configuration parameters, and other configuration information to the devices on the network. The dynamic addressing portion of the protocol also means that computers can be added to a network without manually assigning them unique IP addresses. In fact, devices can be issued a different IP address each time they connect to the network. In some networks, a device's IP address can even change while it is still connected.

13. **Answer: B**. If a filter is put on the DSL connection, the Internet connection might not work correctly.

14. **Answer: D**. DSL modems require an external power source to function.

15. **Answer: C**. The Dynamic Host Configuration Protocol (DHCP) is an Internet protocol that can be used to automatically assign IP addresses to devices on a network using TCP/IP. Using DHCP simplifies network administration because software, rather than an administrator, assigns and keeps track of IP addresses.

16. **Answer: D**. The most efficient way to test network cable is to use a cable tester to check its functionality.

17. **Answer: C**. TCP/IP is the most widely used network protocol today due mainly to the Internet. No matter what type of computer platform or software is being used, the information must move across the Internet in the form of TCP/IP packets.

18. **Answer: D**. The File Transfer Protocol (FTP) is used to upload and download files to and from an FTP server. Large files take considerably longer to send to and download from an FTP server than an email server.

19. **Answer: C**. The Secure Sockets Layer (SSL) protocol is used to authenticate organizations or e-commerce servers on the Internet and to encrypt/decrypt messages using a security process called *public-key encryption*. Most e-commerce transactions are protected under SSL.

Objective 5.2

1. **Answer: A**. The user must learn to reconfigure her network connection to automatically obtain an IP address, subnet mask, gateway address, and DNS address from the host network. DHCP is used to manage these assignments automatically and is particularly convenient when traveling with portable PCs to automatically obtain DHCP information from network hosts such as hotels and airport kiosks that provide high-speed Internet connections for their customers. Because the user is connected to a business network in the office, she probably needs to be given administrative rights to change her network configuration.

2. **Answer: B**. A hardwired network printer is connected to the network through a built-in ethernet LAN adapter and operates at UTP-compatible speeds—10Mbps, 100Mbps, or 1000Mbps (1Gbps).

3. **Answers: A, B, D**. When the TCP/IP protocol is installed, it can require several pieces of configuration information to fully implement it. In a simple local area network, such as a peer-to-peer residential network, only an IP address and a subnet mask setting are required. However, if you are connecting the residential local area to the Internet, you are also required to provide a default gateway, or router address, as well as an IP address for a DNS server.

4. **Answer: A**. The presence of the activity light indicates that the NIC sees network traffic.

5. **Answer: B**. In a typical peer-to-peer network arrangement, the users connected to the network can share access to different network resources, such as hard drives and printers.

6. **Answer: B**. In a client/server network, dependent workstations (clients) operate in conjunction with a dedicated master computer (server). The network control tends to be very centralized. The server typically holds the programs and data for its client computers. It also provides security and network policy enforcement.

Objective 5.3

1. **Answer: D**. By default, PCs running TCP/IP can communicate only with other computers that are on the same network. If multiple networks are involved, or you are connected to the Internet, you must configure the address of the router (default gateway) on each PC. Therefore, if you cannot access the Internet, but you can access resources on the local area network, the gateway address is most likely configured incorrectly.

2. **Answer: A**. You can use the PING command to test both the name and IP address of the remote unit. If you know the hostname of a computer on the network, you can use PING *hostname* to determine its IP address.

3. **Answer: A**. The TCP/IP loopback test enables you to verify that TCP/IP has been successfully loaded in the local computer. If the test fails to return a reply, the problem is with the installation of TCP/IP on the local machine. If the test responds with a Reply, the TCP/IP protocol is installed and functioning correctly.

4. **Answer: C**. The first step in troubleshooting local network connectivity is to try to obtain a connection with the network. Check to see that the computer is physically connected to the network and check the activity/status lights on the back plate of the LAN card to determine whether the network recognizes the adapter. If the lights are glowing, the NIC sees network traffic and the connection is alive. If not, check the adapter in another PC.

5. **Answer: A**. You must ping address 127.0.0.1 to perform a loopback test that verifies TCP/IP has been successfully loaded in the local computer.

6. **Answer: D**. Because the user can ping other users or devices on the network, the local network adapter, its drivers, and its network cable must be good. With TCP/IP disabled, the printer would not be able to reply to a ping sent to it.

7. **Answer: B**. When dealing with portable PCs that have built-in wireless networking, you should check that your wireless network adapter's radio module is switched on. Some laptops come with buttons that can be used to disable the wireless network function when not in use. This is a power-saving feature used to extend the battery life cycle.

8. **Answers: A, D**. A blinking link light on a switch typically indicates that information is passing through that port. In this case, no other ports are connected to anything to generate traffic. However, one of the most troubling types of NIC failure occurs when the problem device captures all the network data and continuously retransmits it erroneously. This condition, known as a *jabbering NIC,* shuts down all the computers on the affected segment and thereby complicates the troubleshooting problem. Each computer may have to be tested individually. The other possibility here is that the switch or just this port is bad and is generating the blinking light.

9. **Answer: C**. IPCONFIG is available in both Windows 2000 and Windows XP. You can start the IPCONFIG command-line utility with two important option switches: /renew and /release. These switches are used to release and obtain new IP settings received from a DHCP source. The /release switch dumps the old TCP/IP configuration, and the /renew command requests a new set of TCP/IP information to use.

10. **Answer: A**. IPCONFIG enables you to determine the current TCP/IP configuration (MAC address, IP address, and subnet mask) of the local computer. With these TCP/IP configuration settings, you can troubleshoot network connectivity problems.

11. **Answer: B**. The TRACERT utility traces the route taken by ICMP packets sent across the network and displays the hostname, IP address, and roundtrip time for each hop in the path. Because the TRACERT report shows how much time is spent at each router along the path, it is helpful to determine where network slowdowns are occurring.

Objective 5.4

1. **Answer: D**. A networked or online computer has more opportunity to contract a virus than a standalone PC because viruses can enter the unit over the network or through the modem. Therefore, all computers with connections to the Internet should be protected by an antivirus solution before they are ever attached to the Internet. Conducting regular virus scans of the system's memory and HDD is critical when using the Internet.

2. **Answer: A**. To minimize the risk of security compromise on a wireless LAN, the IEEE 802.11 standard provides a security feature called Wired Equivalent Privacy (WEP). WEP provides a 128-bit mathematical key encryption scheme for encrypting data transmissions and authenticating each computer on the network. Enabling the WEP function adds security for data being transmitted by the workstations.

3. **Answer: A**. Cabling can become a trip or catch hazard if not managed properly. Cables should be run neatly and out of the walkway. If possible, signal and power cables should be just long enough to make the necessary connections without creating stress on the connector. Additional cable lengths should be coiled and secured neatly. If temporary cabling must be run in or across a walkway, it should be taped down to the floor or covered with a protective cover strip to prevent it from becoming a trip hazard.

Domain 6.0

Objective 6.1

1. **Answer: C**. Session hijacking is a method of gaining unauthorized access to someone's computer by stealing cookies from one of his legitimate Internet sessions. In a type of session stealing called *Man in the Middle attack*, the attackers can use a packet sniffer to capture cookies as they are passed across the network, or they can steal the cookie information from the PC if they can trick it into believing the code it is receiving is from a trusted location, such as the server. After attackers have obtained the cookie information, they can gain access to other privileged information and take over use of the legitimate user's session ID, which identifies him to the site as a legitimate user. In yet another session hijacking version, called *IP spoofing*, the attacker is able to insert commands into an active communication by pretending to be an authenticated user.

2. **Answer: C**. Users should never talk about their passwords with anyone, other than known system administrators, no matter how harmless or legitimate such conversation might seem. This includes third-party service personnel who might find it convenient to temporarily use the operator's password to perform work on that person's PC. These technicians should be granted the proper level of access and their own temporary access information from the network administrator. Such discussions should be conducted in person, and never over the telephone or through email. Otherwise, the user should stand by and enter the password each time it is needed.

3. **Answer: B**. In Windows 2000 and Windows XP, significant events (such as system events, application events, and security events) are routinely monitored and stored. These events can be viewed through the Event Viewer utility. Security events are produced by user actions such as logons and logoffs, file and folder accesses, and creation of new Active Directory accounts. Security events are recorded and displayed according to how the configuration of the system's audit policy has been configured through the Group Policy editor. To view login events for the entire network, you would need to access the Event Viewer on the domain controller. Likewise, local logon information can be obtained through the Event Viewer on each local machine.

4. **Answers: A, D**. Windows XP Home does not provide the variety of account options found in Windows 2000 or XP Professional. Windows XP Home provides only Limited and Administrative rights options for controlling access to system resources. When a user is given a Limited account, she is enabled to access programs already installed on the computer but cannot install software or hardware components or change her account name or type. The user cannot create a new user because this activity is relegated to computer administrators.

5. **Answer: A**. In Windows 2000 and Windows XP, the administrator has the tools to limit what the user can do to any given file or directory. This is accomplished through two types of security permissions: share permissions and NTFS permissions. The sharing function is implemented at the computer that hosts the folder or resource (*resources* are devices capable of holding or manipulating data). To access the shared remote resource, the local operating system must first connect to it. After the connection has been established, the level of access to the resource is controlled by the share or NTFS permissions (or a combination of the two) configured (or inherited) for the resource.

6. **Answer: A**. In Windows 2000 and XP, the administrator has lockout policy settings for how many times account access can be attempted before the account is locked out—the account lockout threshold. The default value for this setting is 0, which disables the account lockout function.

7. **Answer: C**. Group Policies are the Windows 2000/XP tools for implementing changes for computers and users throughout an enterprise. The Windows 2000 and XP Group Policies can be applied to individual users, domains, organizational units, and sites. With Group Policies, administrators can institute a large number of detailed settings for users throughout an enterprise, without establishing each setting manually. The drawback of using Local Computer Policies is that each system would need to be configured individually. In this case, the administrator can create and configure a Group Policy that will push the installation of the database application to the users in the group when they log in.

Objective 6.2

1. **Answer: C**. Encryption is treated as a file attribute in Windows 2000 and Windows XP. Therefore, to encrypt a file, you need to access its properties page by right-clicking it and selecting its Properties option from the pop-up menu. Move to the Advanced area under the General tab and click the Encrypt Contents to Secure Data check box.

2. **Answer: A**. *Spoofing* is an activity whereby a person or program masquerades as someone else by falsifying data. With email, this is accomplished by making the email look as though it came from someone else. On the Internet, phishing sites spoof (pretend to be) reputable sites with the intent to acquire user information such as usernames, passwords, and credit card information. Phishing expeditions typically begin with an email or instant messenger communication that points the target toward the spoofed site.

3. **Answers: A, C**. If one of the WPA versions is not an option, you should enable WEP with 128-bit encryption. In addition, after you've installed and authenticated all the wireless clients, you should set the SSID Broadcast option to Disabled so that outsiders do not use SSID to acquire your address and data. Also change the SSID name from the default value if you have not already done so.

4. **Answer: C**. You can configure the ICF function with filters to enable specific traffic to enter the network, such as web or FTP services running on the internal network that must be made available to external customers. Then you can configure a filter to open the firewall to let just that service pass through. For email SMTP and POP services, the port settings involved are 25 and 110.

Objective 6.3

1. **Answer: A**. In Windows XP, the administrator has been given tools that can be used to limit what the user can do to any given resource. Non-hot-swappable devices such as local printers cannot be added to Windows 2000 or Windows XP systems without Administrator permissions. In a Domain environment, members of the Print Managers group can normally add printers to the system. Likewise, members of the Local Users group can add network printers to the system. All these capabilities are based on the default permission settings for these groups; with the exception of the Administrators group, the capabilities of these groups can be modified through Group Policy settings.

2. **Answer: B**. WEP is a strong encryption method, but serious hackers can crack it. This has led the wireless industry to create a stronger Wi-Fi Protected Access (WPA) standard. A newer version of WPA, called *WPA2*, fully implements the security mechanisms for wireless networks called for in the IEEE 802.11i standard.

Objective 6.4

1. **Answer: B**. Social engineers exploit people's human nature to fool them into providing information about themselves, their business, or their computer/network. They accomplish this by using trickery, deceit, lies, gifts, or acts of kindness to first establish a level of trust. They then use this trust relationship to gain information.

2. **Answer: A**. Some social engineering efforts, such as phishing or pharming, can go to great lengths to get users to surrender their login information. For instance, the programmer may design a login screen that exactly mimics a login screen that you expect to see from a trusted site or company. In the background, the login screen passes your information back to the programmer. You should know to ignore the request, delete the email message, and report the incident to your supervisors. However, you should not forward the request because doing so also poses a security risk.

Objective 7.0

Objective 7.1

1. **Answers: A, B**. To protect PC equipment from electrostatic discharge (ESD), wear an antistatic wrist strap to release any static present on your body. You can also install an antistatic mat to carry away static from the work area. Most electronics work areas include antistatic mats made out of rubber or other antistatic materials where technicians can stand while working on the equipment. This is particularly helpful in carpeted work areas because carpeting can be a major source of ESD buildup. Some antistatic mats have ground connections that should be connected to the safety ground of an AC power outlet.

2. **Answer: D**. Use a simple solution of water and fabric softener to clean the exterior of the monitor and remove static buildup from the display. Then apply a clear water rinse to the monitor. Water and electricity make a dangerous and possibly deadly mixture. Therefore, any liquid you use should not saturate the applicator or be applied directly to the monitor. Make sure that the monitor's power cord is disconnected from any power source before washing it.

3. **Answer: D**. In the case of a complete shutdown, or significant sag, the best protection from losing programs and data is to use an uninterruptible power supply (UPS). These battery-based systems monitor the incoming power and kick in when unacceptable variations occur in the power source.

4. **Answer: A**. The presence of water in the work area from other sources, such as leaking pipes or ceilings, should always be a cause for alarm and correction. Water leaks in the work area are generally the responsibility of the building maintenance supervisor. If the business does not have someone on staff who is responsible for building infrastructure, you should report the situation to whoever is responsible for the PCs and/or network so that person can properly shut down the systems.

5. **Answer: A**. Brownouts are significant sags that can last for a protracted period of time. In the case of a complete power shutdown, or significant sag, the best protection against losing programs and data is an uninterruptible power supply (UPS).

Objective 8.0

Objective 8.1

1. **Answers: A, C**. You may run into situations in which you do not speak the same language as the customer. When this occurs, you need to find someone who can interpret for you to perform the customer-questioning segment of the troubleshooting process. You should contact your management to see if someone in the organization has the ability to interact with this customer. Finally, you may be able to communicate with the customer on a graphical level using drawings.

2. **Answer: A**. Never break copyright regulations by illegally loading, or giving away, software. One of the leading causes of computer virus infection is pirated software. Not only do you run this risk in giving away copies, but it's illegal and can introduce you to various people you never really wanted to meet, such as lawyers and judges. On top of that, it could cost you your job. Tell customers who ask you to install suspected software that it is illegal to do so and you cannot do it for them.

3. **Answer: A**. If a problem runs beyond the scope of your position or your capabilities, take the initiative to move it to the next level of authority. Never leave customers hanging without a path to get their problems addressed. Provide alternatives when possible: downtime scheduling, loaner equipment availability, and so on. This is also true for requests for work to be performed that are outside your assignment or your company's agreement with the customer. Escalate the request so that management can take proper action in deciding how the particular customer should be handled.

4. **Answer: B**. Along with reporting damage to customers when it occurs, you will occasionally have to give customers other types of bad news, such as you can't repair the system or recover the data from a damaged drive. The best way of giving bad news is to simply give it to the customers as soon as you have determined the extent of the problem and be honest with them about the extent of the problem they have. Avoiding giving customers the bad news or delaying it only wastes the customers' time and can cause them to doubt your abilities.

5. **Answer: A**. The best tool for training users is typically the actual equipment or software they will be expected to use. If you are coaching one or two users, it is best to pull up a chair and get to an equal level with them. This allows you to make the training more personable and less formal. Use the documentation that comes with the hardware or software as part of the training process. Point out and mark key topic areas in the documentation that you know the users will need after you're gone. However, do not read the manuals to them; this is an instant cure for insomnia and very ineffective training. Also be careful to use language that the users can relate to. Use proper terminology; avoid jargon or industry slang when coaching users.

6. **Answer: A**. On some occasions customers may not be ready for you. They may have had things come up between the time they scheduled your appointment and the time you arrived that changed their need for the equipment. Always ask if they are ready for you to work on their machines before you begin your work.

7. **Answer: B**. There are two main issues involved here. The first is the rules that cover what types of software are permissible for different employees, and the second is the use of your time. Check to determine whether the software you are being asked to install is legal software, whether the company policy allows for this person to have this software. You might want to make sure that this activity does not take up more time than you can afford to give up. If both of these concerns can be overcome, install the software for the user.

8. **Answer: D**. If possible, you should take this opportunity to educate your fellow employee by guiding him through the process so that he will know how to do this in the future.

Objective 8.2

1. **Answer: A**. If you are working on a piece of equipment at the customer's facility, you could check to see who is calling. If the call is from someone you think you should speak with, or is a call you think it is important to take, answer the call, keep the conversation to a minimum, and call the other party back after you finish the customer's job. If you are in the customer's immediate presence when you see that a call could be important, tell the customer that you must take the call and excuse yourself from her presence to respond to the call.

2. **Answer: C**. If you are exposed to illegal software or pornographic material on a customer's computer, you should report this to your supervisor. If you discover illegal software or pornographic material on one of your company's computers, report it to the proper authority in your organization (provided you are not authorized by your company's policies to handle this situation yourself).

3. **Answer: B**. If you damage a customer's property in the process of your work, you should take responsibility for the damage. Hiding inflicted damage or passing it off on the customer can put you and your company in an embarrassing situation if it comes into question. When damage occurs, make sure that you document the extent of the damage and the circumstances surrounding how it occurred. Let your management know and then let the customer know. Your company probably has policies in place that spell out your responsibilities in this area.

4. **Answer: A**. You may also encounter situations in which you should not assume accountability for different things. For example, working in a customer's residence when she is not there can be problematic. If the customer decides something is missing and you were there by yourself, guess whose problem it will become. Even when she finds the item later, the damage has been done. Likewise, never assume responsibility for anyone's children or being alone with children.

5. **Answer: A**. In residential settings, you may be subject to the presence of children who could be a distraction or a problem in getting your work completed in an efficient manner. If this is the case, you should explain this to the customer and ask him to remove the children from the work area. This is not your responsibility and could cause problems if you directly confront the children.

6. **Answer: A**. If you decide to take a call at a customer's business (or residence), and it begins to look as though it is going to take some time, you really should tell the other party that you will have to reconnect at a different time. Customers will notice that you are on the phone and, if they are paying for your time, will feel like they aren't getting good value from you.

7. **Answer: A**. If you can reach the Internet from the infected machine, you can download several free removal tools and scanning utilities and run them to identify and possibly remove viruses from the infected machine. There are also virus definition sites that you can find on the Internet. These sites list the virus, what it does, and where it is installed in the system. Microsoft also offers a Malicious Software Removal Tool for Windows 2000 and Windows XP. This tool is available as a download from the Microsoft Update, Windows Update, or Microsoft Download Center.

8. **Answer: C**. Because this PC has already been in your shop several times, you must sell your abilities to the customer and then deliver. Simply starting at the beginning again and asking the customer to tell you what is wrong (for the fourth time) does not accomplish this. Attempt to de-escalate the situation. This usually involves letting the customer get pent-up frustrations off his chest by simply listening to him. When you reply, remain calm, talk in a steady voice, and avoid making inflammatory comments. Also, try to avoid taking a defensive stance because this signals a conflict point. Realize that criticism given out by a customer is generally not personal, so don't take it personally. Information delivered with an aggressive attitude normally leads to an aggressive or retaliatory response from the customer. Work with the customer to redirect the conversation to creating solutions to the problems. Reassure the customer that you are fully capable of fixing the problem and then follow up by fixing the problem and returning the system to working order. As part of the customer service effort, you need to go over the important details, one at a time, and explain how you plan to handle each concern (or whom you must turn to for a final answer).

9. **Answer: D**. Attempt to de-escalate the situation. This usually involves letting the customer get pent-up frustrations off his chest by simply listening to him. When you reply, remain calm, talk in a steady voice, and avoid making inflammatory comments. Also, try to avoid taking a defensive stance because this signals a conflict point. Realize that criticism given out by a customer is generally not personal, so don't take it personally. Information delivered with an aggressive attitude normally leads to an aggressive or retaliatory response from the customer. Work with the customer to redirect the conversation to creating solutions to the problems. Reassure the customer that you are fully capable of fixing the problem and then follow up by fixing the problem and returning the system to working order.

10. **Answer: B**. If a problem runs beyond the scope of your position or your capabilities, take the initiative to move it to the next level of authority. Never leave customers hanging without a path to get their problems addressed. Provide alternatives when possible: downtime scheduling, loaner equipment availability, and so on. This is also true for requests for work to be performed that are outside your assignment or your company's agreement with the customer. Escalate the request so that management can take proper action in deciding how the particular customer should be handled.

CHAPTER THREE

Remote Support Technician Exam

Practice Questions

Domain 1.0: Personal Computer Components

Objective 1.1: Install, configure, optimize, and upgrade personal computer components

1. One of your customers is a training video producer who has created a new safety movie. He wants to transfer the movie to portable media that can be distributed as a demo. The total size of the video file is 6.5GB. What media could you suggest to this customer as the best solution for the project?

   ○ **A.** A CD-R disc

   ○ **B.** A single-sided, single-layer DVD+R disc

   ○ **C.** A single-sided, dual-layer DVD-R disc

   ○ **D.** A double-sided, dual-layer DVD-RW disc

Quick Answer: **281**
Detailed Answer: **286**

2. When you receive a new system board to upgrade a customer's desktop PC, you notice that the box says it is "SLI Ready." The customer wants to know what this means. What can you tell the customer about this statement?

- ○ **A.** The system board supports simultaneous onboard and card-mounted video controllers.
- ○ **B.** The system board features multiple processor sockets.
- ○ **C.** The system board supports scalable linear integration upgrades.
- ○ **D.** The system board supports dual PCIe video controllers.

3. The integrated video feature has died on one of your customer's system boards. He needs to get the system back into operation as quickly as possible. You tell him that he should be able to disable the integrated video controller through the CMOS Setup utility and then install a video adapter card in the machine and put it back in operation. He wants you to bring him a video card and install it in the machine, so you ask him to describe the slots he has available on this particular system board. Which of the following expansion slot types could typically be used to host video adapter cards in a desktop PC? (Select all that apply.)

- ○ **A.** An AGP slot
- ○ **B.** A PCIe slot
- ○ **C.** An AMR slot
- ○ **D.** A PCMCIA slot

4. You are working on a charity project to recondition used PCs donated by a local Fortune 500 company for use in a retirement community. All the hard drives have been removed, so you must install new drives in each system. The system boards feature two IDE interface connections, but the signal cables were removed with the drives. Which cable type should you obtain to connect the new PATA drives to the IDE interface on these system boards to ensure maximum performance from the new drives?

- ○ **A.** 34-conductor ribbon cable with 34-pin mini-Centronics connectors
- ○ **B.** 36-conductor serial cable with 36-pin Centronics connectors
- ○ **C.** 40-conductor ribbon cable with 40-pin socket connectors
- ○ **D.** 80-conductor ribbon cable with 40-pin socket connectors

5. Your national sales director spends a considerable amount of time on airplanes each month. It is time to upgrade his notebook PC. You have settled on the fact that he needs one of the low power-consumption chipsets and processors, and now you are evaluating which battery types might be available to provide power over the duration of longer flights. Which battery type offers the longest battery life in a portable PC?

- ○ **A.** NiCD
- ○ **B.** Li-ion
- ○ **C.** Lead acid
- ○ **D.** Alkaline

6. You are working with a small advertising firm whose art development person will be traveling a lot over the next six months in conjunction with a big project she is working on. The art developer needs a notebook PC to travel with, but the display has to be very good for her to prepare the types of artwork required for the project. What should you recommend as the best display type for this notebook PC?

- ○ **A.** Dual-scan technology
- ○ **B.** Active-matrix TFT technology
- ○ **C.** Passive-matrix technology
- ○ **D.** CSTN/DSTN technology

7. What are your options for installing drivers not directly supported by the Windows XP operating system? (Select two correct answers.)

- ○ **A.** Obtain an OEM installation disk or CD for the device that has the Windows XP drivers.
- ○ **B.** Devices not directly supported by Windows cannot be installed.
- ○ **C.** Use a driver from a similar model from the same manufacturer in the Add Hardware Wizard's list of supported devices.
- ○ **D.** Attempt to locate the specific device in the Add Hardware Wizard's list of supported devices.

8. If the system's PnP function does not recognize a network adapter card you are trying to install, where can you go to install it in a Windows XP Professional system?

  ○ **A.** Navigate to the Device Manager, expand the Network Adapters node, and configure the driver options for the new card.

  ○ **B.** Click on the Network Connections icon in the Control Panel and configure the settings for the new card.

  ○ **C.** Click on the Add Hardware icon in the Control Panel and use the Add Hardware Wizard to install drivers for the new card.

  ○ **D.** Navigate to Control Panel/System and select the Hardware tab. Then click on the Hardware Profiles button to configure the new card.

9. Your notebook PC is running out of battery power faster than it should. What should you do to correct this? (Select all that apply.)

  ○ **A.** Place the battery in a commercial battery charger overnight to build the level of charge in the battery backup.

  ○ **B.** Keep the external AC power adapter plugged into the notebook whenever possible to increase the amount of charge in the battery.

  ○ **C.** You must fully discharge the battery and then recharge it over repeated cycles.

  ○ **D.** Purchase another battery for the notebook.

10. When you get to your job assignment, you discover that the system you are working on has a defective PS/2 mouse and that it does not support USB devices. You have only USB mouse devices with you. What should you do under these circumstances?

  ○ **A.** Install an adapter card–mounted USB port.

  ○ **B.** Return to the shop to get a PS/2-compatible version.

  ○ **C.** Install a USB/wireless converter that allows the USB mouse to communicate wirelessly with the host PC.

  ○ **D.** Install a USB-to-PS/2 converter for the new mouse.

11. What is the first step in troubleshooting any problem?

  ○ **A.** Identify the problem.

  ○ **B.** Analyze the problem.

  ○ **C.** Inspect components.

  ○ **D.** Establish a plan of action.

12. Your machine does not run; you look inside and see that it uses RIMM for memory. You also notice that there is one vacant slot on the board. What do you need to do to get the machine to run with this type of memory installed?

- ○ **A.** Install a blank RIMM module in the empty slot.
- ○ **B.** Remove the RIMM modules and install standard DDR modules.
- ○ **C.** Install a CRIMM in the empty slot.
- ○ **D.** Remove the existing memory modules and install matched RIMM pairs in all the slots.

13. You installed a new video card in a desktop PC system that doesn't have onboard video. When you start up the system, there is no display. What should you do to correct this condition?

- ○ **A.** Swap the display unit with a known good unit of the same type.
- ○ **B.** Restart the system, enter CMOS Setup, and ensure that the default, onboard video option is disabled.
- ○ **C.** Replace the video adapter card with a known good card.
- ○ **D.** Restart the system in Safe Mode, remove the old video driver, and restart the system so that Windows can detect the new card and install the proper drivers for it.

Objective 1.2: Identify tools, diagnostic procedures, and troubleshooting techniques for personal computer components

1. You've installed one IDE hard drive, and it is working fine. You install a second IDE hard drive, and neither hard drive works. What could be the problem?

- ○ **A.** The hard drives are connected in the wrong order on the IDE cable.
- ○ **B.** The second hard drive is on the secondary IDE port with its jumper set in the slave position.
- ○ **C.** Both hard drives are connected to the primary IDE port, and the jumpers on both drives are set as masters.
- ○ **D.** One drive is connected as primary master and the other as secondary master, but the power connector isn't connected to the secondary master.

2. If you turn the sound volume in Windows 2000 entirely to the right channel, and the sound comes out the speaker marked "Left," what is wrong?

Quick Answer: **281**
Detailed Answer: **288**

- ○ **A.** The software for the CD player needs to be reinstalled.
- ○ **B.** The audio cable is bad.
- ○ **C.** The right speaker is bad.
- ○ **D.** The speakers are sitting on the wrong sides.

3. One of your customers has called you because he was attempting to perform a RAM upgrade on his machine when he felt a small snap on his fingertip. Now the system does not start up to the desktop. What should you do in this situation?

Quick Answer: **281**
Detailed Answer: **288**

- ○ **A.** Try to determine the exact damage done and then educate the customer about ESD.
- ○ **B.** Tell the customer it's a lot less expensive to call you in the first place and then install new memory modules in the PC.
- ○ **C.** Tell the customer that he should wear an antistatic wrist strap if he is going to be working on his own equipment. Then replace the system board.
- ○ **D.** Replace the RAM with new modules and install an antistatic mat under the PC.

4. In the process of any type of troubleshooting effort, what should you do after you've identified a problem and repaired it?

Quick Answer: **281**
Detailed Answer: **288**

- ○ **A.** Document the steps you've performed.
- ○ **B.** Educate the customer about how you fixed the problem.
- ○ **C.** Train your coworkers about the steps you took to repair the problem.
- ○ **D.** Identify any additional steps needed.

Quick Check

5. After you install a PCI network adapter card, you try to start the PC and nothing happens. What is the most likely cause of this condition?

Quick Answer: **281**
Detailed Answer: **288**

   ○ **A.** The adapter is not seated properly in the expansion slot. Remove it and reinstall it.

   ○ **B.** You've forgotten to reconnect the PC to the AC power outlet.

   ○ **C.** The adapter is incompatible with the operating system version that's installed. Check its HCL for a compatible replacement.

   ○ **D.** The installed drivers do not operate the new adapter card. Remove the existing video driver and allow the PnP process to find it and load the correct drivers.

6. A friend has called you after attempting to install a new video card, and it doesn't produce any video output. When you examine the system, you see that the system board has an onboard video connector. What should you do to get the system running?

Quick Answer: **281**
Detailed Answer: **289**

   ○ **A.** Remove the adapter card–based video adapter card and restart the system.

   ○ **B.** Restart the system in Safe Mode, access the Device Manager utility, and disable the driver for the onboard video adapter.

   ○ **C.** Restart the system and use the Recovery Console to update the video driver.

   ○ **D.** Restart the system and access the CMOS Setup utility to disable the onboard video feature.

7. What conditions could cause the Device Manager utility to display an exclamation point on a yellow background next to a PC Card adapter?

Quick Answer: **281**
Detailed Answer: **289**

   ○ **A.** The PC Card device might be faulty.

   ○ **B.** The PC Card controller in the notebook might be faulty.

   ○ **C.** The operating system does not support the installed PC Card device.

   ○ **D.** The PC Card slots have been disabled in the CMOS.

8. After you upgrade a video adapter card's driver in Windows XP, the video display is scrambled. What action should you take to revert to the old driver version?

Quick Answer: **281**
Detailed Answer: **289**

- ○ **A.** Boot into Safe Mode with the command prompt only and remove the driver.
- ○ **B.** Boot into Safe Mode and run the Driver Rollback feature from the Device Manager.
- ○ **C.** Use the SFC utility to start up the system and roll back the driver.
- ○ **D.** Use the Recovery Console to reboot the system and then roll back the driver.

9. When you turn on your computer, the floppy drive fails to work. Also, you notice that the floppy drive operating light is on continuously. What is the problem?

Quick Answer: **281**
Detailed Answer: **289**

- ○ **A.** The floppy drive is bad and needs to be replaced.
- ○ **B.** The motherboard BIOS needs to be upgraded.
- ○ **C.** The floppy drive cable has been connected backward.
- ○ **D.** The power supply connection to the floppy drive is bad.

10. During an attended local installation of Windows XP Professional on a new SATA hard drive, you receive a `Blue Screen - Inaccessible Boot Device` STOP error. What can you do to overcome this error and install the operating system?

Quick Answer: **281**
Detailed Answer: **289**

- ○ **A.** Run the Recovery Console from the distribution disc.
- ○ **B.** Partition the drive before beginning the installation process.
- ○ **C.** Install third-party drivers for the SATA drive.
- ○ **D.** The MBR area of the hard drive has physical damage that the install program cannot work around. You must replace the hard drive.

11. A user has called in to report that her PS/2 keyboard does not work. She has just set up the system in a new location. It was working fine before the move. What should you have this user do?

  ○ **A.** Install a PS/2-to-USB converter on the end of the keyboard's signal cable and test the keyboard's operation from the USB port.

  ○ **B.** Move the keyboard connector to the other PS/2 connector and try it.

  ○ **C.** Enable the keyboard in the CMOS Setup utility and reboot the system.

  ○ **D.** Use the Device Manager utility to troubleshoot the keyboard's device driver.

Objective 1.3: Perform preventative maintenance on personal computer components

1. You have been put in charge of producing a preventative maintenance schedule to present to a small law firm that has just hired you to maintain its PCs. One of the operations you have to schedule is periodic defragmentation operations for each machine. How often should you perform a defrag operation on a desktop PC used in an office setting?

  ○ **A.** Weekly

  ○ **B.** Monthly

  ○ **C.** Yearly

  ○ **D.** Daily

2. What does the command-line CHKDSK / R statement do?

  ○ **A.** It realigns the magnetic domains on the disk.

  ○ **B.** It provides the full path to each folder on the disk.

  ○ **C.** It locates bad sectors on the disk and recovers readable information.

  ○ **D.** It performs a faster, reduced intensity check of the disk.

3. Which of the following products are recommended for manual cleaning of the R/W heads in a tape drive?

Quick Answer: **281**
Detailed Answer: **289**

    ○ **A.** Soft cloths

    ○ **B.** Cotton swabs

    ○ **C.** A pencil eraser

    ○ **D.** Foam swabs

4. You have wavy lines on a new CRT monitor, what should you do?

Quick Answer: **281**
Detailed Answer: **289**

    ○ **A.** Reinstall the video driver.

    ○ **B.** Replace the video card.

    ○ **C.** Degauss the monitor.

    ○ **D.** Replace the monitor.

Domain 2.0: Operating Systems

Objective 2.1: Identify the fundamental principles of using operating systems

1. Which of the following is not part of the normal System State Data backup operations performed by Windows 2000 or Windows XP?

   ○ **A.** The Registry

   ○ **B.** The system startup files

   ○ **C.** The COM+ class registration database

   ○ **D.** The System Information database

   Quick Answer: **281**
   Detailed Answer: **290**

2. In the Windows 2000/XP environment, where do you go to access the system's administrative tools from a centralized location?

   ○ **A.** Start/Settings/Control Panel/Administrative Tools

   ○ **B.** Start/All Programs/System Tools

   ○ **C.** Start/Settings/Control Panel/System/Administration

   ○ **D.** Start/Run/Administration Tools

   Quick Answer: **281**
   Detailed Answer: **290**

3. Which Windows 2000 utility is designed to enable administrators to configure drives and volumes located in remote computers?

   ○ **A.** Hierarchical Storage Manager

   ○ **B.** Volume Manager

   ○ **C.** FDISK.EXE

   ○ **D.** Disk Management

   Quick Answer: **281**
   Detailed Answer: **290**

4. You are working in the Recovery Console, and you want to move to another directory to check for the presence of specific files there. Which command-line statement do you use to move between directories?

Quick Answer: **281**
Detailed Answer: **290**

- ○ **A.** CD
- ○ **B.** MD
- ○ **C.** RD
- ○ **D.** GD

5. After receiving an `NTLDR is Missing` message on a Windows 2000 Professional system, you boot the machine using the Windows distribution CD kit and gain access to the system's Recovery Console. When you examine the contents of the drive, you do not see the NTLDR file in the root directory. You suspect that the file is not apparent because it is a hidden system file. Which of the following actions enables you to change the attributes of the file so that you can verify its presence?

Quick Answer: **281**
Detailed Answer: **290**

- ○ **A.** Restart the system in Safe Mode, access the Windows Explorer, right-click on the C: drive, select Properties from the pop-up list, move to the General page, and click on the desired attribute box.
- ○ **B.** Run the `attrib -r -s -h c:\ntldr` command from the command line.
- ○ **C.** Restart the system in Safe Mode, access the Windows Explorer, click the View menu, select the Folders entry, click the View tab, and check the Show All Files box.
- ○ **D.** Run the `attrib +r +s +h c:\ntldr` command from the command line.

6. When you start up your PC, several unfamiliar icons appear in the notification area of the taskbar, and the system's startup response is noticeably slow. What Windows utility should you use to troubleshoot these symptoms?

Quick Answer: **281**
Detailed Answer: **290**

- ○ **A.** The ASR utility
- ○ **B.** The Device Manager utility
- ○ **C.** The `MSCONFIG` utility
- ○ **D.** The SFC utility

7. Where do you go to enable Driver Signature Verification in Windows XP Professional?

Quick Answer: **281**
Detailed Answer: **290**

  ○ **A.** Navigate Start/All Programs/Accessories/System Tools and select the Driver Signing option from the sub-menu.

  ○ **B.** Navigate Start/Control Panel/System icon and then select the Hardware tab and click the Driver Signing button.

  ○ **C.** Navigate Start/Control Panel/Administrative Tools/Computer Management and select the Driver Signing option from the System Tools snap-in.

  ○ **D.** Navigate Start/Control Panel/Add Hardware and click on the Enable Driver Signing option in the Add Hardware Wizard Welcome page.

Quick Answer: **281**
Detailed Answer: **290**

8. You want to make a source document you've prepared for your staff a read-only file so that it cannot be altered. Which of the following methods can you use in Windows Explorer to change the file's attributes?

  ○ **A.** Edit the appropriate Registry entry for the file using Regedt32.

  ○ **B.** Right-click on the file, select Properties, and place a check mark in the Read Only check box.

  ○ **C.** Highlight the file, choose the Select Options entry in the System Tools menu, and select the Read Only option.

  ○ **D.** Highlight the file, choose the Select Options entry in the View menu, and select the Read Only option.

Quick Answer: **281**
Detailed Answer: **290**

9. You need to share a folder with several of your coworkers. What is the path you must use to establish sharing on this folder in Windows XP Professional?

  ○ **A.** Right-click on the desired folder, select the Properties option from the menu, and then click on the Sharing and Security tab.

  ○ **B.** Navigate Start/Control Panel/Administrative Tools and click on the Enable button on the Sharing tab.

  ○ **C.** Right-click on the desired folder and select the Sharing and Security option from the menu.

  ○ **D.** Navigate Start/Control Panel/Add or Remove Programs or Windows Components and select the Sharing option from the menu on the left side of the page.

10. Your Windows XP system refuses to start up. You have been unable to recover the system using other methods, including Safe Mode, the Last Known Good Configuration option, and the Recovery Console. What else can be done in a Windows XP system to recover the system?

Quick Answer: **281**
Detailed Answer: **290**

- ○ **A.** Run the Automated System Recovery (ASR) backup operation.
- ○ **B.** Run the Automated System Recovery (ASR) restore operation.
- ○ **C.** Run the Windows XP Repair Disk program (RDISK.EXE) from the command line of the ASR disk.
- ○ **D.** Run the Windows XP SFC utility from the command prompt.

11. What command-line statement can be used to create a new directory on a hard disk drive?

Quick Answer: **281**
Detailed Answer: **291**

- ○ **A.** CD
- ○ **B.** MD
- ○ **C.** RD
- ○ **D.** GD

12. Which Windows utility would you employ to control programs that run at startup?

Quick Answer: **281**
Detailed Answer: **291**

- ○ **A.** Safe Mode
- ○ **B.** MSCONFIG
- ○ **C.** SFC
- ○ **D.** Dr. Watson

13. What command-line statement is used to reconfigure a FAT32 volume into an NTFS volume in a Windows XP system?

Quick Answer: **281**
Detailed Answer: **291**

- ○ **A.** Change C:/FS:NTFS
- ○ **B.** Convert C:/FS:NTFS
- ○ **C.** Format C:/FS:NTFS
- ○ **D.** Connect C:/FS:NTFS

14. What command-line statement would you use to remove the Read Only attribute from a file?

Quick Answer: **281**
Detailed Answer: **291**

- ○ **A.** RA *path\filename*
- ○ **B.** ATTRIB +R *path\filename*
- ○ **C.** ATTRIB -R *path\filename*
- ○ **D.** MK RO *path\filename*

15. Which utilities can be used to partition hard disk drives in Windows XP? (Select all that apply.)

Quick Answer: **281**
Detailed Answer: **291**

- ○ **A.** Format
- ○ **B.** Disk Management
- ○ **C.** Partition Magic
- ○ **D.** DISKPART.EXE

16. Which Windows utility can be used to save and restore System State data?

Quick Answer: **281**
Detailed Answer: **291**

- ○ **A.** The ASR utility
- ○ **B.** The MSCONFIG utility
- ○ **C.** The FAST utility
- ○ **D.** The Recovery Console

17. What is the basic function of the HKEY_CURRENT_USER Registry key in Windows XP?

Quick Answer: **281**
Detailed Answer: **291**

- ○ **A.** User logon data
- ○ **B.** User-specific configuration
- ○ **C.** PnP status data
- ○ **D.** Current information about installed devices

18. What is the basic function of the HKEY_CURRENT_CONFIG Registry key?

Quick Answer: **281**
Detailed Answer: **291**

- ○ **A.** User logon data
- ○ **B.** Current information about hardware devices
- ○ **C.** PnP dynamic status data
- ○ **D.** User-specific configuration

19. Which file gathers system hardware information and passes it to NTLDR?

Quick Answer: **281**
Detailed Answer: **291**

- ○ **A.** BOOT.INI
- ○ **B.** NTOSKERNAL
- ○ **C.** HAL.DLL
- ○ **D.** NTDETECT

20. When a file is deleted from the Recycle Bin, what happens to the file?

Quick Answer: **281**
Detailed Answer: **292**

- ○ **A.** It goes to the trash.
- ○ **B.** It may be recovered.
- ○ **C.** It is restored.
- ○ **D.** It is unrecoverable.

21. What happens to information that was deleted from removable media?

Quick Answer: **281**
Detailed Answer: **292**

- ○ **A.** It is archived and held for later deletion.
- ○ **B.** It is moved into the Recycle Bin.
- ○ **C.** It is relocated to the System Backup directory.
- ○ **D.** It is deleted from the file system.

22. How do you identify a compressed file in Windows 2000? (Select all that apply.)

Quick Answer: **281**
Detailed Answer: **292**

- ○ **A.** The file or folder is listed in a second color.
- ○ **B.** The file or folder is listed in italic.
- ○ **C.** The file or folder shows an archive/compressed attribute listing in Windows Explorer when the Advanced Attributes option is selected.
- ○ **D.** The file or folder is given a vice-clamp icon.

Objective 2.2: Install, configure, optimize, and upgrade operating systems

1. You have a Windows XP–based portable system, and you want to use different I/O equipment when the system is in its docking station than when you are using it on the road. You don't want to have to reconfigure the computer each time you leave the office and return. What Windows XP feature can you use to avoid this situation?

Quick Answer: **282**
Detailed Answer: **292**

- ○ **A.** If the system is PnP compliant, different hardware profiles are created by the Windows XP operating system when the computer is docked and undocked. So, simply turn on the system in both configurations and accept the profiles generated.

- ○ **B.** Manually configure the computer with both hardware profiles you want to use. Select the desired profile from the Start menu after startup.

- ○ **C.** Allow the Windows operating system to detect the notebook configuration when it is out of the docking station. Then manually configure a hardware profile for when the docking station is connected. Select the desired profile from the Start menu after startup.

- ○ **D.** Allow the Windows operating system to detect the notebook configuration when it is in the docking station. Then manually configure a hardware profile for when it is not connected to the docking station. Select the desired profile from the Start menu after startup.

2. Where in Windows XP can you optimize the virtual-memory management?

Quick Answer: **282**
Detailed Answer: **292**

- ○ **A.** Help and Support Center
- ○ **B.** All Programs/Accessories/System Tools
- ○ **C.** System Tools/Control Panel/Advanced tab
- ○ **D.** Control Panel/System/Advanced

3. Where in Windows XP can you find the Defragmenter utility for optimizing the hard drive?

Quick Answer: **282**
Detailed Answer: **292**

- ○ **A.** Control Panel/System Tools
- ○ **B.** Administrative Tools/Computer Management Console
- ○ **C.** Control Panel/Computer Management Tools
- ○ **D.** Administrator Management Console

4. When you try to run an XCOPY command from a Windows XP machine, you receive an error message stating `Bad Command or File Name`. What is the most likely reason for this message to occur in a Windows XP system?

- ○ **A.** You do not have administrative privileges.
- ○ **B.** XCOPY does not run in Windows XP.
- ○ **C.** XCOPY is a hidden command, so you must first change its attributes.
- ○ **D.** The operating system is not configured to find XCOPY.

5. Since your company upgraded its PCs to Windows XP Professional, you have encountered numerous problems associated with employees loading manufacturer's drivers for particular equipment they work with. In many cases, the new drivers have created hardware conflicts and operational failures in the systems. What can you do to stop this practice from occurring and to force the employees to use drivers that are known to work with Windows XP?

- ○ **A.** Access the Driver Signing Options page located under the Control Panel/System icon/Hardware tab/Driver Signing button to establish how the system responds when it detects an unsigned driver. Set the option to Substitute.
- ○ **B.** Access the Driver Signing Options page located under the Control Panel/System icon/Hardware tab/Driver Signing button to establish how the system responds when it detects an unsigned driver. Set the option to Warn.
- ○ **C.** Access the Driver Signing Options page located under the Control Panel/System icon/Hardware tab/Driver Signing button to establish how the system responds when it detects an unsigned driver. Set the option to Disable.
- ○ **D.** Access the Driver Signing Options page located under the Control Panel/System icon/Hardware tab/Driver Signing button to establish how the system responds when it detects an unsigned driver. Set the option to Block.

6. You want to upgrade to Windows XP Professional, but you're not sure that your system can support it. What should you do to make sure that the system will support the upgrade?

Quick Answer: **282**
Detailed Answer: **293**

- ○ **A.** Run the HCL.EXE utility from the distribution CD.
- ○ **B.** Run the ACL.EXE utility from the distribution CD.
- ○ **C.** Run the Upgrade.exe utility from the distribution CD.
- ○ **D.** Run the Checkupgradeonly utility from the distribution CD.

7. You have been called in to troubleshoot a PC whose hard drive appears to be running slow. The system is not connected to the Internet and has only occasional usage. When you examine the system, you see that the primary hard drive is nearly full. What actions are required to clear up this condition? (Select all that apply.)

Quick Answer: **282**
Detailed Answer: **293**

- ○ **A.** The MSCONFIG utility needs to be run.
- ○ **B.** A defrag operation should be run.
- ○ **C.** The drive needs to be repartitioned and reformatted.
- ○ **D.** The Windows Disk Cleanup utility needs to be run.

8. After updating your network adapter card in your Windows XP system, you want to update its drivers. What is the path you need to navigate to update the network adapter drivers?

Quick Answer: **282**
Detailed Answer: **293**

- ○ **A.** Navigate Start/All Programs/Accessories/System Tools/System Configuration and then select the Upgrade Driver option from the menu.
- ○ **B.** Navigate Start/Control Panel/Add Hardware. The Hardware Wizard then detects the new driver and installs it.
- ○ **C.** Navigate Start/My Network Places/Connections/Properties and then click on the Update Driver button.
- ○ **D.** Navigate Start/Control Panel/System/Hardware tab/Device Manager and then expand the Network Adapters node. Select the desired network adapter, click on the Driver tab, and then click on the Update Driver button.

9. Where do you go to adjust virtual memory after receiving a Low `Virtual` Memory error from a Windows XP Professional system?

Quick Answer: **282**
Detailed Answer: **293**

   ○ **A.** Navigate Start/Control Panel/Administrative Tools/Computer Management/Device Manager. Then access the Performance snap-in and check the Let Windows Control Virtual Memory check box.

   ○ **B.** Navigate Start/Control Panel/System/Advanced/ Performance/Settings. Then access the Advanced tab and click on the Change button in the Virtual Memory area.

   ○ **C.** Navigate Start/Control Panel/Performance/Settings. Then access the Advanced tab and click on the Change button in the Virtual Memory area.

   ○ **D.** Navigate Start/All Programs/Accessories/System Tools. Then access the Performance option in the menu and input a new value for the Maximum Swap file size.

10. One of your technicians is trying to establish a connection between a PC and a remote network printer. He has called you because he is not sure how to specify the path to the printer. You tell him that he needs to input the universal naming convention path to the printer. What two items are needed to establish a UNC connection? (Select all that apply.)

Quick Answer: **282**
Detailed Answer: **293**

   ○ **A.** Full Control permissions for the remote resource

   ○ **B.** The URL of the shared resource

   ○ **C.** The shared resource name

   ○ **D.** The path to the shared resource

11. Your company is expanding its operations into several new countries. You have been asked to check out Microsoft's Multilingual User Interface and determine whether it would be a good option for bringing on new network users from these countries. Which of the following are reasons why your company might be interested in using the MUI packs? (Select all that apply.)

Quick Answer: **282**
Detailed Answer: **293**

   ○ **A.** To provide easier administration in multilingual environments

   ○ **B.** To facilitate the Language and Locale support function

   ○ **C.** To decrease the cost of configuration changes in a multilingual environment

   ○ **D.** To provide document translation through Windows Office products

12. You use your Windows XP notebook in the office and when you travel. To shorten the startup time and extend the useful battery time when you are flying, you want to stop certain Windows services from loading when you start up the system on the airplane. Which Windows tool would you use to accomplish this task?

- ○ **A.** The Services snap-in
- ○ **B.** The Startup snap-in
- ○ **C.** The Security snap-in
- ○ **D.** The Performance snap-in

13. How is a UNC path from a local computer to a remote printer or a directory located on a remote computer specified?

- ○ **A.** \\Computer_name\shared_resource_name
- ○ **B.** //computer_name/shared_resource_name
- ○ **C.** \\shared_resource_name
- ○ **D.** //shared_resource_name

14. You are preparing to upgrade from Windows 2000 Professional to Windows XP Professional. The system currently has a striped array installed. What, if anything, should you do differently in this upgrade?

- ○ **A.** Don't perform the upgrade because Windows XP Professional doesn't support striping.
- ○ **B.** Back up everything on the striped array before you start the upgrade.
- ○ **C.** Perform a clean Windows XP install instead of an upgrade so that the new operating system can install its own drivers for the array.
- ○ **D.** Check the RAID installation on the Windows XP HCL to make sure that it is supported.

15. Which of the following does the Windows Disk Cleanup utility NOT do?

- ○ **A.** Removes unused Installed Windows Components from the system
- ○ **B.** Removes discarded files from the Recycle Bin
- ○ **C.** Removes temporary Internet files from the system
- ○ **D.** Removes quarantined antivirus files from the system

16. One of your customers wants to upgrade her PC from Windows 95 to Windows XP Professional. What options can you provide for performing this upgrade? (Select all that apply.)

   ○ **A.** The customer can perform a clean install of Windows XP Professional.

   ○ **B.** The customer can upgrade directly from Windows 95 to Windows XP Professional.

   ○ **C.** The customer must upgrade to Windows 98 or Windows Me before she can upgrade to Windows XP.

   ○ **D.** The customer can upgrade to Windows XP from any Windows version provided you purchase the correct upgrade version.

17. What types of utilities can prevent Windows operating system upgrades from occurring?

   ○ **A.** Multiple-OS loader managers

   ○ **B.** Archival utilities

   ○ **C.** Compression utilities

   ○ **D.** Antivirus applications

18. What is required to create a dynamic volume in Windows 2000 or Windows XP?

   ○ **A.** Convert a FAT32 volume using the Disk Management tool.

   ○ **B.** Convert a primary volume using the Disk Management tool.

   ○ **C.** Convert a basic volume using the Disk Management tool.

   ○ **D.** Convert an extended volume using the Disk Management tool.

19. You are installing a Windows 2000 upgrade on a computer at home, and you need to create the four-disk set of boot disks in case you have any problems. What is the correct method of creating these disks?

   ○ **A.** Format the disks using Windows 2000 and then copy over the `NTLDR`, `NTDETECT`, and `BOOT.INI` files.

   ○ **B.** Download the disk images from the Microsoft Support website and run them on the computer.

   ○ **C.** Run the `Makeboot` utility from the distribution CD to create the disks.

   ○ **D.** Insert the Windows distribution CD and type `WINNT/ox` at the command prompt.

20. What group must you be a member of to install a non-hot-swappable device in a Windows XP system?

- ○ **A.** Administrators
- ○ **B.** Guest
- ○ **C.** Users
- ○ **D.** Power Users

Quick Answer: **282**
Detailed Answer: **294**

21. Before you install a new piece of hardware in a Windows 2000 system, what precaution should you take?

- ○ **A.** The Windows 2000 HCL should be consulted to make sure that the device is listed on it.
- ○ **B.** The device's driver should be checked to ensure that it has been signed by Microsoft.
- ○ **C.** The device's operating speed should be examined to make sure that it will run at Windows 2000–compatible compatible speeds.
- ○ **D.** The BIOS should be flashed to make sure that it has the latest hardware support information.

Quick Answer: **282**
Detailed Answer: **295**

Objective 2.3: Identify tools, diagnostic procedures, and troubleshooting techniques for operating systems

1. If you install a new video card in a Windows XP machine, and the display is skewed when the system is started, what action should you take to gain control of the system?

- ○ **A.** Restart the system and select the Safe Mode option from the Advanced Options menu.
- ○ **B.** Restart the system and select the Last Known Good Hardware Configuration option from the Advanced Options menu.
- ○ **C.** Restart the system and select the Normal option from the Advanced Options menu.
- ○ **D.** Restart the system and select the VGA mode option from the Advanced Options menu.

Quick Answer: **282**
Detailed Answer: **295**

2. The Device Manager displays a red X symbol at a device's icon when _____.

   ○ **A.** the device is disabled due to some type of conflict

   ○ **B.** the device is experiencing a direct hardware conflict with another device

   ○ **C.** the selected device is not present on the system

   ○ **D.** the selected device is not operating properly and requires repair

3. How do you activate the Windows XP System Restore Wizard?

   ○ **A.** Navigate the Start/All Programs/Accessories/System Tools path and then select the System Restore option from the menu.

   ○ **B.** Navigate the Start/Settings/Control Panel/System path and then select the System Restore option from the Properties tab.

   ○ **C.** Navigate to the Start menu's Help and Support option, select the Performance and Maintenance option from its menu, and click on the Run the System Restore Wizard option.

   ○ **D.** Navigate to the Start menu's Accessories menu option, select the Performance and Maintenance option from its menu, and click on the Run the System Restore Wizard option.

4. Which of the following information cannot be obtained using the Windows XP System Information utility?

   ○ **A.** System summary

   ○ **B.** Group Policy settings

   ○ **C.** I/O components in the system

   ○ **D.** A description of the Windows Internet Explorer

5. What does the exclamation point (!) inside a yellow field mean when used by the Windows Device Manager?

   ○ **A.** It indicates expandable and collapsible information branches.

   ○ **B.** The device is experiencing a direct hardware conflict with another device.

   ○ **C.** The device has been disabled due to a user selection.

   ○ **D.** The device is not installed properly.

6. A coworker has a driver that failed during a Windows 2000 startup, and he needs to know which Event Viewer log he should look in. Which log holds this information?

- ○ **A.** System
- ○ **B.** Application
- ○ **C.** Security
- ○ **D.** Failed Audit

Quick Answer: **282**
Detailed Answer: **295**

7. Which of the following is not a function of the Emergency Repair Process in Windows 2000? (Select two correct answers.)

- ○ **A.** Repairing the disk drive's boot sector
- ○ **B.** Repairing the system's startup files
- ○ **C.** Repairing corrupted data files
- ○ **D.** Repairing failed applications

Quick Answer: **282**
Detailed Answer: **295**

8. The _____ in Windows 2000 and Windows XP can be used to remove nonfunctioning applications from the system.

- ○ **A.** Close Program tool
- ○ **B.** Task Manager tool
- ○ **C.** Close Application tool
- ○ **D.** Computer Management tool

Quick Answer: **282**
Detailed Answer: **295**

9. The old Last Known Good Hardware Configuration settings are not replaced until _____.

- ○ **A.** A user logs on to the system
- ○ **B.** A user shuts down the operating system
- ○ **C.** A user boots the operating system
- ○ **D.** A user logs off the system

Quick Answer: **282**
Detailed Answer: **295**

10. After the system has successfully completed the POST, you see an error message saying NTLDR is missing. What type of problem is this?

- ○ **A.** Operational problem
- ○ **B.** Configuration problem
- ○ **C.** Hardware problem
- ○ **D.** Bootup problem

Quick Answer: **282**
Detailed Answer: **296**

11. The Windows Recovery Console does all the following except
_____.

   ○ **A.** copy files

   ○ **B.** control startup of services

   ○ **C.** format volumes

   ○ **D.** uninstall programs

12. After you add a new software application to your Windows XP PC,
it refuses to restart. You get a message that a DLL file has been
corrupted. What can you do to troubleshoot this problem?

   ○ **A.** Start the system in Safe Mode and use the Dr. Watson
utility to identify the failing DLL so that it can be
removed.

   ○ **B.** Start the system in Safe Mode and access the
`%SystemRoot%\Windows\system32\`
`dllcache` folder to copy the correct files into the
`%SystemRoot%\system32` directory.

   ○ **C.** Boot to the Windows distribution CD and reinstall
Windows.

   ○ **D.** Use the SFC utility to extract the original correct
versions of the files from Windows files.

13. A customer has asked you to troubleshoot her Windows XP Home
system. The system tries to boot, but you receive a `Missing`
`NTLDR` error message. You want to start the system in Safe
Mode. What of the following items don't load during a Windows
XP Home Safe Mode startup? (Select all that apply.)

   ○ **A.** Mouse

   ○ **B.** Network adapter

   ○ **C.** Hard drive

   ○ **D.** Printer

14. You are setting up a small help desk operation for your company
and need to configure Remote Assistance for the employees
involved in the new operation. Which group can run the Remote
Assistance function?

   ○ **A.** The Administrators group

   ○ **B.** The RemoteAssistance group

   ○ **C.** The Power Users group

   ○ **D.** The HelpAssistant group

Quick Check

15. You have been called to troubleshoot a desktop PC system that produces frequent, intermittent shutdowns, produces blue screen errors, and makes loud clicking sounds. What is the cause of these problems?

Quick Answer: **282**
Detailed Answer: **296**

- ○ **A.** The microprocessor is failing.
- ○ **B.** The hard disk drive is failing.
- ○ **C.** The microprocessor cooling system is failing.
- ○ **D.** The power supply fan is failing.

16. A user on your network has complained that he cannot access a mapped drive on a PC that is located several floors above where he is working, but he can access mapped drives on other machines in the building. The users tells you that he has successfully connected to that machine before today. When you examine the system, you see a red X beside the drive icon. Which of the following could cause this problem? (Select all that apply.)

Quick Answer: **282**
Detailed Answer: **296**

- ○ **A.** The drive map link has expired.
- ○ **B.** The permissions level for the mapped drive has been changed by an administrator.
- ○ **C.** The router for that segment of the network has failed.
- ○ **D.** The machine containing the mapped drive is turned off.

17. You have installed a new widescreen plasma display as the output device for your Windows XP Media Center Edition (MCE). Next, you install a wireless mouse so that you can get far enough away from the large screen to be comfortable. However, after you install the new mouse driver, it stops working. What do you need to do to get the Windows XP MCE system back to an operational level?

Quick Answer: **282**
Detailed Answer: **296**

- ○ **A.** Try the mouse receiver in the other USB port connection.
- ○ **B.** Run the Device Manager's Driver Rollback operation to load the previous driver.
- ○ **C.** Start the system in Safe Mode and remove the `mouse.dll` driver file. Then restart the system so that it can detect and install the new driver.
- ○ **D.** You are out of range. Move the mouse closer to the screen and PC.

18. A user reports that she can't print to her local inkjet printer; no paper comes out and nothing is printed. When you examine the Printers and Faxes page of the Windows XP system, you see that only an HP Laser 1100 printer is showing on the page. What is the most likely cause of this problem?

   ○ **A.** The printer is not installed in the system.

   ○ **B.** The print spooler has been disabled on the system.

   ○ **C.** The wrong printer driver has been installed in the system.

   ○ **D.** The default printer setting has been set incorrectly on the printer.

19. Which Windows XP utility would you use to replace a single Registry key?

   ○ **A.** RegEdit

   ○ **B.** Device Manager

   ○ **C.** Add New Hardware Wizard

   ○ **D.** MSCONFIG

20. After installing a new application on a customer's PC, you receive a .dll file error message. You run the SFC utility from the command prompt but still receive the corrupted file system error messages. What should you do next to correct his problem?

   ○ **A.** Run SFC with the /scanboot switch.

   ○ **B.** Run SFC with the /revert switch.

   ○ **C.** Run SFC with the /scannow switch.

   ○ **D.** Run SFC with the /purgecache switch.

21. One of your technicians has called to let you know that he is trying to initiate a Remote Assistance request with you so that you can help him troubleshoot a problem with a remotely located PC. However, he has no email service on the remote machine. If this employee cannot email you, how else can he initiate a Remote Assistance request with you?

   ○ **A.** Use an FTP service to send the Remote Assistance request.

   ○ **B.** Use Telnet to conduct the Remote Assistance session.

   ○ **C.** Use Windows Messenger to send the Remote Assistance request.

   ○ **D.** Use the Microsoft Updates site to forward the request over the Internet.

22. A user accidentally erased the `PAGEFILE.SYS` file from her Windows XP Professional system. How can she recover it?

Quick Answer: **282**
Detailed Answer: **297**

- ○ **A.** Place the Windows XP distribution CD in the drive and run the Recovery Console to restore the swap file.
- ○ **B.** You must send the user a copy of a `PAGEFILE.SYS` file from a similar PC.
- ○ **C.** The user can download a replacement `PAGEFILE.SYS` file from the Windows Update service.
- ○ **D.** The `PAGEFILE.SYS` file will be regenerated automatically when Windows starts up.

23. You have installed a new application and want to give all the network users access to it. When the users log in to the network, they can't find the new application. What do you need to do to provide the users with access to this application?

Quick Answer: **282**
Detailed Answer: **297**

- ○ **A.** Move the application's shortcut to the All Users folder.
- ○ **B.** Create a new group, place all the employees in the group, and then grant them all access to the application's setup files through the group membership.
- ○ **C.** Assign the Everyone group access permissions to the application's setup files.
- ○ **D.** Assign the Guest account access permissions to the application's setup files.

24. After you update a driver for your SCSI boot drive, the system doesn't start up to the desktop. After removing the driver and allowing Windows to install a driver, you still can't get the system to boot. What options do you have left for repairing this problem?

Quick Answer: **282**
Detailed Answer: **297**

- ○ **A.** Run the `SFC/SCANNOW` option to repair the corrupted driver.
- ○ **B.** Start the system in Safe Mode and use the `Extract` command from the command prompt to extract the SCSI drivers from the Windows distribution CD.
- ○ **C.** Run System Restore and select a Restore Point from before the driver update was made.
- ○ **D.** Run Windows Update Service to download the latest service packs and patches for the operating system.

25. Which Windows utility can be used to verify the integrity of the Windows XP operating system files?

   ○ **A.** SFC

   ○ **B.** CHKDSK

   ○ **C.** Dr. Watson

   ○ **D.** MSCONFIG

Quick Answer: **282**
Detailed Answer: **297**

26. Who can request a Remote Assistance session?

   ○ **A.** The network administrator

   ○ **B.** The local user

   ○ **C.** The local technician

   ○ **D.** The remote technician

Quick Answer: **282**
Detailed Answer: **298**

27. You are called to a site where the user complains that he cannot access the network on his machine, which has just been upgraded to Windows XP Professional. When you arrive, you instantly notice that the My Network Places icon is missing from the desktop. Which of the following is the most likely cause of this condition?

   ○ **A.** No network drivers were installed during the Windows XP installation process.

   ○ **B.** There is no problem; you simply need to run the Windows XP Connection Wizard from the Control Panel.

   ○ **C.** The computer is not networked.

   ○ **D.** The icon has been dropped in the Recycle Bin by mistake and should be retrieved.

Quick Answer: **282**
Detailed Answer: **298**

Objective 2.4: Perform preventative maintenance for operating systems

1. You have just completed a new installation of Windows XP on a client's PC and want to download the latest updates from the Windows Update service. When you attempt to perform this operation, you can get to the Internet but cannot get the Windows Update service to run. Why might this be? (Select all that apply.)

   ○ **A.** The Windows XP Security setting is set to High by default and needs to be adjusted in the Control Panel's Security Center.

   ○ **B.** The Windows Firewall is configured to stop all traffic until it is reconfigured for use.

   ○ **C.** You do not have sufficient permission levels to run the Windows Update service.

   ○ **D.** The operating system has not been activated yet.

Quick Answer: **282**
Detailed Answer: **298**

2. Which of the following is a valid reason for running Windows Update?

   ○ **A.** To obtain the latest operating system release

   ○ **B.** To download the latest antivirus signatures

   ○ **C.** To download the latest security updates and patches

   ○ **D.** To download the latest application links

Quick Answer: **282**
Detailed Answer: **298**

3. What types of files can be downloaded from the Windows Update service? (Select all that apply.)

   ○ **A.** Internet protocol files

   ○ **B.** Critical files

   ○ **C.** Security files

   ○ **D.** Windows application files

Quick Answer: **282**
Detailed Answer: **298**

4. How do you configure the Automatic Updates feature for Windows 2000?

   ○ **A.** Use the Add Components utility to add the Automatic Updates feature to the system.

   ○ **B.** Double-click on Automatic Updates in the Control Panel and then click on Automatic.

   ○ **C.** Use the Add/Remove Programs utility to install the Windows Automatic Updates utility.

   ○ **D.** Access the Microsoft Windows Update web page and click on the Automatic Updates option.

Quick Answer: **282**
Detailed Answer: **298**

Domain 3.0: Printers and Scanners

Objective 3.1: Identify the fundamental principles of using printers and scanners

1. What printer type produces print by squirting ink at the page?

   ○ **A.** Laser

   ○ **B.** Thermal

   ○ **C.** Inkjet

   ○ **D.** Dot matrix

Quick Answer: **282**
Detailed Answer: **299**

2. Which of the following printers can produce photographic-quality, continuous-tone images?

   ○ **A.** Dot matrix printer

   ○ **B.** Dye sublimation printer

   ○ **C.** Direct thermal printer

   ○ **D.** Thermal wax transfer printer

Quick Answer: **282**
Detailed Answer: **299**

3. What type of printer uses small heated pins to transfer multicolor images onto the paper?

   ○ **A.** Dye sublimation printer

   ○ **B.** Thermal wax printer

   ○ **C.** Solid ink printer

   ○ **D.** Thermal autochrome printer

Quick Answer: **282**
Detailed Answer: **299**

4. Which of the following printer types requires special paper?

   ○ **A.** Laser

   ○ **B.** Thermal

   ○ **C.** Dot matrix

   ○ **D.** Inkjet

Quick Answer: **282**
Detailed Answer: **299**

5. You have been asked to install a new desktop PC in a customer's front office. A laser printer was attached to the parallel port of the old computer and is supposed to be moved up to the new system. However, no one can find the old signal cable. What type of cable must you get to connect the old printer to the new PC?

- ○ **A.** RS-485
- ○ **B.** IEEE-1394
- ○ **C.** IEEE-1284
- ○ **D.** HDMI

6. In a laser printer, a thermal fuse is used to prevent _____.

- ○ **A.** heat-sink failure
- ○ **B.** a fuser from overheating
- ○ **C.** a high-voltage power supply from overheating
- ○ **D.** a low-voltage power supply from overheating

7. What is the major purpose of a tractor-feed mechanism, and where is it most commonly used?

- ○ **A.** It is used on color laser printers that handle single sheet forms.
- ○ **B.** It is used on inkjet printers that handle multipart forms.
- ○ **C.** It is used on laser printers that handle continuous, multipart forms.
- ○ **D.** It is used on dot matrix printers that handle continuous, multipart forms.

8. The primary corona wire (conditioning roller) of a laser printer _____.

- ○ **A.** transfers toner to the paper
- ○ **B.** applies a uniform negative charge to the drum
- ○ **C.** presses toner into the paper
- ○ **D.** transfers characters to the paper

Objective 3.2: Install, configure, optimize, and upgrade printers and scanners

1. What is the recommended clear distance and the maximum angle specified for IrDA printer connections?

    ○ **A.** 3 meters, 45°

    ○ **B.** 2 meters, 30°

    ○ **C.** 1 meter, 15°

    ○ **D.** 4 meters, 60°

Quick Answer: **283**
Detailed Answer: **299**

2. How do you increase the density of a printout from an inkjet printer?

    ○ **A.** Mark everything on the page for boldface when creating it.

    ○ **B.** Print the page twice to double the amount of ink applied to the paper.

    ○ **C.** Use a thicker type of ink.

    ○ **D.** Adjust it in the printing software.

Quick Answer: **283**
Detailed Answer: **299**

3. A customer has purchased a new scanner and found that the USB cable from her old scanner cannot be plugged into the new scanner. What should you tell her to do? (Select all that apply.)

    ○ **A.** Return the scanner to the place of purchase and exchange it for one with an interface type she can use.

    ○ **B.** Consult the new scanner's documentation for other interface type options.

    ○ **C.** Send the scanner back to the original manufacturer for credit.

    ○ **D.** Get a USB cable for the scanner that will work with the PC system.

Quick Answer: **283**
Detailed Answer: **299**

4. What is it called when you adjust the color settings of a monitor, printer, and scanner to a standard?

    ○ **A.** Registration

    ○ **B.** Calibration

    ○ **C.** Cross-referencing

    ○ **D.** Color management

Quick Answer: **283**
Detailed Answer: **300**

5. After installing a new web camera on your PC, you decide to remove it. Now, when you try to scan pictures using one of your graphic design applications, the scanner's light comes on, but you only get an error message. What is the most likely cause of this problem?

- ○ **A.** The scanner's light positioning mechanism is locked.
- ○ **B.** The application has not been configured correctly for the scanner model being used.
- ○ **C.** The scanner has not been configured correctly for the application trying to use it.
- ○ **D.** The scanner's TWAIN drivers are corrupted.

6. Which interface is widely used to connect a variety of wireless devices to wireless printers?

- ○ **A.** Bluetooth
- ○ **B.** IrDA
- ○ **C.** 802.11x
- ○ **D.** USB

7. What is the last step in installing a new laser printer at a customer's office?

- ○ **A.** Run a test page from the printer.
- ○ **B.** Reboot the computer.
- ○ **C.** Run a test page from the host computer.
- ○ **D.** Reset the printer's page counter.

8. One of your customers wants to be able to print on both sides of his paper. What can you tell him about setting up this type of printing operation?

- ○ **A.** He should enable the Duplex Printing option in the printer's Properties page.
- ○ **B.** He may need to download special duplexing software for his printer model.
- ○ **C.** His printer may not be able to physically perform duplex printing operations.
- ○ **D.** He must install duplex printer drivers using the Device Manager's Update Driver function.

9. You have just installed a service kit in a customer's laser printer as part of a regularly scheduled maintenance plan. What is the last step you should perform before leaving the customer's office?

○ **A.** Run a test page from the host computer.

○ **B.** Reboot the computer.

○ **C.** Reset the printer's page counter.

○ **D.** Give the customer the bill.

Quick Answer: **283**
Detailed Answer: **300**

Objective 3.3: Identify tools, diagnostic procedures, and troubleshooting techniques for printers and scanners

1. What is a common reason for not seeing a remote printer in Windows XP's Printers and Faxes page?

○ **A.** File and printer sharing is not enabled on the remote host.

○ **B.** Inadequate permissions have been established.

○ **C.** An improper printer name has been entered in the path.

○ **D.** No printer driver is loaded.

Quick Answer: **283**
Detailed Answer: **301**

2. You receive a document from your laser printer that has random sections of missing print. What laser printer component is typically associated with this type of symptom?

○ **A.** The laser-scanning module

○ **B.** The drum

○ **C.** The transfer corona wire

○ **D.** The fuser's compression roller

Quick Answer: **283**
Detailed Answer: **301**

3. Which of the following actions would correct the problem in which the tops of characters are missing from the print output by a dot matrix printer? (Select all that apply.)

○ **A.** The carriage assembly might need to be adjusted to the proper height and angle.

○ **B.** Reseat the printhead in the printhead carriage.

○ **C.** Reseat the platen.

○ **D.** Reverse the ink ribbon.

Quick Answer: **283**
Detailed Answer: **301**

4. You are troubleshooting a printing problem with your production room's dye sublimation printer. When you examine the print queue of the local printer, you see three files in print queue and nothing is coming out of the printer. What is first step you should take to correct this problem?

   ○ **A.** Cycle the printer's power on and off until the jam clears.

   ○ **B.** Right-click on the Printer's icon, click on Properties, and then select Details. From this point, select Spool Settings and select the Print Directly to the Printer option to bypass the spooler to get out your print job.

   ○ **C.** Delete all the files from the print spooler queue and resend your print job to the printer.

   ○ **D.** Double-click on the printer's icon and select the Restart option from the Documents menu.

5. What is the first step you should take if your laser printer is producing faint print?

   ○ **A.** Replace the toner cartridge.

   ○ **B.** Adjust the laser alignment.

   ○ **C.** Adjust the printer contrast control setting.

   ○ **D.** Remove the toner cartridge, inspect it, and gently shake it.

6. You have been called to an advertising firm that has a new flatbed scanner that does not scan. When you test it, the scanning light is on, but it does not move across the page. Which of the following is the most likely cause of the problem?

   ○ **A.** The resolution setting of the scanning software is not compatible with the size of the picture being scanned.

   ○ **B.** The picture being scanned is too big for the resolution setting and memory available in the host system.

   ○ **C.** The scanner's light positioning mechanism is locked.

   ○ **D.** The scanner's signal cable is faulty.

7. You install new ink cartridges in an inkjet printer. Afterward it does not print anything. What should you do now? (Select all that apply.)

   ○ **A.** Remove and reinstall the cartridges so that they seat properly.

   ○ **B.** Remove the tape covering from the cartridges' print nozzles.

   ○ **C.** Restart the printer so that it will detect the new cartridges.

   ○ **D.** Reboot the PC so that it will clear the error message it received from the printer.

8. What type of output is generated by a dot matrix printer when the paper advance mechanism does not work?

   ○ **A.** A black page

   ○ **B.** One or more dark lines running down the page

   ○ **C.** One dark line across the page

   ○ **D.** A blank page

9. What types of problems can cause smudged or disfigured print in an inkjet printer? (Select all that apply.)

   ○ **A.** Misaligned platen

   ○ **B.** Worn-out paper-feed rollers

   ○ **C.** Improperly set paper thickness selector

   ○ **D.** Worn-out ribbon

10. If you have cleared a paper jam from a laser printer, but the printer still indicates that a jam is present, what action should you take first?

    ○ **A.** Remove the paper tray from the printer.

    ○ **B.** Open and close the main access cover to clear any interlock errors.

    ○ **C.** Open the unit to check for additional bits of paper that may have been left behind.

    ○ **D.** Press the Clear button to reset the machine.

11. You receive a page from your laser printer that is completely black. Which of the following components is most likely to be involved in this type of problem?

Quick Answer: **283**
Detailed Answer: **302**

- ○ **A.** The drum is bad.
- ○ **B.** The fuser's compression roller is always on.
- ○ **C.** The primary corona wire has failed.
- ○ **D.** The transfer corona wire is bad.

12. What causes the printout from a dot matrix printer to get lighter from left to right?

Quick Answer: **283**
Detailed Answer: **302**

- ○ **A.** Wrong spacing between the platen and printhead carriage rod
- ○ **B.** Bad printhead
- ○ **C.** Bad ribbon
- ○ **D.** Bad toner cartridge

13. Where are paper jams likely to occur in a laser printer? (Select all that apply.)

Quick Answer: **283**
Detailed Answer: **302**

- ○ **A.** Pickup area
- ○ **B.** Registration area
- ○ **C.** Fusing area
- ○ **D.** Control area

Domain 4.0: Networks

Objective 4.1: Identify the fundamental principles of networks

1. Windows XP Home includes what type of networking as its default?

   ○ **A.** Peer-to-peer

   ○ **B.** Client/server

   ○ **C.** Wireless

   ○ **D.** Ethernet

Quick Answer: **283**
Detailed Answer: **303**

2. Anonymous authentication is used for which type of Internet service?

   ○ **A.** Web server

   ○ **B.** Print server

   ○ **C.** FTP server

   ○ **D.** Secure server

Quick Answer: **283**
Detailed Answer: **303**

3. How can you identify when an Internet website is using the Transport Layer Security or Secure Sockets Layer protocols?

   ○ **A.** Its address starts with FTP.

   ○ **B.** Its address starts with HTTPS.

   ○ **C.** Its address ends with SSL.

   ○ **D.** Its address starts with www.

Quick Answer: **283**
Detailed Answer: **303**

4. What feature do all members of a domain share?

   ○ **A.** A security database

   ○ **B.** Client licenses

   ○ **C.** A printer

   ○ **D.** Applications

Quick Answer: **283**
Detailed Answer: **303**

5. Which of the following is a valid APIPA address?

   ○ **A.** 169.254.0.1 with a subnet mask of 255.255.0.0

   ○ **B.** 10.0.0.1 with a subnet mask of 255.0.0.0

   ○ **C.** 127.0.0.1 with a subnet mask of 255.0.0.0

   ○ **D.** 192.0.0.1 with a subnet mask of 255.255.255.0

Quick Answer: **283**
Detailed Answer: **303**

6. A customer is setting up a small home office network, and he is calling you from a consumer electronics store. The store offers both hubs and switches for basic network connectivity. What should you tell the customer about the major difference between network hubs and switches?

Quick Answer: **283**
Detailed Answer: **303**

- ○ **A.** Switches provide link ports for connecting to the Internet.

- ○ **B.** Switches possess more built-in intelligence than hubs do.

- ○ **C.** These connectivity devices are designed to serve different physical topologies.

- ○ **D.** Hubs have the capability to direct packets to the correct network segment using MAC addresses.

7. Which of the following are legitimate parts of a fully qualified domain name? (Select all that apply.)

Quick Answer: **283**
Detailed Answer: **303**

- ○ **A.** Protocol type
- ○ **B.** Hostname
- ○ **C.** Destination address
- ○ **D.** Domain name

8. Which of the following encryption protocols can be used for 802.11g wireless networking? (Select all that apply.)

Quick Answer: **283**
Detailed Answer: **303**

- ○ **A.** WEP
- ○ **B.** SSID
- ○ **C.** WPA2
- ○ **D.** MS-CHAP

9. Which of the following statements are true concerning Telnet?

Quick Answer: **283**
Detailed Answer: **303**

- ○ **A.** It runs in a pop-up window on the remote PC.
- ○ **B.** It sends encrypted data across the connection.
- ○ **C.** It allows others to gain control of your PC.
- ○ **D.** It allows you to use the resources of computers running other operating systems.

10. What does the DNS service do for PCs and other networking equipment connected to the Internet?

Quick Answer: **283**
Detailed Answer: **304**

- ○ **A.** It resolves last names to IP addresses.
- ○ **B.** It resolves user names to IP addresses.
- ○ **C.** It resolves computer names to IP addresses.
- ○ **D.** It resolves host names to IP addresses.

11. What function does the LDAP protocol provide for Windows network users?

Quick Answer: **283**
Detailed Answer: **304**

- ○ **A.** It safeguards communication in a virtual private network.
- ○ **B.** It is the standard protocol for Windows Active Directory clients to search the network for information such as the location of a remote printer or someone's email address.
- ○ **C.** It encrypts data fro transmissions between Internet hosts.
- ○ **D.** It provides access protection for Windows network environments.

12. Which security protocol is associated with HTTPS sites?

Quick Answer: **283**
Detailed Answer: **304**

- ○ **A.** WPA2
- ○ **B.** TSL/SSL
- ○ **C.** LDAP
- ○ **D.** VPN

13. Which of the following protocols is traditionally used to upload and download files to and from the Internet?

Quick Answer: **283**
Detailed Answer: **304**

- ○ **A.** HTTP
- ○ **B.** Telnet
- ○ **C.** FTP
- ○ **D.** HTTPS

14. Which of the following protocols is normally used to access a World Wide Web server?

Quick Answer: **283**
Detailed Answer: **304**

- ○ **A.** HTTP
- ○ **B.** FTP
- ○ **C.** Gopher
- ○ **D.** NTFS

15. What is the maximum transmission speed on a residential ISDN service?

    O **A.** 256kbps

    O **B.** 128kbps

    O **C.** 66kbps

    O **D.** 33kbps

16. An intranet is _____ network, typically established by an organization for the purpose of running an exclusive site not open to the public.

    O **A.** a local area

    O **B.** an extranet

    O **C.** a wide area

    O **D.** a TCP/IP-based

Objective 4.2: Install, configure, optimize, and upgrade networks

1. Where would you go in a Windows 2000 system to establish parameters for local and wide area networking?

    O **A.** The Network Neighborhood icon

    O **B.** The Network and Dial-Up Connections option

    O **C.** The Network Manager icon

    O **D.** The Network Control Panel

2. You have purchased a new copy of Windows XP because you want to use its Internet Connection Sharing (ICS) feature to provide a central Internet connection for your home computer network. Where is the ICS feature located in Windows XP?

Quick Answer: **283**
Detailed Answer: **305**

○ **A.** Access Network Connections, select the connection to be shared, and then select the Change Settings of This Connection option from the Network Tasks pane. On the Advanced tab, enable the Allow Other Network Users to Connect Through This Computer's Internet Connection setting.

○ **B.** Click on Start/Settings and select the Network and Dial-Up Connections option. Right-click on the connection to be shared and then select the Properties option from the pop-up menu. Under the Internet Connection Sharing tab, select the Enable Internet Connection Sharing for This Connection check box.

○ **C.** Click on Start/Local Network Connections. Right-click on the connection to be shared and then select the Properties option from the pop-up menu. Under the Internet Connection Sharing tab, select the Enable Internet Connection Sharing for This Connection check box.

○ **D.** Click on the Internet icon in the Control Panel, select the Internet Connection Sharing option from the menu, and designate the computers to provide connection sharing with.

3. If a shared file is located on another computer in your network and you need to access it, what method should you employ to specify the path to this file?

Quick Answer: **283**
Detailed Answer: **305**

○ **A.** Use the UNC convention.

○ **B.** Use the URL entry.

○ **C.** Use the `Path` command.

○ **D.** Use the IE interface to connect to it.

4. You are installing a new network for a company. It recently acquired workstations with the Windows XP Professional operating system and has a hub and DSL modem. Due to costs, the company does not want to pay for a new server or router but would still like to have the Internet available to all workstations. It would therefore be willing to pay for extra cabling and network interface card costs. Which of the following is the best solution for this scenario?

- ○ **A.** Establish ICS.
- ○ **B.** Employ VMM.
- ○ **C.** Install a LAN adapter.
- ○ **D.** Activate ACL.

5. Which of the following does an 802.11a access point use for authentication?

- ○ **A.** The SSID
- ○ **B.** An encryption key
- ○ **C.** The antenna type
- ○ **D.** A channel setting

6. You are trying to set up security on a small wireless office network. This 802.11g wireless AP/router has an option to implement WEP. Which of the following items are required to configure the AP/router and set up encryption? (Select all that apply.)

- ○ **A.** The SSID name
- ○ **B.** An encryption key
- ○ **C.** The antenna type
- ○ **D.** A channel setting

7. You are setting up a wireless network, in a large factory building, which requires multiple access points to provide complete coverage. Which of the following items must be configured to provide wireless users access to the network throughout the building? (Select all that apply.)

- ○ **A.** A unique SSID on each AP
- ○ **B.** A universal SSID on all APs
- ○ **C.** A universal channel setting on all APs
- ○ **D.** A unique channel setting on each AP

8. What tool is typically used to configure an 802.11x wireless access point?

Quick Answer: **283**
Detailed Answer: **306**

- ○ **A.** The Windows Network Monitor utility
- ○ **B.** A web browser
- ○ **C.** A floppy disk
- ○ **D.** An OTDR

26. What is the maximum distance that an 802.11b-rated wireless network card should be located away from its designated access point?

Quick Answer: **283**
Detailed Answer: **306**

- ○ **A.** 1 mile
- ○ **B.** Less than 110 feet
- ○ **C.** Less than 500 feet
- ○ **D.** Up to 5 miles

10. In networking terms, a hot spot is _____.

Quick Answer: **283**
Detailed Answer: **306**

- ○ **A.** a communication zone where wireless connectivity can be established
- ○ **B.** an electrically active zone where wireless transmissions can experience interference
- ○ **C.** an electrically active zone where wireless connectivity is excellent
- ○ **D.** a wireless network access zone set up by businesses to enable portable wireless units to access the Internet

11. Which of the following pieces of configuration information is not typically needed to configure an account in an email application?

Quick Answer: **283**
Detailed Answer: **306**

- ○ **A.** DNS server name or IP address
- ○ **B.** Email account name
- ○ **C.** SMTP server name or IP address
- ○ **D.** POP3/IMAP server name or IP address

12. What type of cabling is associated with the CAT5/5e cable rating?

Quick Answer: **283**
Detailed Answer: **306**

- ○ **A.** UTP
- ○ **B.** Thin coaxial
- ○ **C.** STP
- ○ **D.** Thick coaxial

13. Which of the following protocols was designed for use with a Novell network?

- ○ **A.** TCP/IP
- ○ **B.** IrLAN
- ○ **C.** IPX/SPX
- ○ **D.** NetBEUI

Objective 4.3: Identify tools, diagnostic procedures, and troubleshooting techniques for networks

1. Which Windows tools are employed to administer and troubleshoot network-related problems?

- ○ **A.** TCP/IP utilities
- ○ **B.** DHCP utilities
- ○ **C.** DNS utilities
- ○ **D.** WINS utilities

2. When you attempt to access another computer on the network, you can't see any folders or directories. What is most likely to be the cause of this problem?

- ○ **A.** Your computer has a missing or corrupted network protocol.
- ○ **B.** Your computer needs a network adapter.
- ○ **C.** The other computer is password protected.
- ○ **D.** The other computer has no shared drives or folders.

3. After you install a new local area network adapter card and attach it to the local switch, you cannot access or see any other computers on the network. What item should you most likely check first?

- ○ **A.** The cabling between the NIC and the switch
- ○ **B.** The switch
- ○ **C.** The NIC
- ○ **D.** The NIC's drivers

4. After you install a new system, it appears that the customer's network connection is down. What action can you take to run a local loopback test to verify the TCP/IP installation's integrity?

◯ **A.** Run the TRACERT /t command from the command prompt.

◯ **B.** Run the PING 127.0.0.1 command from the command prompt.

◯ **C.** Run the NBSTAT /t command from the command prompt.

◯ **D.** Run the ARP 127.0.0.1 command from the command prompt.

5. Which Windows XP TCP/IP utility would you use to identify all the connections between source and destination computers?

◯ **A.** ARP

◯ **B.** PING

◯ **C.** NETSTAT

◯ **D.** TRACERT

6. The computer you are working on is able to contact other systems in the local network using TCP/IP. However, it is unable to contact other systems outside the local network. What is the most likely cause of this problem?

◯ **A.** There is an IP addressing conflict.

◯ **B.** The default gateway is not configured properly.

◯ **C.** The DNS service is not configured properly.

◯ **D.** The DHCP service is not configured properly.

7. What two well-known TCP ports are associated with FTP functions?

◯ **A.** 20

◯ **B.** 21

◯ **C.** 25

◯ **D.** 80

8. You have multiple WAPs, and you think you are losing bandwidth because outside users are sharing your wireless connection. What can you do to ensure that no one else is using your wireless network connection? (Select all that apply.)

   ◯ **A.** Turn off SSID broadcasts.

   ◯ **B.** Move the WAPs away from the outside walls of the residence.

   ◯ **C.** Set up WEP with a strong encryption key.

   ◯ **D.** Install a shielded antenna.

9. After setting up a new Windows XP computer on the network, you run IPCONFIG /ALL. The results show that you have an IP address of 169.254.0.1, along with a subnet mask of 255.255.0.0. What utility can you use to find this address?

   ◯ **A.** The NSLOOKUP server is not available.

   ◯ **B.** Nothing is wrong; you have a valid Class B IP address configuration.

   ◯ **C.** The DNS server is not working.

   ◯ **D.** The DHCP server is not working.

10. You have a new workstation with a known valid IP address, but it cannot browse the network. What utility can you use to check connectivity to a nearby computer?

   ◯ **A.** ARP

   ◯ **B.** IPCONFIG

   ◯ **C.** NETSTAT

   ◯ **D.** PING

11. You are performing a site survey for a customer, and you need to determine where to place desks to provide the best performance over the wireless network. Which Windows XP utility can you use to monitor the performance of the wireless network throughout the customer's facility?

   ◯ **A.** Performance Logs and Alerts

   ◯ **B.** The Windows Wireless Network Connection Status dialog box

   ◯ **C.** The Network Monitor utility

   ◯ **D.** The Task Manager utility

12. When you start your networked computer, you receive a
Duplicate IP address error message. What action should
you take to remove this error?

Quick Answer: 284
Detailed Answer: 307

  ◯ **A.** Run IPCONFIG/Relinquish from the
command prompt.

  ◯ **B.** Run IPCONFIG/Renew from the command prompt.

  ◯ **C.** Run IPCONFIG/ALL from the command prompt.

  ◯ **D.** Run NSLOOKUP/release from the command
prompt.

13. You are troubleshooting a network performance problem on a
customer's network. The network is already running very slowly,
so you want to add as little traffic to the network as possible.
Which of the following TCP/IP utilities would you employ to check
the network while using the least network bandwidth?

Quick Answer: 284
Detailed Answer: 307

  ◯ **A.** Ping the gateway address.

  ◯ **B.** Ping the loopback address.

  ◯ **C.** Run the TRACERT utility.

  ◯ **D.** Run the IPCONFIG /ALL utility.

14. One of the users on your network cannot access or see any other
computers on the network. Other users on other network seg-
ments are not having this problem. Which of the following items
should you check first in troubleshooting this problem?

Quick Answer: 284
Detailed Answer: 307

  ◯ **A.** The activity lights on the user's network adapter card

  ◯ **B.** The router that the user's PC is connected to

  ◯ **C.** The network cable connection to the user's network
adapter

  ◯ **D.** The user's network adapter drivers

15. A building contractor has contacted you for information about
how to secure a residential network he is putting in a new home.
He needs to know the difference between using a software-based
firewall to protect the network and using a hardware-based firewall. What are the differences between hardware and software
firewalls? (Select all that apply.)

Quick Answer: 284
Detailed Answer: 307

  ◯ **A.** A hardware firewall typically offers higher levels of
protection than a software firewall.

  ◯ **B.** A software firewall protects only the machine it is
installed on.

  ◯ **C.** A hardware firewall protects only the machine it is
installed on.

  ◯ **D.** A software firewall typically offers greater performance
than a hardware firewall.

16. Which well-known TCP port is reserved for HTTP traffic?

- ○ **A.** 23
- ○ **B.** 25
- ○ **C.** 80
- ○ **D.** 443

17. One of your network users cannot see a WINS server on the network, but he can see other servers on the network. What is the most likely cause of this problem?

- ○ **A.** The DNS server is not working.
- ○ **B.** The DHCP server is not working.
- ○ **C.** The WINS server is not working.
- ○ **D.** The NSLOOKUP server is not available.

18. Which two TCP/IP utilities display the address of a known remote location?

- ○ **A.** PING
- ○ **B.** NETSTAT
- ○ **C.** IPCONFIG
- ○ **D.** NSLOOKUP

19. Which of the following causes a mapped drive to disappear from a system when it is shut down and restarted?

- ○ **A.** The Reconnect at Login option was not checked when the drive was mapped.
- ○ **B.** The name of the mapped folder has been changed.
- ○ **C.** The path to the mapped folder has changed.
- ○ **D.** The host computer for the mapped folder is turned off.

20. When you are trying to diagnose the cause of networking problems, where do you enter commands to run TCP/IP troubleshooting utilities?

- ○ **A.** At the command prompt
- ○ **B.** On the TCP/IP Properties window
- ○ **C.** In the dialog box that appears when you double-click on the file `tcpip.com`
- ○ **D.** From the dialog box in the Network Neighborhood Control Panel

21. Which TCP/IP utility can you use to release and renew IP address information from a DHCP server?

    ○ **A.** IPCONFIG

    ○ **B.** TRACERT

    ○ **C.** PING

    ○ **D.** NETSTAT

22. One of your users cannot log in to the network. However, other users do not have a problem connecting to the network. Which of the following items should you check first?

    ○ **A.** Check to see if the CapsLock function is engaged.

    ○ **B.** Check the network cable between the user's PC and the local connectivity device.

    ○ **C.** Check the user account information on the local server to make sure that the user's account is still valid.

    ○ **D.** Check the network switch the user is connected to.

Domain 5.0: Security

Objective 5.1: Identify the fundamental principles of security

1. A user can look at the contents of a folder in Windows 2000 but cannot open the files or rename them. What permission does this user have enabled?

   ○ **A.** Read

   ○ **B.** List Folder Contents

   ○ **C.** Read & Execute

   ○ **D.** Modify

Quick Answer: **284**
Detailed Answer: **309**

2. If you move a shared folder with limited rights to a FAT32 partition, what are the effects on folder protection?

   ○ **A.** The permissions follow the folder to the new partition.

   ○ **B.** The permissions for the folder are reduced to Read and Write Only.

   ○ **C.** The folder inherits the permissions set on the partition it is being moved to.

   ○ **D.** The established permissions cannot follow the folder to a FAT32 partition.

Quick Answer: **284**
Detailed Answer: **309**

3. Which NTFS permissions enable you to delete a folder? (Select all that apply.)

   ○ **A.** Full

   ○ **B.** Read

   ○ **C.** Write

   ○ **D.** Modify

Quick Answer: **284**
Detailed Answer: **309**

4. Your boss wants you to configure the company's network of computers so that only approved software can be loaded onto company PCs. What can you do to prevent employees from installing their own applications?

Quick Answer: **284**
Detailed Answer: **309**

- ○ **A.** Create new accounts for all the employees in the Users group and then configure the group to have only Read permissions.

- ○ **B.** Create a new group account for these employees and configure the group with Write and Execute permissions.

- ○ **C.** Create an account for each user, create a special group account, and then move all the user accounts into it. Finally, apply permission settings to the new group account to limit its members to Write permissions.

- ○ **D.** Remove any unauthorized users from the Administrators and Power Users groups and make sure that the Local Administrator and Power Users groups do not contain any Domain User accounts.

5. Your organization is growing, and you need to be able to delegate responsibilities for some network management activities to other members of your team. Which standard Windows group can you use to grant these employees the ability to manage users and groups that they create without making them administrators?

Quick Answer: **284**
Detailed Answer: **309**

- ○ **A.** Administrators
- ○ **B.** Backup Administrators
- ○ **C.** Network Configuration Operators
- ○ **D.** Power Users

6. What is the correct order to grant many users with access to the same resources?

Quick Answer: **284**
Detailed Answer: **309**

- ○ **A.** Create the users, create a group that defines the common needs of the users, and then assign them access rights to the group.

- ○ **B.** Create a group that defines the common needs of the users in question, make all the users members of that group, and then assign the group access permissions for the resources they need access to.

- ○ **C.** Assign access permissions to the default Everyone group so that all the users have access to the resources.

- ○ **D.** Assign access permissions to the Guest account so that all the users have access to the resources when they log in to the network.

7. An employee returns to the company after being gone for several months. She cannot remember her last password. How do you get her back to work?

- ○ **A.** Email the employee her password.
- ○ **B.** Call her with it.
- ○ **C.** Default to the company policy.
- ○ **D.** Make up a password for her.

Objective 5.2: Install, configure, optimize, and upgrade security

1. A user wants to use his new hard drive to store sensitive company data. His computer is running Windows XP Professional. He plans on encrypting all data in his folder and making it so that only a few select users can access the data. What can you do to help him achieve that goal?

- ○ **A.** In the folder's Properties page, access the Advanced screen under the General tab and click on the Encrypt Contents to Secure Data check box.
- ○ **B.** Access the Security window from the Control Panel and then click on the Encrypt Contents to Secure Data check box in the Advanced page.
- ○ **C.** Access the folder's properties, set the Security and Sharing level for that folder, and then establish a password for the folder that can be shared with the designated employees.
- ○ **D.** Create a group with just those people in it, grant that group permissions to the folder, and then prohibit anyone else from logging on to this user's computer.

2. What command is used to encrypt files and folders from the Windows 2000 or Windows XP command line?

- ○ **A.** `Protect`
- ○ **B.** `Uuencode`
- ○ **C.** `Encrypt`
- ○ **D.** `Cipher`

3. What Windows 2000 utility can be used to prevent users other than the user who secured the folders and files from accessing them?

- ○ **A.** File Manager
- ○ **B.** Encrypted File System
- ○ **C.** Microsoft Management Console
- ○ **D.** Windows Explorer

Quick Answer: **284**
Detailed Answer: **309**

4. For Windows XP, the Local Area Connections properties window offers two tabs not available in the Windows 2000 version. What are the two tabs called?

- ○ **A.** Advanced and Authentication
- ○ **B.** Authentication and Encryption
- ○ **C.** Advanced and Encryption
- ○ **D.** General and Advanced

Quick Answer: **284**
Detailed Answer: **309**

5. You have received a file from your supervisor marked "Confidential—Your Eyes Only." When you save this file to your hard drive, you want to protect it by encrypting it. Where do you set up file encryption in your Windows XP desktop PC?

- ○ **A.** Click on the File menu, select the Encryption option from the pull-down list, and click on the Encrypt This File option.
- ○ **B.** Create a new folder, right-click on it, and then select the Encrypt option from its Properties menu. Then move the file into the encrypted folder.
- ○ **C.** Right-click on the file in Windows Explorer and check the Encrypt Contents to Secure Data check box.
- ○ **D.** Navigate to the Control Panel/Administrative Tools/Computer Management console and click on the Disk Management option. Then select a drive and choose the Encrypt Files on This Drive option from the menu.

Quick Answer: **284**
Detailed Answer: **309**

6. One of your customers has research work on his notebook PC that he wants to protect. In the event that the notebook is stolen, he wants more authentication than a simple user name and password login for his PC. What can you recommend that will be easy to implement, cost effective, and adequately protect the information on his notebook?

- ○ **A.** Employ an encryption algorithm for login.
- ○ **B.** Install a retinal scanner on the PC.
- ○ **C.** Employ a Shared Secret login scenario.
- ○ **D.** Install a fingerprint scanner on the notebook.

7. Your boss is worried about the security of the financial information on his office computer. He wants you to install the Encrypted File System on his computer to provide additional security for this information. What is required to install and run EFS on his PC?

- ○ **A.** You have to download the EFS upgrade from the Windows Update service.
- ○ **B.** The information must be converted into the EFS format in Windows Explorer.
- ○ **C.** The information must be located on an NTFS partition.
- ○ **D.** You have to install a copy of the EFS utility from his Windows distribution CD.

8. Which of the following strategies provides the best protection from viruses and worms?

- ○ **A.** Change the Administrators account password from the default.
- ○ **B.** Make as many people part of the Administrators group as possible.
- ○ **C.** Place only as many users as needed in the Admin group.
- ○ **D.** Put all the users in the Security group.

9. Your company wants to inexpensively create more secure communications between its remote offices. What can you recommend to your management to accomplish this?

- ○ **A.** Implement Remote Access Service (RAS) at each office.
- ○ **B.** Encrypt all communications using the MS-CHAP protocol.
- ○ **C.** Use VoIP communications.
- ○ **D.** Implement a VPN that connects all the offices.

Objective 5.3: Identify tools, diagnostic procedures, and troubleshooting techniques for security issues

1. When you start up your PC at the beginning of your workday and try to log in to the network server, you receive a The system could not log you on error message. You have logged in to this server several times before, so which of the following could be the cause of this message? (Select all that apply.)

   - ○ **A.** You have mistyped your username or password.
   - ○ **B.** The network server is down, so you cannot be authenticated.
   - ○ **C.** You have been locked out by the network's password policy.
   - ○ **D.** Your network's NSLOOKUP server is not available.

Quick Answer: **284**
Detailed Answer: **311**

2. You have been called because one of your customers wants to encrypt a folder on her drive. However, when she accesses the folder's properties, there is no option to encrypt it. Why might this be?

   - ○ **A.** The folder is located on a FAT partition.
   - ○ **B.** The customer does not have adequate permissions to change the attributes of this folder.
   - ○ **C.** The folder has been marked as Read Only.
   - ○ **D.** The folder is inheriting its attributes from the partition it is installed in.

Quick Answer: **284**
Detailed Answer: **311**

3. You are working with a public school to improve its networking capabilities. As you survey the wireless signal strength levels throughout the facility, you find a hidden unauthorized WAP sitting on top of a filing cabinet in a main office. What is this type of WAP called?

   - ○ **A.** A hidden WAP
   - ○ **B.** A secret WAP
   - ○ **C.** A rogue WAP
   - ○ **D.** A guerilla WAP

Quick Answer: **284**
Detailed Answer: **311**

Objective 5.4: Perform preventative maintenance for security

1. A person in your building comes up and introduces herself as a new employee and then starts asking questions about the company's network configuration. This person may be _____.

   ○ **A.** a social engineer

   ○ **B.** a corporate security agent

   ○ **C.** a spammer

   ○ **D.** naturally inquisitive

2. You purchase a used gaming computer through an online auction service. When you receive the computer and set it up, the operating system doesn't load. You see a black screen with an ENTER Password message. What action should you take?

   ○ **A.** Go into the CMOS Setup utility and disable the User Password setting so that you can access the system.

   ○ **B.** Restart the system in Safe Mode and use the MSCONFIG utility to systematically investigate the system's startup process. Then remove the programs and services preventing you from getting to a desktop display.

   ○ **C.** Boot to a floppy boot disk and run FDISK on the computer to repartition it.

   ○ **D.** Restart the system, move into the CMOS Setup, and reconfigure the password setting.

3. You receive an email from your Internet service provider asking you to go to its secure site and update your credit card information. When you click on the link supplied in the email, you are taken to the ISP's site, where you are told to update your payment information. What should you do at this point?

   ○ **A.** Forward the email to your supervisor for follow-up.

   ○ **B.** Encrypt your information and return it to the ISP.

   ○ **C.** Ignore the email and delete it.

   ○ **D.** Forward the email to your local police department.

Domain 6.0: Professionalism and Communication

Objective 6.1: Use good communication skills, including listening and tact/discretion, when communicating with customers and colleagues

1. You are training a new help desk employee. Which of the following should you tell the new person to avoid when dealing with angry customers on the telephone?

   ○ **A.** Telling the customers that you understand their frustrations

   ○ **B.** Putting the customers on hold

   ○ **C.** Using technical terminology to refer to pieces of equipment

   ○ **D.** Going over details of your conversation to reaffirm commitments made

Quick Answer: **285**
Detailed Answer: **312**

2. Which of the following are good attributes of an effective customer service person? (Select all that apply.)

   ○ **A.** Active listening

   ○ **B.** Ability to focus on the customer

   ○ **C.** Personality

   ○ **D.** Analytical skills

Quick Answer: **285**
Detailed Answer: **312**

3. What is the most important key to handling irate customers?

   ○ **A.** Remaining calm regardless of the customers' attitudes

   ○ **B.** Restating the customers' key points so that they know you are listening to them

   ○ **C.** Defending your credibility so that they know they are dealing with a competent professional

   ○ **D.** Telling them that you know they are frustrated and leaving them alone until they have a chance to cool down

Quick Answer: **285**
Detailed Answer: **312**

4. Which of the following activities are involved in active listening? (Select all that apply.)

- ○ **A.** Not getting unfocused
- ○ **B.** Repeating back the customer's key points
- ○ **C.** Making written notes about the customer's key points
- ○ **D.** Not getting thrown by the customer's demeanor

5. After you inspect a failing printer that is under warranty, you determine that the cause of the problem has been improper use of the machine. When you attempt to explain what has happened with the printer and why it is not covered by the warranty, the customer does not accept your explanation of the situation. What should you do under these circumstances?

- ○ **A.** Provide the customer with a step-by-step technical explanation of the problem and the warranty's policies.
- ○ **B.** Tell the customer that you are leaving because you cannot complete the work without his agreement.
- ○ **C.** Agree to disagree with the customer and start working on the problem knowing that your company is going to bill the customer for the work.
- ○ **D.** Escalate the discussion to your supervisor.

6. Your customer has been given a specific timeframe for completion of work you are doing. As the deadline approaches, you can tell that the work is not going to be completed on time. What should you do first in this situation?

- ○ **A.** Tell the customer the work cannot be done by the deadline and ask the customer for an extension.
- ○ **B.** Call your supervisor to let her know the work will not be done on time.
- ○ **C.** Keep working until the customer checks on your progress.
- ○ **D.** Tell the customer that you can't get the work done on time and that you will keep working until the job is completed.

7. A customer is explaining a problem that you recognize, but his assumption about the cause is incorrect. How should you handle this?

Quick Answer: **285**
Detailed Answer: **312**

- ○ **A.** Give the customer a complete technical description of the situation so that he sees the error in his thinking.

- ○ **B.** After the customer finishes, explain what you know the problem to be.

- ○ **C.** Stop the customer and tell him that you're pretty sure that you know what is going on with the machine.

- ○ **D.** After the customer finishes, go to work and fix the problem.

8. If you have to pick up a problem from another technician who has already been working with a customer, how should you enter the process? (Select all that apply.)

Quick Answer: **285**
Detailed Answer: **313**

- ○ **A.** Apologize for any questions you may need to ask that have already been asked.

- ○ **B.** Have the customer start from the beginning and describe everything about the problem.

- ○ **C.** Have the other technician give you his notes on the problem.

- ○ **D.** Go directly to work on the equipment so as not to cost the user more time than he has already expended.

9. While working at the help desk, you receive a call from a customer who complains that she has called in several times about things not working on her new PC system. How should you handle this call?

Quick Answer: **285**
Detailed Answer: **313**

- ○ **A.** Refer to the company policy for returns and service and guide the user appropriately.

- ○ **B.** Offer the customer a full refund for her system so that the repair efforts stop eroding the profits from selling her the system.

- ○ **C.** Be frank with the customer and let her know that there's nothing wrong with her PC and that there is nothing more you can do for her.

- ○ **D.** Offer the customer a partial refund for her system to resolve the issue and end the call.

10. You are setting up a progression chart for your technical support staff to use when handling incoming contacts from customers. The chart begins at the far left side of the page with a block that represents the technician who first receives the complaint from the customer. Which of the following should you use to title this block?

    ○ **A.** Lead Technician

    ○ **B.** Initial Problem Owner

    ○ **C.** Primary Technician

    ○ **D.** Access Owner

Quick Answer: **285**
Detailed Answer: **313**

11. When a support organization is dedicated to making sure that a customer's problem is handled, this is called what?

    ○ **A.** Taking ownership of the customer's problem

    ○ **B.** Active problem solving

    ○ **C.** Total Quality Service (TQS)

    ○ **D.** Complete Customer Service (CCS)

Quick Answer: **285**
Detailed Answer: **313**

12. You are on a customer support call with a peripheral supplier's help desk. The first-level technician has not been able to identify and correct your problem, so he escalates your call to a second-level technician. However, to keep you from having to repeat your entire problem to the new tech, the first-level technician briefs the new technician for you. When you facilitate the new contact for both parties, this is called a _____.

    ○ **A.** cold handoff

    ○ **B.** warm handoff

    ○ **C.** hot handoff

    ○ **D.** direct transfer

Quick Answer: **285**
Detailed Answer: **313**

Objective 6.2: Use job-related professional behavior including notation of privacy, confidentiality, and respect for the customer and customer's property

1. After completing a repair on one of your customer's computers, you discover a folder of pornographic pictures on the computer. What should you do about this discovery?

   ○ **A.** Report it to your supervisor.

   ○ **B.** Deny access to the user.

   ○ **C.** Remove the offensive material from the machine.

   ○ **D.** Move the information to a server to secure the network audience.

Quick Answer: **285**
Detailed Answer: **313**

2. When an irate customer begins to use profanity in discussions with you, what action should you take?

   ○ **A.** Walk away in protest so that the customer knows you are offended.

   ○ **B.** Withdraw from the situation as soon as possible and report the customer to your supervisor.

   ○ **C.** Withdraw from the conversation and report the customer to her supervisor.

   ○ **D.** Tell the customer you don't appreciate the use of such language and leave her presence.

Quick Answer: **285**
Detailed Answer: **313**

3. On a repair job, the customer asks you for the personal cell phone number of another technician at your company. He says that he knows the other technician and would like to get in touch with him. How should you handle this request? (Select all that apply.)

   ○ **A.** Offer to relay the information and have the other person call the customer.

   ○ **B.** Give the customer the other technician's number.

   ○ **C.** Call the other technician to see if he wants his number released to this person.

   ○ **D.** Tell the customer that you do not know the number to avoid any kind of potential problems from giving out the number.

Quick Answer: **285**
Detailed Answer: **314**

4. You are working on a PC at a customer's desk, and you come to the conclusion that you need to disassemble the machine to replace the system board. How should you do this?

Quick Answer: **285**
Detailed Answer: **314**

- ○ **A.** Quickly do the work at the customer's desk and get the machine back in operation as quickly as possible.
- ○ **B.** Remove the PC to a proper workspace to work on it.
- ○ **C.** Replace the unit with a temporary unit instead of repairing it at the customer's desk.
- ○ **D.** Arrange to come back after the office is closed to work on the PC without interrupting the user.

5. One of your customers has given you a request for work that is prohibited by your company's written policies. What should you tell the customer?

Quick Answer: **285**
Detailed Answer: **314**

- ○ **A.** Tell the customer you can't do it; the request is against your company's policies.
- ○ **B.** Tell the customer you will see if there is some allowable alternative that you can offer.
- ○ **C.** Tell the customer to contact your supervisor.
- ○ **D.** Perform the requested work on your own time so that you keep your customer happy without breaking the company's policy.

6. When work is requested that is outside the scope of your company's agreement with the customer, what should you do?

Quick Answer: **285**
Detailed Answer: **314**

- ○ **A.** Call your supervisor, describe the requested additional work, and proceed as directed.
- ○ **B.** Offer to do the work after hours because this is such an important customer.
- ○ **C.** Refuse the work because it is not part of the scope of work you have been given.
- ○ **D.** Inform the customer that the additional work will cost extra and perform the requested work.

7. While talking with an employee, you notice that he is illegally downloading music on a company computer. What should you do about this?

Quick Answer: **285**
Detailed Answer: **314**

- ○ **A.** Advise your supervisor.
- ○ **B.** Remove the download utility from the machine.
- ○ **C.** Tell the user to stop the unauthorized activity.
- ○ **D.** Do nothing because this is not your responsibility.

8. Which of the following is the best method of training users to operate the new equipment you've just installed?

- ○ **A.** Reading the equipment's documentation to the users and having them highlight the parts they will need after you are gone.

- ○ **B.** To avoid putting the users to sleep with a long technical discussion of the equipment's operation, give them the quick version of the most important points, avoiding technical terms whenever possible.

- ○ **C.** Suggest that they purchase an extended training class from your company to ensure that they are fully acquainted with the new device or system.

- ○ **D.** Use their new equipment to show them how it operates.

Quick Check Answer Key

Objective 1.1

1. C	6. B	11. A
2. D	7. A, D	12. C
3. A, B	8. C	13. D
4. D	9. C, D	
5. B	10. D	

Objective 1.2

1. C	5. B	9. C
2. D	6. D	10. C
3. A	7. A	11. B
4. A	8. B	

Objective 1.3

1. B	3. D
2. C	4. C

Objective 2.1

1. D	9. C	17. B
2. A	10. B	18. B
3. D	11. B	19. D
4. A	12. B	20. B
5. B	13. B	21. D
6. C	14. C	22. A, C
7. B	15. B, D	
8. B	16. A	

Quick Check Answer Key

Objective 2.2

1. A	8. D	15. D
2. D	9. B	16. A, C
3. B	10. C, D	17. D
4. A	11. A, C	18. C
5. D	12. A	19. C
6. D	13. A	20. A
7. B, D	14. B	21. A

Objective 2.3

1. D	10. D	19. A
2. A	11. D	20. D
3. A	12. D	21. C
4. B	13. B, D	22. D
5. B	14. D	23. B
6. A	15. B	24. C
7. C, D	16. C, D	25. A
8. B	17. B	26. B
9. A	18. A	27. C

Objective 2.4

1. C, D	3. B, C
2. C	4. B

Objective 3.1

1. C	4. B	7. D
2. B	5. C	8. B
3. B	6. B	

Quick Check Answer Key

Objective 3.2

1. C
2. D
3. B, D

4. D
5. D
6. A

7. C
8. C
9. C

Objective 3.3

1. A
2. A
3. A, B
4. D
5. D

6. C
7. A, B
8. C
9. B, C
10. B

11. C
12. A
13. A, B, C

Objective 4.1

1. A
2. C
3. B
4. A
5. A
6. B

7. B, D
8. A, C
9. D
10. D
11. B
12. B

13. C
14. A
15. B
16. D

Objective 4.2

1. B
2. A
3. A
4. A
5. A

6. A, B
7. B, D
8. B
9. C
10. D

11. A
12. A
13. C

Quick Check Answer Key

Objective 4.3

1. A	9. D	17. C
2. D	10. D	18. A, D
3. A	11. B	19. A
4. B	12. B	20. A
5. D	13. A	21. A
6. B	14. A	22. B
7. A, B	15. A, C	
8. A, C	16. C	

Objective 5.1

1. B	4. D	7. C
2. D	5. D	
3. A, D	6. B	

Objective 5.2

1. D	4. A	7. C
2. D	5. C	8. C
3. B	6. D	9. D

Objective 5.3

1. A, B, C	3. C
2. A	

Objective 5.4

1. A	3. C
2. C	

Quick Check Answer Key

Objective 6.1

1. B	5. D	9. A
2. A, B	6. D	10. B
3. A	7. D	11. A
4. A, B, D	8. A, C	12. B

Objective 6.2

1. A	4. B	7. A
2. B	5. B	8. D
3. A, C	6. A	

Answers and Explanations

Domain 1.0

Objective 1.1

1. **Answer: C**. Three disc types can be used to accommodate the 6.5GB capacity required for this project: the single-sided, dual-layer DVD (8.5GB); the double-sided, single-layer DVD (9.4GB); and the double-sided, dual-layer DVD (17.1GB). However, CDs and single-sided DVD formats do not offer enough capacity to store the movie files. On the other hand, the double-sided, dual-layer DVD is overkill in both capacity and cost. In addition, the -RW capability means that potential customers can simply record over the demo that your customer distributed.

2. **Answer: D**. A good game system would provide the fastest video adapter card and its supporting expansion slot. This involves PCIe adapter slots and video cards with as much video memory onboard as possible. Some newer chipsets designed to support gaming applications include support for dual 16X PCIe slot video cards. This specification is called the Scalable Link Interface (SLI) specification and enables both cards to operate simultaneously. Additional advances have yielded twin, dual-slot (quad) PCIe system boards to host four video adapters.

3. **Answers: A, B**. Three common expansion slot types are used with video cards. The oldest is the original PCI bus. However, the AGP slot found on a great number of ATX system boards was designed specifically for video adapter cards. Most new PCs use the 16X PCIe slot for video controllers. In some high-end gaming systems, dual PCIe slots are used for the video adapter subsystem.

4. **Answer: D**. When you are installing the PATA signal cable in an IDE-based system, you should recall that two similar types of cables are used with PATA devices. The newer ATA-4/Ultra ATA 66, Ultra ATA 100, and Ultra ATA 133 IDE enhancements provide higher data throughput by doubling the number of conductors in the signal cable to 80 while keeping the connectors at 40 pins.

5. **Answer: B**. Most portable PC designs have switched to nickel metal-hydride (NiMH), lithium-ion (Li-ion), or lithium-ion polymer batteries. These batteries typically provide in excess of two or three hours of operation. The actual life of a laptop computer battery may vary from just under one hour to over six hours in each sitting, depending on the particular notebook PC type and configuration, the way it is being used (lots of disk/disc accesses), and the battery type and its age.

6. **Answer: B**. An improved type of LCD places a transistor at each of the matrix row-column junctions to improve switching times. This technology produces an active-matrix display that employs thin-film transistor (TFT) arrays to create between one and four transistors for each pixel on a flexible, transparent film. TFT displays tend to be brighter and sharper than dual-scan displays. However, TFT-based LCD panels also tend to require more power to operate and are more expensive to produce than panels using other LCD technologies.

7. **Answers: A,D**. If Windows XP does not support the device, obtain an OEM installation disk or CD for the device that has the Windows XP drivers. It is necessary to click the Have Disk button in the Hardware Installation Wizard window and supply the file's location to complete the installation process if the driver disk does not have an AutoStart function (A). If the wizard does not detect the hardware, the user can attempt to locate the device in the Add Hardware Wizard's list of supported devices (D).

8. **Answer: C**. The Windows XP Add Hardware icon brings the Add Hardware Wizard into action. It initially asks whether you want to add/troubleshoot a device or uninstall/unplug a device. If the system does not detect any new hardware, it asks you to choose a hardware device to troubleshoot. If the device must be installed manually because Windows could not detect it, Windows produces a Choose a Hardware Device component list and guides the manual installation process from this point and prompts you for any necessary configuration information. If the device is not present in the list, you can also click the Have Disk button to manually load drivers supplied by the device's manufacturer.

9. **Answers: C, D**. To correct battery memory problems, you must start the portable computer using only the battery and allow it to run until it completely discharges the battery and quits. Then recharge the battery for at least 12 hours. Repeat this process several times, watching for consistently increasing operating times. If this procedure fails to revive the battery or extend its usefulness, you need to purchase a new battery for the portable.

10. **Answer: D**. Simple USB-to-PS/2 converters are included with many mouse models. These simple, passive devices reroute mouse control and data signals to the proper pins for each interface.

11. **Answer: A**. Gather information to identify the nature of the problem. This can involve questioning the user and identifying any changes that have been made to the system. After identifying the problem, you should assess the problem systematically and divide complex problems into smaller components to be analyzed individually. Next, you should analyze the potential causes of the individual problems and make an initial assessment of whether they are hardware or software related. During this analysis, you should verify even obvious potential causes: The classic is the unplugged power cord.

12. **Answer: C**. The RAMBUS design requires that its memory modules be installed in sets of two. Any unfilled memory slots must have terminators (referred to as *CRIMMs*).

13. **Answer: D**. Because this system board does not have a built-in video adapter function, there should be no option in the CMOS Setup to enable or disable this function. You simply need to roll back or remove the new driver and get one that works installed. Click on the Properties button on the Adapter tab. Select the Driver tab and select Uninstall, Roll Back, or Update the Display Adapter's Driver. If you uninstall the current driver, you can simply restart Windows and allow it to detect the display adapter and attempt to install the correct driver. The Windows XP Roll Back Driver feature returns the system to the driver that was being used before the current video display driver. The Update Driver option asks you to select a driver to use from several options.

Objective 1.2

1. **Answer: C**. If a working IDE hard drive fails because a second IDE hard drive has been installed, the reason is probably that they are connected to the same IDE interface connector and both drives are set as master. On IDE drives, there can be only one master drive selection on each IDE channel.

2. **Answer: D**. When the speakers are placed on the wrong sides, increasing the volume on the right speaker instead increases the output of the left speaker. The obvious cure for this problem is to physically switch the positions of the speakers.

3. **Answer: A**. The snap the customer felt was ESD, and the fact that the system does not operate indicates that damage has occurred with one of the system's integrated circuit devices. All you can do at this point is try to determine the extent of the damage and educate the customer about the causes and effects of ESD. MOS devices are sensitive to voltage spikes and static electricity discharges. The level of static electricity present on your body may be high enough to destroy the inputs of an MOS device if you touch its pins with your fingers (in practice, this level of damage may require multiple electrostatic discharges). Professional service technicians employ a number of precautionary steps when they are working on systems that may contain MOS devices. These technicians normally use a grounding strap that can be placed around the wrist or ankle to ground themselves to the system being worked on. These straps release any static present on the technician's body and pass it harmlessly to ground potential.

4. **Answer: A**. Finally, document your activities, actions, and outcomes. Good notes become a technician's personal knowledge base and can be used over and over. They also provide documentation when questions arise concerning how a problem was handled.

5. **Answer: B**. If "nothing is happening" when you try to start the system, your first thought should be about a power-related problem. When checking a dead system, perform a careful visual inspection of the system. Check the outside of the system first. Look for loose or disconnected cables. Consult all the external front-panel lights. If no lights are displayed, check the power outlet, plugs, and power cords, as well as any power switches that may affect the operation of the system. You may also want to check the commercial power-distribution system's fuses or circuit breakers to ensure that they are functional.

6. **Answer: D**. Many new system boards provide onboard VGA video as part of their chipsets and architecture. To upgrade the video capabilities of these systems, you must disable the onboard video capabilities before using an adapter card–based video display system. To do so, you must access the CMOS Setup utility and disable the onboard video function there.

7. **Answer: A**. If the adapter's icon shows an exclamation mark on a yellow background, the card is not functioning properly. Turn off the system and reinsert the device in a different PC Card slot. If the same problem appears, there are three possible sources of problems: The card might be faulty, the PC Card controller in the PC might be faulty, or the operating system might not support the device in question.

8. **Answer: B**. Windows XP includes an option that can be used to revert to an older device driver when a driver upgrade causes problems with a device. This feature is called *Driver Rollback* and can be implemented through the Windows XP Device Manager.

9. **Answer: C**. A reversed FDD signal cable causes the FDD activity light to stay on constantly.

10. **Answer: C**. In this case, you must install third-party device drivers to support the drive and continue the installation process. Windows Setup provides an F6 function key option to pause the installation process so that these mass storage device drivers can be installed.

11. **Answer: B**. In ATX and BTX systems, the mouse and keyboard can both use identical 6-pin, PS/2 mini-DIN connectors. It is quite possible to plug these devices into the wrong connector if the color-coding system is not followed. Always check for this possibility when you have PS/2 devices that are not functioning.

Objective 1.3

1. **Answer: B**. Monthly activities: Defragment the system's hard drive using the DEFRAG utility. Remove unnecessary temporary (.TMP) files from the hard drive. Check software and hardware manufacturers for product updates that can remove problems and improve system operation. Back up the entire hard disk drive.

2. **Answer: C**. The CHKDSK command is a command-line utility that has remained in use with Windows 2000 and XP and is used to recover (and remove, if necessary) lost allocation units from the hard drive. The /R switch locates bad sectors on the disk and recovers readable information.

3. **Answer: D**. To manually clean read/write heads, use isopropyl alcohol on a foam swab. Cotton swabs can shed fibers that can contaminate the drive and damage portions of its R/W head.

4. **Answer: C**. If a CRT presents wavy lines in the display, you might need to remove built-up electromagnetic fields from the screen through a process called *degaussing*.

Domain 2.0

Objective 2.1

1. **Answer: D.** Backing up the System State data includes the contents of the Registry, system startup files, files under Windows File Protection in Windows XP, and the COM+ class registration database (a database of information about Component Services applications).

2. **Answer: A.** In a Windows 2000 environment, the system's administrative tools are stored in the Computer Management console, which can be accessed through the path Start/Settings/Control Panel/Administrative Tools.

3. **Answer: D.** The Windows 2000/XP Disk Management utility contains a Dynamic Volume Management feature with a new user interface that enables administrators to configure drives and volumes located in remote computers.

4. **Answer: A.** The CD command displays the name of the current directory or switches to a new directory.

5. **Answer: B.** From the command prompt environment, you can use the `Attribute` command to verify that the hidden system files have been successfully copied to the disk (that is, `attrib -r -s -h c:\ntldr` to make it visible and to remove its read-only, system, and hidden status).

6. **Answer: C.** The system's slow startup performance is likely due to the number of items being loaded along with the operating system, as indicated by the number of icons appearing in the taskbar. Start the `MSCONFIG` utility from the command prompt and move to the Startup tab. Remove the checks from any applications that you do not want to run at startup. You should perform this action with some forethought; generally, you do not want to disable anything in the `\Windows` folder. Using the `MSCONFIG` utility allows you to disable applications, try the system, and then restore them if you need to—as opposed to deleting them from the Startup folder.

7. **Answer: B.** Driver signing is controlled through the Windows 2000/XP Control Panel's System icon. In the System applet, select the Hardware tab and click on the Driver Signing button. The Driver Signing Options page appears. On this page you can establish how the system should react when it detects an unsigned driver.

8. **Answer: B.** To change a file's attributes in Windows Explorer, right-click on the desired file, select the Properties option from the pop-up list, move to the General page, and click on the desired attribute boxes.

9. **Answer: C.** In Windows operating systems, you can establish sharing for a folder by right-clicking on it and selecting the Sharing (Sharing and Security in Windows XP) option from the menu. This produces the Sharing tab of the folder's Properties page.

10. **Answer: B.** The Windows XP ASR tool is a function of the Windows Backup utility (`NTBACKUP.EXE`) and is used to back up and restore the System State information, along with all the files stored on the system volume. The ASR feature is considered to be the last resort that is used when you have been unable to recover the system using

other methods, including Safe Mode, the Last Known Good Configuration option, and the Recovery Console.

11. **Answer: B**. The MD *path\newfolder* (Make Directory) statement creates a new subdirectory named *newfolder* in the path indicated.

12. **Answer: B**. The Selective Startup option located on the General tab of the System Configuration Utility dialog box interactively loads device drivers and software options according to the check boxes enabled. Start the troubleshooting process with only one box checked. If the system starts up with that box checked, add another box to the list and restart. When the system fails to start, move into the tab that corresponds to the last option you enabled and step through the check boxes for that file one at a time until the system fails again.

13. **Answer: B**. The CONVERT command is used in Windows 2000 and Windows XP to convert volumes from FAT-based disks into NTFS volumes that typically provide more efficient disk management. The format for using this command is C:\>CONVERT C: /FS:NTFS. This converts a FAT-based volume C into an NTFS-based volume C: by installing the NTFS file system on the volume.

14. **Answer: C**. To change the file's attribute from Read Only, use the ATTRIB command and the file's name, along with the -R switch to remove the attribute from the designated file.

15. **Answers: B, D**. In Windows 2000 and Windows XP, you perform the disk partitioning function using the Disk Management utility. You can use this utility to partition drives and see the basic layout of the system's disks. DISKPART.EXE is a Windows XP command-line–based disk-partitioning utility used to establish and manage logical structures on a hard disk drive. It is one of Windows XP's major disk management tools. You can access it through the Recovery Console.

16. **Answer: A**. The ASR tool is used to back up and restore the System State information, along with all the files stored on the system volume. The ASR feature is a function of the NTBACKUP.EXE (Windows Backup) utility and is considered to be the last resort that is used when you have been unable to recover the system using other methods, including Safe Mode, the Last Known Good Configuration option, and the Recovery Console.

17. **Answer: B**. The HKEY CURRENT_USER key holds the data about the user-specific configuration settings of the system, including color scheme, keyboard, desktop, and startup settings.

18. **Answer: B**. The HKEY_CURRENT_CONFIG key works with the HKEY_LOCAL_MACHINE branch containing current information about hardware devices.

19. **Answer: D**. During the Windows startup process, NTLDR runs NTDETECT to gather system hardware information. NTDETECT checks the system for key hardware items. The process then initializes the drivers prepared by NTLDR and uses the NTDETECT information to create a temporary Hardware hive in memory. Finally, NTOSKRNL creates the Registry's HKEY_LOCAL_MACHINE\HARDWARE key from the information gathered earlier by NTDETECT and executes additional device drivers.

20. Answer: B. The Recycle Bin is a storage area for deleted files. It enables you to retrieve such files if they are deleted by mistake. If files have been thrown out of the bin but have not been overwritten, they can be recovered using a third-party software utility for recovering deleted files.

21. Answer: D. In the case of removable media such as floppy disks, a network drive, or removable drives (for example, tape drives, ZIP disks, USB drives, SD drives, and so on), the Recycle Bin does not retain the files deleted from the media. When a file or folder is removed from one of these devices, the file information is deleted directly from the file system. The same is true for files deleted from the command line and for deleted compressed files.

22. Answers: A, C. (A) Compressed files can be marked so that they are displayed in a second color for easy identification. You accomplish this through the Folder Options setting in the Control Panel. (C) The other indication that you can have concerning a compressed or encrypted file or folder is an attribute listing when Windows Explorer or a folder is configured to display attributes as part of the Details option in the View menu.

Objective 2.2

1. Answer: A. The Windows XP Professional operating system uses hardware profiles to determine which drivers to load when the system hardware changes (docked or undocked). It uses the Docked Profile to load drivers when the portable computer is docked and the Undocked Profile when the computer starts up without the docking station. These hardware profiles are created by the Windows XP operating system when the computer is docked and undocked if the system is PnP compliant. You can also configure Windows to prompt you to select a profile during the Windows startup process.

2. Answer: D. You can increase the performance of Windows XP by manipulating the size and placement of their virtual-memory swap file (`Pagefile.sys`). You can manipulate page files in Windows XP under the Advanced tab in the Control Panel's System applet. Click on the Settings button in the Performance field and then click on the Advanced tab.

3. Answer: B. The Windows XP Defragmenter utility is available through the Administrative Tools/Computer Management Console. It is also available through the All Programs/Accessories/System Tools path.

4. Answer: A. In the Windows 2000/XP environment, users may not have permissions that enable them to access different files and folders or perform different activities. This is the result of an administrative decision and can be overcome only by an administrator establishing permission levels that permit access. XCOPY is actually an old "external" DOS command and retains the error messages associated with the operation of those commands. The `Bad Command or Missing File Name` error indicates that a syntax error has occurred; either the name has been entered incorrectly, the path to the location of the file is incorrect, or the file is missing or corrupted. The location for external commands such as XCOPY in Windows XP is `C:\Windows\System32`. If the file is moved, the system would not be able to find it. However, this is not likely to happen in Windows XP.

5. **Answer: D**. The drivers that the employees are downloading are not working with the hardware under the new operating system. Microsoft has a program called *driver signing* that allows hardware manufacturers to verify that their drivers work with given Microsoft operating systems. To prevent the employees from installing drivers that don't work, you need to enforce the use of driver signing to verify drivers before they are installed. On the Windows XP Driver Signing Options page, you can establish how the system should react when it detects an unsigned driver. The Block option does not permit any unsigned drivers to be loaded into the system.

6. **Answer: D**. Before you install Windows XP Professional from the CD, it is recommended that you run the Windows XP version of `Checkupgradeonly`. This file checks the system for possible hardware compatibility problems and is located on the installation CD under `\i386\winnt32`.

7. **Answers: B, D**. The defragmentation process optimizes the operation of the disk drive by reorganizing its data into logically contiguous blocks. With data being arranged in this manner, the system does not need to reposition the drive's read/write heads as many times to read a given piece of data. The Windows 2000/XP Windows Disk Cleanup utility can be used to identify certain types of applications and temporary files that are not required for operation of the system. The temporary files that you can normally afford to remove from the system to gain needed disk space include Windows, Internet, and multimedia temp files.

8. **Answer: D**. You can use the Device Manager to identify installed ports, update device drivers, and change I/O settings, as well as troubleshoot device driver issues. To update a driver in the Device Manager, select the network adapter entry that needs to be updated, click on its Driver tab, and click on the Driver Update button.

9. **Answer: B**. To access the virtual memory settings in Windows XP, you must navigate to the Settings button in the Performance area of the Control Panel's System properties. Clicking on this button produces the Performance Options dialog box. To manually configure the virtual memory settings, access the Advanced tab and click on the Change button in the Virtual Memory area.

10. **Answers: C, D**. The path to the shared resource contains the remote computer's name and shared resource name (directory or printer). It also must be expressed using the Universal Naming Convention (UNC) format. The format begins with a pair of backslashes, \\. Each name in the path is separated by a single backslash.

11. **Answers: A, C**. MUI interface packs add language resources to the base operating system without modifying any core system binaries. This greatly eases desktop administration in multilingual computing environments and considerably lowers the cost of desktop change and configuration management.

12. **Answer: A**. Unused system services should be stopped or disabled to optimize system responsiveness and performance. In Windows XP, you can launch the Services control applet either through the Control Panel/Administrative Tools/Services path or by running the `SERVICES.MSC` command-line utility. This utility produces a listing of all the user-controllable services running in the system. From this list, you can stop or switch services to manual startup configuration. You should not disable any service unless you are absolutely sure that you will not need it and that no other vital service needs it.

13. **Answer: A**. The path to the shared resource contains the remote computer's name and shared resource name (directory or printer). It also must be expressed using the Universal Naming Convention (UNC) format. The format begins with a pair of back-slashes, \\. Each name in the path is separated by a single backslash.

14. **Answer: B**. Windows XP Professional is capable of managing only a RAID0 striped array. In this case, you should be able to upgrade to Windows XP. However, you should make sure to back up the existing information from the array because the upgrade to Windows XP may destroy the existing disk parameters, and all data on the drives will be lost.

15. **Answer: D**. The Windows 2000/XP Windows Disk Cleanup utility can be used to identi-fy certain types of temporary files that are not required for operation of the system. The temporary files that you can normally afford to remove from the system to gain needed disk space include Windows, Internet, and multimedia temp files. It also emp-ties the Recycle Bin if the Recycle Bin option is checked. However, the Disk Cleanup utility does not manipulate files that have been placed in quarantine by an antivirus utility.

16. **Answers: A, C**. Systems running Windows 95 or Windows NT Workstation 3.51 oper-ating systems cannot upgrade directly to Windows XP. Instead, they must have inter-mediate upgrades to bring them up to a Windows version that does support direct upgrading to Windows XP.

17. **Answer: D**. Active antivirus software might prevent Windows from being installed on a system. These utilities see changes to the operating system's core files as a virus activity and work to prevent them from occurring. Any antivirus programs should be disabled prior to running Windows Setup. You can re-enable the program after com-pleting the setup process.

18. **Answer: C**. Basic volumes are converted to dynamic volumes using the Disk Management tool (follow the path Start/Run, enter **DISKMGMT.MSC** into the text box, and then click on OK). A basic disk is a physical disk that contains partitions, drives, or volumes created with Windows NT 4.0 or earlier operating systems. Dynamic disks can hold only dynamic volumes (not partitions, volumes, or logical drives). Windows 2000 and XP dp not support dynamic volumes on portable computers.

19. **Answer: C**. Under Windows 2000, you must place the distribution CD in the drive and launch the Makeboot utility to create the four disk images for its Windows 2000 Setup disks. You can also create Setup disks from the command prompt using the MAKEBT32.EXE file for Windows 2000. These disks can also be made from the Start/Run/Browse/CD-ROM path. From the CD, select the BOOTDISK option followed by the MAKEBT32.EXE command.

20. **Answer: A**. In Windows XP, the administrator has been given new tools that can be used to limit what the user can do to any given resource. Non-hot-swappable devices such as local printers cannot be added to Windows 2000 or Windows XP systems without Administrator permissions. In a domain environment, members of the Print Managers group can normally add printers to the system. Likewise, members of the Local Users group can add network printers to the system by. All these capabilities are based on the default permission settings for these groups; with the exception of the Administrators group, the capabilities of these groups can be modified through Group Policy settings.

21. **Answer: A.** To determine what components Windows 2000 supports, you need to consult the Hardware Compatibility List to make sure that the device is listed on it.

Objective 2.3

1. **Answer: D.** The VGA mode option was introduced into the Windows NT/2000/XP line expressly for the purpose of managing video driver problems. Under this option, the system starts normally except that it loads the standard Windows VGA display driver that every VGA adapter should run with.

2. **Answer: A.** When a red X appears at the device's icon, the device has been disabled due to a user selection. The disabled device continues to consume system resources, but no protected mode driver is loaded for it.

3. **Answer: A.** To activate the Windows XP System Restore Wizard, navigate the Start/All Programs/Accessories/System Tools path and then select the System Restore option from the menu.

4. **Answer: B.** The Windows 2000/XP System Information utility provides five subfolders of information about the system. These folders include a system summary, a list of hardware resources being used, a list of I/O components in the system, a description of the system's current software environment, and a description of the Windows Internet Explorer.

5. **Answer: B.** The Device Manager displays an exclamation point (!) inside a yellow field whenever a device is experiencing a direct hardware conflict with another device. The nature of the problem is described in the device's Properties dialog box.

6. **Answer: A.** You should access the Event Viewer utility and expand the System node to view the event log of system events, such as loading the networking services. Even if no desktop is available, you can restart the system in Safe Mode and access the Event Viewer to use this log to isolate the cause of the error.

7. **Answers: C, D.** In Windows 2000, you can use the Emergency Repair Process to repair the boot sector, repair the startup files, and replace the system files. However, you should be aware that the Windows 2000 Emergency Repair Process is designed to repair the operating system only and cannot be of assistance in repairing application or data problems.

8. **Answer: B.** In Windows 2000 and Windows XP, you can use the Task Manager to determine which applications in the system are running or stopped, as well as which resources are being used. You can also determine what the general microprocessor and memory usage levels are. A nonfunctioning application can be terminated using Task Manager in Windows 2000 and XP.

9. **Answer: A.** The Last Known Good Hardware Configuration mode of Windows 2000/XP Startup causes the system to start up using the configuration information that it recorded the last time a user successfully logged on to the system. This configuration information is not replaced until a user actually logs on to the system.

10. **Answer: D**. The system produces a single beep indicating that it has completed its POST and initialization process. Because the system reaches the single beep, you can tell that the basic hardware in the system is working okay. After the beep tone has been produced in the startup sequence, the system shifts over to the process of booting up and begins looking for and loading the operating system components. Errors that occur between the beep and the presentation of the operating system's user interface (command prompt or desktop GUI) are bootup or operating system startup problems.

11. **Answer: D**. You can use the Recovery Console to perform tasks such as copying files to the hard disk used for booting; controlling the startup state of services; adding, removing, and formatting volumes on the hard disk; repairing the MBR or boot sector of a hard disk or volume; and restoring the Registry. You cannot use it to uninstall programs.

12. **Answer: D**. The System File Checker utility, `SFC.EXE`, is a Windows 2000/XP command-line utility that checks the system's protected files for changed, deleted, or possibly corrupted files. If it finds such files, it attempts to extract the original correct versions of the files from Windows files in the `%SystemRoot%\windows\ system32\dllcache` folder.

13. **Answers: B, D**. When you start a system in Safe Mode, only basic device drivers and files are loaded in the system (for example, the mouse, keyboard, mass storage, and VGA video drivers, along with default system services and no network connections).

14. **Answer: D**. HelpAssistant is a special Windows XP account used with its Remote Assistance utility to authenticate users connecting through it. This account is enabled whenever a remote assistance invitation is created, and it is automatically disabled when all invitations have expired.

15. **Answer: B**. Although several symptoms are presented here, the loud clicking sound associated with hard disk drive problems is the key to this scenario. This is not a symptom associated with the other components. Start the system and listen for sounds of the hard drive spinning up (a low whine or clicking noise). If a loud clicking noise comes from the drive, the drive has lost its alignment and is looking for its starting track.

16. **Answers: C, D**. If a red X appears on the icon of a properly mapped drive, this indicates that the drive is no longer available or that the connection to it has been lost. Its host computer may be turned off, the drive may have been removed, or it may no longer be on the same path. Likewise, the router for the segment could have failed removing the pathway to the mapped drive. If an administrator changes the permission levels to the mapped resource, the system does not produce the red X mentioned. Instead, it simply produces an error message saying the connection to the drive has not been restored.

17. **Answer: B**. In Windows XP, the Device Manager includes a new Driver Rollback option that can be used to replace an upgraded driver whenever it causes problems with the system. To roll back the driver, right-click on the device in the Device Manager listing and select the Properties option. Click on the Driver tab and then the Roll Back Driver button.

18. **Answer: A**. Normally, if a printer is not producing anything in a Windows environment even though print jobs have been sent to it, you should check the print spooler to see whether any particular type of error has occurred. To view documents waiting to be printed, you would double-click on the desired printer's icon. While viewing the print spooler queue, you should check to make certain that the printer has not been set to the Pause Printing setting. However, in this scenario, the customer is trying to print to an inkjet printer, but only a laser printer has been defined for use. The local inkjet printer must be added and defined in the local computer's Printers and Faxes list using the Add Printer Wizard.

19. **Answer: A**. Windows 2000 includes two Registry editors: RegEdit and RegEdt32. RegEdit is an older Registry editor that was used with previous Windows versions but retains some features not available in the newer RegEdit version. Both utilities enable you to add, edit, and remove Registry entries and to perform other basic functions. Under Windows XP, the RegEdt32 option has been reduced simply to a small program that launches REGEDIT.EXE.

20. **Answer: D**. Windows XP keeps a copy of the system's DLL files in the %SystemRoot%\System32\Dllcache folder. When you run the SFC utility, the system goes to this folder looking for the file to install when it discovers that the current version is incorrect. Using the /purgecache switch purges the dllcache folder and immediately scans all protected system files. This causes the system to request the distribution CD for a clean copy of the required files.

21. **Answer: C**. Remote Assistance invitations can be sent directly to the helper using a Windows Messenger account or as an email attachment using Outlook. You can also create the invitation as a file and save it to a folder that the helper has access to or send it as an email attachment. The email attachment or saved file is given an .msrincident extension.

22. **Answer: D**. The PAGEFILE.SYS file is automatically regenerated when Windows starts up.

23. **Answer: B**. This is one of the two methods of associating user accounts that have common needs. Create the group, make all users a member of the group, and then assign the group access permissions to the resource (in this case, the application's setup files). The other method involves assigning each user individual permissions to the resource. The latter approach would make it difficult and time-consuming to troubleshoot effective access rights due to repeating the long list of user accounts for the shared resource.

24. **Answer: C**. The Windows XP System Restore utility enables administrators to roll back the Windows XP Professional operating system to a previous operational state and configuration—without affecting any user's personal data. This feature extends the Last Known Good Configuration operation by allowing the system to be rolled back to predetermined Restore Points established when the system was operational.

25. **Answer: A**. The System File Checker utility (SFC.EXE) is a Windows 2000/XP command-line utility that checks the system's protected files for changed, deleted, or possibly corrupted files. SFC can be used to verify that the protected system files are the appropriate versions and to verify and replace files in the dllcache folder. The latter ensures that files used to replace invalid operating system files are actually valid.

26. **Answer: B**. Conducting a Remote Assistance session requires that both the user and helper actively participate in establishing the connection. A Remote Assistance session is established in three phases: The user requiring support sends a Remote Assistance invitation to the helper, the helper responds to the invitation, and the user accepts the helper's assistance.

27. **Answer: C**. If the My Network Places window is empty, or if its icon is missing, networking connections may have not been established. If this is the case, you must correctly configure networking on the local unit to connect to any other computers on the network. The other possibility is that the Desktop icons are simply hidden (as they generally are by default). This can be corrected through the Start/Control Panel/Display/Desktop tab/Customize Desktop button/General tab path.

Objective 2.4

1. **Answers: C, D**. Automatic Updates can be configured to download and install updates on a specified schedule or to notify the user when high-priority updates become available. You can click on the Automatic (Recommended) option button and then enter day and time settings for Windows to install the updates under the Automatically Download Recommended Updates for My Computer and Install Them option. You must be logged on as an administrator or a member of the Administrators group to complete this procedure. Beginning with Windows XP SP1, Microsoft began requiring that the copy of Windows be activated before access to Windows Updates is provided. Therefore, if you are running Windows XP under the 30-day grace period, without performing the activation process, you will be denied access to updates. Conversely, the Windows Firewall does not block all traffic; it blocks only unsolicited traffic. Automatic Updates is initiated from inside Windows, so returning traffic from this site is not blocked. The default setting for Internet Security in Windows Internet Explorer is Medium High. This setting does not stop interaction with Windows updates.

2. **Answer: C**. Microsoft offers an online Windows Update service to deliver its patches, service packs, and security updates to users.

3. **Answers: B, C**. Microsoft offers an online Windows Update Service to deliver updates to users. These updates include security updates, critical updates, or service packs.

4. **Answer: B**. In Windows 2000 and Windows XP, you can double-click on the Automatic Updates icon in the Control Panel. In either operating system, you can configure Automatic Updates to download and install updates on a specified schedule or to notify the user when high-priority updates become available. You can click on the Automatic (Recommended) option button and then enter day and time settings for Windows to install the updates under the Automatically Download Recommended Updates for My Computer and Install Them option.

Domain 3.0

Objective 3.1

1. **Answer: C**. Inkjet printers produce characters by squirting a precisely controlled stream of ink drops onto the paper. The drops must be controlled very precisely in terms of their aerodynamics, size, and shape; otherwise, the drop placement on the page becomes inexact, and the print quality falters.

2. **Answer: B**. In the dye sublimation printer, a heating element strip is used to transfer the color substance on a plastic film to the paper. The heating element contains thousands of small heat points that create fine patterns of color dots. Different temperatures can be applied to the element to produce different shades.

3. **Answer: B**. In a thermal wax transfer printer, a thermal printhead melts dots of wax-based ink from the transfer ribbon onto the paper. When the wax cools, it is permanently attached to the page.

4. **Answer: B**. Thermal printers relied on special heat-sensitive or chemically reactive paper to form characters on the page. Thermal printing techniques use heated elements to burn or melt dot pattern characters on special paper. There are two types of thermal printers: direct thermal printers and thermal wax transfer printers.

5. **Answer: C**. The IEEE has established specifications for bidirectional parallel printer cables (IEEE-1284). These cables affect the operation of EPP and ECP parallel devices.

6. **Answer: B**. A thermal fuse protects the fuser assembly from overheating. If the temperature of the fuser is not controlled correctly, it might cause severe damage to the printer, as well as present a potential fire hazard.

7. **Answer: D**. Tractor feeds are used with very heavy forms, such as multiple-part continuous forms, and are most commonly found on dot matrix printers.

8. **Answer: B**. A high voltage, applied to the primary corona wire, creates a highly charged negative field that conditions the drum to be written on by applying a uniform negative charge (–600V) to it.

Objective 3.2

1. **Answer: C**. As with all IrDA connections, the distance and angle of transfer are limited. The recommended clear distance between the two devices is 1 meter, and the maximum angle between the transmitter and receiver is 15°.

2. **Answer: D**. The density of the printout from an inkjet printer can be adjusted through its printing software. However, when the print becomes noticeably faint or the resolution becomes unacceptable, the cartridge needs to be replaced.

3. **Answers: B, D**. Most "new" scanners offer a USB port. If the old USB cable does not connect correctly to the new scanner (Type A versus Type B USB connectors), it should be a simple matter of locating the correct USB cable type for your scanner. However, it is not uncommon for scanners to feature a variety of connection options.

The scanner's interface circuitry may be able to handle different interface types, such as Centronics parallel, RS-232 serial, SCSI, USB, IEEE1394, or IrDA interfaces.

4. **Answer: D**. Color management is a set of tools used to establish and maintain consistent image appearance between different devices, such as cameras, displays, scanners, and printers. Each of these devices has different color responses when displayed. Also, no direct correlation exists between RGB color in monitors and CYMK colors in printers. However, color management acts to coordinate the appearance of these color types between the devices. The output from scanners can be converted into either RGB or CYMK color models.

5. **Answer: D**. One of the most common types of drivers associated with scanners is the TWAIN driver. The TWAIN interface specification was designed to enable different types of image acquisition devices to communicate with TWAIN-compatible applications. If a TWAIN file is missing or damaged, the TWAIN application generates an error message when you try to perform a scan operation. The scanner application software installs the TWAIN drivers when it is installed. You should uninstall and reinstall the scanner's TWAIN software.

6. **Answer: A**. The Bluetooth option enables users to print directly from notebook PCs, PDAs, or cell phones. Bluetooth can be added to an existing USB or parallel port printer through a small Bluetooth receiver that plugs into the port. It also makes printer placement a simple and dynamic activity. You need only to position the printer within the specified range (generally, 20 feet—the maximum range for low power Bluetooth is 10 meters/32 feet) of the Bluetooth device to achieve connectivity. Also, you can pick up the printer and relocate it to another room or office.

7. **Answer: C**. Because this is a new printer installation, before you leave the office, you should verify that the printer installation runs correctly from the host computer through the printer. In the case of a network-ready printer, you should verify that the customer can print from different locations in the network.

8. **Answer: C**. It is not unusual for commercial office printers to offer several types of add-on components for their machines, such as a duplexer—a device that reroutes paper through the printer so that copies can be made on both sides. However, duplexers are not typically a standard part of the printer. Therefore, your customer will likely have to purchase a duplexer for his machine before he can carry out duplex printing operations. If the duplexing hardware is installed on the printer, he should enter the printer's Properties page and enable the Duplex Printing option. However, this option can also be enabled from the Print Preferences settings of many applications.

9. **Answer: C**. As with other printer types, you should maintain laser printers in accordance with the manufacturer's guidelines. This includes installing the manufacturer's maintenance kit designed for that printer. Don't forget to reset the page counter on those copiers and laser printers that have them. This should be the last step before turning the printer over to the customer because service agreements are often based on page counts.

Objective 3.3

1. **Answer: A**. The remote computer that the printer is connected to, referred to as the *print server*, should appear in the Windows My Network Places window of the local computer. If the local computer cannot see files and printers at the print server station, file and print sharing may not be enabled there. Inadequate access rights do not prevent you from "seeing" the printer.

2. **Answer: A**. Missing print in a laser printer is normally attributed to the laser scanning module. If the laser scanning module is not correctly installed or positioned, it cannot deliver lines of print to the page.

3. **Answers: A, B**. If the tops of characters are missing, the printhead is misaligned with the platen. It might need to be reseated in the printhead carriage, or the carriage assembly might need to be adjusted to the proper height and angle.

4. **Answer: D**. If the printer operation stalls during the printing operation, some critical condition must have been reached to stop the printing process (that is, the system was running but stopped). First, access the print spooler's Document menu and try to restart the printer. If the printer still does not print, delete backed-up spool files (`.SPL` and `.TMP`) in the `%SystemRoot%\System32\Spool\Printers` directory. Begin by simply deleting the first print job to determine whether it is the source of the problem. If so, it is likely that the other print jobs will go ahead and print and allow your print job to process. Unnecessarily deleting other users' print jobs is poor networking etiquette.

5. **Answer: D**. Faint print in a laser printer can be caused by a number of things. If the toner level in the cartridge is low, empty, or poorly distributed, or the contrast control is set too low, the print quality can appear washed out. Correcting these symptoms is fairly easy. First, remove the toner cartridge, inspect it, shake it gently (if it is a sealed unit), and retry it. This is the most intuitive option because the toner runs out and can get unevenly dispersed in the cartridge. Also, the printer's contrast control is not likely to change during normal usage. The next step depends on the outcome from shaking the cartridge. If the cartridge feels as though it should have plenty of toner in it, try adjusting the printer's contrast control to see whether you can improve the print quality. If the cartridge feels as though it is empty, replace the cartridge before trying to adjust the contrast setting.

6. **Answer: C**. Some scanners have locking mechanisms that prevent the light source from moving inside the housing during transportation. If the light source is on but does not move when the system applies a scan request, refer to the scanner's documentation to determine whether your scanner has a locking mechanism. If so, check to make sure that the scanner is unlocked.

7. **Answers: A, B**. First you should check to make sure that the new ink cartridges are seated properly. If not, they do not make good electrical contact with the printer's firing circuits and are not able to produce any output. Inkjet cartridges are shipped with a piece of tape covering the jet to prevent ink from dripping out during shipping. Failure to remove this tape causes an error and prevents the jet from delivering ink to the page.

8. **Answer: C**. When the paper does not advance, the output is usually a thick, dark line across the page.

9. **Answers: B, C**. (B) Bad paper-feed rollers cause an inkjet printer to produce wavy graphics. If the paper thickness settings are correct but the print output is disfigured, you need to replace the paper-feed rollers. (C) If an inkjet printer's paper thickness selector is set improperly, the paper can slip as it moves through the printer and cause wavy graphics to be produced. Check the printer's paper thickness settings. If they are correct and the print output is disfigured, you need to replace the paper-feed rollers.

10. **Answer: B**. Many times, a paper-jam error remains even after the paper has been removed from the laser printer. This is typically caused by an interlock error. Simply opening the printer's main access door should clear the error. If the error continues after opening and closing the printer's main access cover, the next step would be to reopen the printer and check for bits of paper that may have been left behind in the paper removal process.

11. **Answer: C**. A bad primary corona can cause black pages to be produced. When this occurs, no uniform charge is placed on the drum to repel toner.

12. **Answer: A**. If the output of the printer gets lighter as it moves from left to right across the page, you might need to adjust the spacing between the platen and the printhead carriage rod to obtain proper printing.

13. **Answers: A, B, C**. Due to the extreme complexity of the laser printer's paper-handling system, paper jams are a common problem. This problem tends to increase in frequency as the printer's components wear from use. Basically, paper jams occur in all three main sections of the printer. These sections are the pickup area, registration area, and fusing area.

Domain 4.0

Objective 4.1

1. **Answer: A**. Windows XP Home and XP Media Center Edition are derivative operating systems designed for the home or small office/home office market. These versions include peer-to-peer local area networking function as an integral part of the system. The Home edition does not provide for connecting the PC to a domain-based network.

2. **Answer: C**. Most public FTP sites allow anonymous authentication for access to the site. Anonymous authentication is an interaction that occurs between the local browser and the FTP host without involving the remote user (that is, no user name or password is required to gain access).

3. **Answer: B**. When a website URL address starts with https://, it uses the Transport Layer Security (TLS) protocol (or the older Secure Sockets Layer [SSL] protocol) for secure e-commerce activities.

4. **Answer: A**. The members of the domain share a common directory database and are organized in levels. Every domain is identified by a unique name and is administered as a single unit having common rules and procedures.

5. **Answer: A**. If no DHCP server is found, Windows computers default to a random IP address in the range of 169.254.X.X and a subnet mask of 255.255.0.0. The Automatic Private IP Address (APIPA) feature is useful in smaller, single-segment networks because it effectively autoconfigures such a network.

6. **Answer: B**. A switch connects network devices together to form a local area network. Instead of repeating a received message at all its other ports, the switch can direct the information to its intended receiver if the address of the receiver is known.

7. **Answers: B, D**. A fully qualified domain name (FQDN) is a human-readable address that describes the location of the site on the Internet. It contains the host name, the domain name with any subdomains, and the top-level domain name. For example, the name "www.oneworld.owt.com" is an FQDN. The letters "www" represent the host name. The host name specifies the name of the computer that provides services and handles specific Internet requests for specific Internet addresses. In this case, the host is a World Wide Web server. The `.owt` portion represents the organization as a domain listed under the top-level domain (`.com`). The `.oneworld` portion is a subdomain of the `.owt` domain and must be locally administered by the OWT organization.

8. **Answers: A, C**. WEP is a strong encryption method, but serious hackers can crack it. This has led the wireless industry to create the stronger Wi-Fi Protected Access (WPA) standard. A newer version of WPA, called WPA2, fully implements the security mechanisms for wireless networks called for in the IEEE 802.11i standard.

9. **Answer: D**. Telnet is a service that enables you to establish a connection into another computer so that you can utilize its resources in a command-line interface environment. The client computer doesn't have to be running the same operating system as the remote server. This is a good solution for situations in which the PC environment is radically different from that of the other computer (such as a Linux or Novell system, or a mainframe computer).

10. **Answer: D**. When a DNS client submits a name resolution request to a DNS server, the server searches through its DNS database and, if necessary, through the hierarchical DNS system until it locates the host name or FQDN that was submitted to it. At this point it resolves the requested host name to the corresponding IP address and returns it back to the client.

11. **Answer: B**. The Lightweight Directory Access Protocol (LDAP) is a standardized protocol employed by many vendors, including Microsoft, to access directory databases such as Windows Active Directory.

12. **Answer: B**. The Hypertext Transfer Protocol Secure (HTTPS) is used to access linked documents on the World Wide Web that are located on a secure server. A secure server typically requires that a password be entered before access is granted. In some applications, https:// means that documents are encrypted using the Transport Layer Security (TLS) protocol—or the older Secure Sockets Layer (SSL) protocol—before sending them to a user who connects to the secure site. A connection to a certificate server that employs SSL/TLS presents a URL that begins with https://. For example, a site called https://buy.now.com is a secure site in which messages between the browser and server are encrypted. The browser indicates that the connection is secure by displaying a locked padlock, or key, near the bottom corner of the browser.

13. **Answer: C**. The File Transfer Protocol (FTP) is used to upload files to and download files from the Internet. Large files take considerably less time to send and download through an FTP operation than they would using an email server. FTP also can reconnect after a communications break and start sending information again from the point where it was interrupted. This is not true of emails with attachments.

14. **Answer: A**. The World Wide Web (WWW) is a menu system that ties together Internet resources from around the world. Web servers inventory the Web's resources. Hypertext Transfer Protocol (HTTP) is a client/server protocol used to download files from the Internet. A client, which can be any network workstation or a standalone computer connected to the Internet through an ISP, sends a request to a web server for files contained at the server. The server responds to the request by sending the files to the client. Nearly any file type can be sent using HTTP. Most Internet applications on the WWW use HTTP.

15. **Answer: B**. The BRI ISDN, which is used mostly in residential service, can transfer voice and data information in a pair of 64kbps channels.

16. **Answer: D**. An intranet is a private network built on the TCP/IP protocol that belongs to a single organization. It is, in essence, a private Internet. Like the Internet, intranets are designed to share information and services, but they are accessible only to the organization's members, with authorization. In an intranet system, a local server provides Internet applications, such as HTTP, email, FTP, and browsing for the network.

Objective 4.2

1. **Answer: B**. In Windows 2000, the Network and Dial-Up Connections page provides several key functions associated with local and wide area networking. It is used to install new network adapter cards and change their settings, change network component settings, and install TCP/IP.

2. **Answer: A**. To establish Internet Connection Sharing (ICS), you must log on to the computer using an account that has Administrator rights. In Windows XP, access the Network Connections by clicking on My Network Places and then selecting the View Network Connections option from the Network Tasks pane. Next, right-click on the connection to be shared and select the Properties option from the drop-down menu. On the Advanced tab, enable the Allow Other Network Users to Connect Through This Computer's Internet Connection setting. (You can also access the connection's properties by selecting the Change Settings of This Connection option in the Network Tasks pane, provided the Show Common Tasks in Folders option is selected in the Tools/Folder options menu.)

3. **Answer: A**. If the file is located on another machine that you can access across a network and is shared, you need to use the Universal Naming Convention (UNC) path to access the machine, and then the shared folder, and finally the desired file (that is, *computername**sharename**filename*).

4. **Answer: A**. Sharing an Internet connection enables several computers to be connected to the Internet through a single dial-up connection. These connections can be made individually or simultaneously. To establish Internet Connection Sharing (ICS), you must log on to the computer using an account that has Administrator rights. NAT is another option for enabling multiple computers to use a single channel for Internet access. Windows servers and routers are often used to implement the NAT function in larger networks. In this scenario, the company did not want to expend the money to install these types of devices to provide this function.

5. **Answer: A**. If no encryption method is configured, wireless clients can authenticate with a wireless AP using the service set identifier (SSID) name. The SSID is a 32-character identifier that is attached to the front end of packets sent across wireless networks. This is referred to as *Open System* authentication. However, with an encryption method such as WEP or WPA/WPA2 enabled, the AP and client must authenticate using a shared key (that is, all the computers in the network must be configured to use the same key to communicate). WEP provides a 128-bit mathematical key encryption scheme for encrypting data transmissions and authenticating each computer on the network.

6. **Answers: A, B**. During the AP configuration process, you need to enter a password, service set identifier (SSID) name, and an AP channel. Next, you are asked to enable encryption and security features. If the Wireless Network Configuration Wizard provides for multiple encryption levels, you should select the highest (strongest) level of encryption. To implement WEP, you need to enable it and enter the WEP key value (password), either in the form of a hexadecimal number string or as an ASCII character string. Record this string for use with the network's client computers. Each client computer needs to have the key installed the next time it attempts to connect to the network. When requested by the system, enter and confirm the WEP key.

7. **Answers: B, D**. The service set identifier (SSID) settings of all the clients and the APs should match. If you are adding an AP to a network that already has one, set the second AP to a different channel. Never set two APs in the same network to the same channel. This enables users to roam seamlessly between the different APs.

8. **Answer: B**. After the best location for the AP has been established, and it has been connected to the network host, you need to configure it for operation. Most APs provide their own browser-based wizard for this purpose. Other APs come with CD-based configuration programs. In either event, you need to start a browser on one of the network's computers, usually one that's permanently or temporarily wired to the AP, and gain access to the AP's configuration utility.

9. **Answer: C**. Type 802.11b cards have a limited range of operation (about 500 feet). This estimation relies on a clear, unobstructed pathway existing between the card and the access point. The signals used under this wireless specification do not travel well through objects.

10. **Answer: D**. Notebook computers are natural selections for use as wireless networking clients. Because they are portable, they can be used anywhere within any wireless access point's hot spot. Many enterprises are creating hot spots to enable traveling computer users to access the Internet through their access point (for a fee).

11. **Answer: A**. When setting up an email account, you must supply the configuration information (that is, email account name, password, POP3 server address, and SMTP server address).

12. **Answer: A**. Unshielded twisted-pair (UTP) is categorized in different ratings for different networking applications. CAT5e cabling is currently the most widely used specification for data communication wiring.

13. **Answer: C**. IPX/SPX is a Novell network protocol for LANs.

Objective 4.3

1. **Answer: A**. When TCP/IP is installed in a Windows 2000 or Windows XP system, a number of TCP/IP utilities designed to check out network-related problems are automatically installed with it.

2. **Answer: D**. If you can browse the network but cannot use certain resources in other locations, sharing is not turned on in the remote unit, or your account does not have proper access permissions to that resource.

3. **Answer: A**. Cabling is the single largest cause of networking problems. Because this is a new installation, the cabling and its connections are particularly suspect.

4. **Answer: B**. The loopback function is reserved under IP network 127.x.x.x and can be engaged through the PING utility.

5. **Answer: D**. The TRACERT (or traceroute when dealing with UNIX/Cisco Systems and tracepath when dealing with Linux) utility traces the route taken by packets sent across an IP network. Routers along the path return information to the inquiring system, and the utility displays the host name, IP address, and roundtrip time for each hop in the path.

6. **Answer: B**. If users can see other local computers in a TCP/IP network but cannot see remote systems on other networks, you may be having routing problems. Determine whether the address for the default gateway (router) listed in the TCP/IP properties is valid.

7. **Answers: A, B**. If web or FTP services are running on the internal network and must be made available to external customers, you can configure a filter to open the firewall to let just that service pass through. Normally, these filters are configured around services recognized by the TCP and UDP Transport layer protocols. These protocols use port numbers to identify specific processes such as HTTP or FTP. The port numbers for FTP services are 20 and 21.

8. **Answers: A, C**. If one of the WPA versions is not an option, you should enable WEP with 128-bit encryption. In addition, after you've installed and authenticated all the wireless clients, you should set the SSID Broadcast option to Disabled so that outsiders do not use SSID to acquire your address and data. Also change the SSID name from the default value if you have not already done so.

9. **Answer: D**. If a Windows client cannot locate a DHCP device when it starts up on the network, it defaults to an unused, pseudorandom IP address in the 169.254.X.X network and a subnet mask of 255.255.0.0. This provides an important clue that DHCP problems are occurring in a DHCP environment.

10. **Answer: D**. Attempt to ping a known IP address. PING is a tool used to check connectivity between IP hosts, such as between workstations or between workstations and servers.

11. **Answer: B**. The Windows Wireless Network Connection Status utility is built into all Windows XP versions and provides connection status, network name (SSID), length of current connection time, connection speed and signal strength, and number of packets sent and received.

12. **Answer: B**. The IPCONFIG utility can be started with two important option switches: /renew and /release. These switches are used to release and update IP settings received from a DHCP server. Normally, the /renew option often works without a preceding /release operation. However, this approach sometimes fails, requiring the /release operation to be performed first.

13. **Answer: A**. The loopback address and IPCONFIG utilities work locally and do not send traffic across the network. TRACERT shows connections, but it uses slightly more bandwidth than performing a PING operation on the local gateway address.

14. **Answer: A**. First, check the link light on the card; if present, the card and cable are good. The router affects everyone else on the network segment, so if it were defective, other users would also be having problems. The second most efficient check is the cabling; cabling is the leading cause of network problems.

15. **Answers: A, C**. Hardware firewalls do typically offer higher levels of protection than software-based firewalls. Hardware firewalls are typically installed between the modem and router (in some cases, they are built into the router). So, they protect the connection between the outside network and the internal network. On the other hand, software firewalls, such as the Windows Firewall utility, protect only the computer where they are installed from outside threats.

16. **Answer: C**. TCP/UDP port 80 is reserved for HTTP services.

17. **Answer: C**. The WINS server is not working, so the user is not receiving Windows Naming Service information.

18. **Answers: A, D**. (A) PING enables you to verify connections to remote hosts. You can use the command to test both the name and IP address of the remote unit. (D) NSLOOKUP is a TCP/IP utility found in Windows 2000 and Windows XP that can be entered at the command prompt to query Internet (DNS) name servers for information about hosts and domains.

19. **Answer: A**. The Reconnect at Logon option must be selected in the Map Network Drive page for the drive mapping to be a permanent part of the system. If this option is not selected when the user logs off, the mapped drive information disappears and needs to be remapped for future use. On the other hand, if a red X appears on the icon of a properly mapped drive, this indicates that the drive is no longer available. Its host computer might be turned off, the drive might have been removed, or it might no longer be on the same path. If the drive was mapped to a particular folder and the folder name has been changed, the red X also appears.

20. **Answer: A**. TCP/IP troubleshooting utilities are controlled by commands entered and run from the command prompt.

21. **Answer: A**. The IPCONFIG utility can be started with two important option switches: /renew and /release. These switches are used to release and update IP settings received from a DHCP server.

22. **Answer: B**. Because no other users are having a problem accessing the network, the problem is local to the user. This involves his PC, network adapter card, and drop cabling to the closest connectivity device. Because the vast majority of all network problems are associated with cabling, the NIC, cabling, and local connectivity device are normally checked first in situations like this. However, it is also possible that the problem is associated with the user or PC. The CapsLock setting can keep the system from logging in the user, and his account may be expired. Although user account problems and login errors can keep the user from accessing the network, they are not typically the first things you check unless you have some indication these items might be involved.

Domain 5.0

Objective 5.1

1. **Answer: B**. When users of a Windows 2000 system complain that they can see files in a folder but cannot access any of the files, they might have been assigned the List Folder Contents permission at the folder level. The List Folder Contents permission enables users only to view the contents of the folder, denying them all other permissions, including Read and Execute.

2. **Answer: D**. When files and folders from an NTFS partition are moved to a FAT partition, their NTFS attributes and security features are lost. Even moving files between different NTFS partitions on different drives can change the security level of the files. Migrating NTFS data to a partition that has lower permission levels than the original partition causes the data to inherit the lesser permissions of the target folder.

3. **Answers: A, D**. The Modify permission enables users to modify and delete the file and to perform all the activities associated with the Read, Write, and Read & Execute permissions. The Full Control permission enables the user or group to take ownership of the file and to change its permissions, as well as perform all the other activities possible with all the other permissions.

4. **Answer: D**. By default, only members of the Administrators and Power Users groups have the ability to install applications in a Windows domain. Members of other Windows groups do not have this ability unless they are given it by a Group Policy or inherit it through a group association.

5. **Answer: D**. Power Users is a special group that has permissions to perform many management tasks on the system but does not have the full administrative privileges of the Administrator account. Power Users can create and manage users and groups that they create. Also, they do not have access to files and folders on NTFS volumes unless they are granted permissions to them through other sources. There are no members in this group when it is created.

6. **Answer: B**. The most efficient method of assigning large groups of users access to the same resources is to (1) create the group, (2) make all users a member of the group, and (3) assign the group access permissions to the resource.

7. **Answer: C**. In matters of security, such as handling of passwords, you should always fall back on the company's policies to protect the company, its employees, its proprietary information, its intellectual properties, and yourself.

Objective 5.2

1. **Answer: D**. You must establish a group (or select an appropriate existing group) and give group members access to the folder with proper permission levels. Simply setting up encryption on the folder does not work here because you want to share the folder with other users. Under the EFS system in Windows 2000 and Windows XP, only the person currently logged in when the files were encrypted can decrypt them. You can't give that permission to a group.

2. **Answer: D**. Files and folders can be encrypted from the command line using the `Cipher` command. Files can also be encrypted through their Properties pages in the Windows Explorer.

3. **Answer: B**. The Windows 2000 NTFS system provides an Encrypted File System (EFS) utility that is the basis of storing encrypted files on NTFS volumes. After a file or folder has been encrypted, only the user who encrypted it can access it. Other users cannot open or share the file (although they can delete it).

4. **Answer: A**. The Windows XP Local Area Connections properties window offers two tabs not available in the Windows 2000 version: Advanced and Authentication. The Advanced tab is used to enable the Windows XP Firewall. The Authentication tab is used to configure authentication protocols.

5. **Answer: C**. Encryption is treated as a file attribute in Windows 2000 and Windows XP. Therefore, to encrypt a file, you simply need to access its Properties page by right-clicking on it and selecting its Properties option from the pop-up menu. Move to the Advanced Attribute window under the General tab and click the Encrypt Contents to Secure Data check box.

6. **Answer: D**. Biometric scanners are getting significantly more sophisticated—including facial-scanning devices, searchable databases, and supporting application programs. However, the biometric authentication device most widely used with PCs is the finger-print scanner. Some manufacturers offer miniature touchpad versions that sit on the desk and connect to the system though a cable and USB connector. Other fingerprint scanners are built into key fobs that plug directly into the USB port. Some manufactur-ers even build these devices into the top of the mouse.

7. **Answer: C**. Windows 2000 and XP Professional users can implement the EFS option to encrypt their files and folders on NTFS drives. To do so, they simply click on the Encrypt Contents to Secure Data check box in the file's or folder's Advanced Attributes window. Users can open these files and folders just as they would any ordinary files or folders. However, if someone gains unauthorized access to the computer, that person cannot open the encrypted files or folders (unless she can log in as you, or she has access to effective password-cracking software). EFS is simple to use because it is actually an attribute that can be established for files or folders.

8. **Answer: C**. Under general user accounts, the virus and worms cannot gain access to system-level files (admin rights are required for this). Therefore, give as few users as possible administrative rights.

9. **Answer: D**. Digital certificates are another major security feature in the Windows 2000 and Windows XP operating systems. Digital certificates are password-protected, encrypted data files that include data that identifies the transmitting system and can be used to authenticate external users to the network through Virtual Private Networks (VPNs). VPNs use message encryption and other security techniques to ensure that only authorized users can access the message as it passes through public transmis-sion media. In particular, VPNs provide secure Internet communications by establish-ing encrypted data tunnels across the WAN that cannot be penetrated by others.

Objective 5.3

1. **Answers: A, B, C**. Access to network accounts is based on your user account name and password, which the network asks for each time you log on. Forgetting or misspelling either item results in your being denied access to the network. Password entries are typically case sensitive, so forgetting to properly capitalize key characters or having the Caps Lock key engaged prevents the system from authenticating you and providing access. On the other hand, if the network server is down, there is no component in the network to authenticate you and log you in. Finally, if you violate one of the network's established password policies, you may be locked out and prevented from logging in for a predetermined amount of time.

2. **Answer: A**. It is a good security move to convert any FAT or FAT32 partitions to NTFS so that the stronger NTFS and share permissions can be used to provide stronger control over access to data on the drive. This also allows you to use the NTFS encrypting file system to protect files on the drive. When a file is moved from an NTFS partition to a FAT partition, the NTFS-specific attributes are discarded.

3. **Answer: C**. Transmissions from wireless network devices cannot be confined to the local environment of a residence or business. Although the range is typically limited to a few hundred feet, RF signals can easily be intercepted even outside the vicinity of the stated security perimeter. Any unauthorized mobile terminal can accomplish this using an 802.11 receiver. Any unauthorized WAP in a wireless network is referred to as a *rogue access point*. These APs can be used for either malicious purposes, or simply to gain free access to a wireless network connection.

Objective 5.4

1. **Answer: A**. Social engineers exploit people's human nature to fool them into providing information about themselves, their business, or their computer/network. They accomplish this by using trickery, deceit, lies, gifts, or acts of kindness to first establish a level of trust. They then use this trust relationship to gain information.

2. **Answer: C**. Social engineering efforts can go to great lengths to get users to surrender their login information. For instance, the programmer may design a login screen that exactly mimics a login screen that you expect to see from a trusted site or company. In the background, the login screen passes your information to the programmer. The best option for this situation is to repartition and reformat the drive to remove any potential threat.

3. **Answer: C**. This is a classic description of a phishing expedition. These expeditions typically begin with an email or instant messenger communication that points the target toward the spoofed site. These sites are often look-alikes for sites where financial activities are conducted. Users should be educated about how to handle suspicious requests properly. They should know to ignore the request, delete the email message, and report the incident to their supervisors. However, they should not forward the request because doing so also poses a security risk.

Domain 6.0

Objective 6.1

1. **Answer: B**. Avoid putting customers on hold if possible. If you must put them on hold, make certain to get their name and phone number in case anything happens. If you expect that a customer may be on hold for more than a couple of minutes, ask if you can call the customer back.

2. **Answers: A, B**. One of the attributes that makes a good customer service person is the ability to actively listen to the customer. Real listening means not just hearing what the customer has to say, but trying to pin down what she means. The technique for doing this is called *active listening*. Using active listening involves focusing on the customer's comments, repeating key information to let the customer know that you are following what she is saying, and avoiding distractions such as visual or audible activities that draw your attention away from the customer.

3. **Answer: A**. When customers become angry, attempt to de-escalate the situation. This usually involves letting customers get pent-up frustrations off their chest by simply listening to them. The best thing to do is let customers vent verbal frustrations without reply. It can be very frustrating to let customers vent without interrupting them, but that is an important part of successfully handling irate customers. When you do reply, remain calm, talk in a steady voice, and avoid making inflammatory comments. Also, try to avoid taking a defensive stance because this signals a conflict point. Realize that criticism given out by customers is generally not personal, so don't take it personally. Information delivered with an aggressive attitude normally leads to an aggressive or retaliatory response from customers.

4. **Answers: A, B, D**. The art of active listening involves focusing on the customer's comments, repeating key information to let the customer know that you are following what he is saying, and avoiding distractions such as visual or audible activities that draw away your attention away from the customer.

5. **Answer: D**. If a problem runs beyond the scope of your company's agreement with the customer, take the initiative to move it to the next level of authority. This allows your management to take proper action in deciding how the particular customer should be handled.

6. **Answer: D**. Always notify customers as soon as possible about any appointment changes, service delays, complications, or setbacks that may occur. Apologize for the inconvenience and ask how they would like to proceed. These things happen to everyone, and your best defenses against customer dissatisfaction are promptness and good communication.

7. **Answer: D**. Even if you are sure that you know what is going on after the first sentence, have the patience to listen to the customer's complete description. This is not only common courtesy, but also serves to uncover extra data about the problem.

8. **Answers: A, C**. Because the customer has probably explained everything at least once, you should begin by apologizing for any repetition the hand-off might create. You still need to ask all the relevant questions to get yourself up to speed, and this may annoy a customer who has a broken piece of equipment and has been through the process without success. Having the other technician give you his notes on the problem can also help you minimize the repetitive questions the customer might need to answer.

9. **Answer: A**. Although this is an extreme circumstance, you are governed by the company's policies regarding returns and repairs. In most cases this would involve escalating the customer's problem to a higher authority level to be dealt with.

10. **Answer: B**. The person who makes the original contact with the customer is the initial problem owner until that person has reached a point where the customer service plan indicates that the problem should be handed off to another level or section of the customer service organization. If the problem falls within the scope of the initial problem owner's responsibilities, problem ownership should remain with that technician.

11. **Answer: A**. Taking ownership of a customer's problem means that there is a program and/or personal dedication in place to make sure that the customer gets his problem resolved in an efficient and direct way. The support mechanism is constructed in such a way that there is no way to pass off a customer to someone else and forget about him. At each level, the technician is responsible for resolving the customer's complaint, problem, or issue. This may involve handling the customer's problem personally or setting up a connection between the customer and someone directly qualified to handle the nature of problem the customer is having. Even then, the first-level technician is required to follow up to make sure that customer's problem was taken care of.

12. **Answer: B**. The term *warm hand-off* generally is used within the call-center industry to describe a situation in which a caller is handed from one technician to another without having to call again or re-establish the context in which the call is being made. This can mean, for example, that a first-level customer service technician makes a new connection to a second-level technician and explains the customer's problem to the new technician. It may also include situations in which customer information is electronically transferred or made available to the second technician.

Objective 6.2

1. **Answer: A**. Pornographic materials on computers fall into the same category as illegal copies of programs. Having such materials on a PC is reason for immediate termination in most companies. If you are exposed to illegal software or pornographic material on a customer's computer, you should report this to your supervisor. If you discover illegal software or pornographic material on one of your company's computers, report it to the proper authority in your organization (provided you are not authorized by your company's policies to handle this situation yourself).

2. **Answer: B**. If the customer is too angry to work through the details with you, conclude the encounter by trying to do, or offer, something to lessen her frustration level, and make certain to follow up as you've indicated. As soon as possible, withdraw from the confrontation and let the situation cool off. Inform your supervisor of the situation as quickly as possible so that you have inside support and so that a plan of relief can be implemented.

3. **Answers: A, C.** Even if you know the other person's number, you should respect his right to privacy and offer to intercede between the customer and other technician. If you have the other technician's number, call it and arrange the call between them and the customer. If you don't have the number, offer to have the technician call the customer when you see him next.

4. **Answer: B.** Consider the impact your work will have on the customer or user's work area. In this example, you need to consider the best location to perform this operation: Should you work at the user's desk, work at some convenient place within the facility, or take the machine to your work area? This decision may be dictated by time pressures (does the PC need to be returned to service as quickly as possible?) or by appearance (would the appearance of a disassembled computer on a user's desk be improper for the facility you are working in?). Also, the user may need to do other things at her desk while her computer is down. Another element you may need to consider is the availability of proper grounding options to prevent ESD damages.

5. **Answer: B.** Try never to leave customers hanging without a path to get their problems addressed. If this request cannot be performed under your company's policies, there may be nothing you can offer. However, you should always check to see whether there is some other option available that you are not aware of.

6. **Answer: A.** If a problem runs beyond the scope of your position or your capabilities, take the initiative to move it to the next level of authority. This is also true for requests for work to be performed that are outside your assignment or your company's agreement with the customer. Escalate the request so that management can take proper action in deciding how the particular customer should be handled.

7. **Answer: A.** If you discover illegal, improper, or pornographic material on one of your company's computers, report it to the proper authority in your organization (provided you are not authorized by your company's policies to handle this situation yourself).

8. **Answer: D.** The best tool for training users is typically the actual equipment or software they are expected to use. If you are coaching one or two users, it is best to pull up a chair and get to an equal level with them. This allows you to make the training more personable and less formal. Use the documentation that comes with the hardware or software as part of the training process. Point out and mark key topic areas in the documentation that you know the users will need after you're gone. However, do not read the manuals to them; this is an instant cure for insomnia and very ineffective training. Also be careful to use language that the users can relate to. Use proper terminology. Avoid jargon or industry slang when coaching users.

CHAPTER FOUR

Depot Technician Exam

Practice Questions

Domain 1.0: Personal Computer Components

Objective 1.1: Install, configure, optimize, and upgrade personal computer components

1. The types of connectors usually associated with speaker and microphone ports are _____.

   - ○ **A.** 25-pin, D-shells
   - ○ **B.** 1/8″ mini plugs and jacks
   - ○ **C.** RJ-11 jacks and plugs
   - ○ **D.** 15-pin, D-shells

Quick Answer: **360**
Detailed Answer: **364**

2. You are installing an OEM processor upgrade that calls for you to install a faster Pentium 4 processor in an existing system. Although OEM processors do not include a fan and heat-sink unit, you suspect that you need to upgrade the system's cooling capabilities to accommodate the faster processor. However, you are not sure which fan and heat-sink module needs to be installed. What should you do to ensure proper cooling for this processor?

Quick Answer: **360**
Detailed Answer: **364**

- ○ **A.** Flash the BIOS to upgrade it for the new processor. The Flash program contains updated fan control information for the new processor.

- ○ **B.** Because both processors are Pentium 4s, there is no need to change the fan unit. The BIOS will adapt to the new processor automatically.

- ○ **C.** Install the fastest compatible fan unit available. The BIOS will automatically adjust the fan speed to compensate for any additional heat and you will have ensured that enough cooling capability is available.

- ○ **D.** You must research and locate a proper cooling system for this processor by matching its operating temperature specification to the fan unit.

3. How many pins are on a Socket A microprocessor?

Quick Answer: **360**
Detailed Answer: **364**

- ○ **A.** 370
- ○ **B.** 423
- ○ **C.** 462
- ○ **D.** 478

4. The key to inserting a microprocessor is to _____.

Quick Answer: **360**
Detailed Answer: **364**

- ○ **A.** make sure to orient the writing on the top of the chip with that of the previous processor

- ○ **B.** align the notch in the chip with the notch in the socket

- ○ **C.** reattach the fan unit properly

- ○ **D.** look for the arrow on the chip and align it with the arrow on the PC board

5. What specification must you observe when upgrading a power supply?

Quick Answer: **360**
Detailed Answer: **364**

- ○ **A.** Maximum current capabilities
- ○ **B.** Maximum wattage rating
- ○ **C.** Output voltage levels
- ○ **D.** Internal resistance

6. What are the consequences of mixing RAM types and speeds within a system? (Select all that apply.)

Quick Answer: **360**
Detailed Answer: **364**

- ○ **A.** It causes the system to lock up.
- ○ **B.** The system runs slower.
- ○ **C.** Hard-memory errors occur.
- ○ **D.** There is no effect.

7. How many devices can be attached to a single Universal Serial Bus (USB) host?

Quick Answer: **360**
Detailed Answer: **364**

- ○ **A.** 32
- ○ **B.** 64
- ○ **C.** 127
- ○ **D.** 255

8. What is the recommended maximum length of an RS-232 cable?

Quick Answer: **360**
Detailed Answer: **364**

- ○ **A.** 100 feet (30 meters)
- ○ **B.** 30 feet (9 meters)
- ○ **C.** 10 feet (3 meters)
- ○ **D.** 50 feet (15 meters)

9. You are thinking about setting up a simple striped array on your email server at the office. What is the minimum number of drives required to implement a RAID0 solution?

Quick Answer: **360**
Detailed Answer: **365**

- ○ **A.** 1
- ○ **B.** 2
- ○ **C.** 3
- ○ **D.** 4

10. RAID0 is also known as _____.

Quick Answer: **360**
Detailed Answer: **365**

- ○ **A.** disk duplexing
- ○ **B.** disk mirroring
- ○ **C.** a striped disk array
- ○ **D.** a disk parity array

11. Which of the following components make up the Pentium processor cooling system? (Select all that apply.)

Quick Answer: **360**
Detailed Answer: **365**

- ○ **A.** The heat sink
- ○ **B.** The fan unit
- ○ **C.** The socket
- ○ **D.** The chipset

12. Identify the SATA signal connecter from the diagram that follows.

Quick Answer: **360**
Detailed Answer: **365**

- ○ **A.** A
- ○ **B.** B
- ○ **C.** C
- ○ **D.** D

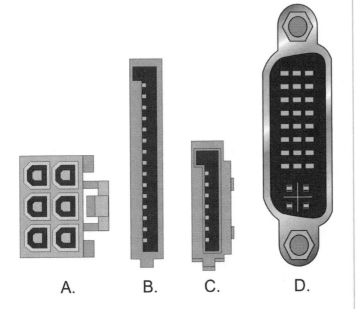

A.   B.   C.   D.

Connector Types

13. Identify three sources of determining the speed of the currently installed microprocessor in a Windows XP Professional PC.

Quick Answer: **360**
Detailed Answer: **365**

- ○ **A.** Through the System Information utility
- ○ **B.** Through the Device Manager utility
- ○ **C.** Through the Control Panel's Processors icon
- ○ **D.** Through the System Properties dialog box

14. Identify two sources for determining the amount of RAM currently installed in a Windows XP Professional PC.

Quick Answer: **360**
Detailed Answer: **365**

- ○ **A.** Through the System Information utility
- ○ **B.** Through the Device Manager utility
- ○ **C.** Through the Control Panel's Memory icon
- ○ **D.** Through the System Properties dialog box

15. Which of the following properly describes the correct technique for installing thermal compound between a new microprocessor and its heat sink?

Quick Answer: **360**
Detailed Answer: **365**

- ○ **A.** Run a thin layer on the top of the processor.
- ○ **B.** Run an even layer on the top of the heat sink.
- ○ **C.** Run a bead around the edges of the heat sink.
- ○ **D.** Run a bead around the edges of the microprocessor.

16. What voltages are present on the power supply's 4-pin Auxiliary (disk drive) power connector?

Quick Answer: **360**
Detailed Answer: **366**

- ○ **A.** +5/+12 VDC
- ○ **B.** +9/+14 VDC
- ○ **C.** +7 VDC and ground
- ○ **D.** +5 VDC and ground

17. What action must be taken to restore the system if the CMOS supervisory password is forgotten in an ATX system?

Quick Answer: **360**
Detailed Answer: **366**

- ○ **A.** Unplug the computer from the power outlet and remove the CMOS backup battery.
- ○ **B.** Physically remove and reinstall the CMOS backup battery.
- ○ **C.** Remove the microprocessor for 2 minutes to let the information dissipate from the system.
- ○ **D.** Change the Password Enable setting in CMOS.

18. Where is system hardware configuration information stored in a notebook PC?

Quick Answer: **360**
Detailed Answer: **366**

- ○ **A.** In the BIOS
- ○ **B.** In the CMOS area of the RTC
- ○ **C.** In the microprocessor's configuration registers
- ○ **D.** On the hard drive in the swap file

19. After you physically install a sound card in a desktop PC's expansion slot, what is the first step in starting up the system?

Quick Answer: **360**
Detailed Answer: **366**

- ○ **A.** Connect the microphone to the MIC jack.
- ○ **B.** Connect the speakers to the speaker jacks of the sound card.
- ○ **C.** Turn on the computer and let Windows detect and install the correct drivers for the card.
- ○ **D.** Plug the computer into the AC power source and turn it on.

20. Which TCP/IP utility can you use to determine whether the network adapter is receiving an IP address?

  ○ **A.** PING

  ○ **B.** TRACERT

  ○ **C.** IPCONFIG

  ○ **D.** NBSTAT

Quick Answer: **360**
Detailed Answer: **366**

21. Which of the following connector types are typically used for video output in a PC? (Select all that apply.)

  ○ **A.** VGA

  ○ **B.** HDMI

  ○ **C.** PS/2

  ○ **D.** USB

Quick Answer: **360**
Detailed Answer: **366**

22. How much information can you store on a double-sided, single-layer DVD?

  ○ **A.** 4.7GB

  ○ **B.** 9.4GB

  ○ **C.** 700MB

  ○ **D.** 17.1GB

Quick Answer: **360**
Detailed Answer: **366**

23. You have been called to a customer's residence to examine his high-end gaming computer. He is frustrated because its performance level is not as good as he had been led to believe. When you examine the system, you notice that the system board has two 16X PCIe video slots. One has a video adapter installed, and the other is empty. What type of system board is this likely to be, and what can you do to increase the system's performance?

  ○ **A.** The system board is probably SLI Ready, and you should install an additional SLI video card to improve performance.

  ○ **B.** The system board is probably MLI Ready, and you should install an adapter card–based MLI RAM accelerator.

  ○ **C.** The system board is probably Next Ready, and you should install an adapter card–based NR disk drive accelerator.

  ○ **D.** The system board is probably Game Ready, and you should replace the existing video adapter with a dual-channel Game Ready card.

Quick Answer: **360**
Detailed Answer: **367**

24. Under what circumstances can you install an NLX system board in a Micro ATX case?

Quick Answer: **360**
Detailed Answer: **367**

- ○ **A.** None; the two form factors are incompatible with each other.
- ○ **B.** Always; the two form factors are compatible with each other.
- ○ **C.** When you install an NLX-to-MATX adapter kit.
- ○ **D.** Only in PC versions that use a universal tower case.

25. How many devices can an ATX Pentium system board support if it employs EIDE technology with ATA-**2** enhancements?

Quick Answer: **360**
Detailed Answer: **367**

- ○ **A.** 2
- ○ **B.** 4
- ○ **C.** 8
- ○ **D.** 16

26. You have been tasked with upgrading the existing RAM in one of the production room's PCs. What are the most important considerations you must take before ordering new RAM for this machine?

Quick Answer: **360**
Detailed Answer: **367**

- ○ **A.** The PC's current RAM type and speed
- ○ **B.** The speed of the PC's current microprocessor
- ○ **C.** The PC's front-side bus speed
- ○ **D.** The PC's total RAM capacity

27. Which peripheral interfaces listed require that the system be shut down to change devices? (Select all that apply.)

Quick Answer: **360**
Detailed Answer: **367**

- ○ **A.** Parallel port
- ○ **B.** Serial port
- ○ **C.** USB port
- ○ **D.** FireWire port

28. When you are installing a ribbon cable for a PATA drive, the color stripe should point to _____.

Quick Answer: **360**
Detailed Answer: **367**

- ○ **A.** pin 80
- ○ **B.** pin 34
- ○ **C.** pin 40
- ○ **D.** pin 1

29. You are installing new PATA hard drives and DVD drives in new systems you are building for a client. The system boards you are using feature two IDE interface connections. Which cable type would you use to connect the new PATA drives to the IDE interface on these system boards?

- ○ **A.** 34-conductor ribbon cable with 34-pin headers
- ○ **B.** 36-conductor serial cable with Centronic connectors
- ○ **C.** 50-conductor ribbon cable with 50-pin headers
- ○ **D.** 80-conductor ribbon cable with 40-pin headers

30. If you are installing a new PATA hard drive upgrade that will be the only drive in the system, how should you configure it?

- ○ **A.** As the primary slave
- ○ **B.** As the secondary master
- ○ **C.** As the secondary slave
- ○ **D.** As the primary master

31. After you've completed the physical installation of a new SATA drive in the system, you want to install Windows XP on the drive. During the installation process, you receive this error message: Setup did not find any hard disk drives installed in your system. What should you do to correct this problem?

- ○ **A.** Partition the drive and use it.
- ○ **B.** Configure the drive's jumpers.
- ○ **C.** Load OEM drivers for the new drive.
- ○ **D.** Load Microsoft signed drivers for the drive.

32. What size socket is required to install a second-generation Athlon 64 processor?

- ○ **A.** Socket 939
- ○ **B.** Socket 775
- ○ **C.** Socket 750
- ○ **D.** Socket 439

33. After you upgrade a desktop PC by installing a new PC133 DRAM module, you start the system and see that it is still identifying the RAM as PC100. What action should you take to determine why this is occurring? (Select all that apply.)

    ○ **A.** Flash the BIOS with the latest updates for this system.

    ○ **B.** Check the front-side bus speed of the installed processor.

    ○ **C.** Check the installed RAM to make sure that it is all PC133 DRAM.

    ○ **D.** Check the CMOS Setup to confirm that the system is configured properly for the new RAM.

34. What is the minimum RAM type that should be used with a 133MHz FSB?

    ○ **A.** PC133

    ○ **B.** PC166

    ○ **C.** DDR133

    ○ **D.** PC100

35. You are assembling a new system for a friend, and you see that the system uses 240-pin memory modules. What type of memory modules should you purchase to build your friend's system?

    ○ **A.** DDR DIMMs

    ○ **B.** DDR2 RIMMs

    ○ **C.** DDR SODIMMs

    ○ **D.** DDR2 DIMMs

36. Which of the following are legitimate system board form factors? (Select all that apply.)

    ○ **A.** MicroATX

    ○ **B.** HTX

    ○ **C.** ATX

    ○ **D.** NLX

37. Which option must be enabled in the CMOS Setup to support large hard drive sizes and allow the IDE controller to convert the sector/head/cylinder addresses into a physical block address that improves data throughput?

- ○ **A.** Normal
- ○ **B.** Auto
- ○ **C.** LBA
- ○ **D.** ECHS

38. Which of the following are legitimate PATA drive configuration options? (Select all that apply.)

- ○ **A.** Master
- ○ **B.** Cable Select
- ○ **C.** ID Source
- ○ **D.** Slave

39. Which RAID type employs mirroring?

- ○ **A.** RAID0
- ○ **B.** RAID1
- ○ **C.** RAID2
- ○ **D.** RAID5

Objective 1.2: Identify tools, diagnostic procedures, and troubleshooting techniques for personal computer components

1. If a system produces an error message before the single beep during bootup, what type of problem is normally indicated?

- ○ **A.** Configuration
- ○ **B.** Hardware
- ○ **C.** Operating system
- ○ **D.** Bootup

2. What happens when you mix different IDE drive types, such as a UDMA 100 hard drive and a UDMA 66 hard drive, on a single signal cable?

Quick Answer: **360**
Detailed Answer: **369**

- ○ **A.** Only the master device is disabled.
- ○ **B.** Only the slave device is disabled.
- ○ **C.** Both master and slave devices are disabled.
- ○ **D.** The disk drive system works normally but at the slowest device speed.

3. You need to locate where an ethernet cable ends. What device can be used to locate it?

Quick Answer: **360**
Detailed Answer: **369**

- ○ **A.** A multimeter
- ○ **B.** An oscilloscope
- ○ **C.** An ethernet loopback dongle
- ○ **D.** A Time Domain Reflectometer (TDR)

4. Which of the following questions would be helpful to ask computer operators when they present a problem to you?

Quick Answer: **360**
Detailed Answer: **369**

- ○ **A.** Are you still under warranty?
- ○ **B.** What were you doing when the problem happened, and when did it occur?
- ○ **C.** How long have you been operating a computer?
- ○ **D.** Where are you located?

5. A friend has asked you to check out her PC. She has tried to upgrade its CPU and RAM using a "How To" book purchased at the local bookstore. The system shows no signs of operating except that the power light comes on when you hit the On/Off switch. When you open the system unit, you notice that the fan and heat-sink unit are simply sitting on top of the processor and not locked down. Also the processor sockets locking arm is not clamped down, and the processor is not all the way down in the socket. What should you do first in this situation?

Quick Answer: **360**
Detailed Answer: **369**

- ○ **A.** Lock the processor securely in place by closing the socket's locking arm.
- ○ **B.** Check for thermal grease on the heat sink.
- ○ **C.** Check the processor for bent pins.
- ○ **D.** Snap the fan/heat-sink unit into position and make sure that its power connection is properly attached.

6. What are the effects of microprocessor fan failures on the system?

Quick Answer: **360**
Detailed Answer: **369**

   ○ **A.** The system slows down noticeably.

   ○ **B.** The system displays Excessive Temperature Failure error messages.

   ○ **C.** The system continuously fails and then restarts.

   ○ **D.** The system locks up after a short period of operation.

7. The Windows Recovery Console does all the following except _____.

Quick Answer: **360**
Detailed Answer: **369**

   ○ **A.** copy files

   ○ **B.** control startup of services

   ○ **C.** format volumes

   ○ **D.** uninstall programs

8. After you upgrade a video adapter card's driver in Windows XP, the video display is scrambled. What action should you take to revert to the old driver version?

Quick Answer: **360**
Detailed Answer: **370**

   ○ **A.** Boot into Safe Mode with the command prompt only and remove the driver.

   ○ **B.** Boot into Safe Mode and run the Driver Rollback feature from the Device Manager.

   ○ **C.** Use the SFC utility to start up the system and roll back the driver.

   ○ **D.** Use the Recovery Console to reboot the system and then roll back the driver.

9. What conditions could cause the Device Manager utility to display an exclamation point on a yellow background next to a PC Card adapter? (Select all that apply.)

Quick Answer: **360**
Detailed Answer: **370**

   ○ **A.** The PC Card device might be faulty.

   ○ **B.** The PC Card controller in the notebook might be faulty.

   ○ **C.** The operating system does not support the installed PC Card device.

   ○ **D.** PC Card slot support has been disabled in the CMOS Setup.

10. When you are checking the power supply unit with a digital multimeter, it should be set to _____.

Quick Answer: **360**
Detailed Answer: **370**

- ○ **A.** DC current
- ○ **B.** DC voltage
- ○ **C.** AC current
- ○ **D.** AC voltage

11. Which symptom would the POST not identify?

Quick Answer: **360**
Detailed Answer: **370**

- ○ **A.** A corrupt CMOS RAM location
- ○ **B.** A bad keyboard controller
- ○ **C.** A failing hard drive
- ○ **D.** A RAM memory module that fails at high temperature

12. You have added a second hard drive to a working system. When the system boots, an error message appears on the screen, and the system fails to boot up. What is the most likely cause?

Quick Answer: **360**
Detailed Answer: **370**

- ○ **A.** The new drive is defective.
- ○ **B.** The cable is defective.
- ○ **C.** Both drives are set to master.
- ○ **D.** Only one drive can be connected at a time.

13. You build your first PC at home. When you turn on your computer, the floppy drive fails to work. Also, you notice that the floppy drive operating light is on continuously. What is the problem?

Quick Answer: **360**
Detailed Answer: **370**

- ○ **A.** The floppy drive is bad and needs to be replaced.
- ○ **B.** The motherboard BIOS needs to be upgraded.
- ○ **C.** The floppy drive cable has been connected backward.
- ○ **D.** The power supply connection to the floppy drive is bad.

14. As you begin to troubleshoot a coworker's PC, you realize that the power supply fan is not working. What items should you check to determine why this problem has occurred? (Select all that apply.)

Quick Answer: **360**
Detailed Answer: **370**

- ○ **A.** Check to make sure that the system unit's air vents are clear.
- ○ **B.** Check the system's CMOS configuration to make sure that the fan circuitry is enabled there.
- ○ **C.** Check the external voltage selector switch setting on the back of the power supply unit.
- ○ **D.** Check the fan's power connection.

15. After you install an 80GB drive in a desktop PC, only 20GB is displayed when the system is started. No extra disk space is shown in Windows Explorer. How can you make use of the rest of the space on the disk without losing data?

   ○ **A.** Use the Disk Manager utility to partition the rest of the disk space on the drive.

   ○ **B.** Use the Device Manager to recalculate the geometry of the disk to use the additional space on the drive.

   ○ **C.** You must back up the data on the disk and reformat it to include the additional space.

   ○ **D.** You must repartition the drive and start over from the beginning.

16. One of your customers has called you in to determine why a new Media Center PC he's assembled is not performing well. As you investigate the system, you see that it has an Ultra ATA-100 drive that does not seem to be performing up to its full potential. Which of the following could be causing this problem?

   ○ **A.** The technician who assembled the system did not enable the LBA mode in the CMOS.

   ○ **B.** The disk drive has been placed on the same IDE channel as the CD/DVD-RW drive, which slows the operation of the channel significantly.

   ○ **C.** The technician who assembled the system did not use an 80-wire EIDE cable.

   ○ **D.** The swap file has become too large and should be moved to another drive.

17. One of your associates has contacted you about using isopropyl alcohol that was included in his standard field supply kit. His understanding is that it is not a good idea to use alcohol to clean PC components. Which of the following is true concerning using isopropyl alcohol in PC maintenance programs?

   ○ **A.** Isopropyl alcohol corrodes metal components.

   ○ **B.** Isopropyl alcohol evaporates and leaves a residue that can prevent contact between electrical components.

   ○ **C.** Isopropyl alcohol is extremely flammable.

   ○ **D.** Isopropyl alcohol can damage the plastic portions of the PC.

18. After you install a new processor in a desktop PC, you notice that the system stops after running awhile. What is most likely the cause of this problem?

Quick Answer: **360**
Detailed Answer: **371**

- ○ **A.** You installed the wrong processor type.

- ○ **B.** You failed to configure the CMOS Setup for the new processor values.

- ○ **C.** You failed to install the processor fan assembly properly.

- ○ **D.** You failed to flash the BIOS to logically upgrade the system for the new processor.

19. What is the easiest way to test a video display monitor?

Quick Answer: **360**
Detailed Answer: **371**

- ○ **A.** Plug the monitor into another working PC.

- ○ **B.** Replace its video adapter and allow the PnP process to detect the monitor.

- ○ **C.** Restart the system in Safe Mode to load the minimal VGA driver for the monitor.

- ○ **D.** Replace the monitor with a known working model.

20. A customer has tried to upgrade her system from Windows 2000 Professional to Windows XP Home. Different I/O error messages appear when she tries to start the system. What can you do to correct these errors?

Quick Answer: **360**
Detailed Answer: **371**

- ○ **A.** Reinstall Windows 2000 Professional.

- ○ **B.** Upgrade to Windows XP Professional.

- ○ **C.** Use the Device Manager to locate the defective driver and load the old driver from the Windows 2000 distribution disc.

- ○ **D.** Use the Device Manager to locate the defective driver and load the newest drivers for the failing device.

21. You are called out to troubleshoot a system that doesn't start up and makes a repetitive loud clicking sound when you turn it on. Which component is most likely the cause of these problems?

Quick Answer: **360**
Detailed Answer: **371**

- ○ **A.** The hard disk drive
- ○ **B.** The video adaptor
- ○ **C.** The network adapter card
- ○ **D.** The microprocessor fan

22. How can a CD be retrieved from a disabled CD-ROM drive?

   ○ **A.** Insert a straightened paper clip into the tray-release access hole in the front panel.

   ○ **B.** Press the Open/Close button.

   ○ **C.** Eject the disk using the operating system.

   ○ **D.** Use a thin knife to gently pry open the door.

Quick Answer: **360**
Detailed Answer: **371**

Objective 1.3: Perform preventative maintenance of personal computer components

1. Speakers are checked using the _____ setting of a multimeter.

   ○ **A.** volt

   ○ **B.** amperage

   ○ **C.** capacitance

   ○ **D.** ohms

Quick Answer: **361**
Detailed Answer: **371**

2. What must you do first if you want to troubleshoot a USB problem on a Windows 2000 system?

   ○ **A.** Open the Device Manager.

   ○ **B.** Log on as a member of the Administrators group.

   ○ **C.** Select the USB driver and click the Properties button.

   ○ **D.** Restart the system.

Quick Answer: **361**
Detailed Answer: **371**

3. What condition is indicated by the `Hard Drive Boot Failure` error messages?

   ○ **A.** The MBR is missing or corrupt.

   ○ **B.** The drive is not formatted.

   ○ **C.** Operating system files are missing or corrupt.

   ○ **D.** The hard drive signal cable is not attached.

Quick Answer: **361**
Detailed Answer: **371**

4. What meter reading would you expect from an open speaker?

   ○ **A.** 4 ohms

   ○ **B.** Infinite (or a blank display)

   ○ **C.** 8 ohms

   ○ **D.** 0 ohms

Quick Answer: **361**
Detailed Answer: **371**

5. What effects does leaving off expansion slot covers after an upgrade have on the operation of the system? (Select all that apply.)

Quick Answer: **361**
Detailed Answer: **371**

   ○ **A.** It permits dust to accumulate in the system unit.

   ○ **B.** It disrupts airflow patterns inside the case.

   ○ **C.** It diminishes the ground potential of the system.

   ○ **D.** It has no discernible effect on the system.

6. _____ rearranges noncontiguous files into a more efficient contiguous arrangement on the disk.

Quick Answer: **361**
Detailed Answer: **371**

   ○ **A.** DEFRAG

   ○ **B.** SCANDISK

   ○ **C.** CHKDSK

   ○ **D.** FDISK

7. What is the best type of cleaning tool for use on the exterior of computer components?

Quick Answer: **361**
Detailed Answer: **372**

   ○ **A.** Damp cloth

   ○ **B.** Vacuum cleaner

   ○ **C.** Brush

   ○ **D.** Antistatic spray

8. Under what conditions should you update a system's BIOS?

Quick Answer: **361**
Detailed Answer: **372**

   ○ **A.** Anytime there is an update available

   ○ **B.** When you are installing a new microprocessor

   ○ **C.** When the update has functions that are important to the security or operation of the system

   ○ **D.** When you are installing additional memory modules

9. Which of the following can cause system overheating? (Select all that apply.)

Quick Answer: **361**
Detailed Answer: **372**

   ○ **A.** Open slot covers in the back panel of the system unit

   ○ **B.** Excessive open space in the system unit case

   ○ **C.** Low humidity conditions

   ○ **D.** High humidity conditions

10. You are in charge of maintaining several PCs located in an open-air warehouse. The area is very dusty due to trucks entering and leaving the warehouse, as well as from exhaust created by fork trucks used to move materials in the warehouse. When you perform periodic preventative maintenance procedures on these machines, what extra step should you take to compensate for their environment?

Quick Answer: **361**
Detailed Answer: **372**

- ○ **A.** Wash down the PCs with fabric softener to lessen dust buildup due to static charges.
- ○ **B.** Install pusher fans to exhaust warm air out of the system unit case and prevent dirty air from entering.
- ○ **C.** Remove their front panels and clean the air vents.
- ○ **D.** Close off the air vents in the front of the case to prevent dust and moisture from entering the system.

11. Which of the following are common sources of heat buildup that can be found around a PC installation? (Select all that apply.)

Quick Answer: **361**
Detailed Answer: **372**

- ○ **A.** Direct sunlight
- ○ **B.** Location of heaters
- ○ **C.** Excess body heat
- ○ **D.** Papers piled on equipment

12. Which of the following is an acceptable method of cleaning oxide buildups from adapter board contacts?

Quick Answer: **361**
Detailed Answer: **372**

- ○ **A.** A wet, soft cloth
- ○ **B.** Warm, soapy water
- ○ **C.** Electrical contact cleaner spray
- ○ **D.** A nylon cloth

13. Your company is sending you to install several PCs in a facility located in the desert southwest portion of the United States. The area is very hot and dry in the summer months and is prone to dust storms in the spring and fall of the year. Which of the following is the best scenario for installing the PCs under these circumstances?

Quick Answer: **361**
Detailed Answer: **372**

- ○ **A.** Install the PCs in a dust-free area.
- ○ **B.** Install the PCs in an air-conditioned area.
- ○ **C.** Install foam dust filters in the air intake vents of the PCs.
- ○ **D.** Install systems with water-cooled processors.

14. At what point does heat buildup become a problem for most PCs?

   ○ **A.** Room temperatures above 85° F

   ○ **B.** Room temperatures above 90° F

   ○ **C.** Room temperatures above 95° F

   ○ **D.** Room temperatures above 100° F

Quick Answer: **361**
Detailed Answer: **372**

15. Which solution can be used for antistatic cleaning?

   ○ **A.** A water and fabric softener solution

   ○ **B.** A water and ammonia solution

   ○ **C.** A water and bleach solution

   ○ **D.** A hydrogen tetrachloride solution

Quick Answer: **361**
Detailed Answer: **372**

16. What product is recommended for manual cleaning of floppy disk drives and tape drive R/W heads?

   ○ **A.** Soft cloths

   ○ **B.** Cotton swabs

   ○ **C.** A pencil eraser

   ○ **D.** Foam swabs

Quick Answer: **361**
Detailed Answer: **372**

Domain 2.0: Laptop and Portable Devices

Objective 2.1: Identify the fundamental principles of using laptops and portable devices

1. You are working with a small advertising firm whose art development person will be traveling a lot over the next six months in
   conjunction with a big project she is working on. The art developer needs a notebook PC to travel with, but the display has to be
   very good for her to prepare the types of artwork required for the
   project. What should you recommend as the best display type for
   this notebook PC?

   ○ **A.** Dual-scan technology

   ○ **B.** Active matrix TFT technology

   ○ **C.** Passive matrix technology

   ○ **D.** CSTN/DSTN technology

Quick Answer: **361**
Detailed Answer: **373**

2. Which peripheral devices are more likely to use infrared
   communication? (Select all that apply.)

   ○ **A.** A keyboard

   ○ **B.** A printer

   ○ **C.** A mouse

   ○ **D.** A scanner

Quick Answer: **361**
Detailed Answer: **373**

3. What type of wireless communication is typically carried out
   directly between portable PCs?

   ○ **A.** Infrared

   ○ **B.** Bluetooth

   ○ **C.** Cellular

   ○ **D.** 802.11x

Quick Answer: **361**
Detailed Answer: **373**

4. The LCD display on a portable computer is powered by _____.

   ○ **A.** low-voltage AC

   ○ **B.** high-voltage AC

   ○ **C.** low-voltage DC

   ○ **D.** high-voltage DC

Quick Answer: **361**
Detailed Answer: **373**

5. Which Windows XP power conservation mode used in portable PCs turns off selected components, such as the hard drive and display, until a system event, such as a keyboard entry or a mouse movement, occurs?

Quick Answer: **361**
Detailed Answer: **373**

❍ **A.** Hibernate mode

❍ **B.** Suspend mode

❍ **C.** Standby mode

❍ **D.** Shutdown mode

6. What functions are performed by the external power supply of a portable computer system?

Quick Answer: **361**
Detailed Answer: **373**

❍ **A.** Increase the voltage of commercial power for the computer

❍ **B.** Convert commercial DC voltage into AC voltage for system usage and battery charging

❍ **C.** Store commercial power to recharge the battery

❍ **D.** Convert commercial AC voltage into DC voltage for system usage and battery charging

7. The main objective of portable system manufacturers is to produce portable computers that can travel efficiently. Therefore, they are typically striving to _____. (Select all that apply.)

Quick Answer: **361**
Detailed Answer: **373**

❍ **A.** create systems that use less energy

❍ **B.** create systems that have larger displays

❍ **C.** create systems that have smaller keyboards

❍ **D.** create systems that are smaller

8. In a portable PC that has PCMCIA slots, the _____ portion of the operating system's socket services delivers the correct device driver for an installed PC Card when it is hot-swapped into the system.

Quick Answer: **361**
Detailed Answer: **373**

❍ **A.** Card Services

❍ **B.** Autodetect

❍ **C.** Driver Bank

❍ **D.** Universal PnP

9. One of the biggest problems for portable computers is _____.

Quick Answer: **361**
Detailed Answer: **374**

  ○ **A.** heat buildup inside the case

  ○ **B.** lack of full-sized keys on their keyboards

  ○ **C.** lack of expandability due to a limited number of I/O ports

  ○ **D.** lack of disk drive capacity

Objective 2.2: Install, configure, optimize, and upgrade laptops and portable devices

1. You have just completed a major upgrade of a notebook PC. You upgraded the notebook's processor to a faster version and doubled the RAM capacity by installing an additional 512MB of new DDR2 RAM. When you start up the system, it shows only 956MB of memory installed. What is the cause of this discrepancy?

Quick Answer: **361**
Detailed Answer: **374**

  ○ **A.** One of the memory modules is bad.

  ○ **B.** The new memory modules do not match the existing modules.

  ○ **C.** The system is set up to use split bank addressing.

  ○ **D.** The system is using shared video memory.

2. What is the proper way to remove a USB device from a Windows-based notebook PC system?

Quick Answer: **361**
Detailed Answer: **374**

  ○ **A.** Click on the Safe Hardware Removal icon in the systray.

  ○ **B.** USB devices are hot-swappable and can be installed or removed at any time.

  ○ **C.** Use the New Hardware Wizard to remove the device from the system and then disconnect it.

  ○ **D.** Disable the device in the Device Manager and then physically remove it from the system.

3. What must you do to replace a system board in a given notebook computer model?

Quick Answer: **361**
Detailed Answer: **374**

   ○ **A.** Obtain an exact replacement for the board being removed.

   ○ **B.** Check the compatibility of the replacement board with the other components in the notebook. This can be accomplished by accessing the portable manufacturer's website.

   ○ **C.** Obtain a Flash program for the new BIOS to make sure that it is compatible with the existing architecture of the notebook.

   ○ **D.** Store the contents of the old BIOS configuration on a floppy before changing out the boards. This permits you to reload your existing settings back into the new system after the installation.

4. You've been asked to upgrade the processor in an old Pentium II notebook PC to gain some performance increase. What should you tell the customer about this upgrade?

Quick Answer: **361**
Detailed Answer: **374**

   ○ **A.** The customer needs to upgrade the RAM instead.

   ○ **B.** You will upgrade the processor as far as possible.

   ○ **C.** This processor can't be upgraded in a notebook PC.

   ○ **D.** Upgrading the processor in this system is probably not worthwhile.

5. You increase the amount of RAM in the notebook PC of a friend who is using it to play graphics-intensive video games. However, there is no noticeable sign of performance improvement in the game after the upgrade. Why is this?

Quick Answer: **361**
Detailed Answer: **374**

   ○ **A.** Only so much shared memory is available in a notebook PC.

   ○ **B.** The shared memory allocation must be increased in the PC.

   ○ **C.** Without upgrading the BIOS, the memory upgrade does not take effect.

   ○ **D.** To generate a performance improvement, you should have performed a microprocessor upgrade instead.

Objective 2.3: Identify tools, diagnostic procedures, and troubleshooting techniques for laptops and portable devices

1. If you purchase a spare battery for a new notebook computer, how should you store the second battery if you don't anticipate needing it for several months?

   ○ **A.** Store it fully charged in a refrigerator.

   ○ **B.** Fully charge it and store it at room temperature.

   ○ **C.** Fully discharge it and store it at room temperature.

   ○ **D.** Fully discharge it and then store it in the refrigerator.

   Quick Answer: **361**
   Detailed Answer: **374**

2. Which of the following are functions of the Fn key on a notebook PC? (Select all that apply.)

   ○ **A.** To access hidden functions on the hard drive

   ○ **B.** To access additional functions from the keyboard

   ○ **C.** To access additional display devices attached to the system

   ○ **D.** To access additional Windows features from the keyboard

   Quick Answer: **361**
   Detailed Answer: **374**

3. Your national sales director spends a considerable amount of time on airplanes each month. It is time to upgrade his notebook PC. You have settled on the fact that he needs one of the low power-consumption chipsets and processors, and now you are evaluating which battery types might be available to provide power over the duration of longer flights. Which battery type offers the longest battery life in a portable PC?

   ○ **A.** NiCD

   ○ **B.** NiMH

   ○ **C.** Lead acid

   ○ **D.** Alkaline

   Quick Answer: **361**
   Detailed Answer: **375**

4. You notice that the length of time that your portable computer can run on the battery before it shuts down is significantly shorter than it used to be. What can you do to restore some additional usage to the battery?

Quick Answer: **361**
Detailed Answer: **375**

  ○ **A.** Place the battery in a commercial battery charger overnight to build the level of charge in the battery backup.

  ○ **B.** Keep the external AC power adapter plugged into the notebook whenever possible to increase the amount of charge in the battery.

  ○ **C.** You must fully discharge the battery and then recharge it over repeated cycles.

  ○ **D.** Take the battery out of the computer and warm it in an oven on low heat for an hour.

5. You have received a notebook PC for repair. The work ticket on the machine indicates that the PC is producing numbers instead of letters when some characters are typed on the keyboard. What is the most likely cause of this problem?

Quick Answer: **361**
Detailed Answer: **375**

  ○ **A.** The Regional Language setting has been established incorrectly in the operating system.

  ○ **B.** The Windows Character Map is configured incorrectly.

  ○ **C.** The numeric keypad feature is enabled.

  ○ **D.** The Fn key has been pressed by mistake.

6. A coworker has asked your advice on a new notebook PC he has never seen before. The notebook is supposed to have built-in wireless networking, but he cannot get the internal radio module to work. What is the first thing you should tell him to check?

Quick Answer: **361**
Detailed Answer: **375**

  ○ **A.** To determine whether TCP/IP has been configured in Windows

  ○ **B.** To determine whether the 802.11x wireless radio is turned on

  ○ **C.** To determine whether the 802.11x antenna has been installed

  ○ **D.** To determine whether the SSID and WEP functions have been established

7. After traveling to an international conference in Europe, you remove your notebook PC from your travel bag and start it up. When the system starts, the cursor randomly hops around the screen when you touch the touchpad. The notebook was working perfectly before you boarded the airplane. What action is required to correct this problem?

Quick Answer: **361**
Detailed Answer: **375**

- ○ **A.** Replace the touchpad unit.

- ○ **B.** Clean the touchpad surface.

- ○ **C.** Install new touchpad drivers.

- ○ **D.** Reconnect the touchpad's signal cable to the system board.

8. How do you normally add an external monitor to a notebook PC?

Quick Answer: **361**
Detailed Answer: **375**

- ○ **A.** Plug the external monitor into the external VGA connector and press the appropriate function key combination.

- ○ **B.** Turn off the notebook and plug the monitor into the external VGA connector; then restart the system.

- ○ **C.** Plug the external monitor into the external VGA connector and reboot the notebook until the external monitor is recognized.

- ○ **D.** Simply plug the external monitor into the external VGA connector, and the system will detect it.

9. You want to configure your Windows XP–based notebook PC to go into Hibernate mode when you close the cover. This will enable you to save battery power when you have to relocate from one location to another. From the Windows XP Control Panel, how do you force the notebook into Hibernate mode when the cover is closed?

Quick Answer: **361**
Detailed Answer: **375**

- ○ **A.** Start/All Programs/System Tools/Power Options/Hibernate

- ○ **B.** Start/Control Panel/Power Options/Hibernate tab/Enable Hibernation

- ○ **C.** Start/Control Panel/Power Options/Advanced tab/Enable Hibernate Support

- ○ **D.** Start/Settings/Power Options/Hibernate/Enable

10. You are examining a user's notebook PC because she has complained that the LCD display is producing a fuzzy, blurry image. What is the most likely cause of this condition?

❍ **A.** The notebook's video is not working in its native resolution.

❍ **B.** LCDs cannot produce fuzzy images.

❍ **C.** The wrong drivers have been installed for the video display and need to be replaced.

❍ **D.** The notebook's video resolution is set incorrectly.

11. You have a notebook PC with no display on the built-in LCD panel. What should you do first to troubleshoot this condition?

❍ **A.** Plug an external video monitor into the external VGA connector and redirect the video output to that port.

❍ **B.** Restart the system, enter CMOS Setup, and ensure that the default, onboard video option is enabled.

❍ **C.** Press the Fn key and F5 function key to redirect the video output to the LCD display.

❍ **D.** Reboot the notebook until the internal display is recognized.

12. What is the fastest way to verify that a PC Card is being recognized by a Windows 2000 system and that it is working correctly?

❍ **A.** Access the Windows Event Viewer in the MMC and verify that the PC Card is functioning.

❍ **B.** Access the Hardware Profile tab under the Control Panel's System icon and check the status of the PC Card.

❍ **C.** Access the Add New Hardware Wizard in the Control Panel and check the status of the PC Card.

❍ **D.** Access the Device Manager under the Control Panel's System icon and check the status of the PC Card.

13. If the mouse attached to your portable computer does not work but the touchpad unit does, what step should you take to get the mouse working correctly?

○ **A.** Switch the mouse to the other USB slot to access the enabled USB port connection.

○ **B.** Switch the mouse to the other serial port connector to access the correct COM port.

○ **C.** Switch the mouse to the other PS/2 mini-DIN connector because it must be plugged into the connector for the full-size keyboard.

○ **D.** Check the computer's documentation for an Fn key combination requirement for the mouse.

Domain 3.0: Printers and Scanners

Objective 3.1: Identify the fundamental principles of using printers and scanners

1. How does a dot-matrix printer place characters on a page?

   ○ **A.** Magnetically controlled pins place dots on the paper.

   ○ **B.** Magnetically charged ink particles are attracted to an ionized form on the paper.

   ○ **C.** It squirts precisely controlled drops of ink onto the paper.

   ○ **D.** Fully formed metal characters force ink from a ribbon onto the paper.

Quick Answer: **361**
Detailed Answer: **377**

2. What is the major purpose of a tractor-feed mechanism, and where is it most commonly used?

   ○ **A.** It is used on color printers that print multipart forms.

   ○ **B.** It is used on inkjet printers that print continuous forms.

   ○ **C.** It is used on laser printers that print continuous, multipart forms.

   ○ **D.** It is used on dot matrix printers that print continuous, multipart forms.

Quick Answer: **361**
Detailed Answer: **377**

3. Which laser printer subsystem is responsible for bonding toner to the paper?

   ○ **A.** Fuser assembly

   ○ **B.** Laser

   ○ **C.** Primary corona wire

   ○ **D.** Conditioning roller

Quick Answer: **361**
Detailed Answer: **377**

4. The primary corona wire (conditioning roller) in a laser printer
   _____.

   ○ **A.** transfers toner to the paper

   ○ **B.** applies a uniform negative charge to the drum

   ○ **C.** presses toner into the paper

   ○ **D.** transfers characters to the paper

Quick Answer: **361**
Detailed Answer: **377**

5. Which scanner component converts the scanned image into a digital format?

Quick Answer: **361**
Detailed Answer: **377**

- ❍ **A.** The LED module
- ❍ **B.** The scan head
- ❍ **C.** The diodes in the light detector array
- ❍ **D.** The scanner's digitizer module

6. Which of the following file types are typically associated with scanned images?(Select all that apply.)

Quick Answer: **361**
Detailed Answer: **377**

- ❍ **A.** JPEG
- ❍ **B.** DLL
- ❍ **C.** BMP
- ❍ **D.** TWN

7. Which of the following printer types require special paper?

Quick Answer: **361**
Detailed Answer: **377**

- ❍ **A.** Laser
- ❍ **B.** Thermal
- ❍ **C.** Dot matrix
- ❍ **D.** Inkjet

8. In a laser printer, a positive charge on the transfer corona wire causes _____.

Quick Answer: **361**
Detailed Answer: **377**

- ❍ **A.** the positive image to appear on the print drum
- ❍ **B.** the toner to be transferred from the drum to the paper
- ❍ **C.** the excess toner to be dislodged from the drum after printing
- ❍ **D.** the negative image to appear on the print drum

9. What is the purpose of the thermal fuse in a laser printer?

Quick Answer: **361**
Detailed Answer: **377**

- ❍ **A.** It heats the fusing unit.
- ❍ **B.** It protects the paper from burning.
- ❍ **C.** It fuses the toner image to the paper.
- ❍ **D.** It monitors the temperature of the unit.

Objective 3.2: Install, configure, optimize, and upgrade printers and scanners

1. You have been asked to set up a new laser printer that a customer has purchased from your store. When you examine it, you find that a number of connectivity options are available with the printer, including wireless RF, Bluetooth, infrared, and USB connections. Which printer interface is fastest for a local printer?

   ○ **A.** USB 2.0

   ○ **B.** Bluetooth

   ○ **C.** IrDA

   ○ **D.** FireWire 400

Quick Answer: **362**
Detailed Answer: **378**

2. What is the recommended clear distance and the maximum angle specified for IrDA printer connections?

   ○ **A.** 3 meters, 45°

   ○ **B.** 2 meters, 30°

   ○ **C.** 1 meter, 15°

   ○ **D.** 4 meters, 60°

Quick Answer: **362**
Detailed Answer: **378**

3. What is the first thing you should do with a new inkjet printer installation after physically installing it and connecting it to the host PC?

   ○ **A.** Print a test page from the printer.

   ○ **B.** Print a test page from the host computer.

   ○ **C.** Remove the shipping ink cartridges and install new ones.

   ○ **D.** Load its drivers on the host PC.

Quick Answer: **362**
Detailed Answer: **378**

4. A customer has called you because she is trying to determine whether to upgrade her current duplexing laser printer or purchase a new one. What can you tell her about when it is a good idea to upgrade a printer? (Select all that apply.)

Quick Answer: **362**
Detailed Answer: **378**

- ○ **A.** It is always more economical to upgrade an existing laser printer than to buy a new one.

- ○ **B.** It is always better to buy a new laser printer than spend money on an upgrade due to how quickly they wear.

- ○ **C.** The customer should decide based on how often she is having maintenance performed on the current printer.

- ○ **D.** The customer should decide this on whether there are new features available that she needs for her operations.

5. The best way to ensure good print resolution when using an inkjet printer is to _____.

Quick Answer: **362**
Detailed Answer: **378**

- ○ **A.** use the best-quality paper available
- ○ **B.** use fresh ink cartridges
- ○ **C.** use only the black color function to print
- ○ **D.** use high-resolution cartridges

6. How is a UNC path created from a local computer to a remote printer or a directory located on a remote computer?

Quick Answer: **362**
Detailed Answer: **378**

- ○ **A.** \\Computer_name\shared_resource_name
- ○ **B.** //computer_name/shared_resource_name
- ○ **C.** \\shared_resource_name
- ○ **D.** //shared_resource_name

7. You want to use a printer connected to another computer running Windows XP in the network. What must that other computer have enabled to permit you to print through it?

Quick Answer: **362**
Detailed Answer: **378**

- ○ **A.** Resource Sharing for Windows
- ○ **B.** Network Printing for Windows
- ○ **C.** File and Printer Sharing for Windows
- ○ **D.** Simple File Sharing for Windows

Objective 3.3: Identify tools, diagnostic methods, and troubleshooting procedures for printers and scanners

1. Which inkjet printer setting can adversely affect troubleshooting procedures?

    ○ **A.** Maintenance Mode

    ○ **B.** Page Feed

    ○ **C.** Self-Test

    ○ **D.** Tray Selector

Quick Answer: **362**
Detailed Answer: **379**

2. You have been given an image scanner that does not scan. When you test it, the scanning light comes on, but it does not move across the page. Which of the following is the most likely cause of the problem?

    ○ **A.** The resolution setting of the scanning software is not compatible with the size of the picture being scanned.

    ○ **B.** The USB signal cable is unplugged from the host PC.

    ○ **C.** The scanner's light positioning mechanism is locked.

    ○ **D.** The scanner's positioning motor is defective.

Quick Answer: **362**
Detailed Answer: **379**

3. What is the most basic test you can perform when you encounter an image-printing problem?

    ○ **A.** Print a test page from the printer.

    ○ **B.** Print a test page from the host computer.

    ○ **C.** Print a test page from a disk.

    ○ **D.** Run a self-test on the printer.

Quick Answer: **362**
Detailed Answer: **379**

4. You are trying to set up an IrDA connection between a PC and a laser printer. When you attempt to print a test page, nothing happens. Which of the following could be preventing the print job from being carried out? (Select all that apply.)

    ○ **A.** Items are blocking the line of sight between the PC and the printer.

    ○ **B.** The COM Port settings are not configured correctly in the CMOS.

    ○ **C.** The amount of ambient light in the room is overpowering the IrDA signal.

    ○ **D.** The printer is too close to the PC's IrDA port, so it cannot "see" the complete beam coming from the port.

Quick Answer: **362**
Detailed Answer: **379**

5. A user reports that he can't print to his local inkjet printer; no paper comes out and nothing is printed. When you examine the Printers and Faxes page of his Windows XP system, you see that only an HP Laserjet 1100 printer is showing on the page. What is the most likely cause of this problem?

- ○ **A.** The printer is not installed in the system.
- ○ **B.** The printer spooler has been disabled on the system.
- ○ **C.** The wrong printer driver has been installed in the system.
- ○ **D.** The default printer setting has been set incorrectly on the printer.

6. What is the last step in installing a new laser printer at a customer's office?

- ○ **A.** Run a test page from the printer.
- ○ **B.** Reset the printer's page counter.
- ○ **C.** Run a test page from the host computer.
- ○ **D.** Give the customer the bill.

7. You notice that there are smudges on all the pages scanned from a multifunction device in your work area. What should you do to correct this condition?

- ○ **A.** Clean the glass plate on the scanning bed portion of the device.
- ○ **B.** Turn off the device, let it cool, and then clean the scanner's light bar.
- ○ **C.** Replace the toner cartridge.
- ○ **D.** Calibrate the scanner.

8. What would cause excess toner to collect in a laser printer?

- ○ **A.** A defective cartridge
- ○ **B.** Not using the manufacturer's suggested toner
- ○ **C.** A worn cleaning pad
- ○ **D.** A defective high-voltage power supply

9. What item should be checked first when troubleshooting printer problems?

- ○ **A.** The signal cable connections
- ○ **B.** The print drivers
- ○ **C.** The power switch setting
- ○ **D.** The lights and messages on the control panel

10. What are two consequences of incorrectly setting the paper tray switches in a laser printer?

- ○ **A.** Paper does not feed.
- ○ **B.** Pages are sized incorrectly for the actual paper size.
- ○ **C.** Pages are smudged.
- ○ **D.** Pages are all white.

11. How do you test a portable battery to see if it is seated properly in a portable PC?

- ○ **A.** Unplug the AC adapter.
- ○ **B.** Check the battery level monitor.
- ○ **C.** Test its connections using a multimeter.
- ○ **D.** Turn on the portable and check to see whether the battery indicator icon appears.

12. You have a laser printer that is producing repetitive vertical spots on all print jobs. What items should you check to isolate the cause of this problem? (Select all that apply.)

- ○ **A.** The laser module
- ○ **B.** The installed printer driver
- ○ **C.** The drum
- ○ **D.** The fuser

13. Which of the following would correct the problem in which the tops of characters are missing from a dot matrix printer? (Select all that apply.)

- ○ **A.** The carriage assembly might need to be adjusted to the proper height and angle.
- ○ **B.** Reseat the printhead in the printhead carriage.
- ○ **C.** Reseat the platen.
- ○ **D.** Replace the ribbon.

14. What are two symptoms of an inkjet printer cartridge going dry?

Quick Answer: **362**
Detailed Answer: **380**

- ○ **A.** Print becomes noticeably faint.
- ○ **B.** Resolution becomes unacceptable.
- ○ **C.** One dark line crosses the page.
- ○ **D.** Black streaks run down the page.

15. What causes an inkjet printer to produce wavy graphics? (Select two correct answers.)

Quick Answer: **362**
Detailed Answer: **380**

- ○ **A.** Bad paper-feed rollers
- ○ **B.** Low ink
- ○ **C.** Improper paper thickness setting
- ○ **D.** Mismatched ink cartridge

16. What type of problem produces blank pages from a laser printer? (Select all that apply.)

Quick Answer: **362**
Detailed Answer: **380**

- ○ **A.** The laser-scanning module is bad or misaligned.
- ○ **B.** There is a failure in the fusing section.
- ○ **C.** Contrast is set too low.
- ○ **D.** The corona wire is broken, contaminated, or corroded.

17. When you receive your copy of a document from the office laser printer, you notice that small white spots occur at regular intervals along the length of the page. Which laser printer component is normally associated with a symptom such as this?

Quick Answer: **362**
Detailed Answer: **380**

- ○ **A.** The primary corona has a flat spot on it.
- ○ **B.** The drum has been contaminated.
- ○ **C.** The transfer corona wire is dirty.
- ○ **D.** The laser circuitry is failing.

18. What does it mean if the printer produces a satisfactory self-test printout but does not print from the computer?

Quick Answer: **362**
Detailed Answer: **381**

- ○ **A.** The printer is the problem.
- ○ **B.** The printer is not the problem.
- ○ **C.** The cabling is the problem.
- ○ **D.** The computer is the problem.

19. Paper jams in a laser printer can be caused by _____. (Select all that apply.)

  - ○ **A.** using paper of the wrong thickness
  - ○ **B.** incorrect paper settings
  - ○ **C.** using coated paper
  - ○ **D.** using colored paper

Objective 3.4: Perform preventative maintenance of printer and scanner problems

1. You should never expose the drum of a laser printer to _____.

  - ○ **A.** cold
  - ○ **B.** a strong light source
  - ○ **C.** air
  - ○ **D.** toner

2. You have just installed a service kit in a customer's laser printer as part of a regularly scheduled maintenance plan. What is the last step you should perform before leaving the customer's office?

  - ○ **A.** Run a test page from the host computer.
  - ○ **B.** Reboot the computer.
  - ○ **C.** Reset the printer's page counter.
  - ○ **D.** Give the customer the bill.

3. You have been directed to install a new laser printer in the loading dock facility at your company's manufacturing operations. The facility is located in the southeastern portion of the United States. The area is very hot in the summer months and is humid most of the year. Which of the following is the best scenario for installing the printer under these circumstances?

  - ○ **A.** Install the printer in a shady, dust-free area of the warehouse.
  - ○ **B.** Install the printer in the dock manager's air-conditioned office area.
  - ○ **C.** Install foam dust filters in the printer's air-intake vents and install it out of the sunlight.
  - ○ **D.** Install a dust cover on the printer and install it under the shipping documents table to keep it in the shade.

4. Which of the following are good ways to prevent paper jams from occurring in a printer? (Select all that apply.)

Quick Answer: **362**
Detailed Answer: **381**

   ○ **A.** Buy the best-quality paper available.

   ○ **B.** Make sure that the paper used has the correct weight for the printer you are using.

   ○ **C.** Oil the gears and detector mechanisms on a regular basis.

   ○ **D.** Make sure that the paper used has the correct thickness for the printer you are using.

5. Your laser printer has just been repaired for the fourth time in four months. The paper-handling mechanism is wearing out too quickly. Which of the following is the most likely cause of this accelerated wear?

Quick Answer: **362**
Detailed Answer: **381**

   ○ **A.** The paper being used is too coarse.

   ○ **B.** The paper size is set wrong in the printer tray.

   ○ **C.** The paper being used is too heavy.

   ○ **D.** The toner type is incorrect.

6. What are the consequences of using a solvent to unclog an inkjet nozzle?

Quick Answer: **362**
Detailed Answer: **381**

   ○ **A.** Clogged inkjets

   ○ **B.** Improper drop placement

   ○ **C.** Discolored ink

   ○ **D.** Ink running into the printer

7. What item in a dot matrix printer requires the most attention?

Quick Answer: **362**
Detailed Answer: **381**

   ○ **A.** The ribbon cartridge

   ○ **B.** The printhead

   ○ **C.** The tension knob

   ○ **D.** The Control Panel

8. What prevents ink from leaking out of an inkjet when it is not printing?

Quick Answer: **362**
Detailed Answer: **381**

   ○ **A.** Electrical current

   ○ **B.** Closed valve

   ○ **C.** Hydraulic pressure

   ○ **D.** Surface tension

Domain 4.0: Security

Objective 4.1: Identify the names, purposes, and characteristics of physical security devices and processes

1. What type of system is more susceptible to a virus?

   ○ **A.** A networked computer

   ○ **B.** A standalone computer

   ○ **C.** A laptop computer

   ○ **D.** A personal digital assistant

Quick Answer: **362**
Detailed Answer: **382**

2. One of your customers has begun to work on a new product that could potentially earn a patent. He is worried about the security of his files because his design information is located on a FAT16 drive in his Windows 2000 Professional PC. What can be done to improve protection for his information on this type of drive?

   ○ **A.** Give the files hidden, read-only attributes.

   ○ **B.** Move the files to CD-RW discs.

   ○ **C.** Install a new hard drive in the system and convert the original drive to a removable external drive.

   ○ **D.** Convert the drive to NTFS and establish encryption on the files.

Quick Answer: **362**
Detailed Answer: **382**

3. Which of the following represents the best option for protecting the operating system from the effects of malicious software?

   ○ **A.** Enable the Windows Firewall feature on the machine.

   ○ **B.** Establish a unique SSID on each machine.

   ○ **C.** Enable a WEP key for each machine.

   ○ **D.** Configure MS-CHAP authentication on each machine.

Quick Answer: **362**
Detailed Answer: **382**

4. Which of the following security devices are typically not used with a direct connection to one of the PC's standard I/O ports?

   ○ **A.** Voice recognition devices

   ○ **B.** Fingerprint scanners

   ○ **C.** Retinal scanners

   ○ **D.** Smart card readers

Quick Answer: **362**
Detailed Answer: **382**

5. Which of the following are advantages of smart cards over disk-based security options?

Quick Answer: **362**
Detailed Answer: **382**

- ○ **A.** No moving parts
- ○ **B.** Security
- ○ **C.** Acceptance
- ○ **D.** Capacity

6. Which of the following represent the most secure password type?

Quick Answer: **362**
Detailed Answer: **382**

- ○ **A.** Smith
- ○ **B.** smith01
- ○ **C.** Sm1th!
- ○ **D.** tims

Objective 4.2: Install Hardware Security

1. Which of the following is a biometric authentication device?

Quick Answer: **362**
Detailed Answer: **382**

- ○ **A.** A smart card
- ○ **B.** An intelligent key
- ○ **C.** A fingerprint scanner
- ○ **D.** A password

2. What is the advantage of using smart cards to control access to the information in a PC?

Quick Answer: **362**
Detailed Answer: **383**

- ○ **A.** Multiple users can effectively share the same card and still maintain a high level of security.
- ○ **B.** Smart cards can be deactivated if lost or stolen.
- ○ **C.** Smart cards work with personal identification numbers that are known only to their owners.
- ○ **D.** Smart cards can easily be reprogrammed if compromised.

3. Which of the following security devices enables you to track access to a controlled area?

Quick Answer: **362**
Detailed Answer: **383**

- ○ **A.** A key lock
- ○ **B.** A combination lock
- ○ **C.** A logbook
- ○ **D.** A magnetic keycard

Quick Check

Quick Answer: **362**
Detailed Answer: **383**

4. While reviewing your email in the morning, you receive an offer for a free memory upgrade to your system if you update your business information on a product manufacturer's website. How should you handle this offer?

- ○ **A.** Forward the email to your supervisor for follow-up.
- ○ **B.** Encrypt your information and return it to the ISP.
- ○ **C.** Ignore the email and delete it.
- ○ **D.** Forward the email to your local police department.

Domain 5.0: Safety and Environmental Issues

Objective 5.1: Identify potential hazards and proper safety procedures including power supply, display devices, and environment

1. The local weather report indicates that an electrical storm with severe winds is likely to occur in your area overnight. What reasonable precautions should you take to protect your computers?

   ○ **A.** Monitor the computers until the storm passes.

   ○ **B.** Plug the computers into a surge protector.

   ○ **C.** Turn off the computers.

   ○ **D.** Unplug the computers.

Quick Answer: **363**
Detailed Answer: **384**

2. What are the voltage levels commonly found in a CRT?

   ○ **A.** 250,000V

   ○ **B.** 250V

   ○ **C.** 25,000V

   ○ **D.** 25V

Quick Answer: **363**
Detailed Answer: **384**

3. Which voltage level is more dangerous—110V AC at 5 amps or 25,000V DC at 5 microamperes?

   ○ **A.** The 25,000V level is much more dangerous than the 110V level.

   ○ **B.** Neither is particularly dangerous.

   ○ **C.** Both are extremely dangerous.

   ○ **D.** The 5 amp level is much more dangerous than the 5 microampere level.

Quick Answer: **363**
Detailed Answer: **384**

4. When would it be inappropriate to use an ESD wrist strap?

   ○ **A.** While working on hard disk drives

   ○ **B.** While working on system boards

   ○ **C.** While working on CRT video monitors

   ○ **D.** While working on printers

Quick Answer: **363**
Detailed Answer: **384**

5. A _____ is a passive device used to protect computer equipment from very small overvoltage occurrences.

Quick Answer: **363**
Detailed Answer: **384**

- ○ **A.** USPS
- ○ **B.** passive UPS
- ○ **C.** surge suppressor
- ○ **D.** preliminary ESD filter

6. The best protection against data loss caused by power failure is _____.

Quick Answer: **363**
Detailed Answer: **384**

- ○ **A.** a surge suppressor
- ○ **B.** a tape backup
- ○ **C.** a UPS
- ○ **D.** a RAID system

7. Which peripheral item is most subject to problems created by environmental dust?

Quick Answer: **363**
Detailed Answer: **384**

- ○ **A.** Printer
- ○ **B.** Hard drive
- ○ **C.** Mouse
- ○ **D.** Keyboard

8. Which type of printer can be a source of electrocution, eye damage, and burns?

Quick Answer: **363**
Detailed Answer: **384**

- ○ **A.** Laser
- ○ **B.** Dot matrix
- ○ **C.** Inkjet
- ○ **D.** Daisy wheel

9. You find water dripping from the ceiling in the server room. Which of the following should you do first?

Quick Answer: **363**
Detailed Answer: **384**

- ○ **A.** Notify building maintenance.
- ○ **B.** Notify the network administrator.
- ○ **C.** Place a note in the server room logbook.
- ○ **D.** Turn off the servers.

Quick Check

10. The laser light in a high-quality laser printer is classified as a Class A laser device. What does this rating mean to technicians working on this laser printer?

Quick Answer: **363**
Detailed Answer: **384**

   ○ **A.** Never shine the light on your skin.

   ○ **B.** Never shine the light on any part of your body.

   ○ **C.** Never shine the light in your eyes.

   ○ **D.** Never touch the light while it is in operation.

11. After you've removed the outer case from a CRT display, what precaution should you take before troubleshooting it?

Quick Answer: **363**
Detailed Answer: **385**

   ○ **A.** Make sure that it's discharged.

   ○ **B.** Get clearance from your supervisor.

   ○ **C.** Put on an antistatic wrist strap.

   ○ **D.** Disconnect the monitor from the AC power source.

12. You are checking over a system that has failed when you discover that it failed because one of the power supply wires running to the system board was damaged. How should you handle this situation?

Quick Answer: **363**
Detailed Answer: **385**

   ○ **A.** Cut off the wire even with the power supply housing and troubleshoot the system board for possible faults.

   ○ **B.** Splice the two ends of the cable together and apply heat-shrink tubing over the repaired area of the wire.

   ○ **C.** Cap off the cable using electrical tape.

   ○ **D.** Replace the power supply unit.

13. When you arrive at your workstation, you find three desktop PCs sitting on the floor in front of your workbench. You will have to lift them onto the workbench to work on them. Which of the following describes the correct way to lift a personal computer from the floor?

Quick Answer: **363**
Detailed Answer: **385**

   ○ **A.** With knees bent, lift with your back.

   ○ **B.** With knees bent, lift with your arms.

   ○ **C.** With knees straight, lift with your back.

   ○ **D.** With knees straight, lift with your arms.

14. Your company is establishing a depot repair facility for notebook PCs, and you have been asked to suggest a workspace layout for the technicians. Which of the following items should you include in your recommendation? (Select all that apply.)

Quick Answer: **363**
Detailed Answer: **385**

- O **A.** Antistatic wrist straps
- O **B.** Carpeted floors in all work areas
- O **C.** Dehumidifiers
- O **D.** Antistatic pads on all workbenches

15. Damaging electrostatic discharge is most likely to occur when
_____.

Quick Answer: **363**
Detailed Answer: **385**

- O **A.** working around rubber mats
- O **B.** using test instruments on a system
- O **C.** the humidity is low
- O **D.** you unplug a power supply unit

16. Which of the following actions can cause a system board to short out when you change an adapter card?

Quick Answer: **363**
Detailed Answer: **385**

- O **A.** Not wearing an antistatic wrist strap
- O **B.** The PnP function not being configured properly
- O **C.** Placing the adapter card in the wrong type of expansion slot
- O **D.** Not removing the power cord from the AC power source

17. The _____ of a dot matrix printer generates a great deal of heat and can be a burn hazard when working on these units.

Quick Answer: **363**
Detailed Answer: **385**

- O **A.** paper tray
- O **B.** platen
- O **C.** ribbon
- O **D.** printhead

Quick Check Answer Key

Objective 1.1

1. B.	14. A, D	27. A, B
2. D.	15. A	28. D
3. C.	16. A	29. D
4. B	17. A	30. D
5. B	18. B	31. C
6. A, B, C	19. C	32. A
7. C.	20. C	33. B, C
8. D.	21. A, B	34. A
9. B	22. B	35. D
10. C	23. A	36. A, C, D
11. A, B	24. A	37. C
12. C	25. B	38. A, B, D
13. A, B, D	26. A	39. B

Objective 1.2

1. B	9. A, B, C	17. D
2. C	10. B	18. C
3. D	11. D	19. A
4. B	12. C	20. B
5. C	13. C	21. A
6. D	14. C, D	22. A
7. D	15. A	
8. B	16. C	

Quick Check Answer Key

Objective 1.3

1. D	7. A	13. B
2. B	8. C	14. A
3. A	9. A, D	15. A
4. B	10. C	16. D
5. A, B	11. A, B, D	
6. A	12. C	

Objective 2.1

1. B	4. C	7. A, D
2. A, B, C	5. C	8. A
3. D	6. D	9. A

Objective 2.2

1. D	3. A	5. B
2. A	4. D	

Objective 2.3

1. C	6. B	11. A
2. B, C	7. D	12. D
3. B	8. A	13. D
4. C	9. B	
5. C	10. A	

Objective 3.1

1. A	4. B	7. B
2. D	5. C	8. B
3. A	6. A, C	9. D

Quick Check Answer Key

Objective 3.2

1. A
2. C
3. A

4. C, D
5. B
6. A

7. C

Objective 3.3

1. A
2. C
3. A
4. A, B
5. A
6. C
7. A

8. D
9. D
10. A, B
11. A
12. C, D
13. A, B
14. A, B

15. A, C
16. A, D
17. B
18. B
19. A, C

Objective 3.4

1. B
2. C
3. B

4. B, D
5. C
6. D

7. A
8. D

Objective 4.1

1. A
2. D
3. A

4. C
5. B
6. C

Objective 4.2

1. C
2. C

3. D
4. C

Quick Check Answer Key

Objective 5.1

1. D	**7.** A	**13.** B
2. C	**8.** A	**14.** A, D
3. D	**9.** A	**15.** C
4. C	**10.** C	**16.** C
5. C	**11.** A	**17.** D
6. C	**12.** D	

Answers and Explanations

Domain 1.0

Objective 1.1

1. **Answer: B**. The microphone (audio in) and speakers (audio out) are plugged into the appropriate 1/8″ mini-jacks on the back of the sound card.

2. **Answer: D**. For Pentium 4 processors, the recommended operating temperature is 35° C. You must find a fan that is rated to work with that processor's temperature/speed specification. However, most fans are sold for the particular processor they are intended to support. This guarantees that you're getting not only the correct temperature coverage, but also the proper surface-area coverage for the processor. Regardless of what a fan is supposed to do, if it doesn't cover the entire processor, hot spots can occur that can lead to failure.

3. **Answer: C**. The Socket A specification employs a 462-pin ZIF socket and is supported only by two available chipsets.

4. **Answer: B**. The notches, beveled pin patterns, and dots on the various ICs are used to identify the location of the IC's number 1 pin. You may also have to check the silkscreen printing around the socket to verify the pin 1 location. The main thing to be sure of when inserting a microprocessor in a socket is to make sure to correctly align the IC's pin 1 with the socket's pin 1 position.

5. **Answer: B**. When you are upgrading a power supply, one thing to take into account is its wattage rating requirements. The wattage rating is a measurement of the total power the supply can deliver to the system. More heavily equipped systems (that is, more disk drives and peripherals) require power supplies with higher wattage ratings.

6. **Answers: A, B, C**. Generally, when you add memory modules to an existing system that have different speed ratings than the existing modules, at best the system will operate at the speed of the slowest modules (B). However, mixing significantly different RAM types and speeds in a system can also cause the system to lock up (A) and produce hard-memory errors (C).

7. **Answer: C**. The Universal Serial Bus (USB) provides a fast, flexible method of attaching up to 127 peripheral devices to the computer. The peripherals can be daisy-chained, or networked together, using connection hubs that enable the bus to branch out through additional port connections.

8. **Answer: D**. The recommended maximum length of an RS-232 cable is 50 feet (15 meters). However, some references use 100 feet as the acceptable length of an RS-232C serial cable. Serial connections are tricky enough without problems generated by the cable being too long. Make the cable as short as possible.

9. **Answer: B**. At least two identical disk drive units are required to implement RAID0. If the drives are not identical, the array's data capacity is limited to the number of drives times the smallest drive's capacity.

10. **Answer: C**. RAID0 is also known as *striped disk array* without fault tolerance, which uses the drives in a parallel array.

11. **Answers: A, B**. All Pentium processors require the presence of a heat-sinking device (A) and a microprocessor fan unit (B) for cooling purposes.

12. **Answer: C**. Component C in the figure represents the SATA signal cable connector. The connector depicted as A is a 6-pin PCIe power connector used to supply power to PCIe cards. Connector B is the 15-pin SATA power connector that supplies power to SATA drives, and connector D is a digital visual interface (DVI) connector used for high-end video connections.

13. **Answers: A, B, D**. In a Windows-based PC, you can go to three places to determine the speed of a currently installed microprocessor. You can view the microprocessor's speed through the System Properties page. To access this location, right-click on My Computer and then select Properties from the menu. Click the General tab and view the microprocessor information displayed in the Computer area (A). You can also view the microprocessor's information through the System Information utility. To view the microprocessor's speed through this path, click on the Start button and select the Run option. In the Run dialog box, type **Msinfo32**, click OK, and then select the System Summary option. The processor speed is displayed in the Processor line (B). Finally, you can use the Device Manager to determine the current microprocessor's speed. Click on the Start button and select the Run option. In the Run dialog box, type **Devmgmt.msc** and then click OK. Expand the Processors node to view the micro-processor information (D).

14. **Answers: A, D**. There are two simple ways to determine the amount of RAM currently installed in a Windows-based PC. You can examine the installed RAM information through the System Information utility. To view the installed RAM information through this utility, click on the Start button, navigate the Programs (All Programs in XP)/Accessories/System Tools path, and then select the System Information option. The total physical memory size is presented in the details pane, along with information about the operating system name, version, manufacturer, and directory location. You can also access this information by typing Msinfo32.exe in the Start menu's Run dia-log box (A).

The other path where system memory information is displayed is through the Computer Management console. To use this path, access the Administrative Tools applet through the Control Panel and open the Computer Management Console. Right-click the Computer Management (Local) option in the console tree and then click on the Properties option to view the Computer Management (Local) Properties, which includes the system's installed memory (D).

15. **Answer: A**. A special thermal compound (thermal grease) is placed between the heat sink and the processor to increase the rate of heat transfer to the heat sink. A small drop of this compound (generally the size of a BB) should be applied to the surface of the processor at its center. Then use the pressure from the heat sink to evenly spread

the compound across the surface. A small amount is all that's needed to create a thin layer to fill the imperfections in the metal and create a more efficient heat transfer between the processor and the heat sink.

16. **Answer: A**. In addition to the system board's power connector(s), other power supply bundles are used to supply power to optional devices, such as the disk drives, CD-ROM/DVD drives, and tape drives. These bundles provide a +5 and a +12V DC supply. The larger 4-pin connector, referred to as the *peripheral power connector*, is carried over from older PC designs, whereas the smaller 4-pin floppy connector has gained widespread usage with smaller form factor disk drives. The 4-pin connector also can be used to power other devices such as additional case fans.

17. **Answer: A**. Because the CMOS password controls access to all parts of the system, even before the bootup process occurs, there is some inconvenience in the event that the user forgets his password. When this occurs, it is impossible to gain access to the system without completely resetting the content of the CMOS RAM. On some system boards, this can be accomplished by shorting a special pair of jumpers on the board. With other systems, you need to remove or quickly short across the backup battery to reset the CMOS information. Be careful not to place the short across the battery for more than a second or so; doing so could cause the battery to explode. It also is necessary to unplug the power from the commercial outlet to reduce the voltage to the CMOS registers. When the content of the CMOS is reset, you must manually restore any nondefault CMOS settings being used by the system.

18. **Answer: B**. Each time the system is turned on or reset, the BIOS startup routine checks the system's configuration settings to determine what types of optional hardware devices have been included in the system. PCs feature a battery-powered RAM area that holds some of the system's advanced configuration information. This configuration storage area is known as *CMOS RAM*.

19. **Answer: C**. At this point in the installation scenario, the power cord can be reconnected to the outlet (it should have been unplugged to install any internal adapter card), and the system can be turned on. Next, the operating system should detect the new sound card and either install the correct drivers or prompt the user for action to install the appropriate drivers for the car.

20. **Answer: C**. This command-line utility enables you to determine the current TCP/IP configuration (MAC address, IP address, and subnet mask) of the local computer. It also may be used to request a new TCP/IP address from a DHCP server.

21. **Answers: A, B**. The standard video output connector is a three-row, DE-15 female D-shell connector used with analog VGA displays (A). Higher-end video cards are likely to include more than one VGA connector, as well as other high-performance video connectors, such as DVI/HDMI, S-Video, and Component/RGB jacks (B).

22. **Answer: B**. CDs are created and marketed in two standard storage capacity ratings: as a 74-minute 650MB CD-R version and as an 80-minute, 702MB CD-R/RW. Like CDs, DVDs are available in DVD-ROM (write-once) and DVD-RAM (rewritable) formats. These discs have capacities that range between 4.7GB and 17GB of data. A single-sided, single-layer 120mm DVD can hold up to 4.7GB of data, whereas a single-sided, dual-layer DVD is boosted to a capacity of 8.5GB. Double-sided, single-layer DVDs hold up to 9.4GB, whereas double-sided, double-layer discs can hold 17.1GB.

23. **Answer: A**. A good game system would provide the fastest video adapter card and its supporting expansion slot. This involves PCIe adapter slots and video cards with as much video memory onboard as possible. Some newer chipsets designed to support gaming applications include support for dual 16X PCIe slot video cards. This specification is called the Scalable Link Interface (SLI) specification and enables both cards to operate simultaneously. Additional advances have yielded twin, dual-slot (quad) PCIe system boards to host four video adapters.

24. **Answer: A**. The new low-profile extended (NLX) form factor became a legitimate standard for cases, power supplies, and system boards. However, manufacturers have chosen to produce low-profile units based on microATX and miniATX designs. These form factors followed the ATX design specification but reduced the size of the unit (and its associated costs) by limiting the number of expansion slots. Unless you obtain a universal case design specifically to handle both the NLX and MicroATX form factors, you cannot install the NLX system board.

25. **Answer: B**. Any system board supporting PATA technology can support up to four devices: two (master and slave) on the primary channel and two (master and slave) on the secondary channel.

26. **Answer: A**. You should never mix memory types when upgrading a system board. If the new memory modules are not technically compatible with the existing memory, the old memory should be removed. Remember that just because the memory modules are physically compatible, this does not mean that they will work together in a system. Mismatched memory speeds and memory styles (registered/unregistered, buffered/nonbuffered, ECC, and so on) can cause significant problems in the operation of the system. These problems can range from preventing bootup to creating simple soft memory errors. You must ensure that the memory type and size you want to install are supported by the system board and that it does not already have the maximum amount of memory installed. The system board's documentation includes information on the type, configuration, and size of memory it will accept. In addition, verify that the memory you want to install is compatible with the memory currently installed on the board.

27. **Answers: A, B**. USB and IEEE-1394 FireWire devices can be added to or removed from the system while it is powered up and fully operational. This is referred to as *hot-swapping* or *hot-plugging* the device (A). IEEE-1284 parallel and RS-232 serial ports are both legacy ports designed before plug-and-play or hot-swap capabilities were introduced to the PC (B).

28. **Answer: D**. When you are connecting a ribbon cable to the system board, pin 1 of the connector must line up with the signal cable's red indicator stripe.

29. **Answer: D**. If you are installing a signal cable in an IDE-based system, you should recall that two similar types of cables are used with PATA devices. ATA-4/Ultra ATA 66, Ultra ATA 100, and Ultra ATA 133 IDE enhancements provide higher data throughput than earlier ATA interfaces by doubling the number of conductors in the signal cable to 80.

30. **Answer: D**. The only hard drive in any PC system should be installed and configured to be the master drive on the primary IDE channel. If additional drives are added to the system, they can be connected and configured to be the primary/master drive as long as the original drive is connected/configured for some other position.

31. **Answer: C**. You may need to load device drivers to enable Windows XP to work with the SATA drive. Because SATA drives are not native to Windows operating systems, you may need to install the manufacturer's drivers so that Windows can recognize the SATA device. Download the SATA drivers from the website of the company that manufactured the SATA adapter card (or system board) you are installing.

32. **Answer: A**. The Athlon 64 and Athlon 64FX processors employ the Socket 939 939-pin PGA socket.

33. **Answers: B, C**. In some cases, the system may detect the presence of the new RAM modules but not be able to correctly identify them. If the system's front-side bus speed cannot be increased to the maximum capabilities of the RAM modules, the memory type displayed during the POST does not reflect the actual memory type installed. You should never mix memory types when upgrading a system board. If the new memory modules are not technically compatible with the existing memory, the old memory should be removed. Just because the memory modules are physically compatible does not mean that they will work together in a system. Mismatched memory speeds and memory styles (registered/unregistered, buffered/unbuffered, ECC, and so on) can cause significant problems in the operation of the system. These problems range from preventing bootup to limiting the speed of the FSB to the lowest memory speed or creating soft memory errors.

34. **Answer: A**. Using RAM slower than the FSB speed would create a significant overclocking situation for the RAM modules and cause the system to fail. Using PC166 RAM would be wasteful because the system reduces its operation to 133MHz. There are no DDR133 devices; there are, however, PC-2100 modules that are constructed using DDR 266 chips that operate with a 133MHz bus clock. PC133 devices are backward compatible with PC100 devices, but the reverse is not so.

35. **Answer: D**. Standard DIMM packages come in 168-pin modules for older EDO, FPM, PC66, PC100, and PC133 SDRAM memory; 184-pin boards for DDR memory; and 240-pin boards for DDR2 memory. These modules are designed to work efficiently with different Pentium-class microprocessors and memory bus schemes.

36. **Answers: A, C, D**. MicroATX and NLX are standard form factor definitions for low-profile cases and components. The ATX design has been the standard for Pentium-based systems for many years. However, the newer BTX specification is designed to take over for the aging ATX specification.

37. **Answer: C**. For larger drives, the Large and LBA modes are used. The LBA mode should be selected if drives support LBA mode. In this mode, the IDE controller converts the sector/head/cylinder address into a physical block address that improves data throughput. The ECHS (or Large mode) option is a generic cylinder/head/sector translation scheme that supports older drive geometries up to 1GB.

38. **Answers: A, B, D**. A PATA drive can be configured as the master drive in a single-drive or multidrive system (A) or the slave drive in the same multidrive system (B). It can also be set up for Cable Select (CS) operation, where the system determines its configuration setting (D).

39. **Answer: B**. RAID1 provides redundancy through a mirrored drive arrangement. The second drive has an exact copy of the first drive. If either drive fails, the system continues to operate, and the information can be copied back over to a replacement for the failed drive without interrupting the system's operation.

Objective 1.2

1. **Answer: B**. Errors that occur, or are displayed, before the single beep during the boot-up process indicate that a hardware problem of some type exists.

2. **Answer: C**. Mixing IDE device types creates a situation in which the system cannot provide the different types of control information each device needs. Therefore, the drives and the IDE controller operate at the ATA performance level that the entire channel can use.

3. **Answer: D**. The Time Domain Reflectometer (TDR) is a sophisticated tester that can be used to pinpoint the distance to a break in a cable. It sends signals along the cable and waits for them to be reflected. The time between sending the signal and receiving it back is converted into a distance measurement, which can be used to determine where an ethernet cable ends.

4. **Answer: B**. The user is one of the most common sources of PC problems. In most situations, your first troubleshooting step should be to talk to the user. Gather information regarding the environment the system is being used in, any symptoms or error codes produced by the system, and the situations that existed when the failure occurred.

5. **Answer: C**. If the processor does not appear to sit completely flush in the socket, remove it before clamping it into place. Check for bent pins that may not be lining up properly with the socket. Also make certain the processor's pin configuration lines up properly with the socket. If you force the processor into the socket, you may break off the pin and ruin the processor.

6. **Answer: D**. If the system consistently locks up after being on for a few minutes, this is a good indication that the microprocessor's fan is not running or that some other heat-buildup problem is occurring. The key indicator is that the failure is linked to time required to heat up and cool down.

7. **Answer: D**. You can use the Recovery Console to perform tasks such as copying files to the hard disk used for booting; controlling the startup state of services; adding, removing, and formatting volumes on the hard disk; repairing the master boot record (MBR) or boot sector of a hard disk or volume; and restoring the Registry. You cannot use it to uninstall programs.

8. **Answer: B.** Windows XP includes an option that can be used to revert to an older device driver when a driver upgrade causes problems with a device. This feature is called *Driver Rollback* and can be implemented through the Windows XP Device Manager.

9. **Answers: A, B, C.** If the adapter's icon shows an exclamation mark on a yellow background, the card is not functioning properly. Turn off the system and reinsert the device in a different PCMCIA slot. If the same problem appears, there are three possible sources of problems: The card might be faulty, the PC Card controller in the PC might be faulty, or the operating system might not support the device in question.

10. **Answer: B.** In computer and peripheral troubleshooting, fully 99% of the tests made are DC voltage readings. These measurements most often involve checking the DC side of the power supply unit.

11. **Answer: D.** During the POST, the operation of the microprocessor, RAM, keyboard, hard disk drive, and CMOS RAM are tested. But a RAM chip that fails at high temperature could not be detected at this stage.

12. **Answer: C.** If a working PATA hard drive fails because a second IDE hard drive has been installed, the reason is probably that they are connected to the same IDE channel, and both drives are set as master. With IDE/PATA drives, there can be only one master drive selection on each IDE channel.

13. **Answer: C.** A reversed FDD signal cable causes the FDD activity light to stay on constantly.

14. **Answers: C, D.** If the power supply's fan is not operational, check the power supply unit. In particular, check for the presence of a voltage level selector switch and make sure it is properly set for the AC supply voltage where you are. If this setting is incorrect, the power supply cannot supply the correct voltage levels to the system's components (C). Also check the fan's power supply connection to make sure that it has not been loosened or disconnected from the system board. The fan must have power to be able to turn (D).

15. **Answer: A.** During the setup procedure, you normally create only the partition that will hold the operating system. In Windows 2000 or Windows XP, it is more efficient to create any additional partitions using the Disk Management utility after the installation has been completed. You can use the Create a New Partition option if the hard disk has existing partitions but also has free (unpartitioned) space. Windows Explorer does not show unpartitioned space on a drive.

16. **Answer: C.** With PATA drives, make certain that the correct type of signal cable is being used. Do not get the newer 80-conductor/40-pin version confused with the older and much slower 40-conductor/40-pin version.

17. **Answer: D.** Isopropyl alcohol is an excellent cleaning agent for electrical contacts in the PC; however, it can soften the PC's plastic parts and dry out rubber components such as the friction rollers in a printer. Although alcohol is flammable, it is not likely to ignite under normal circumstances. Isopropyl alcohol with concentration levels above 70% are adequate for cleaning PC boards and contacts. Alcohol with additives such as menthol may leave residues when they dry, which can be a connectivity problem.

18. **Answer: C**. If the system consistently locks up after being on for a few minutes, this is a good indication that the microprocessor's fan is not running or that some other heat-buildup problem is occurring. The key indicator is that the failure is linked to time required to heat up and cool down.

19. **Answer: A**. The easiest step for testing the operation of a video display monitor is to connect it to the video display adapter in a working PC.

20. **Answer: B**. There is no upgrade path from Windows 2000 Professional to Windows XP Home Edition. Drivers for Windows XP Home have overwritten the original Windows 2000 drivers, and the system does not work with the newer drivers it has installed. You must perform a clean install of Windows XP Professional to upgrade the system.

21. **Answer: A**. The loud clicking sound associated with hard disk drive problems is the key to this scenario. This is not a symptom associated with the other components. Start the system and listen for sounds of the hard drive spinning up (a low whine or clicking noise). If there is a loud clicking noise coming from the drive, the drive has lost its alignment and is looking for its starting track.

22. **Answer: A**. If the drive is inoperable and there is a CD or DVD locked inside, you should insert a straightened paper clip into the tray-release access hole that is usually located beside the ejection button. This releases the spring-loaded tray and pops out the disc.

Objective 1.3

1. **Answer: D**. To check the speaker, just disconnect the speaker from the system, select the resistance (ohms) function, and connect a meter lead to each end. If the speaker is good, the meter should read about 8 ohms for most speakers used with PCs (however, 4-ohm speakers are also widely used). If the speaker is defective, the resistance reading should be 0 for an electrical short or infinite for an open circuit.

2. **Answer: B**. To use the Windows 2000 Device Manager utility to troubleshoot USB problems, you must be logged on as an administrator or as a member of the Administrators group.

3. **Answer: A**. A Hard Drive Boot Failure message indicates that the disk's master boot record is missing or has become corrupt.

4. **Answer: B**. If the speaker is defective, the resistance reading should be 0 for an electrical short or infinite for an open circuit.

5. **Answers: A, B**. The missing cover permits dust to accumulate in the system, forming the insulating blanket that traps heat next to active devices and can cause component overheating (A). The missing slot cover interrupts the designed airflow patterns inside the case, causing components to overheat due to missing or inadequate airflow (B).

6. **Answer: A**. The defragmentation process optimizes the operation of the disk drive by reorganizing its data into logically contiguous blocks. With data being arranged in this manner, the system does not need to reposition the drive's read/write heads as many times to read a given piece of data.

7. **Answer: A.** Outer-surface cleaning can be accomplished with a simple soap-and-water solution, followed by a clear water rinse. Care should be taken to make sure that none of the liquid splashes or drips into the inner parts of the system. A damp cloth is easily the best general-purpose cleaning tool for use with computer equipment.

8. **Answer: C.** When a major PC component is upgraded, the system's BIOS (along with any associated BIOS extension devices) should be updated with the latest compatible firmware.

9. **Answers: A, D.** The missing cover permits dust to accumulate in the system, forming an insulating blanket that traps heat next to active devices and can cause component overheating. It also interrupts the designed airflow patterns inside the case, causing components to overheat due to missing or inadequate airflow (A). High humidity can lead to heat-related problems and failures (D).

10. **Answer: C.** In particularly dusty environments, it is a good practice to check the air vents in the system unit chassis and remove any dust buildup present. Even partial blockage of these openings can significantly affect the cooling capabilities of the system.

11. **Answers: A, B, D.** Sources of heat buildup around the computer and its peripherals include direct sunlight from an outside window, locations of portable heaters in the winter, and papers and books piled up around the equipment.

12. **Answer: C.** The oxidation buildup occurring on electrical connectors and contacts reduces the flow of electricity through the connection. Even with proper handling, some corrosion can occur over time. This oxidation can be sanded off with emery cloth, rubbed off with a common pencil eraser or special solvent wipe, or dissolved with an electrical contact cleaner spray. The only acceptable answer offered in this question is the use of contact cleaner.

13. **Answer: B.** Excessive heat can cause premature aging and failure of electronic components. High humidity can also lead to heat-related problems and failures, but this should not be as much of a problem in a desert area. Installing the computers in an air-conditioned environment will enable you to maintain the temperature and humidity levels that the computers will be working in.

14. **Answer: A.** Microcomputers are designed to run at normal room temperatures. If the ambient temperature rises above about 85° F, heat buildup can become a problem.

15. **Answer: A.** The application of an antistatic spray or antistatic solution to the exterior surfaces of the PC and its peripherals prevents the buildup of static charges on the components of the system. A solution composed of 10 parts water and 1 part common household fabric softener makes an effective and economical antistatic solution.

16. **Answer: D.** To manually clean read/write heads, use isopropyl alcohol on a foam swab. Cotton swabs can shed fibers that contaminate the drive and damage portions of its R/W head.

Domain 2.0

Objective 2.1

1. **Answer: B**. An improved type of LCD places a transistor at each of the matrix row-column junctions to improve switching times. This technology produces an active-matrix display that employs thin-film transistor (TFT) arrays to create between one and four transistors for each pixel on a flexible, transparent film. TFT displays tend to be brighter and sharper than dual-scan displays; however, they also tend to require more power to operate and are therefore more expensive.

2. **Answers: A, B, C**. Many system board designs include an IrDA-compliant port standard to provide wireless communications with devices such as keyboards, mouse devices, character printers, personal digital assistants, and notebook computers.

3. **Answer: D**. Each client computer that has a wireless 802.11x network interface can communicate with other wireless-equipped computers or with an access point. Wireless network computers are also able to communicate with wired network computers on an ethernet LAN using the access point as the connection between the two networks. When the wireless adapter is used in this configuration, the communications mode is referred to as *ad hoc mode*.

4. **Answer: C**. The power consumption of LCD displays is very low. The screen is scanned by sequentially activating the panel's row and column electrodes. The pixels appear to be continuously lit because the scanning rate is very high. The electrodes can be controlled (turned on and off) using very low DC voltage levels. The inverter in the LCD panel works with high-voltage AC to provide the backlight, which is part of the display, but not part of the actual LCD panel

5. **Answer: C**. Most notebook computers feature power savings functions through both their BIOS and their operating systems. The standby mode option is the Windows version that turns off selected components, such as the hard drive and display, until a system event, such as a keyboard entry or a mouse movement, occurs.

6. **Answer: D**. The external power supply used with portable systems basically converts AC voltage into a DC voltage that the system can use to power its internal components and recharge its batteries.

7. **Answers: A, D**. Portable computers have two ideal characteristics: They are compact and lightweight. Portable computer designers work constantly to decrease the size and power consumption of all the computer's components.

8. **Answer: A**. Because PC Cards are hot-swappable, the operating system's socket service must update the system when a new card is installed or an existing card is removed. If not, the system would lose track of its actual resources. The card service portion delivers the correct device driver for the installed PC Card. (That is, when a PC Card modem is removed and replaced with a LAN card, the operating system must automatically update its capability of controlling and using the new card.)

9. **Answer: A**. One of the biggest problems for portable computers is heat buildup inside the case. Because conventional power supplies (and their fans) are not included in portable units, separate fans must be designed into portables to carry heat out of the unit. The closeness of the portable's components and the small amount of free air space inside its case also adds to heat-related design problems.

Objective 2.2

1. **Answer: D**. Portable PCs typically use a technique called *shared video memory*. Under shared memory, the system uses a portion of its main memory to hold screen information for the display. One of the disadvantages of shared memory is that it takes up RAM that applications would normally use. It also causes the system to show less memory capacity than is installed because a portion has been reserved for use with the video display.

2. **Answer: A**. The Safely Remove Hardware utility is used to notify the operating system in advance of the removal of USB devices. Because some devices have write caching enabled, corruption or data loss may occur.

3. **Answer: A**. System boards for portable computers are not designed to fit a standardized form factor. Instead, they are designed to fit around all the components that must be installed in the system. Therefore, system boards used in portable computers tend to be proprietary to the model they are designed for. Mounting hole positions are determined by where they will best suit the placement of the other system components.

4. **Answer: D**. Considering the age and lack of support for a portable PC this old, you should probably let the customer know that it is really not worth upgrading the processor in this system.

5. **Answer: B**. In most portable PCs, you can adjust the shared memory allocation through the CMOS Setup utility. Most video-intensive software packages, such as high-end game programs, require at least 64MB of video RAM as a minimum, along with a large installed system memory. To allow your friend's game software to perform to its fullest, you may want to allocate 128MB or more to shared memory for video.

Objective 2.3

1. **Answer: C**. If the battery is expected to be stored for more than 30 days (as you would expect the replacement for a new computer to be), you should fully discharge the battery and store it at normal room temperature.

2. **Answers: B, C**. The portable keyboard normally contains an Fn function key. This key activates special functions in the portable, such as display brightness and contrast. Other common Fn functions include Suspend mode activation and LCD/external-CRT device selection.

3. **Answer: B**. Most portable PC designs have switched to nickel metal-hydride (NiMH), lithium-ion (Li-ion), or lithium-ion polymer batteries. These batteries typically provide in excess of two or three hours of operation. The actual life of a laptop computer battery may vary from just under one hour to over six hours in each session, depending on the particular notebook PC type and configuration, the way it is being used (lots of disk/disc accesses), and the battery type and its age.

4. **Answer: C**. To correct battery memory problems, you must start the portable computer using only the battery and allow it to run until it completely discharges the battery and quits. Then recharge the battery for at least 12 hours. Repeat this process several times, watching for consistently increasing operating times.

5. **Answer: C**. The condition of the NumLock key can cause portable PCs to produce incorrect characters. Notebook PCs do not have separate 10-key numeric keypads. If the Num Lock key function is engaged, the system remaps different keys to the locked numbers. In most cases, the only indicator that the Num Lock key function is engaged is a small light near a small icon representing a numeric keypad. Unless you look closely, you probably won't realize that a numeric keypad is associated with the keyboard (small numbers are embossed on the alpha keys). You can disable the Num Lock On setting using the Fn key along with a designated function key (also denoted by a small numeric keypad icon).

6. **Answer: B**. When dealing with portable PCs, you should check that your wireless network adapter is switched on. Some laptops come with buttons that can be used to disable the wireless network function when not in use. This power-saving feature is used to extend the battery cycle life.

7. **Answer: D**. In this case, the touchpad is probably defective and needs to be replaced. Touchpads are sealed units and typically not susceptible to environmental dirt. However, if a film is allowed to build up on the pad's surface, it can affect its capability to detect the presence of the fingertip and cause erratic operation. In this case, there is no reason for the touchpad to get dirty in your travel bag. Also, there is no reason for the drivers to go bad traveling in your travel bag. There is a chance that the touchpad connection to the system board has become intermittent.

8. **Answer: A**. Most portables offer standard connectors to enable full-size keyboards and VGA monitors to be plugged in. The VGA connector standard is a 3-row, 15-pin D-shell type (DE-15F). The portable's Fn key can be used to redirect the video output to the external VGA port. Check the user's guide for directions in redirecting the video back to the main display.

9. **Answer: B**. In Windows 2000 and Windows XP, the power management functions are located in the Control Panel under the Power Options icon. These functions include options for configuring hard drive and display shutdown times, as well as standby mode timing and system hibernation functions. Standby settings are confgured under the Power Schemes tab, whereas the hibernation function is enabled under the Hibernate tab (Enable Hibernate Support in Windows 2000 and Enable Hibernation in Windows XP).

10. **Answer: A**. The construction of LCD displays prevents them from providing multiple resolution options as an adapter-driven CRT display can. The resolution of the LCD display is dictated by the construction of the LCD panel, and this value is known as its *native resolution*. To display image signals specified in higher or lower resolutions (DVD, HDTV, and so on) requires the video display system to convert the image to the native resolution to be displayed correctly. If the display image has more pixels than the display's native resolution, it loses some of its picture information and sharpness when displayed. On the other hand, if the image has fewer pixels than the display, you see all the pixels displayed, but there is no increased quality because of the additional resolution capabilities of the display. The additional picture elements added to fill in the image might make it look worse.

11. **Answer: A**. If you are having problems with the built-in LCD display, a common practice is to plug an external monitor into the external VGA port and redirect the video output there. This allows you to determine whether the video problem is in the LCD display or in the built-in video display adapter circuitry. *Note:* You can use a bright light to differentiate between problems with the LCD panel and the inverter. Shine the light on the LCD panel to see if anything is present on the screen. In this test, you are using the light source to replace the back light produced by the inverter.

12. **Answer: D**. To verify that the PC Card device is working, access the Device Manager under the Windows Control Panel's System applet. If there is a problem with the PC Card device, it appears in the Device Manager. If the adapter's icon shows an exclamation mark on a yellow background, the card is not functioning properly.

13. **Answer: D**. If the portable's touchpad works, but the external mouse does not, check the documentation for an Fn key combination requirement for the mouse.

Domain 3.0

Objective 3.1

1. **Answer: A.** The printhead is a collection of print wires set in an electromagnetic head unit. Dots are created on the paper by energizing selected electromagnets, which extend the desired print wires from the printhead. The print wires impact an ink ribbon, which impacts the paper.

2. **Answer: D.** Tractor feeds are used with very heavy forms, such as multiple-part continuous forms, and are most commonly found on dot matrix printers.

3. **Answer: A.** After an image has been transferred to the paper in a laser printer operation, a pair of compression rollers in the fusing unit acts to bond the toner particles to the paper. The heated top roller, known as the *fusing roller*, melts the toner to the paper as the paper exits the fusing unit. The lower roller applies pressure to the paper.

4. **Answer: B.** A high voltage, applied to the primary corona wire, creates a highly charged negative field that conditions the drum to be written on by applying a uniform negative charge (–600V) to it.

5. **Answer: C.** A precision positioning motor moves the scan head below the paper. As the head moves, light reflected from the paper is captured and channeled through a series of mirrors. The mirrors pivot to continually focus the reflected light on a light-sensitive diode. The diode converts the reflected light intensity into a corresponding digital value.

6. **Answers: A, C.** Typically, scanners can directly provide image files in BMP, TIFF, and JPEG formats. Some models can even deliver images in PDF format. Bitmap is not always the best format for documents, presentations, and web development. BMP image files are larger than JPEG versions and can become pixelated when manipulated. Therefore, the JPEG format is often preferred over BMP, particularly for photographs.

7. **Answer: B.** Thermal printers relied on special heat-sensitive or chemically reactive paper to form characters on the page. Thermal printing techniques were at one time widely used with PC printing. These printers use heated elements to burn or melt dot pattern characters on special paper. There are two types of thermal printers: direct thermal printers and thermal wax transfer printers.

8. **Answer: B.** The toner is transferred to the paper from the drum because of the highly positive charge the transfer corona wire applies to the paper. The positive charge attracts the more negative toner particles away from the drum and onto the page.

9. **Answer: D.** The thermal fuse protects the fuser assembly from overheating. If the temperature of the fuser is not controlled correctly, it can cause severe damage to the printer, as well as present a potential fire hazard associated with igniting the paper.

Objective 3.2

1. **Answer: A**. Full-speed USB devices operate under the USB 2.0 specification (also referred to as *high-speed USB*) and support data rates up to 480Mbps. The IrDA-SIR standard infrared protocol is used to provide a standard serial port interface with transfer rates ranging up to 115kbps. The IrDA-FIR fast infrared protocol is used to provide a high-speed serial port interface with transfer rates ranging up to 4Mbps. Bluetooth communication occurs at data transfer rates of 723.1Kbps for Bluetooth 1.1 and 1.2 devices and 2.1Mbps for Bluetooth 2.0 devices, whereas FireWire 400 transfers occur at 400Mbps.

2. **Answer: C**. The IrDA specification calls for communication ranges up to 2 meters (6 feet), but most implementations state 1 meter as the recommended maximum range. All IrDA transfers are carried out in half-duplex mode and must have a clear line of sight between the transmitter and receiver. The receiver must be situated within 15° of center with the line of transmission.

3. **Answer: A**. For the most part, the steps for adding a printer to a system are basically the same regardless of the type of printer being installed: Connect the printer's power cord to an AC power source. Connect the printer to the correct I/O port at the computer system. Make sure that the port is enabled. Set up the appropriate printer drivers. Install the paper. Run the printer's self-test and then print a document. However, manufacturers of USB printers are increasingly instructing you to run the installation software that comes with the device before connecting it to the computer and turning on the printer.

4. **Answers: C, D**. There are two good reasons to upgrade any kind of equipment—including printers. If maintenance time on a device is becoming excessive, you should consider replacing it; no one works free on equipment, and the cost of user downtime and lost productivity is added to the cost of repair. The other reason to replace a piece of equipment is to obtain necessary features that the current model does not have.

5. **Answer: B**. The best way to ensure good print resolution when using an inkjet printer is to use fresh ink cartridges. When the print becomes noticeably faint, or the resolution becomes unacceptable, the cartridge needs to be replaced.

6. **Answer: A**. The path to the shared resource contains the remote computer's name and shared resource name (directory or printer). It also must be expressed using the Universal Naming Convention (UNC) format. The format begins with a pair of backslashes, \\. Each name in the path is separated by a single backslash.

7. **Answer: C**. If you want to use a printer connected to another computer running Windows in the network, the printer must be shared with the network users. In the Windows XP system, this is enabled through the File and Printer Sharing for Windows setting. The print server should appear in My Network Places of the remote computer. If the remote computer cannot see any printer at the print server station, print sharing cannot be established there.

Objective 3.3

1. **Answer: A**. During the troubleshooting process, if the printhead assembly does not move at any time, check to see if the printer is in maintenance mode. In this mode, the printer typically keeps the printhead assembly in the home position. If no mode problems are present, the printhead positioning motor should be replaced.

2. **Answer: C**. Some scanners have locking mechanisms that prevent the light source from moving inside the housing during transportation. If the light source is on but does not move when the system applies a scan request, refer to the scanner's documentation to determine whether your scanner has a locking mechanism. If so, check to make sure that the scanner is unlocked.

3. **Answer: A**. Nearly every printer is equipped with a built-in self-test. The easiest way to determine whether the printer is at fault is to run its self-test routine. If the self-test runs and prints clean pages, most of the printer has been eliminated as a possible source of problems. The problem could be in the computer, cabling, or interface portion of the printer. If the printer fails the self-test, it is necessary to troubleshoot the printer's problem.

4. **Answers: A, B**. IrDA communication is based on infrared light, which needs a clear line of sight to travel between the host and peripheral. Ambient light does not interfere with infrared light (A). Under the IrDA specification, the two devices need to be aimed almost directly at each other (within 15°) and less than 2 meters apart. The IrDA feature relies on the PC's serial port circuitry and must be enabled in the CMOS Setup utility before it can be used (B).

5. **Answer: A**. Normally, if a printer is not producing anything in a Windows environment even though print jobs have been sent to it, you should check the print spooler to see whether any particular type of error has occurred. To view documents waiting to be printed, you would double-click on the desired printer's icon. While viewing the print spooler queue, you should check to make certain that the printer has not been set to the Pause Printing setting. However, in this scenario, the customer is trying to print to an inkjet printer, but only a laser printer has been defined for use. The local inkjet printer must be added and defined in the local computer's Printers and Faxes list using the Add Printer Wizard.

6. **Answer: C**. Because this is a new installation, before you leave the office, you should verify that the printer installation runs correctly from the host computer through the printer. In the case of a network-ready printer, you should verify that the customer can print from different locations in the network.

7. **Answer: A**. In a multifunction device, scanning, faxing, and copying operations all begin with the scanner function. Dust, fingerprints, and smudges accumulate on the glass that the scanning light passes through before being reflected off the page holding the image. The dust and smudges affect the passage of the light through the glass on its way to being reflected and detected by the detector. When smudges appear on the documents from a scanner or multifunction device, the first step to correct this condition is always to clean the glass.

8. **Answer: D**. As the laser writes on the drum, the drum turns through the toner powder, which is attracted to the charged image on the drum. The developer roller, in the toner cartridge, turns as the drum turns and expels a measured amount of toner past a restricting blade. A regulating AC voltage assists the toner in leaving the cartridge but also pulls back some excess toner from the drum. Excess toner is recycled within the toner cartridge so that it can be used again. If the regulating AC voltage provided by the high-voltage supply is not correct, excess toner can be spilled out into the body of the printer.

9. **Answer: D**. When troubleshooting a printer, you first should check the lights on the control panel and noise.

10. **Answers: A, B**. The paper trays have a complex set of sensors and pickup mechanisms that must all be functioning properly to begin the paper handling (A). A mechanical arm and photo detector are used to sense the presence of paper in the tray. If these switches are set incorrectly, the printer could print a page that was sized incorrectly for the actual paper size (B).

11. **Answer: A**. If you remove the portable from its AC source, it should run from its DC battery source. If not, its battery may simply be poorly seated, discharged, or it may be defective.

12. **Answers: C, D**. Faults in the print output that occur at regular intervals along the page are usually caused by mechanical problems. When roller and transport mechanisms begin to wear in the printer, bad registration and bad print appear in cyclic form. This can be attributed to the dimensions of cyclic components such as the drum, the developing roller in the toner cartridge, or the fusing roller. When you have cyclic problems, examine the various mechanical components for wear or defects.

13. **Answers: A, B**. If the tops of characters are missing, the printhead is misaligned with the platen. You might need to reseat it in the printhead carriage, or you might need to adjust the carriage assembly to the proper height and angle.

14. **Answers: A, B**. The single item in an inkjet printer that requires the most attention is the ink cartridge (or cartridges). As the ink cartridge empties, the printing eventually becomes faint and uneven, and the resolution of the print on the page diminishes.

15. **Answers: A, C**. Bad paper-feed rollers cause an inkjet printer to produce wavy graphics. If the paper thickness settings are correct, but the print output is disfigured, you need to replace the paper-feed rollers (A). If an inkjet printer's paper thickness selector is set improperly, the paper can slip as it moves through the printer and cause wavy graphics to be produced. Check the printer's paper thickness settings. If they are correct, and the print output is disfigured, you need to replace the paper-feed rollers (C).

16. **Answers: A, D**. A white page indicates that no information is being written on the drum. This condition basically involves the laser scanning module, control board, and power supply (A). White page faults can occur when the corona wire becomes broken, contaminated, or corroded so that the attracting charge between the drum and paper is severely reduced (D).

17. **Answer: B**. When problems occur at cyclic intervals on a printer page from a laser printer, the problem is normally associated with one of the rotating parts (that is, the drum, fuser rollers, developing roller, and so on). In this case, the drum may have

been touched or exposed to a light source so that it has a spot on it that does not hold toner.

18. **Answer: B**. If the printer runs the self-test and prints clean pages, most of the printer has been eliminated as a possible cause of problems. The problem could be in the computer, cabling, or interface portion of the printer.

19. **Answers: A, C**. Using paper that is too thin or too thick for the printer can result in jams, as can overloading paper trays. Using the wrong type of paper can defeat the separation pad and allow multiple pages to be drawn into the printer. In this case, the multiple sheets may move through the printer together, or they might result in a jam (A). Using coated paper stock can be hazardous because the coating might melt, which can cause paper jams or fire (C).

Objective 3.4

1. **Answer: B**. Great care should be taken when installing a new drum unit. Exposing the drum to light for more than a few minutes can damage it.

2. **Answer: C**. As with other printer types, you should maintain laser printers in accordance with the manufacturer's guidelines. This includes installing the manufacturer's maintenance kit designed for that printer. Don't forget to reset the page counter on those copiers and laser printers that have them. This should be the last step before turning the printer over to the customer because service agreements are often based on page counts.

3. **Answer: B**. The air-conditioned office environment is always the best location for printers and other equipment if possible. The air conditioning controls temperature and humidity that can cause the printer to overheat and cause the paper to absorb moisture, creating jams. Dust from the other areas can also collect in the printer and wear its paper-handling mechanisms.

4. **Answers: B, D**. Paper problems can also cause jams to occur. Using paper that is too heavy or too thick can result in jams, as can overloading paper trays (B). Similarly, using the wrong type of paper can defeat the separation pad and allow multiple pages to be drawn into the printer at one time. In this case, multiple sheets can move through the printer together, or they may result in a jam (D).

5. **Answer: C**. Using paper that is too heavy or too thick can wear the pickup pad prematurely and cause jams to occur. This defeats the pickup pad and allows multiple sheets of paper in the tray to be drawn into the printer, producing the jam.

6. **Answer: D**. Using solvents to clear blockages in the jets can dilute the ink and allow it to flow uncontrollably through the jet.

7. **Answer: A**. The single item in a dot-matrix printer that requires the most attention is the ribbon cartridge. It is considered a consumable part of the printer and must be changed often.

8. **Answer: D**. The inkjet nozzle is designed to provide the proper shape and trajectory for the ink drops so that they can be directed precisely toward the page. The nozzles are also designed so that the surface tension of the ink keeps it from running out of the nozzle uncontrollably.

Domain 4.0

Objective 4.1

1. **Answer: A**. A networked or online computer has more opportunity to contract a virus than a standalone unit because viruses can enter the unit over the network or through the modem.

2. **Answer: D**. From a security point of view, it is recommended that FAT partitions be converted to NTFS partitions. The Windows Setup utility provides you with the option to convert the partition to the new version of NTFS, even though it was previously formatted as FAT or FAT32. This conversion process protects existing files—unlike formatting the partition. Windows 2000 and Windows XP both provide effective local hard drive security through their Encrypted File System (EFS) feature. The EFS feature enables the user to encrypt files stored on the drive using keys only the designated user (or an authorized recovery agent) can decode. This prevents theft of data by those who do not have the password or a decoding tool.

3. **Answer: A**. The Windows Firewall feature is designed to provide protection from outside attacks by preventing unwanted connections from Internet devices. Computers connected directly to the Internet are always vulnerable to attacks from the outside.

4. **Answer: C**. Retinal scanners are not readily available for use with PCs, as are the other options. The amount of energy required to scan a retina makes operation from a standard I/O port somewhat difficult. Fingerprint scanners and smart cards typically offer USB connections to the PC. In addition, fingerprint readers are built into many notebook models. Voice recognition products typically use the PC's sound card and a microphone as the input device. In many PCs the sound card is an integral part of the system board. In other systems the sound card can be a PCI device.

5. **Answer: B**. Smart cards employ personal identification numbers (PINs), which are considered to be more secure than encrypted software files. Implementing a PC Card–based smart card system can cost an organization more than $100,000 if it has a large number of employees. In terms of security, the fact that smart cards have no moving parts offers minimal long-term advantages (they do not crash, but they can be affected by environmental factors).

6. **Answer: C**. Complex passwords include some combination of lowercase letters, numbers, symbols, and uppercase characters.

Objective 4.2

1. **Answer: C**. Biometric authentication involves using uniquely personal physiological characteristics to verify people are who they say they are. The qualities most often involved in biometric authentication include voice patterns, fingerprints, palm prints, signatures, facial features, and retinal and iris scans.

2. **Answer: C**. Smart cards are authentication tools that contain information about their owners, such as passwords or personal identification numbers (PINs). The card system combines the users' secret PINs (that is, something the users alone know) with tokens generated by the network's certificate authority *authentication system* to generate a unique *pass code*. The pass code validates the users and their access to different resources.

3. **Answer: D**. Although the logbook can be used to track access through a sign-in/sign-out method, this method depends on the honesty and thoroughness of the people coming and going. The use of intelligent keycards can provide information about who is accessing a particular area and when. In addition, it can also be used to control or limit access to specific areas or at certain times.

4. **Answer: C**. This is a classic description of a phishing ploy. These expeditions typically begin with an email or instant messenger communication that points the target toward the spoofed site. These sites are often look-alikes for sites where financial activities are conducted. Users should be educated about how to handle suspicious requests properly. They should know to ignore the request, delete the email message, and report the incident to their supervisors. However, they should not forward the request because doing so also poses a security risk.

Domain 5.0

Objective 5.1

1. **Answer: D.** Remove all power cords associated with the computer and its peripherals from the power outlet during thunder or lightning storms.

2. **Answer: C.** Extremely high voltage levels (in excess of 25,000V) may be present inside the CRT housing, even up to a year after electrical power has been removed from the unit.

3. **Answer: D.** The 110 VAC at 5 amps is much more dangerous than the 25,000 VDC at 5 microamperes according to the current-delivering capabilities (5 amps versus 5 microamperes) they create.

4. **Answer: C.** Antistatic straps should never be worn while working on higher-voltage components, such as monitors and power supply units.

5. **Answer: C.** A surge suppresser is used to protect computer equipment from very small overvoltage occurrences by passively filtering the incoming power signal to smooth out variations.

6. **Answer: C.** In the case of a complete shutdown or a significant sag, the best protection from losing programs and data is an uninterruptible power supply (UPS). A *UPS* is a battery-based system that monitors the incoming power and kicks in when unacceptable variations occur in the power source.

7. **Answer: A.** Unlike the hard disk drive and the mouse, printers and keyboards are open to the atmosphere and should be vacuumed regularly. Although dust buildup in the keyboard can cause problems with the operation of its key switches and can cause its electronic devices to fail due to overheating, the printer is more susceptible to dust buildup due to its many openings and the presence of fans and moving electro-mechanical parts.

8. **Answer: A.** Unlike other printer types, the laser printer tends to have several high-voltage, high-temperature, and vision hazards inside it. To get the laser printer into a position where you can observe its operation, you may need to place yourself in potential contact with those areas. Be aware that laser printers can be a source of electrocution, eye damage (from the laser), and burns (from the fuser assembly).

9. **Answer: A.** The presence of water in the work area from other sources, such as leaking pipes or ceilings, should always be a cause for alarm and correction. Water leaks in the work area are generally the responsibility of the building maintenance supervisor. If the business does not have someone on staff who is responsible for building infrastructure, you should report the situation to whoever is responsible for the PCs and/or network so that person can properly shut down the systems.

10. **Answer: C.** The laser light is a hazard to eyesight. Great care should be taken to avoid contact between the laser light and your eyes.

11. **Answer: A**. In repair situations, the high-voltage charge associated with video displays must be discharged. This is accomplished by creating a path from the tube's high-voltage anode to the chassis. With the monitor unplugged from the commercial power outlet, clip one end of an insulated jumper wire to the chassis ground of the frame. Clip the other end to a long, flat-blade screwdriver that has a well-insulated handle. While touching only the insulated handle of the screwdriver, slide the blade of the screwdriver under the rubber cup of the anode and make contact with its metal connection. This should bleed off the high-voltage charge to ground. Continue the contact for several seconds to ensure that the voltage has been fully discharged.

12. **Answer: D**. You should replace the power supply unit. Even if you are very good at soldering and repairing damaged cabling, the condition may have caused damage to the power supply's electronics. Also, the cost of your time to repair and test the unit might exceed the cost of installing a new unit.

13. **Answer: B**. Many work-related injuries occur due to improper material handling and lifting techniques. The proper technique for lifting objects is to bend at the knees and lift with your legs, keeping your back straight. In other words, lift with your legs, not with your back!

14. **Answers: A, D**. The work area should include antistatic protection devices to protect static-sensitive devices from electrostatic discharge (ESD). These discharges can build up on moving surfaces (including people) and damage the integrated circuit devices in the PC. The most common antistatic device is a grounding strap placed around the wrist or ankle while a technician is working on equipment. Antistatic mats for the floor and table are advised as well. These devices all work to channel static discharges away from sensitive devices. ESD is more likely to occur under low humidity conditions, so the dehumidifier would not be a good choice.

15. **Answer: C**. ESD is most likely to occur during periods of low humidity. If the relative humidity is below 50%, static charges can accumulate easily. ESD generally does not occur when the humidity is above 50%. Anytime the charge reaches about 10,000V, it is likely to discharge to grounded metal parts.

16. **Answer: C**. System boards are fairly sturdy from an electrical point of view. To create a short circuit in one of them, you must get a powered trace connected to a ground trace. The only option that actually accomplishes this is plugging an adapter card into the wrong type of expansion slot and then turning on the system. Although some areas of the system board have electrical energy applied to them even when the system is turned off, the expansion slots are not one of those areas. Therefore, not removing the power cord does not cause a short to occur while the system is turned off.

17. **Answer: D**. To exchange the printhead assembly, make sure that the printhead assembly is cool enough to be handled. These units can get hot enough to cause a serious burn.

What's on the CD-ROM

The CD-ROM features an innovative practice test engine powered by MeasureUp™, giving you yet another effective tool to assess your readiness for the exam.

Multiple Test Modes

MeasureUp practice tests can be used in Study, Certification, or Custom Mode.

Study Mode

Tests administered in Study Mode allow you to request the correct answer(s) and explanation to each question during the test. These tests are not timed. You can modify the testing environment during the test by selecting the Options button.

You can also specify the objectives or missed questions you want to include in your test, the timer length, and other test properties. You can also modify the testing environment during the test by selecting the Options button.

In Study Mode, you receive automatic feedback on all correct and incorrect answers. The detailed answer explanations are a superb learning tool in their own right.

Certification Mode

Tests administered in Certification Mode closely simulate the actual testing environment you will encounter when taking a licensureexam and are timed. These tests do not allow you to request the answer(s) and/or explanation to each question until after the exam.

Custom Mode

Custom Mode allows you to specify your preferred testing environment. Use this mode to specify the categories you want to include in your test, timer length, number of questions, and other test properties. You can modify the testing environment during the test by selecting the Options button.

Attention to Exam Objectives

MeasureUp practice tests are designed to appropriately balance the questions over each technical area covered by a specific exam. All concepts from the actual exam are covered thoroughly to ensure that you're prepared for the exam.

Installing the CD

System Requirements:

▶ Windows 95, 98, Me, NT 4, 2000, or XP

▶ 7MB disk space for testing engine

▶ An average of 1MB disk space for each individual test

▶ Control Panel Regional Settings must be set to English (United States)

▶ PC only

To install the CD-ROM, follow these instructions:

1. Close all applications before beginning this installation.

2. Insert the CD into your CD-ROM drive. If the setup starts automatically, go to step 6. If the setup does not start automatically, continue with step 3.

3. From the Start menu, select **Run**.

4. Click **Browse** to locate the MeasureUp CD. In the Browse dialog box, from the Look In drop-down list, select the CD-ROM drive.

5. In the Browse dialog box, double-click **Setup.exe**. In the Run dialog box, click **OK** to begin the installation.

6. On the Welcome screen, click **MeasureUp Practice Questions** to begin installation.

7. Follow the Certification Prep Wizard by clicking **Next**.

8. To agree to the Software License Agreement, click **Yes**.

9. On the Choose Destination Location screen, click **Next** to install the software to C:\Program Files\Certification Preparation. If you cannot locate MeasureUp Practice Tests on the Start menu, see the section titled "Creating a Shortcut to the MeasureUp Practice Tests," later in this appendix.

10. On the Setup Type screen, select **Typical Setup**. Click **Next** to continue.

11. In the Select Program Folder screen, you can name the program folder where your tests will be located. To select the default, simply click **Next** and the installation continues.

12. After the installation is complete, verify that **Yes, I Want to Restart My Computer Now** is selected. If you select **No, I Will Restart My Computer Later**, you cannot use the program until you restart your computer.

13. Click **Finish**.

14. After restarting your computer, choose **Start > Programs > Certification Preparation > Certification Preparation > MeasureUp Practice Tests**.

15. On the MeasureUp Welcome Screen, click **Create User Profile**.

16. In the User Profile dialog box, complete the mandatory fields and click **Create Profile**.

17. Select the practice test you want to access and click **Start Test**.

Creating a Shortcut to the MeasureUp Practice Tests

To create a shortcut to the MeasureUp practice tests, follow these steps:

1. Right-click your desktop.

2. From the shortcut menu, select **New > Shortcut**.

3. Browse to C:\Program Files\MeasureUp Practice Tests and select the **MeasureUpCertification.exe** or **Localware.exe** file.

4. Click **OK**.

5. Click **Next.**

6. Rename the shortcut MeasureUp.

7. Click **Finish.**

After you complete step 7, use the MeasureUp shortcut on your desktop to access the MeasureUp products you ordered.

Technical Support

If you encounter problems with the MeasureUp test engine on the CD-ROM, please contact MeasureUp at (800) 649-1687 or email support@measureup.com. Support hours of operation are 7:30 a.m. to 4:30 p.m. EST. In addition, you can find Frequently Asked Questions (FAQ) in the Support area at www.measureup.com. If you would like to purchase additional MeasureUp products, call (678) 356-5050 or (800) 649-1687, or visit www.measureup.com.